A FISH OUT OF WATER

The Lord Mayor and Lady Mayoress, Sir Robin and Lady Gillett.

A Fish out of Water

by

Sir Robin Gillett

The Pentland Press Limited
Edinburgh · Cambridge · Durham · USA

© Sir Robin Gillett 2001

First published in 2001 by
The Pentland Press Ltd.
1 Hutton Close
South Church
Bishop Auckland
Durham

British Library Cataloguing in Publication Data.
A catalogue record for this book is available
from the British Library.

ISBN 1 85821 525 0

Typeset by George Wishart & Associates, Whitley Bay.
Printed and bound by Antony Rowe Ltd., Chippenham.

In loving memory of my late wife Libby who shared many of the experiences recalled in the book and the Officers and men of the Maritime Volunteer Service to whom the proceeds go.

List of Illustrations

Foreword

The first question that any autobiographer should ask is: 'Why am I doing this? What is the objective?'

To make money? – No way.

To justify oneself and one's actions? – Insecure whimpism.

Because my friends persuaded me? – Sycophants all of them.

For the benefit of my children/grandchildren? – Boring.

To keep me out of mischief in my twilight years? – I'll take the mischief.

As an example to the next generation? – Arrogant swine.

Because there is no voice that I would rather listen to, or opinions that I respect more? – Nearer the truth.

Because I am an egotistical, pompous old fart? – Bingo!

You pays your money and takes your choice.

It's my story and I am sticking to it.

I do not mention many names, either because I have forgotten them, or I don't want any libel actions. There is no index, so that it won't be possible to have a quick look to see if your name is mentioned and then not buy it if it isn't. Profits go to the Maritime Volunteer Service, so why should I spoil their chances?

Enjoy.

My Thanks
To Jill Cole who transcribed the whole thing from my dictated tapes and corrected my grammar and spelling – no, delete the latter; as I dictated it any spelling mistakes must be hers (or her spell-checker's)!

Part One

Background – My Parents

My father, born 1890, was the eldest of three children (two sons and a daughter). He was born at Highgate, where my grandfather had moved from Chippenham, Wiltshire, on the purchase by Lloyd's Bank of his branch of Capital and Counties Bank. Father was educated at Durlston Court School and Marlborough College, leaving as Upper School Captain in 1907 to serve his Articles as a Chartered Accountant. Passing his finals in 1914 he became a partner in Dixon, Wilson, Tubbs and Gillett, situated in Basinghall Street, E.C.2, behind Guildhall. Having joined the 7th Battalion Middlesex Regiment as a T.A. 2nd Lieutenant in 1911, he was mobilised in August 1914 and sent as Battalion Transport Officer (now a First Lieutenant) to Gibraltar. 1915 saw him in France as a Captain and Company Commander and by the end of the year awarded the Military Cross.

He met my mother in 1918 when she was billeted as a V.A.D. in Grandfather's house. They were married in 1919 at St. Mary Abbott's Church in Kensington. Returning to the City after the war, Father established himself as one of the first 'company doctors' specialising in saving firms, rather than liquidating them. He joined the Common Council in 1930. In the last war as a Major he commanded the area H.G. He was elected an Alderman in 1948, served as Sheriff in 1952-53 (knighted by the Queen in Guildhall after the Coronation lunch) and became Lord Mayor 1958-59, having been created a Baronet at the end of his term of office. He retired from work at the age of 81 and died in 1976 not quite making 86.

My mother was born in 1894 in Dublin, where her father's regiment, the Duke of Cornwall's Light Infantry, was stationed on garrison duty. Her background was Staffordshire 'county' on her mother's side and Naval and Military on her father's. On the outbreak of the South African war the D.C.L.I. was sent to South Africa where, at the Battle of Paarderberg, her father was killed, leaving my grandmother with my mother aged eight and her younger brother aged four. Whilst the latter went off to Rugby and, in due course, served in the D.C.L.I., my mother was educated by governesses, selected, she used to claim, more for their ability to partner my grandmother on the tennis court or at bridge. After finishing school in Paris and Switzerland, the outbreak of the 1914-18 war saw her enlisted in the Red Cross as a V.A.D. orderly, which is how she met Father. Between the wars, she took an active part in local life at Frinton and built an estate of twenty very high standard houses for local working families, for which she charged a minimal rent. Her constitution was never strong and she died in 1962.

Chapter 1

I was born in a nursing home in Ladbroke Grove, London, on 9th November, 1925. The date has little significance now, but at the time my arrival was considered portentous, particularly by my father and his friends. The ninth of November was (and remained until 1958) Lord Mayor's Day, the day upon which the new Lord Mayor took office and held his grand Show and Banquet at Guildhall. Even then my father had expressed an aspiration to achieve the office, and my birth on this momentous date was bound to be an excellent omen for him. No one considered at the time that it might actually be a good sign for *both* of us! When, in fact, my father eventually succeeded in his ambition, his own Lord Mayor's Show was the last to be held on that particular date. In order to avoid the problem of traffic congestion in the City and also to provide school children with the opportunity to see the Show, it was moved in 1959 to the second Saturday of the month, where it has remained ever since. It was thus that when my own turn came to host the Lord Mayor's Show I was unable to do so on my birthday. My own Show was held on Saturday 13th November, 1976, with the Banquet taking place on the following Monday.

I have no record of the time of my birth. Unlike the system used by the Scots (who tend to be better at these things) my birth certificate merely gives the date and not the *hour* of birth. This, of course, is most disconcerting when one happens to be seeking the advice of an astrologer, who requires such specific information in order to ensure the accuracy of any prediction. It was, I am given to understand, a 'difficult' birth, in so much as my mother was advised not to have any more children. Thus was I condemned to the life of an only child. I say this not as any indication that my childhood was an unhappy one, but I do rather suspect that having siblings enables one to learn very early on about the values of sharing and unselfishness. It also meant that, until I started school, I had no yardstick against which to measure my own progress and development.

I was christened at St. Mary Abbot's Church, Kensington, where my

With Mother.

parents had been married by the Chaplain of my father's regiment. The name Robin was in honour of a cousin of my mother, who had been killed in the 1914-18 War. My other names were also strong family names: Danvers was an ancient line from my father's family tree, which had originally been introduced with William in 1066; Penrose was a name from my mother's side, which had been used by all her forbears as far back as anyone cared to remember. My mother was told that she would be unable to have me christened Robin since it was an abbreviation of Robert and not, therefore, a proper name. Mother was insistent, however, and Robin I became. This only had repercussions once in later life, when a somewhat over-zealous Toastmaster, in an effort to be correct, introduced me as Sir Robert Gillett. It was never to happen again!

My first home was Number 33, Sheffield Terrace, a road leading off to the west of Church Street, Kensington. It was a large, comfortable house and I spent most of my early years on the top floor, where the Day Nursery and an adjacent Night Nursery were situated. This floor also comprised a bathroom, and accommodation for the two house servants: the cook and the parlourmaid. Like all the best young Englishmen I had a Scots Nanny, the redoubtable Nurse Ferguson, who seemed terrifically old to me at the time but probably wasn't, at all. Nanny slept in the Night Nursery, alongside me in my cot. Nurse Ferguson, of whom I grew very fond, brought me up on breakfasts of traditional Scots porridge which (in true Highland fashion) was left to steep overnight in the Day Nursery and which was heated up in the morning for the two of us. I certainly thrived on this diet and I have had a liking for porridge ever since, despite some very dubious variations of the dish that were served up in my later years at school.

Our house had a large garden at the rear and a small front garden. One of my earliest memories is of being outside, for some reason or other, in the garden at the front of our house early one morning. The milkman had called and upon ringing the doorbell was greeted by the house parlourmaid who brought him a cup of tea – I suspect out of a pure generosity rather than because she happened to harbour any particular affection for him. I stood gazing with unabashed curiosity as the milkman proceeded to pour the tea from the teacup into the saucer, blow upon it and then drink noisily from the saucer. Fascinated by this procedure I was determined to try it out at the very next opportunity. Nurse Ferguson was, however, singularly unimpressed with my saucer-slurping and I was severely reprimanded for poor manners the next time she served me tea in the Nursery! Nanny had rather peculiar ideas about diet in general and about good manners, in particular. I recall that she never allowed me to have pepper or vinegar on my food, 'Because,' she explained, 'that's what gives housemaids spots'. These condiments remained, therefore, delicacies unknown to me throughout my pre-school years.

I have other memories of those early years reflecting a picture of London which has long since disappeared. Street-vendors would be strolling about outside; muffin-men ringing bells and flower-sellers displaying their wares. On most days I would be taken out for airings, firstly in my pram and then toddling alongside Nanny, across to Kensington Gardens, which was a short walk away. In the summer months there used to be an old lady who sat under a huge umbrella, just outside the entrance to the park, with a little stall from which she purveyed chocolates and other sweetmeats to the passing children and their escorts. She was known to all and sundry as 'the chocolate lady' and was always extremely cheerful and friendly. I was to discover, later on, that her real name was Mrs Wheelerbread, and I have always held a great affection for her. She was married to a naval pensioner who had a similar stall at the bottom of the road leading up to Kensington Palace. He, too, sat under an umbrella and, from his little stall sold flowers. Together they made a living and they shared a tenement on one of the side streets off Church Street, where I was subsequently to visit them.

Occasionally, Nurse Ferguson used to take time off on a Sunday and I was left in the charge of my father, who was obliged to provide me with fresh air and exercise. In my 'pram period' this would consist of visits to the Round Pond, Peter Pan's statue or a walk beside Rotten Row. Apparently for the latter expeditions, Father would wear a morning coat and top hat, which in the mid-1920s would not have looked at all out of place. All his life, my father was a great 'morning-coat man' and he always cut a very fine figure. When I was big enough to walk, it was duck-feeding at the Pond and sugar lumps for the police horses in the Row. I had a toy sailing boat, which I used to push out across the Round Pond, competing with the many other model craft which would be raced across the water by enthusiasts. Some gentlemen even had model ocean liners, constructed in the finest detail and engine-propelled. When we were out in the park, I would be sent up to Women Police Officers in their topee-like hats and long skirts to ask the time; presumably this was to discourage shyness and also to promote respect for a Police Officer's powers of protection if one were ever in need.

Father was a great walker, and, as I grew stronger and more willing, the length and distance of our forays gradually increased. On at least one occasion we walked from Sheffield Terrace across Kensington Gardens, Hyde Park, Green Park and St. James', all the way to the Houses of Parliament. Thankfully we took the bus home! Although it was certainly a long way for a little lad, my father would tell stories as we walked and the time passed by all too quickly.

One alternative and very exciting form of Sunday morning entertainment was a visit to the Zoo. My father, for some reason which remains unbeknown to me, was a member of the Zoological Society. This entitled him to entry to Regent's Park on Sunday mornings, when the Zoo was closed to the general public. On these expeditions we would set off well-laden with a variety of comestibles to suit the palates of the various species in residence, who would be happy to enjoy our bounty. Unlike the general public we were allowed in to the cages of many of the larger mammals, accompanied, of course, by their keepers. One that I can recall in particular was an Indian elephant able to perform magic: one pushed a penny into an apple until it disappeared, then offered the apple to the elephant. The great beast would snuffle up the apple with his trunk, pop it into his mouth and, after a munch or two, return the penny to your hand before finishing off the apple. There was also a brown bear called 'Winnie', the mascot of some regiment, who simply adored Nestlé's condensed milk. She would drink this straight from the can, we having first of all pierced the requisite holes. It was, on one distinctly memorable occasion, the brown bears who were to prove our downfall, and a severe embarrassment to my father, whose reputation as a competent child-minder were severely jeopardised...

We visited the brown bears' cage regularly. Although we were not permitted in the cage itself, we were allowed into the space in front of the lower barrier which kept the public at bay. The treat for these bears was Tate & Lyle's Golden Syrup which we had in plentiful supply, complete with wooden kitchen spoon to aid consumption. The drill was to twist the wooden spoon in the tin and push it through to the bear, who would grasp the spoon in its forepaws, lick it clean and then wait eagerly as the process was repeated. When the tin was too empty for useful deployment of the spoon, it was handed over to the bear whose long tongue could remove the last sticky

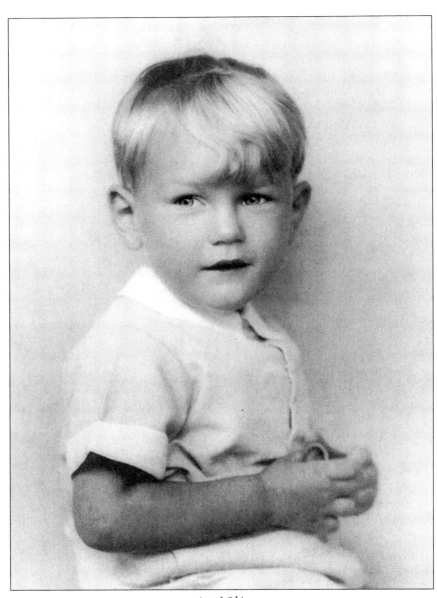

Aged 3¹/₂.

drops. We were all familiar with this routine, the bears, my father and I, and the two of us would share the feeding between us, my father taking the larger bears and me the smaller. On the fateful day, my father made the mistake of handing over the tin before it had been sufficiently emptied. As the bear tilted the tin, a stream of golden syrup escaped. I was immediately below, busily engaged in feeding a smaller bear, and can still vividly recall the sensation of a sticky stream descending on my hair. I moved back before the bear could lick it off, but it took a certain amount of explaining and a great deal of hot water when we arrived back at home.

On Sundays the family sometimes went to lunch with my grandfather who lived in Stanley Crescent. He had an early crystal set and we would listen keenly to the 'magic box' through earphones. If my behaviour ever became too rumbustuous for him, Grandfather would silently retire to his study, where he would await my apology once my father had reprimanded me and sent me in. I recall the very first radio we acquired at home – a Pye so-called 'portable', about the size of a large suitcase, which ran off an accumulator, which was a large acid battery which had to be recharged at fairly frequent intervals. Henry Hall and Jack Payne's bands seemed to dominate the programmes and I was allowed to listen to Children's Hour presented by Uncle Mac. Within the family and among friends my father was always known as Mac because my mother did not care for Harold or Sydney, his real Christian names.

The people who lived next door to us in Sheffield Terrace had a governess, who came to teach their daughter Imogen. I would attend a nursery school, which was held in their house for the benefit of three or four children who lived in the immediate neighbourhood. It was here that I started to learn to read, as well as embark on a number of other useful skills such as producing endless quantities of raffia work for my unfortunate parents. I have never kept in touch with Imogen, but I suppose I could well refer to her as my first girlfriend. She was certainly the next best thing to a sister and I spent a considerable amount of my time in her company.

I was an eager reader, and would practise my new-found skill on the tradesmen's lorries that drove past our house. In those days there was still quite a number of steam lorries about, puffing smoke and making a dreadful racket. Milk floats still had milk churns on the back, from which milk was poured into a can and taken into the house.

11

Family holidays were spent at Frinton-on-Sea, where my parents rented a house. I was introduced to the sea at a very early age, in 1926, and therefore I suppose was quite accustomed to sea air by the time I was to live on the coast permanently. My father was very keen on riding and introduced me to this hobby fairly early on, too: a photograph exists, as evidence, of me aged about eighteen months astride a small pony. My riding was to continue throughout my formative years – firstly with hired ponies and then, eventually, my own.

My first two Christmases were spent in a lovely old Georgian house in Staffordshire, where we stayed with 'Uncle Frank'. I have never to this day discovered quite what relation he was – although of course in those days close family friends were always known as 'auntie' or 'uncle'. Uncle Frank was, in fact, Sir Frank Villiers Foster, a baronet with no heirs, who also happened to be Master of the South Staffordshire hounds. I have very vague memories of this rather grand house, which are embellished, again, with the aid of photographs: one in particular of a somewhat diminutive boy in little wellies, well wrapped up against the cold, in a snowy landscape. One memory I do have is of sleeping in a brass bed on my own – Nanny was in the room next door. There was a fox's mask on the wall, and I can recall wondering where the rest of the fox might be.

In 1930, my parents decided to purchase a house in Frinton, where they had been renting for a number of summers. This now became our permanent out-of-town home, and we used to go down at Easter as well as Summer, taking Cook and the housemaid with us together with all the family baggage which would be transported down independently while we travelled by car, stopping on the way for lunch at a lovely old pub with a restaurant at Witham.

Chapter 2

The lease on 33, Sheffield Terrace must have expired in 1932 and we then moved to a flat in Camden Hill Court, which was up the hill a little way and looked down over Kensington. Here we stayed until 1933 when we decided that we might as well go and live at the house in Frinton; my father's office was reasonably close to Liverpool Street Station and there was a good train service. Thus my father became a commuter and my mother and I took up residence by the sea, where we stayed until after the war. I had been attending a pre-prep school in Kensington, and I now transferred to a mixed pre-prep in Frinton, which was run by two sisters, the Misses MacDonald. It was at this establishment that I experienced my first taste of the battle of the sexes, and learnt just how unpleasant little girls might be toward little boys. During our break times we were permitted out into the gardens where we would chase around; the boys would inevitably gang up on the girls, taunting them with names and pulling their hair, as is their wont. Unfortunately I was the sole boy who stayed on at school for lunch since most of my 'mates' went home. I was thus forced to partake of this meal with a group of girls, mostly older than me, who took full advantage of having one poor hapless little lad to themselves. They would tease me relentlessly, at times reducing me to tears, which of course did not help my cause at all. I would pray for the bell to go to end this torture. The experience, whilst not putting me off girls for life, certainly did nothing to endear me to the species.

In the summer of 1934 I progressed to a very good boys' prep school, Hillcrest, situated only one avenue away from our home. Donning my cap and blazer for the very first time I proudly rode my new bicycle to school on the first day, there to commence my first proper education. The Headmaster and his son, who ran the school together, were both Scots – known, for obvious reasons, as Old Mr Stuart and Young Mr Stuart. I enjoyed life at Hillcrest immensely. Having spent my first term as a day boy, it soon dawned on me that I was something of a 'second class citizen'. There was a sense of comradeship amongst boarders from which day boys were excluded. I also found it difficult to concentrate on homework in the home environment, where distractions such as the radio made it quite hard to do my prep. I therefore announced that I wanted to be a boarder and, strange as it might seem given that we lived only a street away, my parents consented; I suspect they felt that as an only child I would fare better in the company of my peers. A boarder I duly became and remained so for the rest of my time at the school, coming home only occasionally at weekends when I might bring one of my chums home for lunch. On the whole I fared well as a boarder and thoroughly enjoyed myself. The school had a Scout troop, which I joined, when I was old enough. Prior to this I had been a member of the Cubs in the town (again I suspect that my mother was afraid of molly-coddling me as an only child and was determined that I should 'join in' as much as possible, which I felt was not always to my advantage). However, I did acquire a taste for camping and other such pursuits, so it was a natural progression to join the Scouts, where I eventually progressed to the role of Patrol Leader. My father had been a keen supporter of the Scout movement and this was an activity of which he thoroughly approved.

I fared reasonably well at Hillcrest. I was never particularly good at games, although I was quite keen on boxing. However, my early enthusiasm was dampened somewhat after an incident in which I had had my cheekbone cracked when kicking a ball around with some friends; thereafter I would flinch away from my boxing opponents for fear of further damage, which really put paid to my development in the ring. We played soccer in the winter months and cricket in the summer. I never excelled at the latter; in fact I did not particularly *like* cricket, but this meant that when I became more senior I found that I was missing out on all the visits to play other schools and the sumptuous teas that were inevitably provided. I thus procured the job of scorer, which meant all of the benefits without actually having to wield a cricket bat or bowl a wicket. Similarly with soccer, I got myself a job as a linesman which meant, again, that I valiantly accompanied the team with my little flag and was able to watch the game without having to participate.

It may be a consequence of being an only child that I have never been attracted to team games. As a staunch individualist I enjoyed tennis and fencing but have remained consistently averse to what I have in later life rather rudely referred to as 'games' – as opposed to the refinements of 'sport'. 'Games', (such as football and cricket), are as far as I can make out determined by a set of rules; they involve a referee, everyone depends on everyone else and as soon as it is getting exciting someone blows a whistle and the whole thing is over. By contrast a 'sport' might be an activity such as horse riding. It involves only oneself and the horse and whatever one happens to be doing the pleasure and the skill are determined largely by one's own personality, not by another. Sailing is another example, where one is engaged in pitting oneself against the elements, or fishing and shooting where one is reliant solely upon one's own skill and expertise. I rather think I would never have taken kindly to riding a tandem bicycle.

From a very early age I had been set upon a career with horses. We kept our own stables at home, and had a groom who looked after the horses. I had my own pony, Scamp, although he was rather a handful for me and was eventually dismissed to a riding school owned by cousins of ours out in Suffolk. Scamp was replaced by Tinker, an Exmoor pony of whom I was terribly fond and who had won some prize at the Richmond Horse Show. Tinker was a rascal but we got on famously together. We would take part in local gymkhanas and I have photographs still of various triumphs. Our groom was a Yorkshire-man, with an accent so broad that I could barely understand a word he said. However, he had been a Corporal in the Scots Greys, and he

With my pony, Tinker.

15

used to take me out to the beach in the mornings and put me through all kinds of drill on my pony, making me ride without stirrups and do exercises in the saddle. In 1936 I rode Tinker dressed as Dick Turpin in the local parade to commemorate the Coronation of King George VI. Our groom was concerned that Tinker, not having been properly trained, might take fright at the cheering crowds and flag waving. He therefore resorted to an old army trick to keep the pony calm. A mixture of laudanum and chewing tobacco was sewn up in a piece of butter muslin, which was tied to Tinker's bit. Chewing on this kept him happily quiet and docile despite the excitement around him. During the war, when Frinton was declared Front Line, Tinker was sadly evacuated to a farm inland. His ability to open gates was here to prove his downfall; he managed to escape from the field where he was put to graze and was knocked down and killed by a passing army convoy.

For a young boy Frinton was, at that time, an ideal place in which to grow up. In the summer one was already 'at the seaside', surrounded by friends and a perfect beach. The summers in those days always seemed to be long, hot and sunny. I rode every day, usually in the early mornings, with my father or our groom. I played tennis and went to the beach, where we would invariably have a picnic lunch. I also learned to swim. My personal tutor was an ex-naval PT instructor; wearing a set of waders and a waterproof oilskin suit, he would support you in the water with an old bicycle inner tube until you were able to go solo. Living close to the sea, it was not long before I acquired my first boat: a six-foot rowing dinghy, which I proudly bought out of my own savings. Then, when I was eleven years old, I graduated to a lovely ten foot clinker-built standing lug sailing dinghy. The spring and winter holidays were spent riding or cycling round the local countryside, walking, or, if there was snow, tobogganing down the few hills available. Occasionally in the summer I went out fishing with my father in a local sailing boat or trawling in the adjacent Walton Backwaters.

By the age of ten and under the influence of my proximity to and enjoyment of the sea and my reading, I had changed my mind about horses and was inclining strongly towards a seafaring life as a possible career. I did *not* incline towards a civil career and certainly had no desire to follow in my father's footsteps as a Chartered Accountant. In any case, the Household Cavalry was in the process of becoming predominantly mechanised and driving a tank held no place in my imagination. The tales of T.T. Jeans, Bartemeas and my hero worship for Lord Nelson were pushing me inexorably in the direction of the Navy as a way of life. My great great grandfather had been at sea in the Napoleonic wars, and had actually served on the *Victory* for a short while (although not at the Battle of Trafalgar). We had a picture of Nelson hanging in the drawing room over what was referred to in the family as 'Nelson's Box', which was my great great grandfather's Spanish walnut brass-bound box in which he had kept his papers. I would spend hours poring over books of warships and by the age of twelve could have named all the major and many minor ships of the then huge Royal Navy.

My health I think gave my mother some concern. I suffered from what in those days was called acidosis and was regularly fed glucose, or given barley sugars to suck. I was also made to rest for an hour every afternoon. Although this hampered my post-luncheon social life it did improve my general knowledge. I was not required to sleep, just to lie down. This I would do with a book, often a volume of Arthur Mae's Children's Encyclopaedia, or an illustrated history book, 'The Romance of the Nation'. I was suspected of being anaemic due to a naturally pale complexion and ordered to eat raw beef sandwiches at break each day at school – I am not sure of the repercussions of this other than putting me off beef for life! Very occasionally at school I fainted and was regularly car-sick, even on fairly short journeys. I remember though that the likelihood of this was in inverse ratio to the size of the car: especially if sitting in the back. The back seat of a Rolls was fatal; the front of a Morris Minor no problem at all. I recall no sea-sickness during those early years, although it has to be said that the seas I then sailed upon were never very rough. Time was to tell!

At school I was being prepared for the entrance examination to the Royal Naval College at Dartmouth. By 1938, the clouds of war were gathering, evidence of which reached my life at Frinton in a few small ways. I recall that during the Munich Crisis we were all issued with gas masks and the cigarette cards we all used to collect ran a series on ARP equipment. I sat the Dartmouth College exam in the March of '39. Prior to the written exam, you were required to attend a medical and an interview. I think 250 candidates submitted, of which only 70 got through to the written exam. I was, fortunately, among their number, but unfortunately on the day of the exam was suffering from a bad dose of 'flu. It was a tough exam and of the 70 who sat only 33

As a Boy Scout, aged 12¹/₂.

passed. The doors of the Royal College at Dartmouth were thus closed to me, which was a great disappointment. However, there was a second option. I was still determined to go to sea and plumped, instead, for the Nautical College, Pangbourne, now known as Pangbourne College. Founded in 1917 to supply Officers for the Royal and Merchant Navies, it was one of three Nautical Schools, which also included H.M.S. Worcester and H.M.S. Conway. There was an intake into the R.N. from the three schools when one reached the age of 17, in addition to the 'special' entry. Pangbourne thus provided a second chance. In the summer term I took the Common Entrance examination and donned my naval uniform for the first time as a cadet in September, 1939 – concurrent, almost, with the outbreak of the Second World War.

On the morning of 3rd September, my father, mother and I left the beach and met my grandfather at the Esplanade Hotel, where he was staying, to listen to Mr Chamberlain's broadcast on the radio at 11.00 a.m. War, he told us, had been declared on Germany. There must have been few people who thought that our ultimatum would stop Hitler in his invasion of Poland.

What were my feelings about it? I can remember quite clearly that my chief worry was that 'it would be over by Christmas' (why were wars always supposed so to be?!) and that I would have played no part in it. Brought up in a family with a great tradition of service and remembering posters from the '14-'18 War of children saying to their father, 'What did you do in the Great War, Daddy?' the possible disgrace of not having served far outweighed any fears of being killed, or wounded. I need not have worried – the war waited for me!

How selfish can youth be? I never spared a thought for how my parents might have felt about it. It was not until thirty five years later that this was brought home to me. I looked across the breakfast table on my elder son's nineteenth birthday (he was at University at this stage) and said, 'I had my nineteenth birthday in Murmansk. At least you have come this far without a war.' I realised then what parents must feel when their carefully nurtured young go off to battle.

When Frinton was declared Front Line (at the time of Dunkirk) it was impossible to stay in the town unless you had a good reason for being there. My father ran the Home Guard, so we stayed. All of my friends, however, departed and thus began another lonely period in my life. Throughout all of the holidays during the war (before I went to sea, that is, in 1943) I was back to being not only an only child but an only teenager in Frinton. I would accompany the Home Guard on activities, and keep myself busy in many ways, but generally speaking I feel it was a lost period in my life. No dances, no balls . . . none of the usual trappings of teenage years. The local worthies would run social evenings for the troops who were billeted on the town. A little makeshift band was put together to entertain the chaps and I would accompany them on the drums, having nobody to take with me to these dances.

This apart, my excitement was provided for me by the war itself, which was taking place in close proximity. During the Battle of Britain it was possible to go out into the garden and watch the aeroplanes wheeling around, Spitfires chasing Bombers across the sky. Occasionally we were strafed with machine gun fire and one of our neighbours – about five houses down our avenue – was the recipient of a parachute mine, which shook us all up a bit. When returning from inland bombing missions, German planes would ditch any unused bombs on us on the way home. It was excitement, of a sort, but perhaps not the kind any contemporary teenager might relish. Looking back, I cannot help but experience a certain regret that I rather missed out on the fun that ought to accompany one's teenage years.

Chapter 3

September, 1939. We are at war with Germany and I am in the uniform of the service of my choice, a Cadet R.N.R., about to commence training at the Nautical College, Pangbourne; four years to go before I will see active service at sea but a step in the right direction. My mail henceforth will be addressed not to Master Robin Gillett, but to Cadet R.D.P. Gillett R.N.R.: for a thirteen-and-a-half year old, determined to see service, a boost indeed.

The Nautical College, Pangbourne (N.C.P. for short – the car parks had not been invented, then) had been founded in 1917 by the shipowners Devitt and Moore who had, since the latter part of the last century, trained Cadets in their clippers for service as officers in the Merchant Navy. With the First World War and the passing of sail, they decided to found a shore establishment, similar to the Royal Naval College, Dartmouth, to carry on the good work. A public school in uniform, embracing a general educational curriculum, but in place of the classics, instruction in navigation, seamanship, signals and some basic engineering, spread over a four-year period. The routine was pro-active but sustainable; the discipline was strict but fair. Subsequent entry into the Merchant Navy was not obligatory and many went into the R.N. or other services, although with a war on what had been called 'civil life' as a career was seldom an option for the leavers between 1939 and 1945.

For organisational purposes the College was divided into four Divisions (Houses in normal school parlance) and each Division into two Watches, (Port and Starboard). The Divisions took their names from the Devitt and Moore clippers, *Port Jackson, Hesperus, Harbinger* and *Macquorie*, with about fifty-five cadets in each. Each Division had a Chief Cadet Captain in charge, each watch a Cadet Captain plus two Cadet leaders and the Chief Cadet Captain of the College equated to Head Boy elsewhere. There was a Divisional Tutor (Housemaster) for each.

To ease the leap from Preparatory School all Cadets for their first two or three terms went into Port Jackson and then graduated to one

September, 1939: in uniform.

of the other three for the rest of their time. The Cadet Officers for Port Jackson were specially selected and provided from the three senior Divisions.

Routine was governed by bugles and bells, from Reveille at 0645 till Lights Out at 2100. We were paraded and checked five times a day; we marched or doubled everywhere, even into meals. We slept in bunks, which we made every morning with the covers just so and towels made up round the upper rails. Toothbrushes in their mugs on the clothes locker tops had their heads all 'dressed' one way and any clothing found lying about and not stowed in the approved order was put in the scran-bag with a fine of 1d for its recovery. Anyone with 6d's worth at the week's end was beaten. We were a tidy lot!

As one might expect, considerable emphasis was placed on physical fitness and each day started with activity exercises, known as 'akkers' for short. Dragged from a warm bunk, dressed in shirt, shorts and plimsolls, we were paraded at 0700 on the parade ground under the eye of the Chief Instructor, or one of his minions, for fifteen minutes of P.T. In wintertime we were out in the dark, but there was still no chance of missing the eagle eye of the Instructor as he strode amongst us – and woe betide the idle. The parade ground was surfaced with gravel and on dismissal one picked out the stones which were always embedded in the palms of one's hands after press ups. If it was wet we were sent on a route march instead, or on Saturday mornings, when the Instructors had a lie-in, on a run.

This sleep-dispelling exercise was followed by a cold shower, supervised by the duty Cadet Captain, who counted out ten very slow seconds, the minimum time allowed under the freezing water. He himself had a hot shower afterwards. Teeth (still chattering) to be cleansed, bunks to be made and uniform donned we fell in and were marched into breakfast. There followed 'territories'; these were allotted tasks of general cleaning of the grounds, polishing brasswork and other seaman-like domestic chores throughout the College. It also included furious brushing of our uniforms before being fell-in for Divisions. After a careful inspection by the Cadet Captain, ever ready to 'run in' any cadet idle on parade, we were counted and reported – presumably to see none of us had escaped during the night or otherwise absented themselves without reason. The padre then conducted prayers before we were marched off to our studies. During the morning break we had recourse to the canteen, where in the first term, before rationing began to bite, the usual tuckshop-type commodities were on sale. Back to work until 1230 when we returned to the parade ground for drill with the College Band (of cadets) providing the martial music for our manoeuvres till lunch-time. Unlike the other parades, which were by Divisions, this was by Companies of which there were five, graded by height, and regardless of age or seniority.

After lunch we changed into the appropriate sporting rig and paraded again (to weed out absentees) before proceeding to the games fields or the river. For sporting purposes we were divided into 'tops' as in the wooden walls of yore. Fo'c's'le, foretop, maintop and mizzen, according to age, size and ability. Rugger in the Michaelmas Term, hockey in the Lent term, cricket or sailing and rowing in the Summer. There was also boxing and fencing one day a week with tennis in the summer and squash in the winter. Unless one was sick, or excused, you played. There was no swimming pool then, so swimming and life saving, which was compulsory, took place in Old Father Thames. On Saturdays non-players had to watch inter-school matches, and on Sundays hobbies were permitted, or cycling and walking within a five mile radius of the College which, conveniently for the authorities, excluded Reading, the nearest town of any interest.

After Evening Quarters – the last parade of the day and again the usual check on numbers – there was supper, followed by three periods of prep. in our classrooms. On Thursday evenings one period of prep. was omitted and the whole college moved to the gym for boxing bouts, in which each cadet in turn had to participate, according to matched weights. On Saturday nights there was usually a film, or occasionally a Divisional Concert or a play performed by the Dramatic Society. On Sundays there was a big parade followed by Chapel, with Evensong in the evening. Nobody was allowed to do nothing at any time! Divisional Prayers at 8.30 p.m. were followed by Lights Out at 9.00 p.m. There were not many insomniacs, I can assure you.

Discipline was largely in the hands of the Cadet Officers and was in fact an important element in their man-management training. The administration of punishment was far more formalised than it was in normal public school, both in its award and execution. There were three grades of summary jurisdiction for ex-classroom offences. The lowest was House Report for internal Divisional cases presided over by the Chief Cadet Captain of the Division, whose powers were limited to awarding extra drills, extra working parties, referral up to the next 'court' or admonishment. The defendant was marched in and halted before the C.C.C., 'off caps' and the charge read by the 'arresting' cadet officer, who gave evidence. The defendant was then asked if he had anything to say before being told of his punishment. All the proceedings were logged and signed by the C.C.C.

The drill in the next higher court, that of the Chief Cadet Captain of the College, was similar, but his powers of punishment included corporal punishment. It was used for inter-divisional charges, that is when a Cadet Officer of one Division charged a cadet from a Division other than his own, or on a referral up from the House Report in a case where a C.C.C. felt his powers of punishment were inadequate.

The third and final stage was 'Defaulters', where the 'presiding judge' was the Commander who could order beatings, or even expulsion. Recommendations for punishment from the academic staff were processed through this court. Here the Master at Arms presented the case for the prosecution and the cadet's C.C.C. or C.C. was present also. Beating with a cane, six or three cuts, when ordered was carried out by the Chief Cadet Captain of the College in the presence of the Commander, Master-at-Arms (who counted the strokes), the Duty Chief Cadet Captain and the defendant's Chief Cadet Captain. Requests were dealt with by this court also.

Another custom rare, I would think, in other public schools, was the weekly 'pay parade', when we received a one shilling piece, known as a 'Bursar's Bob', in our caps. It wasn't pay, as such, but pocket money, charged on our termly bill. It was a beating offence to have more than ten shillings in your possession at any time. Money could be deposited with your Divisional Tutor and drawn for some sufficient purpose. Many cadets also had Post Office savings accounts in the village. Not that there was much need for money. Once rationing began to come in there was little in the canteen or at the shops. As our trouser pockets were sewn up (to avoid the temptation of sticking one's hands therein) there was nowhere to stow cash anyway.

How did I fit in against such a background, and settle during my first year in the Junior Division? I suppose one thing that we all had in common was that we were all of one mind: to serve, and preferably to serve at sea. We had no thoughts of University, civil life was for 'oddballs' or wimps – although I am not certain that the word had been invented then. Of the twenty-five cadets who joined with me in

1939 twenty-four wanted to join the Royal Navy – the other one was committed to the Merchant Navy at that stage.

The new entry joined a day before term started in order to 'settle in'. We had a medical examination, a talk from the Commander and an intelligence test which, together with the results of our entrance examination, would be taken into consideration to decide in which academic stream we were to be placed. Those who might be expected to sit their School Certificate within two years went into one stream (which included me), the other into a three-year stream. We were drilled, and told that we would not be allowed the use of the bicycles we had brought with us until we could march properly with the rest of the Division (after about two weeks). Because it was the Michaelmas Term the majority of the previous year's intake had moved on to Senior Divisions, but the remainder, who had joined at Lent or Summer Term, were the old hands as far as we 'first termers' were concerned and made us feel pretty inferior until we found our feet. Some whose bicycles ('grids' as we used to call them) were not in a roadworthy state would seek to borrow ours till we were allowed to use them. By the time we could use them, they were all too often in a somewhat less pristine condition than they had been when we arrived. In fact by 1941, in the interest of safety, only Cadet Officers were allowed bicycles at the College.

At the end of our probationary period we were set an exam. to test our knowledge of the College, which included nicknames of College staff, or places within the precincts, traditions, etc. For instance the large lavatory by the Study Area called 'The Crystal Palace' was presided over by a grubby old veteran known as 'Captain Cook', who had permanently clenched between his teeth a battered old pipe whose stem was attached to the bowl by a piece of Bunsen burner piping.

We were allocated our 'tops' for games and as my prep school had been a football school I now had to master the art of rugger (without much success) and likewise hockey in the following term. I elected for fencing as my extra, which I took to well. I subsequently gained my colours and was promoted to Captain before I left the College.

When I joined the College it was presided over by a retired Captain R.N. as Captain Superintendent, but he was recalled to the Navy at the end of the Michaelmas Term and Sir Phillip Devitt, the co-founder with his father, who was Chairman of the Governors, moved into the College with his family and exercised both roles. The Commander, or

Executive Officer, was Jackie Blair, a Commander R.N.R., and he oversaw the day to day running of the place. Later he was to go and was replaced by a Commander R.N. (ret'd) who taught Navigation to us as a civilian, but emerged as Commander MacIwaine R.N. to take over as Executive Officer until the end of the war.

At the end of my first year I was transferred to my Senior Division which was Hesperus, housed then in Bowden Green, a separate house in the grounds some way away from the main complex. The 'phoney war' was by now over and we were alone. Dunkirk was history and the Battle of Britain raged over the skies when I was on leave at Frinton, where I was to find that much had changed. Not only had most familiar faces left, but the familiar sites, too, were altered: the greensward was landmined and the foreshore protected by a grid of scaffolding backed up by concrete anti-tank blocks. There were six-inch gun emplacements opposite the Grand Hotel and pillboxes and roadblocks at strategic places. The L.D.V., subsequently the Home Guard, had been formed and my father, as Major, commanded the area embracing Frinton, Walton, the Kirby's (Upper and Lower), and up to Weeley. Our second house was turned into Home Guard H.Q. Although Tinker had to be evacuated, my father was allowed to keep his horse, Grey Boy, on the Home Guard strength. Our groom was recalled to the army and the horse stabled locally.

The beach huts had been removed, and my dinghy was in the garden. However, for that first summer only I was given a chit by the local R.N. officer to sail my dinghy on the Walton Backwaters (Arthur Ransome's 'Secret Water') in uniform. There were three com-mandeered motor yachts manned by R.N.S.V.R. crews patrolling the creeks and inlets with whom I became very friendly. I was also permitted to go out with the Home Guard as an observer on their local exercises. Alas, the sailing freedom I experienced that summer was never permitted again.

Back to Pangbourne. Air raid shelters adjoined each major residential building and we had several uncomfortable nights when the sirens went, although latterly there was not much activity over us and I do not recall having to go into them again after 1940. The College formed its own Home Guard unit from masters and cadets who were old enough. Static water tanks appeared and we had our own portable pump. We also instituted a fire watch each night on the tower of Devitt House, which had a wonderful view of the surrounding countryside. The more senior cadets kept one and a half hours' watch in pairs throughout the night, and in winter it was very cold. One was excused akkers the next morning and had the reward of a cup of Bovril when the watch was over, but nevertheless it was a bit of a chore, especially when you really needed all the sleep you could get.

By 1941 rationing had begun to take its toll, not only in the contents of the canteen but in the mess room as well. To supplement our meagre diet the pangs of hunger could be assuaged by recourse to the big tins of ship's biscuits placed strategically in the changing rooms. These delicacies were about two inches square and made (so the tin told us) by Spillers of dog food fame. They were brick hard and could be eaten only by bashing a piece off and sucking it into submission before risking one's teeth on it, or soaking it in water first. We learnt that this was what in Nelson's day was known as 'hard tack' – how any weevil, with which they were prone to be infested, ever got into them was hard to imagine.

Speaking of weevils reminds me of the lunch of stew served up one day. It contained a large quantity of pearl barley to augment the small amount of meat. Most of us wolfed it down with enthusiasm, assuming the black spots on the barley were part of the grain, until one slower eater examined his plate more closely and discovered them to be weevils. The news spread rapidly up and down the mess room and soon an ever louder chant began: 'Weevils, weevils, WEEVILS!' It was a scene reminiscent of those old films depicting U.S. prisons with inmates banging their mugs and shouting in riot mode. The Chief Cadet Captain of the College rose from his lonely chair at the top of the mess hall and marched out bearing his plate to the kitchens to complain. Those who had finished suffered no ill effects and probably benefited from the extra protein – the things were dead, after all.

Come the Summer Term of 1941 my stream sat the School Certificate Examination. I passed with two credits and three passes, the minimum required. No great shakes, but it took me into the sixth form. I loved the Summer Term as we spent a lot of time on the river sailing in whalers and 12' dinghies and pulling in gigs. I had always disliked cricket and was happy to let those who were keen on the game uphold the honour of the College on my behalf. In fact I was party, in the classroom, to getting my own back. One day our English tutor, who was very keen on cricket, set us an essay – the usual ploy when a master wanted to leave the classroom for a quick smoke. The subject: 'Cricket'. The rest of the class bent over their pads, pens flying in a frenzy of sycophantic zeal. I sat and gazed blankly at mine and then, in a sudden burst of inspiration, indulged in some positive (or perhaps negative?) thinking: a tactic I have resorted to in later life when faced with this sort of problem. I would make fun of it. And so I tore the noble game to shreds with all the spleen of a theatre critic after a dubious first night. I mocked the principle and execution of the game and really had a ball with the nomenclature of the fielding positions 'silly mid-on', 'slips' and 'square leg', until they sounded like characters from a comic opera. The papers were handed in on the master's return to be marked and reviewed at the next class. On that day they were handed back to their authors with suitable comment. As the names were singled out one by one, my expectation of a detention to try again increased, as mine was not returned. Finally, it was the only one left in the master's hand. I waited for the axe to fall. And then, to my amazement, he said, 'I have given Gillett ten out of ten for his essay. He will now read it out to you. It is a fine piece of original writing!' He had been an overseas correspondent in Paris before the war so perhaps he was sympathetic to my style.

As many a comedian will usually confess, the comic role often goes hand in hand with being slightly out of line at school – puny, no good at games, or whatever, but able to hold one's own in one's peer group by the ability to make them laugh. It certainly worked for me. I was a good mimic and studied each Master's mannerisms to advantage (although not always to mine, in their eyes). One report of mine read: 'Too fond of exercising his ready wit on his superiors'. I was able to quote this to great effect in later life when speaking as Lord Mayor to a distinguished audience, when I would add, 'Of course now I am so bloody superior there's no one left to exercise it on...'

Another time I was summoned to the Director of Studies (Headmaster's) office for reprimand following a complaint from the Senior Maths Master.

'Mr Robinson tells me you are a buffoon,' he said.

'Yes, sir,' I replied.

(Rule 1: If up before the beak, say as little as possible).

'Do you know what a buffoon is?'

'No, sir.' (I lied).

At this point he opened a huge Oxford Dictionary, which was ready before him and tagged at the appropriate place.

'Buffoon: one who makes himself ridiculous to amuse others'.

'Yes, sir,' (I took it as a great compliment to my histrionic ability).

There followed an admonishment on how I was spoiling my chances of passing the R.N. exam – and those of the rest of my class, it would seem. I was given a 'pink card', which had to be signed by each master of every class I attended over the next fortnight to attest to my behaviour and attention. My card was signed – but I was just more careful in future! It was the Director of Studies (D.O.S. for short – an acronym often reversed by the cadets, I fear) himself who gave me the memorable end of term report: 'He sets himself very low targets each term which he then consistently fails to achieve'. Several years later, whilst driving in London, I spotted him and gave him a lift. He was working in the Ministry of Education, far from the worries of humorous cadets . . . but doubtless among many buffoons.

I had become very interested in photography when sailing at home was denied to me after 1940. I constructed a darkroom in the larder of our second house in Frinton (the Home Guard H.Q.) and joined the Photographic Society at the College which had very good equipment and of which I subsequently became the Secretary. By my fifteenth birthday I had acquired, by 'trading up' my cameras, a Lieca IIIA which was a joy to use. I began to think that if I didn't succeed in getting in the R.N. I would go into the R.N.R. for the war and then take up photography professionally after demobilisation. Meanwhile, I paid for my hobby by processing other cadets' films and taking pictures of them (for their girlfriends) and of College events as the semi-official College photographer.

I had obtained a Higher School Certificate subsidiary Physics in 1942 and joined the College Scientific Society. One of the conditions was that you had to give a half hour or one hour lecture on a scientific subject of your choice in any scholastic year. I somewhat naturally plumped for photography, choosing to use the whole hour. The important side issue for me was that up until that time, like many people, one of my worst fears was public speaking. However, I was cured for ever by my lecture. It was on a subject which I knew well and I discovered I had a latent desire to pass on my knowledge with almost evangelical zeal. Fired by my success I joined the Debating Society and the following term instituted a series of six lectures on photography: cameras and lenses; film and filters and exposure; developing; making prints; enlarging, and finishing with the sixth consisting of a short examination with twenty five questions and a prize given by me of a book on photography, 'The All in One Camera Book'. All the lectures contained practical demonstrations and attracted an average attendance of thirty cadets per lecture. It also increased the membership of the Photographic Society considerably.

Another bogey overcome was sensitivity to my Christian name. During the difficult years of puberty I became very self-conscious about it, believing my peers would think it cissy – associations of Christopher Robin and all that. Why couldn't my parents have called me something more masculine, like George or Henry? As attack is always the best form of defence, I hit on the wheeze of publishing it openly before anyone might ask me what the 'R' stood for. I did not, therefore, use my other two names of Danvers or Penrose, but signed myself Robin Gillett, and let anyone dare laugh. None did!

'I am now in my last year. A Cadet Leader and Captain of Fencing. I have survived chicken pox and mumps. I don't think I shall make it into the Royal Navy. They are only taking twelve a year from Pangbourne, 'Worcester' and 'Conway', of which six are Executive, five Engineering and one Royal Indian Navy. I know the competition from the Pangbourne entry and my maths just isn't up to it. I think it will be the R.N.R. for me for the rest of the War, then we shall see.' One could leave the College and become a Midshipman R.N.R. without further examination. My reports and placings varied widely and reflected my tastes; I did well in subjects that I liked, badly in those that I did not. High placings in Divinity, History, English, Seamanship and Physics; low in Maths, French and Geography. In some cases the standard of teaching varied enormously. The war saw many of the best teachers called up and they were substituted by people brought out of retirement or straight from school or university awaiting call-up.

My last term (Summer 1943) was significant in many respects. To start with I did not know at its outset that it was to be my last, as I was expecting to leave at the end of the Christmas Term to go into the R.N.R. The highlight of the Summer Term was Founders' Day, with Prizegiving in the morning and a parade and display in the afternoon. This time the Guest of Honour was H.M. King George VI and because the Queen was unwell he brought Princess Elizabeth instead. It was a lovely day in June and all went well. Little did I realise that this event was to feature in my speech in Guildhall at the lunch to H.M. The Queen on her Silver Jubilee.

I was at that time in my third term as a Cadet Leader but was

Nautical College, Pangbourne. Inspection by H.M. King George VI and H.R.H. Princess Elizabeth.

promoted to Cadet Captain, Acting Chief Cadet Captain of my Division on the departure of the then C.C.C. to join a ship. It was not unusual for those waiting to join the Merchant Navy to be tweaked out mid-term. Some went off to sea a week later, only to be torpedoed on their first trip. 1943 was the height of the U-boat wolf pack attacks in the North Atlantic. This promotion gave me far more responsibility and was the most valuable period of my time at the College. If the academic standards were not those one might have expected at a more famous Public School, the man-management skills were taught and exercised to perfection.

The final and probably most dramatic change of course took place towards the last weeks of term. I knew I was not in the running for R.N. entry and was staying on another term, confirmed in my rank at C.C.C., to join the R.N.R. at Christmas. I had never thought of joining the Merchant Navy. But the Commander saw me and said that the Canadian Pacific Steamship Company (C.P.S.) had asked for a cadet who was on their waiting list, or, if unavailable, another suitable candidate. The cadet in question (actually the Chief Cadet Captain of the College) had been snapped up by the Blue Funnel Line – and so was I interested? I said No, I wasn't – but was told to think about it. I did think about it and, like most important decisions taken in my life, came to a quick conclusion on my own with no advice but on the following reasoning. The C.P.S. was a 'crack' company who only employed the best. If I went in to the R.N.R. I might – only *might* – get a transfer to the R.N. at the end of hostilities. If I did not, I would be de-mobbed at the age of around 20, with no job experience and with many others in the same market. If I took the C.P.S. job I would be starting a proper career which I could leave if I did not like it, or could even transfer to the R.N.R. during hostilities, or stay put if I did like it. I wanted to go to sea. I had spent four years training to that end and the sea was the sea whatever colour the funnel or ensign – and we were all in the same war.

The next day I went back to the Commander and told him I would like the job. I then told my parents and friends, who were somewhat surprised as I had never expressed any interest in a Merchant Navy career before. But it was my life, and my decision and, as it turned out, the right one.

There was one other highlight before I left. Winston Churchill was to receive the Freedom of the City of London in Guildhall and my father, who was then on the Common Council, could invite a guest. I was given leave to come up to town to witness the ceremony. I must be one of the few alive today who was so privileged. I celebrated by buying my first pipe, for use when I left. Smoking at the College was of course not allowed and was a beating offence, and as a Cadet Officer I had to set a good example – or lose my stripes.

And so, at the end of that Summer Term I left Pangbourne. I had made many friends who were to remain so throughout my life. I loved the place, warts and all, and within days of leaving to go to sea I found I was missing the College far more than home.

Chapter 4

Summer Term 1943 ended on 27th July and I came home briefly before catching the night train to Glasgow on 30th July. There was not much respite, or time to sort out my gear. Through the good offices of one of my mother's Rear Admiral cousins I had a first class sleeper. My father came to Euston to see me off, and I shall always remember his parting words: 'Look after yourself – you're the only one we've got'.

I don't remember getting much sleep; it was hot, and bumpy. We arrived at Glasgow about 7.00 a.m. and I had some breakfast at a café opposite the station before reporting to the Canadian Pacific office. From there I took another train to Gourock. A boat took me off to my first ship, the *Empress of Russia*, which was just in from a trooping run round the Cape. I was met by two of her three cadets, both of whom were Old Pangbournians, who had finished their qualifying sea time for their Second Mate's Certificates. They helped me with my baggage and then, along with the other new cadet from H.M.S. *Worcester*, I was shown around and told my duties. As the ship was in sea routine we were on watches, I on the 4-8 (a.m. and p.m.) and the other new cadet on the 12-4. The third cadet was now the senior and would keep the 8-12 with the Third Officer. The Senior Officer of my watch was the First Officer, with the Fourth as his junior. The 12-4 had the Second Officer in charge, and the Fifth Officer as junior.

We were introduced to the Chief Officer, who did not keep a watch, and he took us in to see the Captain, a peppery little Hebridean, mostly bald but with a tonsure of what remained of his bright red hair. He wanted to know why I was dressed 'like a Swiss Admiral' (I still had my Cadet Captain's stripes and anchor on my sleeve). I explained that I had been told at the Head Office to join as I was, as time was short.

'Get it off!' was his only reply.

I felt that I had made a bad start.

I picked up my watch at 4.00 p.m. with my predecessor staying on with me whilst I got the hang of things. An anchor watch is pretty

The Empress of Russia *in her wartime colours.*

boring, but I took bearings every half hour as a check against dragging, watched out for boats coming alongside, and for signals (by Aldis or 10" searchlight) from the signal station on the pier head, or from other ships. Sometimes if the station could not see another ship we had to relay a message for them. As we were at anchor the junior officer of the watch was the only one on the Bridge, and he spent most of his time in the chartroom writing up the Fair Copy of the Deck Log Book for landing to Head Office. There were also two Quartermasters and a deck boy on the Bridge watch, engaged in various chores. We had two Clyde 'puffers', one on each side, putting coal into our bunkers. They merely kept us topped up, as they could give us only 100 tons a day and we burned 90 tons a day at anchor, or 250 tons a day when steaming. We had to go up the Clyde to the King George Dock at Govan to fuel properly, where they could bring coal trucks alongside and pour it in.

By 1943 the *Empress of Russia* must have been the largest coal-burner left afloat. She and her sister ship, the *Empress of Asia*, sunk by the Japanese off Singapore in 1942, had been taken into service for the Canadian Pacific's trans-Pacific run in 1913 and were saved from the scrap-yard in 1939 by the outbreak of war. They had both served in the 1914-18 war as armed Merchant Cruisers and troop ships, and now, well past their sell-by date, they were doing the latter again.

They had been fine looking ships in their day, with their pure white hulls and three buff funnels. They had been manned in the past by Canadian officers (mostly ex-patriate Brits.) and Chinese crews but now had an all-British crew. Like many of the great Liner companies between the wars, the C.P.S. had encouraged their officers to join the Royal Naval Reserve, so in 1939 many were called into the Navy to command escort vessels, like corvettes and frigates, or to navigate submarines. Apart from the Captain of our ships who were left in post, many of the wartime officers were not regular company men, but had been supplied by the 'pool' of Merchant Navy personnel that had been set up. Some had left the sea during the recession of the thirties, and had rejoined for the war.

Our Fourth Officer was typical of the non-company breed. He had served all his time in tramp ships and had been sent to the C.P. from the pool, after being torpedoed. His manner was coarse to say the least and his language often matched it. I think he resented cadets being allowed on the Bridge, unless to paint it. In his early days he had lived with a chipping hammer or an oily rag in his hand, treating the standing rigging. To him, far-back spoken cadets in uniform doing officer-like jobs on the Bridge was an anathema. Having not scored many brownie points on my first meeting with the Captain, I was now to sour relations with my immediate mentor.

It happened thus. In the brief days before setting off, as she would have put it, to 'fight the Hun', my mother whisked me to Gieves to equip me the better for the task ahead. To ensure my comfort she bought me a lovely pair of fleece-lined, leather sea boots. They were very comfy, but rather large, and somewhat resembled Boris Karloff's footwear in the Frankenstein movies. However, what better occasion to try them out than my first night watch from 4.00-8.00 a.m.? At 6.00 a.m., after a cup of tea which the deck boy brought up, and it being summer and consequently daylight by this time, the hands buttoned-on a deck hose and, armed with deck scrubbers, commenced *le lavage du pont*. They had finished the Bridge and were now at work on the lower Bridge when the Fourth Officer emerged from the wheelhouse carrying in both hands the fair copy of the logbook on which he had been working for the last two hours, and, balanced on top, some blotting paper, a pen and a little bottle of washable Quink. These he thrust at me with instructions to take them to his cabin and place them on his bunk – with great care. He returned to the wheelhouse and I set off for the companionway leading to the next deck down. My readers will no doubt already have anticipated the outcome. With no hands free I started my downward journey; on about the fourth step down the boots took charge and I toppled forward. The logbook *et al* flew from my hands, opened its covers and, like a stooping falcon, glided across the wet deck below. Fortunately for me the Quartermaster was washing just below the foot of the ladder and caught my plummeting body in his arms. The Fourth Officer materialised as if by magic at the top of the ladder and my tender, well-brought-up ears were treated to a stream of invective, the like of which I had never heard before. I suppose he had a right to be miffed. I just gazed up at him from the arms of the Quartermaster. Those boots (and I still have them to this day) were to lead me into more trouble, this time from the Captain, who used to complain if I perambulated the Bridge over his head when on watch, or trod all over him (he was small, remember, and I was six foot) going through the blackout screens to the wheelhouse. 'A great lummox' was, I think, the turn of phrase he used, or some such Caledonian expression of endearment. But I anticipate. The next time I met the Captain was the day after the Log Book Incident. We were going up the Clyde to dock and re-fuel. I was on the Bridge at my station which was to keep the Bridge notebook and also the engine movement book in which I recorded the time and orders given on the Engine Room Telegraph to the Engine Room. I was standing, pencil poised ready for the next entry, when the Captain turned to me and said, ' Don't stand there like a monkey with his finger up his backside (or a word to that effect) – look alive, boy, look alive!' I was taken aback. I expected that sort of comment from the Fourth Officer but from a four-ringed Captain? Well!

We stayed about ten days in Glasgow. I kitted myself out with blue battledress which was what most of us wore at sea, bought a C.P.S. cap badge and removed my 'Swiss Admiral' stripes. One cadet had to remain on board each night. The other two were free to sample such delights as Glasgow had to offer. We were hardly big spenders as our pay was only £4.00 per month, plus £5.00 per month 'danger money'. When we had served a year the pay rose by £1.00 per month and the 'danger money' by £5.00. I never could fathom the logic of the latter – why had my life become £5.00 a month more valuable just because I was a year older? We drank a lot of beer and went occasionally to a cinema or dance hall, then it was a ride back to Govan (Shield Hall actually) on a tram for a hot V.C. pie with baked beans served on the dockside by the good ladies of the W.V.S. Price 6d, as I recall.

During the day we made ourselves useful checking the lifeboat stores, running errands for the Chief Officer, or studying. We also got to know our way around the ship. She was old and bore little resemblance to her previous passenger ship state. She had been painted grey all over on the outside and her mainmast removed to give the AA guns a better arc of fire. She carried quite a bit of armament: a 6" gun on the poop, eight oelikons for AA use and a Bofors gun on each side amidships, again mainly for anti-aircraft. There was a 270 radar in a housing on the upper Bridge that looked like a lighthouse and various crafty rocket launches which fired a wire suspended between two parachutes to deter or maim incoming aircraft. To man all this hardware we carried a team of naval ratings (D.E.M.S.) and Royal Artillery Maritime Gunners under the command of a Lieutenant R.N.V.R. The troops were housed in what had been the holds, or cleared 2nd Class or immigrant accommodation. They slept in hammocks. The officers used the old first class cabins, with several to a cabin according to rank. A ship's officer, rated equal to the Second Officer, was Troop Deck Officer (T.D.O.) and was responsible for liaison with the Military Officer commanding troops and his staff.

Our deck officers' accommodation was on the level below the Bridge and abaft the Captain's quarters and the main chartroom. The Senior Cadet had a cabin of his own, but an inside one ventilated only by two small windows high in the bulkhead and opening on to the alleyway. The other two cadets shared a very small cabin about 7' square, on the inboard side, the bunks, one above the other and opposite the door a tall-boy, the like of which I had seen only in the Maritime Museum. When closed it was a fairly flat piece of furniture with a mirror at the top and a rack for brushes, etc. Below this, when a flap was pulled down, a basin appeared, complete with soap dish and toothbrush holder at the side. There was one tap, which produced cold water from a tank behind the mirror. When ablutions were completed, one merely closed the flap and the basin discharged its contents into another tank situated in the lower half of the cabinet. Really quite ingenious, and much used in the previous century. If you wanted hot water a type of watering can could be filled from the boiler in the adjacent pantry. What we learned the hard way was that the lower tank had to be emptied, as indeed the upper one had to be filled. But it was not until it overflowed onto our meagre strip of carpet that the light dawned.

Proceeding around the cabin, there was a hanging cupboard in the corner, which opened over a small settee running on the outboard side below a window. This cupboard, hooks behind the door, drawer under the lower bunk and one under the settee, was the only space available to stow our gear. The inner bulkheads (walls) were made of tongue-and-groove boarding; a delight for the cockroaches, known as 'Jaspers', which moved in and out at will. They also got into the drawers and one had to shake every piece of clothing before donning it in order to get them out.

I mentioned a pantry next door. This contained a steam-heated boiler for fresh washing water, tea making, dhobi etc. Here again, the fresh water tank had to be pumped up by a semi-rotary pump (hand operated) to a holding tank on the deck above from whence it fell by gravity to the pantry below. There was one bath for all the officers. It was fed hot and cold salt water, and one then rinsed off with fresh water carried to the bathroom in a large basin from the pantry. Fresh water was a precious commodity with so many troops on board and was available only during certain periods of the day. We took our meals in what had been the First Class Dining Room and it was strange getting used to an almost pre-war diet, with white bread and lashings of butter.

When, at last, coaling and storing were completed we returned to the 'Tail of the Bank' off Gourock, thence to proceed to New York to embark troops. We were to be independent – that is, with no convoy and no escort. We had no troops on board other than a few R.A.F. for training in the U.S.A. or Canada, so no great loss if we were fished, I suppose. I have always held that the *Empress of Russia* was never torpedoed as the Germans felt she was more use to them afloat and consuming her vast quantities of coal, thereby producing a considerable amount of smoke which conveniently pinpointed a convoy. And so we zig-zagged our way across the Atlantic at high speed, reaching about 23 knots at times. The firemen, spurred on by our lonely state, worked wonders in the boiler rooms and lookouts had never been keener.

Which led me to my next *contretemps* with the Captain. He had a nasty habit of keeping his own lookout – and he had binoculars, which I hadn't – from the lower Bridge or his cabin, then bouncing up to my elbow to say, 'Do you see that ship/mine/suspicious object or whatever?' I had to confess that I couldn't, whereupon he would say, 'Keep on the keevive, boy, Keep on the keevive!' I always saw the source of his anxiety when I looked where he was looking, so I started saying 'Yes, sir', then following his line of sight. It worked, but not for long. One day he bounced up as usual saying, 'You see that ship over there?'

'Yes, sir,' I snapped back.

'Then you've got better eyesight than I have,' came the retort.

Gillett had goofed again! To add to my troubles I was sea sick for my first few days, and even after that did not feel 100%. However, all was well when we reached New York – the first time in my life that I had stepped on to foreign soil.

Approached from the sea the skyline was pure 1920s and I imagined the place peopled by Damon Runyon type characters. The harbour was bustling with ferries like water beetles, plying to and fro with their distinctive tooting, unlike our U.K. horns. After we had been thumb-printed, photographed and issued with passes, we were able to go ashore. We were given a 'sub' against our wages. There were about $5 to the pound in those far-off days and you could do quite well on $5.00. Also, the New Yorkers were very hospitable to us lads; at the British Apprentices Club, run by anglophile ladies of New York society, we were treated so well. Dances were organised, with girls galore, the food was lavish and invitations to people's homes arranged. The weather was a trifle too hot and very humid but we had fun. We learnt to drink American beer (cold, light and gassy) and smoke American cigarettes. We saw the sights, rode the subway and drank at Jack Dempsey's Bar. It lasted for ten days and then we sailed for home, in a troopship convoy. Or so we thought.

We were thrown out of the convoy in disgrace after twenty-four hours. We couldn't keep station and we smoked. Why? Largely because our firemen had discovered that if they gave blood to the Red Cross blood bank they would be reimbursed with $1.00 for each pint. Having practically drained themselves of blood, they then proceeded to replace it with alcohol. Secondly the coal that we had taken on in New York was not good quality, and more prone to smoking. This time, we berthed across the river in Hoboken, not a very salubrious neighbourhood, to await the formation of a freight carrying slow convoy in three days' time.

Whilst in Hoboken I went ashore for some ice cream, in my uniform of white short-sleeved shirt, white shorts, white stockings and white shoes. Our normal R.N. or M.N. tropical uniform (and it was even hotter in Hoboken than on Manhattan Island). In those days Americans did not go in for shorts. Their Navy wore long white trousers and the great American Bermuda shorts had not yet been invented. The young all whistled at me, and the older people looked at me as if I were naked and a threat to civilisation as they knew it. I fled quickly back to the ship clutching my carton of rapidly melting ice-cream.

The voyage home was tedious but uneventful. We floundered along like some great grey elephant among some forty assorted cargo ships. We were not even the Commodore's ship. We parted company in the Western approaches and proceeded independently to the Clyde where we disembarked our Yanks. A thirteen-day trip back, as opposed to nine days going out.

It was up to Glasgow for fuel, and then I got four days' leave, which I spent in London with my parents, who were staying at the Park View Hotel at Hyde Park Corner. It was noisy, as Hyde Park opposite was full of AA guns to ward off Doodlebugs, the current Nazi toy. These were a kind of flying bomb, driven by a jet engine. When the jet engine stopped, the whole thing came down and went off.

The nights were thus disturbed, but I was too tired to care. To sleep in a proper bed was bliss and if they hadn't done for me on the Western Ocean I was not prepared to go down any shelter and lose my beauty sleep. I visited Pangbourne one day to regale my chums with tales of my derring-do, or lack of it. Then it was back to Glasgow for more of the same, although in fact it turned out to be 'something completely different'.

When I returned to the ship I found her a buzz of activity, as they were removing all our guns and the radar and painting the ship's side in preparation for our next voyage. We learned that our destination was to be Gothenburg in Sweden, whence we were going, with the hospital ship *Atlantis*, to repatriate British prisoners of war. What follows is a contemporary article I wrote for our local paper on our return from the voyage:

We sailed with the hospital ship Atlantis from a port which I shall leave un-named on Thursday 14th October. Instead of sailing straight to the Skaggerat we laid our course northwards until we arrived off the German minefields at about the 62nd parallel, when we turned southwards and followed the coast of Norway down to the Skaggerat, keeping well clear of the minefields. We were, of course, unescorted, being protected by

International Law (a none-too sure guarantee in these days). Our main danger was floating mines, especially at night. At the entrance to the clear path through the field we were met by a German minesweeper, which acted as a guide. At several points we passed only a few cables from German occupied Norway, where the defence guns of the enemy were plainly visible and E-boats and aircraft kept a watchful eye on us. It was an amazing sensation to look at the rocky coast, very beautiful in its own rugged way, and think that there, so near to us who were free, were a people in slavery under the heel of a race a few specimens of which we had on board.

Once in Swedish waters we were taken over by Swedish escorts and, after having anchored for one night in neutral waters, we arrived at Gothenburg in the afternoon of Tuesday 19th. The Atlantis proceeded in ahead of us and went on up river, so I did not witness her arrival or reception. The German hospital ship, Rayer, was alongside and full of our lads. A trainload was also drawn up on the quayside. The hills reverberated with cheering, from Tommies and Swedes alike. I had a fine view from my station on the forecastle head. As we drew nearer, questions were hailed across, mainly concerning the price of alcoholic beverages and the quantity of same obtainable on board and at home. Then they began to sing 'Take me back to dear old Blighty', and such like. The Germans we had on board, who had had good food, the run of the ship and cinema shows every day, were not so jubilant. Many came from Hamburg and Mannheim and, as the Tommies pointed out, had nothing to go home to.

As soon as we were made fast and the gangway in place, embarkation began. The Swedish Red Cross and our R.A.M.C. men managed this operation as many of the men were minus limbs, not to mention eyes, and in the case of some poor chaps, their reason. Embarkation continued, intermittently, for the next twenty-four hours or so, both soldiers and civilian internees coming aboard. We also got rid of our Huns. Wild rumours flew about the latter – one being that one of them had thought of better places than home and had jumped overboard into the North Sea! Needless to say, all of this was unadulterated bilge.

On the Wednesday, the Crown Princess of Sweden came on board for a visit. She is a Louis Mountbatten. Great cheers from the troops. The Swedes produced a brass band that played the troops on board. Such was their patriotic zeal that they played 'God Save The King' – all three verses – numerous times, thus rather holding up proceedings. I got caught, once, and had to stand at the salute for the whole thing – did my arm ache!

The Swedes are in a pretty bad way, what with Germans as neighbours and strict rationing, even in restaurants. Cigarettes are very scarce; the men

43

get ten and the women five per day. German cigarettes, too. I tried one, but the mildest description not being printable I shall refrain from a reference to their quality. Both cigarettes and soap were gratefully received by the Swedes who came on board (we were not allowed on shore). Tea is also scarce; the pilot we had drank his first cup for three and a half years with us. They are a grand lot of chaps and very pro-English and anti-German.

Once all were aboard who should be, and those that should not were off, we lost no time in departing. I should tell you that three Swedes tried to come with us to enlist but had to be refused as they might easily have been Nazi agents. We left on the Thursday morning with much band-playing, cheering, 'V' signing and streamer-throwing by the Swedes. The German ship that left just before us received not one wave. Apart from the Atlantis and the Empress there was also a Swedish liner of the Swedish-American Line – the Drottningholm – a lovely ship and incidentally and old C.P.S. boat (the Virginia before she was sold).

On our voyage home we anchored the first night, as on our arrival, in Swedish waters. The next morning on weighing, the Empress's port anchor fouled a ledge of rock and before it was realised, the cable parted and one uniform anchor and two shackles of cable went to Davy Jones' scrap heap. Still, it saved us the trouble of heaving in any more and our spare bower was soon shipped. Apart from a mosey Hun flying boat or two and a few floating mines, the voyage home was uneventful and on Monday we dropped the hook in the Firth of Forth. The Atlantis left us further north and docked at Liverpool a day later.

We were at once invaded by Brass Hats, Peers and Pressmen. The Adjutant-General to the forces delivered a message from the king and said a few kind words and then the 'Reception Party' toured the ship. Every warship that passed gave three rousing cheers and some more, and signals of welcome flew from every ship. Disembarkation was carried out by tenders as Leith cannot hold the Empress. The noise from sirens and whistles at Leith as each new tender arrived was ear-splitting. There, however, our side of the picture ends and so I will close this account with some idea of what the men went through in Germany as related to me by them.

Most of the men had been captured in 1940 and were sent to camps in Poland. Here they were with Poles and, later, Russians. It was bitterly cold and their diet consisted mainly of black bread (one soldier had some with him: it weighed a ton and comprised mainly potato and sawdust). Always the same, and never enough. The Poles and Russians got less and were treated like wild beasts. The Germans used steel whips on the latter and shot them at the slightest provocation. Going to work one day they had to *pass through a village where a German soldier had been murdered the previous night. The Germans had shot every man, woman and child in three streets and left their bodies in the road, just as a gamekeeper hangs vermin in his larder. They also saw many Poles hung and left in conspicuous places, 'as an example'. Typhoid raged and the prisoners died in their thousands, many contracting the disease by wearing the clothes of their deceased fellows. Several men went mad and tried to escape by climbing the barbed wire. They were shot, mutilated with bayonets and left hanging on the wire. When placed in chains they considered themselves lucky, as it excused them work. This was all when Germany was drunk with victory. Things are better now. They even got a little meat during the last few days. As the men, the officers received all bayonet and rifle butt at first, but improved conditions now. They reckoned that with their Red Cross parcels every week they fed far better than the Germans.*

An amusing incident was told me by one officer. A lorry load of British prisoners was passing through a German village and was greeted with showers of mud and stones. Later the burgher master of the place made a formal apology to the British prisoners at the camp – the villagers had mistaken them for Italians!

When they were all disembarked we weighed and proceeded north about Scotland, back to our old hunting ground of Gourock and up to Glasgow to fuel. I snatched a three-day leave to London. The journey was hardly worth the discomfort.

The train, which left Glasgow Central Station about 9.00 p.m. and arrived at Euston about 8.00 a.m. the next morning, was always packed, both in compartments and corridors. If one wanted a seat, one had to join early. I remember one night one of the ship's patrolmen and I had done just that and secured window seats. Not long after we had settled in on our own, a crowd of our firemen came in, dumped their gear on the seats and in the racks and then retired to the station buffet for more beer. Ten minutes or so later, another batch of our lads looked in, saw the luggage but no bodies so heaved it all out into the corridor and settled themselves in. Just before the train left the first lot returned, demanding their seats. However, possession being nine-tenths of the law and the doorway being too narrow for entry and blocked by the largest of the occupants, apart from some pithy invective there was not much to be done. It was the first time I had ever seen two men put nose to nose, like rutting stags. The first few hours of the journey, until they had finished their copious supplies of beer, were spent in alcoholic reminiscence of their

45

voyages so far, with pretty horrific tales of punch-ups and feuds in their messes. I feigned sleep, only to finish up with one of their number slumped and snoring on my shoulder.

Towards the end of November we were to commence what I look back on as the most uncomfortable and tedious of all the periods in my sea-going career. From 26th November to 3rd April we made six round trips to Reykjavik and one to Thorshaven (in the Faroes). We were acting as a glorified ferry-boat carrying U.S. troops to and from the forces then occupying Iceland and the Faroes against invasion. The weather was consistently horrible, it was dark a great deal of the time and for eight hours a day I was cold, wet and seasick. Out on the weather wing of an open Bridge, sometimes almost praying for a kindly U-boat to torpedo us and put me out of my misery. They had more sense – they stayed snug beneath the waves. The only vessels visibly worse off were the two escorting destroyers, H.M.S. *Skate* and H.M.S. *Saladin*, reputedly the oldest in the R.N. Most of the time, we had to moderate our speed for their benefit but even so they were standing on the bows one minute and on their sterns the next, burrowing into waves and disappearing in a welter of sea and foam. What life on board was like I found it hard to imagine. One night we had a Force 12 gale and were really knocked about: guard rails were smashed, a lifeboat flung up from the Promenade Deck (with troops on board we used to have the lifeboats secured alongside the Promenade or the Embarkation Deck) and smashed back into the chocks on the Board Deck above with her back broken. We were unable to serve any hot meals that day.

I was also having a certain amount of 'Captain trouble' during this period. My first Captain had left and was replaced by another – a Canadian from the Company's pre-war Pacific Service. This one was of a more robust stature than his predecessor so unlikely to be walked over (or in to) by me. However he had a very distracting habit of interrupting me when I was trying to concentrate on a task. For instance, we cadets did all the signalling when on watch. One was on one's own with nobody to write down as you read 10" searchlight or Aldis lamp Morse from another ship or station. You had to read each letter, memorise the word and thus the whole signal, which you then reported to the Captain or the Officer of the Watch. Similarly with the radar, which was the old 270 set, manned by D.E.M.S. naval ratings. When they got an echo – or several – on the scan they would ring the Bridge and give range and bearings. Again one would have to memorise these bearings and distances so as to relay them to higher authority. In both instances our gallant Captain would arrive at my side with remarks like, 'What's he saying? What's he saying? . . . Are you getting any of it? Are you getting any of it?' It was particularly difficult when signalling, as you had to acknowledge each word received with a flashed 'T' or it was sent again. If the Captain spotted that he would cry out to the Officer of the Watch, 'He's not getting it! He's not getting it!'

On another occasion his fault was lack of clarity with his orders. For some reason which now escapes me, he turned to me and shouted, 'Stand by below!' – meaning for me to ring 'stand by engines' on the telegraph. I started to leave the Bridge to go down to the Master Gyro to check it with the helmsman's repeater, as they sometimes drifted apart in their readings. I did this routinely twice a watch anyway. The Captain screamed at the Officer of the Watch, 'Where's that fool off to now?' Waving his arms he shouted again 'Stand by below!' The Officer of the Watch rang the telegraph. Gillett had logged another boo-boo.

On 24th March 1944, I made my first flight in an aeroplane. This was in a training Anson from Troon R.A.F. station. It was a scheme to take M.N. officers up to see what ships looked like from the air at various altitudes. We flew over the area from Ailsa Craig to the mouth of the Clyde.

At last, a move was afoot and I left the *Empress of Russia* on 5th April without many regrets. Looking back now I find it was hard to believe it was actually me experiencing that part of my life.

Chapter 5

After a spell of leave in London and Frinton I went to Liverpool on 28th April and joined the *Empress of Australia*. She was a beautiful ship, although built at about the same time (1913) as the old *Empress of Russia*. She had a counter-stern as opposed to a cruiser-stern and was more luxurious, even as a troop ship. She even had an indoor swimming pool, although this was used as a store in wartime. She had been built at the Vulcan-Werke R.G. Stetin Germany and had been launched as the *Tirpitz* and intended for use by the Kaiser for his 'victory tour' after the 1914-18 war. Ironically she was commissioned as a Royal Yacht in May 1939 and carried King George VI and Queen Elizabeth to Canada (they returned as passengers in the *Empress of Britain*).

She carried three cadets but in considerable luxury compared with the Russia. We had what had been a first class cabin at the forward end of the Promenade Deck. It boasted a double-bowl marble wash basin, large wardrobes and a writing desk. There was a single bunk and one-up-one-down metal bunks for two with generous space for a table and chairs mid-cabin. The officers seemed a more civilised lot than I had experienced so far. The Captain (Harry Moore) was a larger-than-life character. He was a Captain R.N.R. and rather miffed at not being called back for R.N. duties in this war as he had been in the 1914-18. He was obviously considered more useful where he was. Physically he was solid, with no discernible neck and a body measuring the same from front to back as from side to side. He seemed impervious to cold and seldom donned a greatcoat. Brought up in sailing ships, he treated the *Empress* as if she were one. He hated Engineers and all they stood for, and if a wisp of smoke should appear from a funnel the Chief Engineer was summoned to the bridge and bawled out like a deck boy – not so much for giving our position away to the enemy but for dirtying his pristine decks. He was, in truth, a real martinet of the old school, who believed that one could not be efficient and popular and therefore the more unpopular one made oneself the more efficient one must be. He was, however, a very fine

The Empress of Australia.

seaman and a Captain I could respect. I soon found that if you saluted him when he appeared on deck, or if wishing to address him, he mellowed visibly. More of him anon.

Like Glasgow, Liverpool was for me virgin territory to explore before we sailed on 4th May for Naples with troops for the Italian campaign. How pleasant after the North Atlantic: smooth water, sunshine, white shirts and shorts instead of pullovers and duffle coats. And what a sight! Twenty-five of the great passenger liners in convoy five columns across with five ships in each. *Strath* boats of the P & O, our own *Empresses* and *Duchesses* of the Canadian Pacific, *Castle* ships of Union Castle, Orient Line O's, Shaw Saville and Royal Mail liners, plus some allied Dutch and French ships which had escaped capture. We cadets who, as I have said before, were the signalmen, were very busy, vying with our opposite numbers on the other ships to be first up with flag hoists or down with the executive signal. The Commodore of the convoy kept us on the hop with exercises like streaming barrage balloons (we all carried a small one which flew from the mizzen mast) or gunnery practice.

The whole convoy was not bound for Naples and broke up before we arrived on 16th May. We did not dally, and were on our way again on the 18th back not to Liverpool but to good old Gourock, thence into Gareloch on the 4th June. Of course 6th June was 'D' Day and I felt very 'out of it' swinging round a buoy whilst many of my Pangbourne chums were driving landing craft or gun or rocket ships. All we were doing was driving our motor lifeboats 'twixt ship and shore.

On 3rd July that year I gave up smoking cigarettes – and in fact have not smoked one since. I had, in any case, only smoked since mid-1942 and really preferred my pipe, which was much more practical at sea, where the wind can demolish a fag in no time at all. On the subject of my pipe-smoking I have, over the years, converted many friends and acquaintances off the smoking of 'coffin nails' to the use of a pipe. They would usually start by saying things like: 'I must try a pipe – you look so bloody contended with it in your mouth'. If they were serious I would instruct them in the mysteries, for to enjoy a pipe requires certain basic training. So many abandon the idea through bad early experience. They buy an unsuitable pipe, fill it inexpertly with the wrong tobacco, cannot keep it alight and burn their tongues in the process – and so it is back to the cigarettes before they have had time to 'break the pipe in'.

Rule 1: The pipe. Choose a shape that suits your style and your teeth, with plenty of wood in the bowl. It does not have to cost a lot; search among the so-called 'rejects' often available in large tobacconists. Often they have been rejected not for their smoking qualities but because they have cosmetic flaws in their finishes.

Rule 2: Choose a moderately strong tobacco, pure Virginia to start with; you can try fancy mixtures later. Avoid fine cuts, or mild tobaccos which burn too fast and therefore overheat the pipe and your tongue and may cause you to smoke 'wet' – that is to dribble into the stem giving rise to bubbling noises!

Rule 3: Until your pipe is 'run in' only fill two thirds of the bowl. Press the tobacco well down but do not ram it in or it will not draw. Too loose, and you are in danger of overheating.

Rule 4: Light evenly with match or gas, never petrol which will spoil the flavour.

Rule 5: If you have packed correctly, (this skill improves with practice until you can do it in the dark, or without looking) you should be able to puff contentedly after a few harder lighting sucks, without further recourse to match or lighter until the end. If you have obviously mis-packed, do not keep trying to make it work – hoick the lot out and start again.

Rule 6: Do not finish a pipe full, knock it out and start another in the same overheated pipe. Let it cool off, or use another pipe.

Rule 7. Keep your pipe clean with frequent use of pipe cleaners. Once your pipe is 'run in' a carbon deposit will build up inside the bowl. This is a good thing if not carried to excess. Modern pipes are often treated inside the bowl to cut down the 'running in' process. Excessive carbon build up should be carefully rimed out, but avoid damaging the wood of the bowl. Be careful how you knock out your pipe or you may snap the stem. Bashing it against a wall is not recommended – the palm of the hand is softer. And make sure the 'dottle' is not still smouldering in an ashtray to cause offence, or in a waste paper basket to cause a fire!

Rule 8: NEVER INHALE. This is what kills most cigarette smokers.

On 18th July, after a spot of leave (most of it spent travelling from Helensborough to Glasgow to London to Frinton and back again) we were off to the Med. again, this time to Algiers. We embarked 8th Army troops returning home. Men who had been fighting in North Africa against Rommel's Africa Korps with great bravery in the desert were often uncomfortable about sleeping below in the mess decks with only one inch or so of hull between them and the sea, with the thought that a torpedo or mine might destroy that flimsy wall at any time. We, on the other hand, accepted this as a fact of life and would have been terrified of lying in a sandy slip trench with enemy tanks threatening to run over us. For those at sea, apart from air attack, the enemy was largely invisible, even when they struck and we were 'all in the same boat' regardless of job, or rank and until that happened we enjoyed our creature comforts.

We returned to the Clyde on 10th August, not without a little 'Captain trouble' for the two junior cadets. I have mentioned before that Captain Moore was a martinet of the old school and his arrivals at anchorages were characteristic. All hands went to 'Stations' fore and aft at Toward Point, about six miles from our anchorage. What the hands aft were supposed to do I have not the slightest idea. He also had leadsman in the 'chains' port and starboard sounding as we went in. On the Bridge both cadets were at their posts, although the chance of signalling was fairly remote and certainly not by flags. Our arrival coincided with lunchtime and the other cadet, one Eric Liddell, knew that we would not get any as the stewards were not going to hang around for cadets. The only option was to ask the Captain if we could relieve each other for this purpose. Eric was braver than me; I would have foregone the meal rather than incur the Captain's wrath, and he approached like Oliver Twist approaching

Bumble to ask for more gruel. He saluted and said, 'Would it be all right if Gillett and I relieve each other for lunch, Sir?' The colour rose on the Captain's countenance like a thermometer in a heat wave. He wagged an admonishing finger at the luckless Eric and boomed, 'No you may not, young man! You must learn to subordinate your stomach to duty!' He then popped another smoked salmon sandwich into his mouth from a silver tray, which his 'tiger' (steward) held out to him.

On another occasion he turned to a newly certificated Fifth Officer and growled, 'Tell the First Officer (on the forecastle head) to let go the starboard anchor.' The lad reached for the telephone to give the order. 'What are you doing with that?' bellowed the Captain. 'Shout the order to him!' The poor fellow picked up a megaphone and squeaked rather ineffectually into it. 'That voice would never carry to the four Royals in a gale!' said the Captain – and proceeded to give a demonstration of what would have, by shouting the order himself.

Up to Glasgow and I managed six days leave, spent at Frinton. The 4th September saw us outward bound for New York in a fast convoy under command of an American Commodore. In their convoys the Americans used VHF radio sets for communication between ships at night and in poor visibility. The sets were military portables, sited on the upper Bridge under a small shelter with a seat and something to write on. The two junior cadets (Eric and I) manned the set on a four hour on, four hour off watch system from one hour before sunset until one hour after sunrise and at any time that visibility was poor. Being late summer in the North Atlantic visibility was often poor and so we were on four on, four off most of the way over.

Our 'passengers' were German P.O.W.s of the nastier variety; arrogant S.S. types who were being shipped to the U.S. well out of harm's way. They were not quite so cocky after the hurricane we encountered on the day and night before we arrived in New York. I wrote this episode up for 'The Log' – the Nautical College Pangbourne magazine, and as it was written contemporaneously I repeat my account here without editing. It represents my 18 year-old's impressions at the time. It was quite a 'famous' hurricane: instead of its track re-curving into the Atlantic it swept up the East Coast of North America wreaking havoc in New York and beyond. We passed through the eye of the storm – a pretty unique experience.

For all her grey war paint, a luxury liner, now serving as one of His Majesty's Transports, impresses one with the sense of comfort and security that induced thousands of travellers to go cruising in the happy days of peace. My service in this type of ship had done nothing to shake this belief. The following story, however, is confined to the exception to the rule, being an account of my experiences in the West Indies hurricane which swept the eastern seaboard of North America last September, uprooting trees in New York and stranding yachts a mile inshore on Long Island.

About noon on September 14th, our convoy being twenty-four hours out from New York, we received a W/T warning of a hurricane that was advancing towards our course from Cape Hatteras. This gave us no undue cause for alarm for hurricanes in this area rarely reach further north than 30 degrees of latitude, before re-curving. The weather was fine, the sky clear, and we were rolling easily to a moderately long southerly swell.

Throughout the afternoon the swell lengthened and the sky assumed the aspect of corrugated iron of a most vile hue. The air became oppressive and the barometer dropped with increasing rapidity. It was apparent that, even if we did not have to contend with the hurricane itself, we were in for a dirty night and even amongst the sceptical, a sense of uneasiness prevailed. As the day wore on and signals from the shore gave no indication of any signs of re-curving, we prepared for heavy weather and waited in expectation of an order from the Commodore to alter course to avoid the hurricane's track. For some reason the order never came, though instructions came from the shore after it was too late to take any avoiding action.

At 1815 the storm struck the convoy and in a matter of minutes the sea was lashed into a boiling turmoil by wind and torrential rain. Our high superstructure was a great disadvantage and becoming unmanageable at convoy speed, we steamed clear. By this time the wind was east-by-south and increasing continually in violence. As the ship was eased up into the wind, she listed heavily to starboard, wind and wave continuing to beat her over mercilessly, until the Chief Engineer reported that the port engine could no longer be worked as the port injectors were out of the water. This handicapped our manoeuvrability still further, but at 1900 she was brought on to the port tack with the sea on the port quarter. The convoy had turned east at 1825 and was fortunately well clear, as we were behaving like an elephant run amok.

By 2000 the full hurricane was upon us. On the bridge, one experienced a feeling rare in this mechanised age – that of a man's childlike helplessness in the hands of the unleashed fury of Nature. Our ship, which was accustomed to riding over the ocean with majestic indifference to her surroundings was debased to the likeness of an orange pip that Father Neptune had swallowed and was vainly trying to disgorge. The wind shrieked and roared like some demented beast of prey, greedily ripping signal and ammunition lockers from their mountings, only to fling them with disgust aside again. Two-inch ports cracked like eggshells and steel doors were torn from their hinges; phosphorescence whipped across the decks like bursts of tracer from some hidden battery. When our smarting eyes were able to snatch a glance through the enveloping curtain of rain and flying spray, the aspect of the sea was sufficient to render its practically continuous obscurity a blessing. Vast mountains of heaving water, with evil, breaking crests towered high above us, hesitating menacingly before rolling down, seemingly to engulf us in their hissing midst. A hundred times they crashed down, burying our forecastle in tons of green water; a hundred times the whole ship listed sickeningly under the impact and a hundred times they rolled beneath us, flinging us up on their foaming peaks where the wind took up the battle until we commenced the long drop down to the depths again.

There must be few who have passed through Pangbourne who have not had one of the College boats lee-rail under in a squall, either intentionally or otherwise. This gives rise to a sensation of speed and savour to the pleasure of sailing, even if carried to the extreme extent of capsizing. However, when the lee-rail of our capstan deck aft went under and stayed long enough to allow quantities of water, measurable in tons, to penetrate below, these sensations were not recaptured. Those of the crew who were most experienced were also most aware of the nature of our position and many of the older hands, who had weathered all types of storm and knew the ship's fine qualities and strength of construction, had many an anxious moment that night.

About 2045, the passage of the storm's centre over us was marked by a sudden lull and appearance of a shaft of clear air that penetrated the whirling mists and clouds above us. It quickly passed and the wind suddenly jumped to south-west. This flung us violently over from the port to the starboard tack. Unnerving as this was on the bridge, it caused havoc below, where moveable objects such as tables and chairs had been secured and wedged in expectation of a heavy but continuous list to starboard. The force of our roll to port broke them all loose, and sent them cascading across the decks in a wave of destruction. The stewards flung themselves to the attack, and triumphed before undue damage was done to ship or life, though a grand piano eluded its captors for a considerable time.

From 2130 the wind began to moderate and we were able to head the sea, much to everyone's comfort and peace of mind. The wind continued to drop; the barometer rose as quickly as it had fallen and the air cleared somewhat. At one o'clock the following morning, the ship was put before the wind, and we steamed slowly eastwards to look for the convoy. The hurricane had scattered it far and wide and, after two hours' search that only revealed isolated ships, we turned west again to make port and lick our sores.

Dawn broke over the still angry sea and the nightmare was over, but as the light increased we were able to see that the night's events had been no dream. The upper bridge was littered with debris swept there from other parts of the ship, and whole weatherboards had disappeared. Tarpaulins had been sliced as if by some giant knife, and handrails had been beaten flat. The falls were all that remained of two lifeboats, and another had been lifted bodily from the embarkation deck, where she was lashed in readiness for an emergency, and replaced in her chocks on the boat deck above.

That afternoon we entered the swept channel under almost perfect weather conditions; the sea was calm, the sun shone benignly down and it seemed hard to believe that last night had been real. But it had been – and none on board wished to undergo a repetition.

Apart from the damage to all the ships in the convoy, we were given to understand that two of the escorting frigates foundered during the night.

Old New York had not changed much since our visit last year – but I had, quite considerably. We were case-hardened old salts now, not tenderfoot first-trippers. We found girl friends with cars, went to Coney Island, Jack Dempsey's Bar and the Rockerfeller centre – and got very little sleep. There were over four dollars to the pound in those days and I was now earning £15 per month, all found. Having loaded up with some 4,000 troops we sailed in another American convoy and it was back to four on, four off for the next eleven days.

We anchored off the Bar Light Vessel (outside Liverpool) on the morning of 1st October, where we were the recipients of our Captain's generosity. The three cadets were relaxing on the upper Bridge in the sun when the Old Man appeared and said, 'You lads have had a pretty rough time of it this trip. You can have the afternoon off'. Big deal, we thought – as we could not go anywhere – but it was a great concession, coming from him, and at least he had noticed us. We docked in Liverpool the next day and two days later it was off to Frinton, via London, for five days' leave.

On 25th October we sailed for Belfast Lough, remained there until the 27th and then returned to Liverpool. On 31st October we left with 5,000 Russians on board, round the top of Scotland, to meet an escort, then ... heigh ho! for Murmansk. We had been kitted out with various cold weather goodies: leather sea boots, Long-John underwear, polo neck sweaters, balaclava helmets, woolly gloves, and socks. Rug making was a favourite hobby of the men at sea and I fear many a sweater was picked to bits to make a rug. Our escort turned out to be enormous for the two troopships. Together with the *Scythia* of Cunard, who carried another 5,000 troops, we were escorted by the cruiser *Berwick*, the aircraft carrier *Campagnia*, six fleet destroyers and eight frigates. What, as they say, was the object of the exercise? On landing on the Normandy coast many labour gangs used by the Germans to build the Atlantic Wall were released. These included many Russians captured by the Germans during their advance into Russia and given the option of death or work in a labour battalion. The Russians now wanted them back – hence our convoy. Many of them did not want to go back, fearing retribution I suppose. Four of our lot jumped overboard at Liverpool, but were all retrieved and sent back on board.

The trip was unusual in that, as we progressed further and further northwards, it was almost always dark. The sun did not rise until about 11.45 and set again by 13.30. It was not as cold as I had imagined it would be but I suppose it was only late autumn, not mid-winter. There were no great excitements and I only recall going to action stations twice, when inquisitive reconnaissance planes appeared. There was also some depth charge activity amongst the frigates forming the outer screen. I was amazed to watch *Campagnia* flying off *Swordfish* – presumably for reconnaissance. These ancient biplanes would stagger to the end of the flight deck and appear to fall into the sea but just lift clear and be on their way. Landing back on when she was pitching looked equally hazardous.

We arrived off Murmansk on 6th November, passing H.M.S. *Royal Sovereign* which we had sold to the Russians some time before. We were not allowed ashore but it hardly looked a swinging town from the anchorage. I asked the Russian pilot, who stayed with us throughout our four days' stay, what was going to happen to these 10,000 men we had brought home to Mother Russia? He replied somewhat cryptically that they would be interrogated and the ones who had a satisfactory explanation would be sent straight to the advancing Russian front. The others . . . he shrugged his shoulders. A pistol in the back of the head or a Gulag in Siberia, I suppose.

Nothing else of note happened other than that I celebrated my nineteenth birthday. How (if at all), I cannot remember. The next day,

10th November, we sailed for home back to Gourock, without incident and were home by the 16th, when I took advantage of my free rail warrant to spend three days in London.

I thought that it was time I equipped myself with the tools of my trade and so bought a very ancient sextant, boasting in the lid of its box a Kew Certificate, dated 1894. It was a lovely little instrument, which only needed it mirrors re-silvering. One of its advantages was that it was of the type (and age) that one would be given to read at an oral examination and the other was that it was cheap – only £8.00 – so if I was torpedoed it would not be too great a loss. In the event I used it throughout my career and still have it in my yacht. Judging by prices being paid at auctions for this type of maritime memorabilia it should fetch £800 today – but then the pound bought more in 1944!

Back in Glasgow we had Christmas on board but as the Scots do not (or did not then) do much about the 25th except work, it cannot be described as being in any way memorable. Two days before Hogmanay we were again at anchor off Gourock, so no celebrations then, either. The 5th January saw us away to the sunny Mediterranean, to Naples via Gibraltar. After three days, it was off to Algiers with P.O.W.s on board, if I remember rightly. One thing I became quite adept at was recognising the nationalities we carried, by smell alone. A crowded troop deck of men in their hammocks gave off a characteristic whiff hard to describe but as unique as colour or language.

It was on this crossing that I had a lesson in tobacco. On board were three Chief Yeomen of Signals, on passage to new postings. Wishing for something to do, they volunteered to come on the Bridge and help with the signalling. We became very chummy and they presented us with a 'prick' of tobacco, or half of one, they had made. Let me explain. In those days, seamen could draw leaf tobacco as their ration. This was popular with pipe-smoking old hands only. The leaves were placed on top of each other, sometimes with a sprinkling of rum between layers, and then rolled up tight. The resulting cucumber-like object was then bound with cod line. The binding was tightened by slinging the hammocks from the hammock-hook via the binding, which compressed the tobacco into a solid plug. To smoke the tobacco it was necessary to slice off a piece, then rub it between the hands to break it down sufficiently to fill one's pipe. It was very strong but smoked very coolly. On first trying this, I filled a pipeful and smoked it with great satisfaction for about half an hour, when I began to feel a bit dizzy. I was due to the Bridge on watch and spent the next four hours with my face over the dodger and my mouth wide open allowing the wind to scour me out. We cadets decided it was too much, taken neat, for our young bodies, but was fine when mixed with ordinary tobacco.

We sailed home from Algiers via Gibraltar, arriving back in the Clyde on the 27th January. This was to be my last voyage in her as I was signed off on 3rd March to go on leave and await my next appointment. This was the first long spell of leave I had enjoyed since going to sea. The quick hops down to London from Glasgow were so exhausting in terms of travel that they were hardly worth the effort but I felt I owed it to my parents to let them see me when they could, just in case one day I never got back. Some time was spent at Frinton. I particularly remember V.E. Day (8th May). That evening there was a dance at the tennis club, where everyone let their hair down and I succeeded in knocking over a very large vase of flowers. The war was over in Europe and although we were still fighting in Japan, the tide had turned in the Allies' favour. The lights came on again: social life in London was beginning to pick up, and I went to several parties and to nightclubs in town. The 'debs delight' phase was about to creep into my life.

A ship at last. On 16th May I went up to Liverpool and joined the *Duchess of Richmond*, one of the two surviving of her class of four 20,000 ton, two funnel passenger ships built in 1928 for the Canadian Pacific's North Atlantic service. Rudely referred to by some as the 'drunken duchess' because of her reputation for rolling in bad weather, she never bothered me; I seemed to have outgrown my propensity for seasickness after leaving the *Empress of Russia* and it did not bother me again. I was the only cadet with a cabin to myself and I kept the 8-12 watch as No. 2 to the Third Officer. My new Captain, named Shergold, was younger than my previous ones and a fine ship handler. He, like Captain Moore, had served in sail, but although he kept everyone on the hop he was not a martinet. He could read Morse code like a Chief Yeoman and would read what you were sending on the Aldis lamp or 10" searchlight by the clack of a shutter. If you misspelled a word when sending he would spot it, or if you were receiving and had to have a word repeated he would have read it out of the corner of his eye, even whilst conning the ship, and would want to know the reason why when you reported to him. Unlike Captain Moore he was a great chum of the Chief Engineer who frequently visited him on the Bridge for a chat. He handled his ship like a motor yacht and it was indeed an education to see him close a pilot cutter instead of waiting for the cutter to close on him. We sailed on 23rd May to Naples, calling at Gibraltar and Malta on the way and arriving on 31st May. There was no convoy, just us, with lights on and in peacetime mode. We then commenced a shuttle around the Med., here, there and everywhere that troops needed moving: from Naples to Marseilles; to Taranto; to Algiers and back to Naples. This time in I went to my first opera. The San Carlo Opera House was back in business and I saw 'Lucia di Lammermoor', in Italian of course, and although I did not understand a word, I thoroughly enjoyed the music and the setting. The only snag was that I could only get into the gods, and stand, surrounded by very enthusiastic but very smelly Italians who I think must have worked in a tannery or some such, and had come straight from the factory. Talk about local flavour!

On June 18th we sailed to Liverpool via Gibraltar. We were back in Naples for a 'quickie' two-day visit then back again to Liverpool by 1st August. My parents were having a holiday at Morton-in-Marsh in the Cotswolds, where I joined them for four days. Whilst we were there, the radio announced the dropping of the first atomic bomb on Hiroshima, on 6th August. I returned to Liverpool the next day, and sailed on the 12th for Canada. I had been two years with the Canadian Pacific and at last I was going there!

We heard of the Japanese surrender whilst on passage, but there was not much we could do in the way of celebration. The war I had worried about being over before I was in it in September 1939 had waited for me after all and I had survived it. I was convinced that I had made the right decision in 1943 and this was the career for me. On 18th August we arrived at Quebec and I went ashore on Canadian soil for the first time. I had not appreciated just how French Quebec was – the locals, it seemed, only speaking English with reluctance, if at all. I bought myself a reasonably good and robust watch, something I had lacked until then. We were back in Liverpool by 27th August and I took the opportunity to help my mother house hunt in London. My parents had decided that, with increasing City commitments, they would look for a small house in London instead of staying in hotels when up from Frinton. We marked out a 'search area' on a street map, bounded by Hyde Park's southern edge to the north, Hyde Park Corner to the east, Brompton Road to the south and

The Duchess of Richmond.

Thurloe Square to the west. Having looked at several, we at last found a gem of a house in the 'hamlet' of Knightsbridge (so called on the old maps). Number 4, Fairholt Street was a three-storey Georgian house with a tiny garden behind, two streets north of, and parallel with, Brompton Road, behind Brompton Square and Montpelier Street and south of Rutland Gate, which was accessible through the 'hole in the wall' (a pedestrian route only) from Rutland Street behind. It was empty and freehold and ready for occupation, having been put on the market by the Countess of Mayo through Harrods Estate Agency. My father bought it for the princely sum of £4,500. I fell in love with the place at first sight and still live here, fifty-five years on – although today one could easily add two more noughts on to the asking price!

Back to the sea. We sailed from Liverpool on 16th September. Destination – Singapore. Amongst other troops embarked we carried R.A.F. teams who were going to reorganise the airfield after the Japanese occupation. The Med. was becoming quite familiar by now, but this was my first experience of a passage through the Suez Canal into Eastern waters. We called, briefly, at Colombo, and arrived at Singapore on 9th October. During the nine days we spent there I managed a fair bit of sightseeing, including a trip across the Causeway to Johore, where we visited the Sultan's palace. The town was buzzing with the clamour of the Chinese business-as-usual verve to remove all traces of the Japanese. When I returned, eventually, some thirty two years later, the place was scarcely recognisable.

We left on 18th October for a brief call at Rangoon (I did not get ashore); thence to Colombo for a day and then back through the Canal to Liverpool where we arrived on 15th November (having spent my 20th birthday in the Med.) Back in London I spent my first leave in the new house. On a visit to the Canadian Pacific office in Waterloo Place I was to learn of my promotion to uncertificated Fifth Officer of the *Duchess*. Away with my cadet's insignia and on with my first stripe! By now, I had nearly completed my time to sit for my Second Mate's Certificate. One more voyage was all that was required.

I went back to Liverpool on 15th December, in time to sail for Gibraltar to relieve the garrison on the Rock who were coming home for Christmas. Alas, it was not to be. We sailed on the 17th but a Levanter was blowing and due to a miscalculation by the Pilot we struck a detached mole on leaving harbour and had to be dry-docked to straighten out our stern which was badly bent in the process. I felt so sorry for the troops whose homecoming had been spoilt, and for the Captain who was unable to rectify the Pilot's error in time. Although we did not have Christmas at home, either, we consoled ourselves with some excellent sherry from Saccone & Speed's Emporium plus a few runs ashore on the Rock. We reached Liverpool on 1st January 1946 and on the 15th I left the *Duchess of Richmond*. On the 15th I came home to commence my studies at Sir John Cass, in the City of London.

Chapter 6

The Sir John Cass Institute at that time embraced one of the many such schools situated in major ports around the country, geared to the preparation of candidates for certificates of competency for Second Mate, First Mate, and Master. The courses lasted three months and covered all subjects in the syllabus for these examinations, both written and oral. I exchanged my uniform for a leather-elbowed sports jacket and cavalry twill trousers and felt very academic. It was an easy ride on the No. 96 bus from Brompton Road to Aldgate where the school was situated. Lectures were from 9.00 a.m. to 5.00 p.m. with a considerable amount of homework for evenings and weekends. The lecturers all held Extra Masters Certificates and were well experienced in translating our practical knowledge into a form acceptable to the examiners. Although re-employment was pretty well guaranteed on qualifying in a company such as mine, like all the other students we were put on the dole during this period, and visited the local Labour Exchange every week to collect our money. We were, in fact, in the 'pool' of M.N. personnel founded during the war to provide cover for the service, though we were exempt from call up whilst we were studying. We had already had our qualifying sea time checked before starting our studies to make sure that we were eligible to sit the examination when ready. Time actually 'signed on Articles' counted; if signed off between voyages it did not. I was allowed one year's remission for having been at Pangbourne, and one year to obtain a probationary Second Mate's certificate in passing. The normal period for a cadet or apprentice was four years. Because of the shortage of officers suffered by the M.N. due to casualties, this length of time was shortened by a year, but the qualifying time for the First Mate's certificate would count only from the completion of 'probation' when your Second Mate's certificate was confirmed.

Despite the hard work the social round was not neglected and evenings found me out and about, mostly with two old chums: John Grafton-Williams, who had joined the college with me in 1939 and had gone into the Coldstream Guards upon leaving, and Basil Kelly who had been in the R.N.R., but on demobilisation had joined the New Zealand Shipping Company and was with me at Sir John Cass. Both had cars – John a very racy red sports car and Basil a rather clapped-out Austin 7. I decided that it was about time that I had some wheels of my own. When I was a youngster my parents had said to me that if I did not ride a motorcycle when eligible at sixteen they would buy me an MG Sports Car at seventeen. As I had no desire then – nor have I had since – to ride the former I was quite content to feast my eyes on the latter. Red would be my preference, I had decided. Alas, Mr Hitler knocked that idea on the head. I seem to remember that not smoking until I was 21 might have been a further condition but the war scuppered that, too. During the relatively short period in which I indulged in cigarette smoking my parents used to give me my favourite Abdullah No. 16's as presents.

On the course with me was a chap whose uncle owned a car showroom and B.S.M. School opposite Pelham Court, not far from us. They had some 1939 second hand Sunbeam Talbots and Hillman Minx drop-head coupés for sale. I wanted a drop-head as I liked to be out in the open air when possible. The Sunbeams were somewhat out of reach of my pocket so I plumped for a Hillman Minx 10 h.p. – black, as this was the only option. I think it cost about £250 and they threw in a free course of driving lessons. I had obtained the provisional licence on reaching my seventeenth year, just in case. Tests had been abandoned during the war and to avoid testing six years of backlog, provisional licences such as mine were upgraded without a test. However, I decided to take the B.S.M. course on offer, which proved to be very thorough. I took delivery of the car as soon as my course was completed. She was a nice little car, but with one snag for a night owl such as me. She only had a six-volt battery. Since side lights were required when parking in the street after dark, I would often return to the car in the wee small hours after a visit to some night club only to find that the battery had gone flat. Like nearly all cars of her vintage she had a starting handle and was not too heavy to push start, which meant we were able to get out of most difficulties. Except, that is, for one memorable night...

I was due to start my exams on Monday 1st April, so decided to spend the preceding weekend quietly revising. On the Saturday morning, however, I received a telephone call from my principal girl friend at the time, Jill Hulbert, the daughter of Claude Hulbert, reminding me that it was Boat Race day and suggesting that we should go out in the evening to celebrate. Both her father and uncle (Jack Hulbert) had rowed for Cambridge in their time, which seemed to me to be as good a reason as any for celebration. It took very little to persuade me that it was not, perhaps, such a bad idea to relax a little before the exam. After all, if I did not know my stuff by now, a weekend was hardly going to make much difference. Cambridge won the race that afternoon. I duly called around to Jill's house in Sydney Place and we collected another girl and her escort, Victor Sylvestor Junior, who was then in the Parachute Regiment. We drove around Trafalgar Square, hooting and yelling triumphantly at 'favoured' fans of Oxford. In those days the Boat Race was much more of an event than it is today, and there were crowds filling the streets in London. We finished up at the Milroy, our favourite nightclub, leaving the car in Berkeley Street. Who should be in the Club but the Cambridge crew, celebrating their victory! At about 2.00 a.m., having shared in the celebrations, we left to go home. Upon arriving at the car we discovered that, as usual, the battery was dead. Cranking yielded no relief but just at that moment the Cambridge crew appeared. Jill persuaded them to give us a push, which they did readily, pushing us enthusiastically into Berkeley Square. Alas, still no joy. The Cambridge crew bade us farewell. Almost immediately, a large, chauffeur-driven Rolls pulled up and the occupant enquired if we needed any help. Gratefully we accepted, and opted for a tow. Between us we had no towrope, but resourcefully tied a travelling rug to the rear bumper of the Rolls. There was insufficient rug to tie another knot on our car, but we hooked it around the front bumper and Victor nobly sat upon our bonnet, holding onto the end of the rug. Away we went! We coursed right around the square in this fashion, without success. Still no life in our engine. The chauffeur suggested at this juncture that he might give us a lift. Victor was the only member of the party for whom this was any use, as the Rolls was not going in our direction. Eagerly Victor hopped into the car and, with a cheery wave, was driven swiftly out of sight. I was left with the two girls. There was absolutely no hope of a taxi at this hour, so we set off to walk home to Sydney Place. I can see it now – three lonely figures, trudging resolutely through the deserted streets of London – not a car or a fellow pedestrian in sight, but fortunately a dry night. Having seen the girls safely to their doors I continued my journey to Fairholt Street, arriving home eventually at about 4.00 a.m. I had barely two hours sleep before I had to be up again and arrange for the car to be towed back to the garage where I kept her. Some rest!

The written examinations continued from that Monday through until the Wednesday. Despite my nocturnal perambulations and consequent lack of sleep that weekend, I passed. The following Monday, 8th April, I had my orals with the much feared Captain Wallace, a name guaranteed to make strong men quail. The oral lasted for one and a half hours and that, too, I passed, even though I seemed to have had every subject in the wide syllabus thrown at me.

On 22nd April I laid up the car, and proceeded the following day to Hull, there to join the *Empire Lance* as Fourth Officer. The *Lance* and her sister ship, the *Empire Cutlass* were run by Canadian Pacific for the Ministry of Transport. They were American-built small troopships, built originally to run to the 'Mulberry' harbour off Aramanches in Normandy but now used to ferry troops between Cuxhaven and Hull, bringing reinforcements for the occupation of Germany and returning others home for de-mob. It was rather like our Reykjavik work, but with a quicker turnaround and better weather. We had a day in Hull, a day across the swept channel through the North Sea minefield, a day in Cuxhaven and a day back to Hull. I made twenty-three round trips before leaving her on 8th August, which included a period in June when I had some leave. On returning to Hull I came up by car, keeping the vehicle there until I left the ship. Those of us not on duty on our evenings in Hull would drive out into the surrounding countryside for a pub-crawl. I had had the foresight to purchase an Ordnance Survey of the area, and we dutifully scanned this for the PH symbol, paying each one a visit. Beer was in short supply in some of the villages and we received some hostile looks from the indigenous population. 'Don't tha' coom 'ere wi' tha collige accents' was the reception in Burton Pidsey, I recall. So much for the well-vaunted Yorkshire hospitality.

During the latter part of the lay-up period I went to Liverpool for three days on a radar course. The Ministry of Defence released redundant radars to the Merchant Navy – these were the 293 model which had a P.P.I. (Plan Position Indicator) display fitted in the wheelhouse and the main guts on the upper bridge. It was a considerable advance on the old 270, to which I referred earlier. For a start it did not require a rating to move the aerial and report any blips on the A scan by telephone. However, there was quite a drill to switching it on, having to blow warm dry air through the wave-guide, and it took at least twenty minutes to bring it into action. *Empire Lance* did not carry this equipment but the course was to prepare me for my next ship, which did. Out-runs ashore in Cuxhaven consisted of (a) exchanging cigarettes with the German ship cleaning staff for occupation Marks, and (b) going to the British Officers' Club, formerly the Cuxhaven Yacht Club, and having a very nice meal with wine for the equivalent of a tin of duty free Capstan cigarettes. Coffee beans were the other currency and many a camera, pair of binoculars or sextant was traded in this way. I acquired a fine folding home-movie cine screen for 1lb coffee beans and fifty cigarettes. What I could never understand was who, in the end, drank the coffee or smoked the cigarettes? Not the traders themselves, I was sure. Such items were valued currency worldwide, however.

I mentioned that we followed a swept channel between Hull and Cuxhaven. This was a mile wide, and buoyed. As well as being lit, these buoys had whistles (worked by the tide) or bells. If ever the captain was lying down for a 'zizz' we would play a trick on him by passing very close to the buoy, keeping inside the lane, so that it would hoot and ring down the ship's side. It usually brought him scurrying on to the Bridge shouting 'You're in the minefield! You're in the minefield!' We did spot the occasional mine which had broken adrift from its moorings. These were always reported and the necessary action taken.

Chapter 7

I left the *Empire Lance* on 8 August 1946 on appointment as Fourth Officer to the cargo ship, *Beaverdell*, which was lying in the Royal Victoria Dock in London. The *Beaverdell* was a new ship, built post-war as part of the replacement programme for the previous pre-war *Beavers* – the prefix given to all the Canadian Pacific's cargo ships. They had all been sunk during the war and were therefore replaced by four new ones, of which the *Beaverdell* was the first. They were fine ships – 9,900 tons gross, turbo-electric and capable of 18 knots. They were 'goal-posters', that is, instead of having masts down the centre line they had them off-set, like a set of goal posts, at each of the hatches, which allowed for further span by the derricks over the side for barges, or the quayside. There was only one disadvantage as far watch-keeping was concerned: the 'goalposts' did produce a mass of masts which meant that there was no one position where you might stand and have a clear view of everything. If you stood amidships you could see through the goalposts, if you moved to one wing or the other you could see on that side but your view was obstructed on the other side. Otherwise, it was a very satisfactory system which had been used in the pre-war *Beavers* as well, and one which made the ships very distinctive. There were six hatches, four forward and two aft, and the number two and three between decks were refrigerated. The number four had deep tanks which could be used for ballasting or alternatively for the carriage of oils or, more particularly in our case, for grain from Canada. There was a new design of sliding steel hatch covers, which would close on runners rather like double doors. They were much stronger than tarpaulins although had a few teething problems in their early days, and they did leak, on occasion. The accommodation for staff officers and crew was all amidships; she had a poop and a fo'c's'le although this was used merely as a storeroom for paint or ropes, or for carrying any special cargo that might need locking away.

At last I was in a ship on a regular run, and on my first cargo ship, carrying freight instead of passengers. This all meant that I had rather a lot to learn. I had been rather frightened when I went for my Second Mate's Certificate that the examiner might over-test my knowledge of cargo handling and stowage – subjects that I had only ever learnt from books at that stage, with no practical experience. I was now to learn very rapidly how it was all done. The *Beavers* were on a regular run in the summer, quite often via the Continent (Antwerp or Rotterdam) to and from Quebec and Montreal. In the winter, when the St. Lawrence froze, we went to St. John, New Brunswick, which was the Eastern rail head of the Canadian Pacific Railway. The average length of passage between Europe and Montreal was eight days; sometimes longer in the winter months, or delayed in the summer by fog and ice. Despite the adverse weather, it did mean that we were never away from home for very long, although in those days, before marriage, this did not worry me over much. My main concern was to build up my watch-keeping time to the statutory requirement before sitting my next exam.

The type of cargoes we were exporting at this period in the late forties and early fifties were generally 'luxury goods'. We had a great deal of cargo of a mechanical kind: cars, vans, tractors and the like. These all took up a lot of space but did not weigh a great deal, which resulted in us being rather light on draught, particularly for'ard, when we were crossing the Atlantic. We filled all the ballast tanks with water, but it still meant we were drawing only about thirteen feet forward at times, and if you did run into bad weather it meant that it was impossible to maintain full speed, as the ship would be liable to 'pound' (come down heavily on the wave tops) and possibly incur damage.

We also transported leather goods, whisky, even animals. Pedigree dogs would be sent out, there not having been any exchange for breeding during the war. My duties as Fourth Officer were to keep the 8-12 watch (evenings and mornings) and to write up the fair copy of the logbook. I was also responsible for maintaining the life saving equipment and ensuring that the four lifeboats we carried were all in working order. Like the rest of the officers I was responsible, on watch, for the navigation of the ship and in port to take my stint as officer of the day and to supervise the loading and unloading of cargo. This meant patrolling the decks, and going down the holds to ensure that everything was stowed correctly. There were four officers in all: the Chief Officer, Second (the Navigator), Third (Cargo Officer) and myself. One of the extra duties that fell upon us when we were loading in London was the supervision of special cargoes: small packages of high value, which like registered mail were all numbered and checked, or cases of whisky and spirits which of course the stevedores were doing their best to pilfer if they could. In what became a rather elaborate game you would have to do your best to stop them, although their skills at removal of an odd bottle were very highly refined and they practised great sleight of hand, managing to slip a bottle from a case and conceal it about their person even as they sat in front of you. Another trick was to build a 'wall' of cases, but to allow a gap behind the wall in which their colleagues might have concealed access to the cases. The dockers in New Brunswick were equally eager to get their hands on the whisky but were not nearly as 'skilled' in their methods: they would, for example, arrange for a case to slip out of the sling and fall on the dockside; when it broke they would all stand there with their mugs draining it off. Not at all subtle, when compared with their Cockney counterparts who had several generations of quiet pilfering behind them. I believe some of these characters even managed to get ashore on occasion with sides of beef stuffed under their rather grubby raincoats.

The securing of cars was a somewhat tricky procedure. Generally speaking, they would be held down by nailing cross batons in front of and behind each wheel and from the front of the car to the back, so that each wheel was 'bedded' in its own little slot. One had to watch fairly carefully to ensure that they were properly nailed together and that the lathes were not just resting on one another. As the dockers were on piece work (i.e. getting paid for the number they stowed) there was every temptation for them to miss out a few, which would have gone unnoticed until we were at sea. Any heavy weather, and we would have been the ones to have suffered. One also had to watch that in their haste the workers did not drive a six-inch nail through the car tyre – although I am glad to say that that was a fairly rare occurrence. Needless to say, we inspected them every day at sea to ensure that they were all secure and not sliding about. On our homeward voyages our cargoes were invariably foodstuffs, in the form of sacks of flour or grain in bulk. We also carried paper, in large rolls and sometimes frozen meat – mainly horsemeat for the continent, which was discharged at Antwerp. Paper products also included what seemed to me to be vast quantities of Kotex tampons, or sanitary towels, which were known to the cockney dockers as 'man-hole covers' – an analogy indicative of their customary wit.

The methods of loading and discharging differed in London and Montreal. In London cargo was loaded from and discharged to the shed, alongside which we were berthed, by means of cranes. Offshore derricks were simultaneously used to load and discharge into lighters which came alongside. In the case of grain, an elevator with a huge vacuum cleaner like apparatus would suck the grain out and discharge it into barges alongside. In London, the dockers would only work during the day, starting in the morning at about 8.00 a.m. and finishing at 5.00 p.m. They worked extremely quickly: generations of dock-labouring skills had clearly produced an ability to shift a great deal of cargo in a relatively short space of time, without the workers themselves actually appearing to be doing very much at all. This was in contrast to their counterparts on the other side of the Atlantic, who always appeared to be working hard but whose output was far lower. In Montreal they worked shifts and continued throughout the night. There were no cranes, neither were there lighters coming alongside, but blocks placed on tracks on top of the warehouse (whips, as they were called) which removed or loaded cargo.

Grain, of course, was shot in via tubes. In order to carry the grain safely, wooden shifting boards or bulkheads (which could be dismantled) had to be constructed within the open holds fore and aft to prevent the grain shifting in the event of heavy weather. The deep tanks were very useful since they were already sub-divided, both transversely and fore and aft.

Whilst all these duties connected with cargo were new for me, duties at sea were ones to which I was well-accustomed. The main difference was in the small number of people compared to those on board a passenger ship. The deck crew, in addition to the officers, comprised twelve men: a boatswain, a carpenter, a storekeeper and then nine either able seamen or deckhands, or ordinary seamen. The boatswain, carpenter and storekeeper did not keep watch; they were on day-work (known as 'idlers' in the old sailing-ship days). The other nine were divided into watches, with three on each watch. Whilst on a watch they would alternate between being at the wheel, being on look-out and on standby. As an officer, one would always have the same team of men with one. During the day, if a look-out was not required (as was often the case) the only man on the Bridge would be the man at the wheel and the other two would be employed by the boatswain to undertake various tasks about the decks: painting, scrubbing, chipping or whatever. When we got into port they went

into their port routine. The watches were broken and the men moved
to day work, working a normal eight-hour day under the instruction
of the boatswain. Thus, when at sea, you would often find yourself
with only one other man on the Bridge for company. At night time, if
the weather was fine, the lookout would be kept on the fo'c's'le head.
We did have a crow's nest, on the crossbeam of the forward goal post,
but this was rarely used. In bad weather the lookout would be joined
by his standby and they would be brought up under the wings of the
Bridge. Whilst you were on watch you did the requisite navigation,
taking bearings both visual and radar and plotting these, and every
half hour you also had to work out the dead reckoning position and
record this in what was known as the 'D.R.' book. This could then be
referred to quickly, in the event of an emergency when you might
suddenly need to know the position of the ship. The officer was also
expected to take sights and check the compass at least twice. As well
as the watch officers there was one radio officer who kept fairly
regular watches. During the night he had an alarm system which
would alert him in the event of a distress signal coming through from
any other ship in the vicinity.

Now that the war was over and the R.N.R. officers who had been
seconded to the Royal Navy had returned, the company once again
boasted a corps of officers – a situation I had not experienced in my
early days. We were quickly to become a cohesive force; there was not
a great number of us and Canadian Pacific had fewer ships now than
they had had pre-war. It was not long before we all knew one another
and when boarding any ship you would invariably meet up with
friends, or a Captain or Senior Officer whom you had served with
before. This made life far less complicated than it had been when you
had no idea whom you would be serving with next. Everyone knew
one another, everyone trusted one another and we worked very much
as a team. Morale was high and the company set very high standards
which we strove to maintain. In some respects I think we were more
pukka than the Navy itself... however, more of that anon.

As you will have gleaned from the pages of this book thus far, I
always made a point of studying my senior officers – and in particular
my Captains – to ascertain any traits or characteristics I might wish to
emulate or, on the other hand, avoid if I could. This process
continued in peacetime. The first Captain of the *Beaverdell* I served
under was one of my favourites. He had been a Commodore in the
war and was a marvellous man, with all the qualities I admired: a

quiet person who never raised his voice or used bad language (I think the worst I ever heard him utter in a time of not inconsiderable stress was 'bother' or 'oh dear!') but who always had a firm grip of the situation. He was known, affectionately, as 'Daddy Grant' by his officers, not as a derogatory term but rather because all who knew him viewed him as a father figure. I learned a lot from him. An example follows:

Writing up the fair copy of the Deck logbook was always quite a chore which took up a great deal of one's time – and the longer it was left, the more there was to catch up on. If you could get the job done whilst on watch, so much the better. I was on watch one evening in the middle of the Atlantic. Conditions were good; you could see for miles all around and nothing was amiss. I therefore went into the chartroom abaft the wheelhouse to do a bit of catching up on the fair copy of the logbook. I cannot recall how long I had been at it, but suddenly the Captain appeared. Looking at me rather quizzically, and without raising his voice, he just said, 'Who is keeping the look-out, Mr Gillett?'

I knew I ought to have been at my post; I had no excuse whatsoever for being in the wheelhouse and I had left the ship with only the lookout and the man at the wheel, forging ahead through the Atlantic without an officer on the Bridge. I felt very small indeed. If he had shouted at me I might have tried to justify myself; as it was, my conscience did all that was necessary and I certainly never did that again.

It being the right time of year, we came into the Gulf of St. Lawrence through the Strait of Belle Isle, which is to the north between Labrador and Newfoundland. In the later months of the year we would come in further south, past Cape Race on the southern tip of Newfoundland. There were laid down recommended tracks that you followed eastbound and westbound, designed, I assume, subsequent to the Titanic disaster to try and ensure that ships were kept clear of the ice. It was impossible, of course, to be completely 'clear of the ice'; it was always there, but there was a fairly sophisticated reporting method in operation to provide as safe a passage as possible. We had radar, but this had its limitations; sometimes it picked up ice and sometimes it did not, the strength of the signal depending on both the shape of the iceberg and on how far it was protruding out of the water. Floating icebergs are a hazard only between April and November, for during the winter months they are frozen in; then the St. Lawrence is completely icebound and there is no passage through.

I had never been further up the St. Lawrence than Quebec; this time we did not stop at Quebec but proceeded up river to Montreal. It is a long stint from the Strait of Belle Isle to Montreal even once you are in pilotage waters; some 1,000 miles in all. The pilot station for the St. Lawrence was at Father Point on the south bank, where we picked up our pilot – one of a team of experienced French Canadians who had worked with our company's ships for many years, and some of whom had known our current Captains when they were mere cadets. Travelling up the St. Lawrence is an unforgettable experience. One can never grow tired of the scenery; as has once been described to me, Canada is 'like Scotland, only bigger'. Eventually we docked at Montreal which was, at that time, as far up river as it was possible to go. The St. Lawrence Seaway, an elaborate canal system intended to transport larger ships to the Great Lakes, was then still under construction. We spent eight days in Montreal before sailing again. Instead of returning directly to the U.K. or Antwerp (our customary route) we called in at St. John's, Newfoundland, where we stayed for a further six days. Then followed another detour with a three day stop in Hamburg. I was not, however, to see the sights of this European city on this occasion. The day before we arrived I reported sick; running a very high temperature and shivering violently. A doctor was brought on board once we were in Hamburg and he diagnosed malaria, of which I appeared to be showing classic symptoms. However, a blood test revealed no traces of the disease and as I had no recollection of having had it before, my illness remained a mystery. I made a full recovery and was quite fit by the time we returned to London, although unfortunately I had not seen the last of these bouts of fever.

Thus ended my first round trip to Montreal, a place which I came to regard as something of a second home, since I was to spend almost as much time there as I did back in London. Montreal was a very pleasant city indeed, its inhabitants divided fairly equally between French and English speaking. The stevedores were all French Canadians who spoke a quaint, rather old-fashioned dialect which had certain Anglicised characteristics (a potato, for example, was not a *pomme de terre* but a *potate*). Here I could get by on my schoolboy French, unlike in Quebec where French was universally spoken. I was, over the years, to become very fond indeed of the place.

We had fifteen days back in London: the time it took for all the discharging and loading of cargo, plus some additional time on account of fog preventing our departure. My time was spent happily in the usual round of 'debs delighting' with my chums. Our second voyage to Montreal coincided with my 21st birthday which was spent somewhere in the middle of the North Atlantic, although celebrations were somewhat muted as there was no drinking at sea. I opened my presents when I was off watch and received, among other things, a lovely pair of binoculars, which were to serve me well in the years to come. I was also given a signet ring, which I solemnly placed on the little finger of my left hand – an indication of my arrival into the adult world! Once in Montreal, where we arrived on 13th November, I was able to celebrate in more style and a birthday party was held for me on board on the 16th.

It was then directly back to London, with no stops *en route* this time. At home, I was struck once again with the dreaded fever and was confined to bed for two to three days. As in Hamburg, no medical explanation could be found, but bed rest seemed to result in a cure and the day after rising from my sickbed I was off once again to sea. By this time the St. Lawrence was frozen and closed to navigation, so our destination was Saint John, New Brunswick. I was soon to discover that this was not, perhaps, the most exciting of Canada's seaboard cities although the locals were hospitable enough. The real disadvantage of the port, from a sailor's point of view, was the extremes of high and low water, which could be a difference in excess of 30 feet. This resulted in considerable work for the officer of the watch; as the ship went down on the tide it was necessary to ease off the forward and aft mooring lines, otherwise the ship would be hanging on her ropes. Likewise as she came up again on the tide it was necessary to heave them in to prevent the ship floating off the side of the wharf. This might have been inconvenient in temperate weather. In wintertime, with temperatures reaching 12° below at night, the wet ropes would freeze like bars of iron. Normal procedure was to keep the ropes bound in a 'figure of eight', but when frozen these became unwieldy and so we would keep two head ropes and two stern ropes on the drums of the capstan fore and aft, with constant patrolling to ensure that the ropes were sufficiently tight. Another problem was that the salt water, used to wash down the decks, would also freeze. The windlasses were electric, rather than steam, which meant they could be operated once freed of any residual lumps of ice which would encrust them on the passage through the icy waters. The ice would be steam-hosed off and we were in operation. Not so, alas, with the lavatory facilities ('heads' as they are called at sea). Generally speaking, ships do not boast the 'chain-flushing' variety of w.c.. The water for flushing is provided by pressure and thus in the cold weather the loos had to be flushed continually since had they been allowed to stop they would have frozen up. The handles were lashed down and lavatories flushed all the time – a phenomenon which resulted in some spectacular icicles from the outboard side of the ship where the water was discharged!

During the day, temperatures rose and it was often reasonably warm and sunny. The adverse effect of this, however, was that everything immediately thawed, only to freeze once again at night. As a result all surfaces became immensely hazardous – not only on board, where decks were as slippery as skating rinks, but on shore too, where the hilly roads of St. John had to be negotiated with care. Our main source of entertainment in town was the ice-hockey rink, where there was exhibition of keen competition between the towns of the local league. Curling was another popular local pastime and we would try our hand at this, as well as, on occasion, the more hair-raising winter sport of ice yachting.

This particular trip was memorable in that I was not to return to London on the *Beaverdell*. Whilst in Canada, I suffered yet another of my fever attacks, which now appeared to be increasing in intensity and frequency. Again, my symptoms puzzled the doctors. My condition was compounded by jaundice, and I was sent home in the *Beaverford*, a rather different ship, without refrigerated decks or goalposts but with conventional masts down the centre. The *Beaverford* also carried twelve passengers (the maximum permitted without having to have a doctor on board) and the crew in this case lived in the poop, with officers and passengers in the central accommodation. I was given the pilot's cabin up by the bridge, where I was confined to my bunk for the duration.

Once home, I was visited by my own G.P. who was as mystified by my fever symptoms as everyone else had been. Eventually, he consulted a colleague who had served in North Africa with the army and it was he who suggested that I might be suffering from amoebic dysentery – detectable not from the blood but from stool samples. Sure enough, he was right and I was packed off to a nursing home just off the Cromwell Road to be treated. The treatment was fairly simple but not particularly comfortable – a course of retention enemas to flush out the system. In order for these to be effective it was necessary to 'hold on' for twelve hours, which was often extremely difficult. One would strive frantically to divert one's mind and think of other things until the urge had passed – and what bliss when the nurse arrived in the evening and announced, 'Right. You can go now!' Eventually I was ready once again for action. The jaundice, too, had disappeared although I was under doctor's orders to refrain from alcohol for six months – an instruction which I found quite devastating at the time, but to which I adhered religiously.

A period of convalescence was spent in Lymington, in the New Forest, where I spent a very pleasant time and took the opportunity to visit several elderly relatives and members of the family. Once back in London, Canadian Pacific sent me on a course at the Sperry Gyro Compass School, whose gyrocompasses were fitted in all of our 'Beavers'. One of the navigator's jobs was to maintain and clean the compass and the course on offer provided one with the knowledge required to take the compass to bits and put it together again.

Chapter 8

I had lost a considerable amount of valuable sea-time towards my Master's Certificate and it was now high time to start making this up. I was appointed to stand by the *Duchess of Bedford* in Glasgow. The two surviving Duchesses, *Bedford* and *Richmond*, had been converted back from troop-carrying to passenger-carrying vessels and were being upgraded to Empresses: the *Duchess of Bedford* was to become the *Empress of France* and the *Duchess of Richmond* the *Empress of Canada*. The ships had been virtually stripped out inside and a Chief Officer and two junior officers were appointed by the company to supervise the conversion work which was taking place at Fairfields Yard. Only one of the junior officers was required to stay on board overnight at any one time; the other (we took it turn and turn about) stayed in digs in the city. We procured a bicycle as a means of transport to and from the Yard for whichever one of us had stayed in town overnight. This bicycle was heaved up during the day to keep it out of the reach of thieving hands and lowered each night for duty. One morning, when it was my turn on the bicycle, I set off as usual from the digs. The route took me down a fairly steep hill which ended at the bottom in a T junction; traffic on this main road was fairly heavy with trams and buses as well as the usual cars and lorries. As I gathered momentum I applied the brakes, only to find, to my horror, that nothing happened at all. I was advancing at high speed towards the main road at the bottom. I thought quickly as I continued my rapid descent. It seemed to me I had two options: one, to try and steer the bike into a side road off to the left, which seemed a fairly precarious manoeuvre or two, to get off. I plumped for the latter; dismounted in haste and managed, somehow, to hold on to the handlebars, running alongside the bicycle and eventually bringing it to a halt with me in a heap in the middle of the road. I was bruised and shaken but alive; aware that had I not been successful I would have faced certain death, if not from the oncoming traffic at the bottom of the hill then from crashing into the plate glass of the building opposite. As I was, at the time, about to enter one of the rather more interesting periods of my life, I am really rather pleased that the incident ended happily.

Needless to say, when I eventually arrived on board I had some very strong words for my fellow officer who had 'forgotten' to tell me that he had noticed that the brakes were not working the night before. However, we got on well and he was forgiven – he was, in fact, one of the cadets I had relieved when I served on the *Empress of Russia* and had been Chief Cadet Captain of the College at Pangbourne during my junior years there. Our duties on board were fairly basic. We merely had to wander around the ship and keep an eye on what was going on, which often was not very much at all. In those days, just after the war, the shipyards were somewhat ill-disciplined, without much enthusiasm for work among the employees. One would often find the labourers sitting around playing cards rather than getting on with the job in hand.

Across the river, in the part of the Yard where building took place, a new Beaver was being fitted out – the *Beavercove*, the last of the four post-war Beavers to be built. As soon as she was ready I was due to join her and recommence the Montreal run. But before that happened, I was to meet someone who was to alter the course of my life forever...

When my father had learned that I was going to Glasgow, he had written a letter of introduction for me to a Mr John Findlay, whom he had met during the war. John Findlay owned a steel broker's office and yard, and made his living buying and selling steel for the shipbuilding industry. Upon my arrival in Glasgow I received a letter from Mr Findlay, inviting me to visit him at his office one evening, from where he would take me to his home just outside the city in order to meet the family. Dressed in my best uniform (the smartest clothes I possessed since rationing was still in effect) I made my way to his office as bidden; we were then chauffeur driven to the village of Carmunnock, just to the south east of the city, where the Findlays lived in a lovely converted farmhouse. The only member of the family who happened to be at home at the time was a small girl aged eleven (the youngest of the children); two other siblings were away and Mrs Findlay was out on a shopping expedition with the eldest daughter and a friend and was not expected back until dinner time. John Findlay retired to his study and I was left with Dorothy Anne ('Dodo' to her family), a young, pig-tailed girl who invited me to play cards. She beat me consistently but succeeded in keeping me amused until the return of other members of the party.

On her arrival, Mrs Findlay caught sight of my cap, which I had left on the hall table, and at once recognised the insignia: her elder brothers had served with the Canadian Pacific and had all been Master Mariners. Her father had been a Hong Kong pilot and after his death her mother had re-married another Canadian Pacific officer. After the First World War the company had started carrying what were colloquially known as 'candy kids' – young girls (mainly the daughters of serving officers in the company) who were given jobs looking after the ships' libraries, running the shops and suchlike. Mrs Findlay had been one such 'candy kid', as had her companion who had come into the house with her, who had been married to a Purser in the Canadian Pacific and who was godmother to the Findlays' eldest daughter.

My cap therefore proved to be the unwitting prompt for a host of memories. As we waited for dinner, Mrs Findlay produced volumes of photographs recording her days at sea – snaps of a young beauty surrounded by youthful officers and cadets many of whom I recognised instantly as my present Captains and Senior Officers. My acquaintance with the Findlays was off to a very good start indeed.

There was a son, John, who was at the time away at University, and a middle daughter, Stella, who was boarding at Cheltenham Ladies College. I was to meet both of them in due course. The eldest of the four children was a very beautiful girl, Elizabeth – known affectionately within the family circle as Libby. Over dinner that evening, I found myself unable to take my eyes off her.

Is there such a thing as love at first sight? All I can say is that I found myself extremely attracted to her. I was also quite intimidated. She was terribly sophisticated; just back from Finishing School in Switzerland, with all the social skills, poise and grace that such an education bestows. I was a rather inexperienced, somewhat gauche twenty one year old sailor, still rather yellow around the gills from my bout of jaundice. No doubt she had a fleet of admirers from the right set in Glasgow. I resigned myself to adoration from afar.

At that stage in my career I was beginning to contemplate the institution of marriage with a philosophical air. One or two of my contemporaries had 'taken the plunge' but it occurred to me that a career at sea did not mix well with married life. I had decided that I would stick to the course of a true professional and concentrate fully on career advancement: marriage, I had more or less concluded, was not to be for me, at least not for the present. My thinking may well have been influenced by my mother's brother; a bachelor uncle of mine who was a career army officer. He never married or had children but was an extremely good uncle – a status which seemed to me to be an excellent compromise, although my own chances of reaching it were somewhat slim given that I had no siblings to produce nephews and nieces for me. However, I was, on the other hand, also quite attracted to the idea of marriage. It would all depend, I resolved, on finding the right girl – one with character, who would be capable of surviving the rather unfair separations that a sea-going career necessarily enforced. My calculations stretched to a mental 'checklist' against which I might run various candidates if they happened to turn up. If it was to be a real partnership for life, far better that the groundwork was covered early on, rather than rushing in, only to rush out again. Of course in those days 'rushing out again' was really not *de rigueur* at all anyway.

What were the qualities that I considered important in future wife material? Not necessarily in any particular order I list them here by way of amusement:

- Sense of humour (essential)
- A kindly disposition, neither arrogant nor overbearing
- Well-educated (in the broadest sense, that is)
- Intelligent
- Having good taste – good dress sense, house-sense and an artistic sensitivity
- Financial prudence (but not mean)
- A good housekeeper, competent at sewing, cooking and other domestic skills
- Good with children (very important)
- From a happy family background
- Reasonably healthy (although not necessarily sporty or athletic)
- One who would enjoy travelling, should the opportunity arise
- As a bonus, I had hoped for a certain musical ability. My fantasy extended to a vision of me sitting by the fire with my pipe and slippers whilst my wife sat at the grand piano in our drawing room . . .

I quite accept that my readers may feel that such cold-hearted analysis could only stem from a dyed-in-the-wool male chauvinist. In my defence I should explain that my list is not to be taken too seriously, but also confess that it does display something of the cautious nature of the experienced mariner.

I do not think that at that first meeting, Elizabeth noticed me particularly. However, every time that I was off duty that July and August I would visit the Findlays when I could, sometimes just going over for dinner if I was not sleeping on board, or spending long weekends with them when my duties did not require me to be on the ship. Over the course of those weeks I was made to feel one of the family; they were without exception warmly hospitable and welcoming and by the time I left I felt as I had got to know them all very well. I did not, then, 'press my suit' with Libby. I was biding my time. She had plenty of boyfriends, and one in particular who was the brother of a school friend of hers. I am uncertain as to whether John Findlay suspected my intentions but I recall that when we went shooting one day he was very careful to ensure that said boyfriend and I were at opposite ends of the line!

Although he was a businessman, John Findlay came from a line of farmers. He was very much an outdoor man, for whom the 12th August held an almost sacred importance, when the whole family decamped to Crawford, where he had two grouse moors. Although I had never been shooting before, I was invited to join the party for a few days. John Findlay believed very firmly in participation in the sport; for any in his party there was no sitting around in butts waiting for beaters. We would form a line and walk the birds up ourselves – for hours and hours over the heather which, as a complete novice, I found exhausting. I also had a propensity to shoot other things. The rule was that anything you shot, you carried; consequently I invariably found myself lumbered with a couple of hares, rabbits and other such things in my game bag even before I had shot any grouse. However, it was all great fun, despite the fact that I was never particularly inclined towards the sport, not least because I rather object to killing animals and birds. At least the birds we were shooting were wild, unlike the pheasants reared specially for the purpose, whose destiny in life was to be released only to be shot as soon as they were airborne.

As indicated, by the time I came to leave Glasgow I really felt as if I had been taken into the bosom of this delightful family. John Findlay himself looked a typical Scot: he was tall and upright, with pure white hair which set off a ruddy complexion and a healthy moustache. He was twelve years older than his wife, Florence; together they formed an extraordinarily happy couple. Aside from his business activities and his beloved outdoor sports John was also a J.P. He had been President of the Iron and Steel Benevolent Fund and during the war had joined the Home Guard where he refused to take a commission and gloried in the rank of Lance Corporal. He also did a certain amount of A.R.P. work as well (firewatching, etc) which was very much an indication of his position in the community. He was a member of the Conservative Party, an interest he shared with his wife.

Florence was not a Scot; her father (the Hong Kong pilot, who was drowned) had been an Ulsterman; her mother was English. She had been born in Singapore but spent most of her formative years in Hong Kong. After his death and her mother's remarriage, Florence went to sea, during which time she spent time with a family in New Orleans, whom she had met as passengers on the Canadian Pacific. A charming woman with seemingly boundless energy, she had married John in 1925. During the war she became vice-president of the local W.R.V.S. as well as being Liaison Officer for the local branch of the Red Cross, which meant plenty of hospital visiting. She had been invited to stand as a Conservative candidate for Rutherglen in the election after the war, but her health was not too good by then and she declined, although would represent her area at Conservative Party Conferences. She collected antiques and had great taste, evident both in the decor of their converted farmhouse and in the beautiful garden she had created from a former field. I was very fond of her indeed, and we got on well.

Libby had been born in 1926 (almost a year after me) and had been educated at school in Glasgow until the outbreak of war, when a governess had been employed to teach her and her sister Stella. Libby went on to Cheltenham and then, with the war over, she spent some time as an *au pair* in the home of a Swiss banker, filling the time before finishing school in Lauserne.

John, the only boy in the family (known as John-John to distinguish him from his father; eldest boys in the family were traditionally called John) had suffered as a child from polio which had left the left side of his body slightly disabled. He was a good pianist and trumpeter and a born engineer – always taking cars to pieces and reconstructing them with the gear lever on the right rather than the left to enable him to use it with his good arm. He frequently lost his licence for speeding and was often disqualified for various stretches. The family possessed an old Wolsey and a Hillman Minx of the same brand as my own, which I felt very comfortable driving and

I would often take John out during his disqualified periods and, once out of sight, permit him to take the wheel and get a bit of driving out of his system, swapping over just before we came back in sight of the house. Like his father, John also thoroughly enjoyed outdoor sports such as shooting and fishing.

Next in line was Stella, who was born in 1929, the year after John. She had shared Libby's governess and went on to Cheltenham Ladies College at the age of twelve. Stella was given to literature, in those days, and would frequently retire to her room with an exercise book under her arm to write plays and books. As with the rest of her family Stella was a charming girl, although I never felt a romantic attraction there. It was, from the outset, Libby who caught my eye.

Last, but not at all least, Dorothy Anne was born in 1937; an 'afterthought', as she used to say herself. Dodo was a bright as a button and a bit of tomboy, who regarded me possessively as her own. I was forever being asked to mend her bicycle or plait her hair, or some such. I suppose that with the difference in our ages she regarded me as some sort of honorary uncle. She, too, was despatched to Cheltenham in due course, where she stayed throughout her school career. Another connection between our families was through a cousin of mine who had been to Cheltenham Ladies College herself and had become Secretary of the Guild, who became acquainted with all of the Findlay girls as they passed through the school.

Finally, no account of the family would be complete without mentioning Nanny. Libby would describe Nanny as looking like Arthur Askey in drag; small, with horn-rimmed spectacles and fiercely possessive of her charges, she had arrived on the scene when John was born and stayed until Stella left for school. She then departed for Eton, where she spent some time as a dame, until Dorothy Anne's arrival at which point she promptly returned to the fold. With only one other short break, she was to remain as the family housekeeper until the day she died. I soon discovered that in order for my success with Libby to be assured it was going to be essential to get on Nanny's right side. She regarded all of the Findlay children – and those with whom they consorted – with a most critical eye, and it was therefore well worth spending some time wooing Nanny in order to be assured of a smooth passage with Libby.

All good things must come to an end, and eventually at the end of August I was transferred from the *Duchess of Bedford* (now the *Empress of France*) to the brand spanking new *Beavercove*, where I was appointed Fourth Officer. My days in Glasgow were sadly numbered and the time finally came to say goodbye to the Findlays, who had become like a family to me.

Chapter 9

We sailed from Glasgow down to London, from where it was back once more to the North Atlantic run to Montreal or St. John, New Brunswick. In October I was promoted to Third Officer; a new Fourth Officer joined and for the first time in my life I had someone under me. This meant that I now switched to the middle watch, from midnight to 4.00 a.m. and from noon to 4.00 p.m. It may seem strange, but I really rather enjoyed this watch. From midnight, one was alone on the Bridge with the ship to oneself, with only the man at the wheel and the look-out for company. On a clear night, there is nothing to compare with the sensation of being at sea, with no land in sight, a multitude of stars above you and the ship purring under you through the dark waters. I would feel, in such circumstances, very much at peace with the world and at one with nature. If conditions were right, one would also, on occasion, be treated to Nature's own fireworks display – the *aurora borealis* – when the sky would be alive with sheets of shifting colour. To pass the time during the night I would philosophise and contemplate Life in all its varied forms. One of my solitary habits would be to mentally reincarnate my hero Nelson, who would come up on to the Bridge with me, where I would show him round, pointing out to him all the various modern gadgets he would not have had in his day and making him realise that although many things had changed, it was still the same sea and the same sense of freedom, that has always made a sailor's life so deeply enjoyable at times. It was during those four hours, alone with a calm and reassuring sea, that I would come to appreciate the vastness of the universe and my very small and humble place within it. Often I would stay on to watch the dawn, a myriad colours on the horizon, which would spread gradually and gloriously across the sky. Colours of such vivid hue that, were one to paint them, one would be scorned for one's impression of nature. A privilege indeed, and a sight that those on land will never appreciate.

Once in harbour, duties changed. Although there was no longer need for watches, one was kept very busy supervising the unloading and loading of cargo, with some time off for visits ashore.

Thus passed the year of 1948 – although not quite without incident. On 9th March, I had the opportunity to go to the Guildhall and watch my father being sworn in as an Alderman. He had been on the Common Council since 1930 and finally the Alderman of his ward had died – it had been a case of 'dead men's shoes' as there was no upper age limit for Aldermen who, in those days, would carry on well into their eighties, and sometimes even their nineties, if they were still of sound mind. I was privileged indeed to witness my father's admission, and the realisation of a cherished ambition of his. It proved to be his first step on the ladder that was to lead, eventually, to the Mansion House. The ceremony was a fascinating spectacle, although I certainly did not dream, as I watched, that I would one day be following in my father's footsteps. At that point in my life I had no thoughts at all of a career away from the sea.

When travelling home from the Royal Victoria Docks in London, back to Knightsbridge, I would usually take the bus, which provided an opportunity to see a bit of London after having been away. Every time we passed the Mansion House thereafter the thought would always cross my mind that Father would be there, one day.

The rest of the year passed fairly uneventfully, habitually to-ing and fro-ing between London and Canada with occasional stops on the Continent *en route*. Only one other incident is worth a mention, here. It occurred on 12th August.

I was on watch, at about 2.30 in the afternoon. Conditions were clear, with neither fog nor ice, and we were ploughing steadily along through untroubled waters. All of a sudden came a terrific bang. The entire ship vibrated from end to end, much like a huge dog shaking itself out of the water. I immediately jumped on to the telegraph and rang them to stop engines, and gradually she settled. The Captain, who had been below (on the lavatory, I think!) at the time, leapt on to the Bridge clasping his trousers, demanding to know what the hell had gone wrong. I professed ignorance – I had certainly seen nothing. We suspected propeller damage, and began to ease the engines slowly ahead once more. At about ten knots she started vibrating badly and we eased off, but decided to proceed, slowly, on our way to London. Once we finally arrived she was taken in to dry dock, where the extent of the damage was revealed. It was, indeed, the propeller, which had lost one entire blade (out of four) with an adjacent blade having been sheared about half way across. The cause remained a mystery. Had we hit a whale? It seemed unlikely. I could not imagine any creature managing to damage the huge propeller, which rotated at such an enormous rate. Possibly a container – rare in those days although a more common feature in today's seas where they tend to float about under the surface and are impossible to see. But we shall never know. We were lucky that we had not lost all of the blades and had been able to continue, limping, homeward.

For once I was at home for Christmas and New Year. I celebrated in style by going to the Chelsea Arts Ball (a feature of London social life which alas no longer exists), which was held in the Albert Hall and attended by some four thousand people. The auditorium was cleared of seating in much the same way as it is for the proms. Guests came in fancy dress and danced the night away; certainly a night to remember and a fine way to enter 1949.

By 4th February I had, at last, completed sufficient sea time to qualify for my First Mate's Certificate. It had taken far longer than I had hoped, with all the various interruptions. I had been in the *Beavercove* for seventeen months, the longest period that I ever served in any one ship, but eventually signed off and on 14th February signed on once more at Sir John Cass. Another period of study and 'debs delighting', and time, too for a car change. The old Hillman was by now well past its sell-by date and thus I decided to trade it in for a Standard 12 drop head coupé – a post-war car and a couple of horsepower up on the Minx. Exams commenced on 11th April and by the 20th, having survived another oral with the dreaded Captain Wallace, I was the proud possessor of the First Mate's Certificate. Only one more stint before I could finally qualify for Master!

On 2nd May I joined the *Beaverlake* as Third Officer and on the 18th I was promoted to Second Officer and Navigator, keeping the 4-8 watch mornings and evenings. My promotion, which made me the senior of the three watch-keeping officers, entitled me to a larger cabin. I enjoyed navigation, which was preferable to cargo work. My duties included having to take sights morning and evening and to be responsible for the navigating equipment (my Sperry course came in useful here); I looked after the gyrocompass and supervised all of the charts. The job was right up my street.

It was company policy within the Canadian Pacific to alternate officers between ships as part of the promotional process. I stayed with the *Beaverlake* until 13th September, and was then sent to

The Beaverlake.

Liverpool to join the *Empress of Canada* (the *Duchess of Richmond* that was), serving once again under Captain Shergold, my favourite captain from my cadet days. I think we were both glad to see one another again; he enjoyed having under him those he had himself 'brought up' as cadets. It was good, too, to be back in a passenger ship. We were on the regular run between Montreal and Liverpool; not quite as convenient for me, of course, but I stayed with the *Empress* only until the end of December before returning to London once more.

My next appointment was to the *Beaverglen*, as Second Officer, but this was not to take place until 22nd December. I therefore had a few weeks' grace, which turned out to be the beginning of a major change in my life.

Chapter 10

I had kept in touch with the Findlays during my absence and would often meet up with John Findlay who would dine with my parents if he was down in London. Stella had come down to the Monkey Club, a girls' finishing school in town, and I would take her out to a nightclub on occasion. I had bought goodies for the family, whom I knew to be great entertainers at Christmas, and I would send them parcels of ingredients for Christmas cakes, puddings and the like, which were still difficult to obtain over here. However, I had not seen Libby since my time in Glasgow. During this period before Christmas I was invited to go and stay with the family.

I travelled up to Scotland with Stella. The Findlays had moved, in the interim, to a place near Paisley, the original farmhouse now proving rather too small for the growing family. The new house was quite grand, with splendid grounds including swimming pool and tennis courts, and I was welcomed there as an old friend. They had not changed at all – with the exception of Dorothy Anne who was now out of her pigtails and had developed into a boisterous young teenager.

Libby was a lovely as ever. I was overjoyed to see her again, and it was now that I realised how very much in love with her I was. In the two years since we had first been introduced, I had changed somewhat. No longer was I the rather naive and jaundiced twenty-one year old who had first appeared at their house. I was now experienced, more of a 'man of the world', and had gained in self-confidence which no longer left me feeling overawed in her presence.

I spent a glorious four days there. There was snow on the ground and we entered fully into the festive spirit, hanging Christmas decorations and preparing food. A large party was held one evening and guests arrived, good-humouredly participating in traditional party games. I recall during a game of sardines desperately hoping to be confined with Libby, only to be monopolised by Dodo who grabbed me by her sticky hand and dragged me off somewhere. Such are little sisters.

The attraction was obviously mutual. I danced with Libby and Libby alone at all the dances we attended and on one evening, the memory still with me now, we had our first kiss. By the time I had to return to London, the family had accepted that we were 'together'. They all came to see me off on the night sleeper from Glasgow, but tactfully left us alone to say our final farewells. I remember to this day looking through the window of the carriage for a final, goodbye kiss. For years afterwards, whenever I felt homesick or lonely without her, I found myself able to revive that picture and that feeling. There was no doubt that I was smitten, and smitten hard.

It was the most miserable Christmas I had ever spent. My parents must have wondered what the trouble was (although I rather suspect my mother's intuition may have informed her why I was suffering so). My time was spent writing long letters to Libby, yearning for the time when we might be together again. I was in love, and separated from my loved one, and only those who have been through it know of the torment this brings.

I was determined we should marry, of that I had no doubt. My practical self dictated that I should obtain my Master's Certificate before 'tying the knot', but this was nearly a year away.

I was back in London in February and Libby came down. We had a glorious few days and I took the opportunity to show her proudly around 'my' London. Unfortunately this coincided with a government clampdown on nightclubs and a law had just been introduced enforcing clubs to serve food. This meant they were all closed – some for good, some for refurbishment. It seemed ironic that in all my times of 'debs delighting' I had chaperoned around the London scene many girls in whom I was not particularly interested, and now that I had someone with me whom I really wanted to impress, everything was closed. However, it mattered little. We were together. We had a whale of time, going out to dinner and to the theatre. On the Saturday (I was due to sail on the Tuesday) I whisked Libby off to Harrods where we chose a rather expensive gold wristwatch; a present to indicate the strength and permanence of my feeling towards her – and a signal to ward off any potential predators in Glasgow! However, the following day my mother quizzed me as to my 'intentions'. I told her that I fully intended to marry Libby.

'Why don't you get engaged, then?' she asked, with straightforward matter of factness.

Why not, indeed?

The following day I collected Libby from her hotel and we drove into Hyde Park.

'Do you know where we're going?' I asked, playfully.

'No,' came the obvious reply.

'We're going to Garrards to buy you an engagement ring'.

This was the nearest I came to going down on one knee and proposing. I had assumed, in my arrogant way, that she would say yes. In fact, she burst into tears. But they were tears of joy, and off we went to choose a lovely ring. A kindly chap served us and booked us for lunch at the Spanish restaurant over the road while he adjusted the ring to fit Libby's finger. He brought the ring over once it was ready and joined us in a glass of champagne. And there we were, engaged.

The first person we told was Nanny. At that time she was with a family in Hampstead, where we drove and had tea. She was delighted with the news. We then went home to tell my parents and telephone Libby's. It had never occurred to me to ask John Findlay for 'permission'; my close relationship with the family assured me of their approval. John was down in London the very next day on business and we went out to dinner, where he confirmed the family's delight.

A new chapter in my life had begun. I went off to sea, leaving behind me for the first of many times the one I loved.

In addition to this important step in my personal life, a career move was also to occur at about this time. I very much wished to join the Royal Naval Reserve and enhance my professional sea-going experience. However the ship owners' lobby had in previous years persuaded the government not to have an R.N.R. They had lost so many of their men to the R.N.R. in 1939 and it was felt that in the event of another war, the Royal Naval Volunteer Reserve (R.N.V.R.) should suffice to cover the Navy's needs, with the Merchant Shipping Officers being far more usefully employed in their own convoy ships. However, it had now been decided to begin reversing this decision and to re-open a restricted officer-only corps, and I was thus able to volunteer. This I did in the February, and in August of that year I was duly interviewed, medically examined and commissioned as a probationary Sub-Lieutenant.

When we came in to London in the March of that year we were due for a re-fit in dry dock, which meant an extended period of time ashore. I took the opportunity to go up to Scotland, not having been

Our Engagement.

since before Christmas. I spent six days with the family and then returned with Libby to London. We had decided, by that time, to get married in September. It seemed pointless waiting until I had my Master's certificate and waste the time that my studies would give us together. I would also be undertaking some R.N.R. training which would, again, allow me to be based at home. Precious time together indeed and it seemed foolish not to take advantage. Thus the date of September 22nd was fixed and preparations commenced.

The year was not without other incident. Canadian Pacific had, at some point, agreed to participate in the making of a documentary film, sponsored by some government department or other, which was designed to demonstrate Britain's exporting capabilities. The film would start out with footage of various factories and production lines and then visit the docks, where shots were taken of loading on to one of our *Beavers*, until the final shots of unloading and of the goods finding their home in Canada. The title of the film was 'Across Deep Waters'. There was a requirement for some scenes to be shot at sea with, preferably, some shots of dramatic weather conditions to lend a bit of excitement to the whole. Two of us on board were quite keen on photography: myself, and a chap called John Waling. It was decided that we would have the cameras and take responsibility for capturing the sea shots. The equipment was cumbersome and very heavy but we were both extremely keen and agreed to share the duty. Fortunately, we encountered some fairly rough weather quite soon on our way out, and managed some effective shots of waves breaking across the bows and sweeping across the decks. I was determined, however, to try for something rather better. I told the officer of the watch to let the ship 'run off'; that is, come off the wind a little and then come back into it, so that the waves would really smack into our port bow, producing a very dramatic image indeed. I made my way to the comparative shelter of the main deck, creeping forward as far as I dared with the protection of a solid bulkhead rather than the open rails, which were to be found on other decks. The camera was rolling as we hit each wave in turn, jolting violently with the impact. A first, then a second . . . and then the third, a colossal wave of green water which swept inboard. I found myself swimming about, clutching on manfully to the camera and grateful for the solid protection of the bulkhead between me and the sea – had I been against open rails I suspect I would have been sucked out! The ship gradually righted herself, the water eventually drained away, and I was left dripping, my sea boots full of water and feeling rather anxious as to the extent of the damage to the camera. It was certainly the end of shooting for that voyage. I took the camera up to my cabin, dried myself off and then proceeded to take it to bits as best I could. It seemed perfectly all right, as far as I could make out, and I suspected that the film had probably survived, protected in its sealed drum. I handed over the camera once we arrived in Montreal and heard nothing further, so can only assume that all was well.

Some six months later 'Across Deep Waters' happened to be showing at the Odeon, Marble Arch as a 'B' film prior to 'The Lavender Hill Mob' with Alec Guinness. Having missed the private showing as I had been away at sea, I was looking forward with interest to see the results of my handiwork. We took our seats and the film commenced. I felt immensely proud to see my name and John Waling's on the credit titles, as 'Sea Scenes by . . . ' Sitting in front of us was a mother with her two small daughters. When the sea scenes came on, with the full force of crashing waves (including the one that had knocked me down) the little girls grew quite excited. Their mother turned to them and said, in knowledgeable tones: 'Of course, you know, they fake all of these scenes in a tank.' Having practically lost my life in the process of acquiring said sea scenes I was tempted indeed to strike the woman. I refrained, but did rather wonder why I had gone to so much trouble!

But to return to the matter of my engagement. Over the next few months I continued the passage to and from Montreal, and in all cases bar one I would either visit Scotland on my return or Libby would come down to London, and on one occasion I took her down to Frinton, where my parents continued to visit. Libby's mother was confined to the London Clinic with a minor heart problem for a while, and thus her visits coincided with visiting her mother, too. At about the same time my father was also in a nursing home, so hospital visiting took up some of our time. Both parents were, fortunately, to recover. Preparations for the wedding continued apace. It was to take place in Scotland, where the vast majority of Libby's friends and relations were. With rationing still in place over here, she went to Paris to buy her trousseau and acquired a magnificent dress, which was to appear subsequently (with Libby wearing it) on cinema screens across Glasgow, in an advertisement by the people who did the photography for us!

There was one important question. Would my ship arrive in time

The Fiancé.

The Fiancée.

for the wedding? We were scheduled to be back in London on the Tuesday, giving me time to sign off and get up to Scotland for the rehearsal on the Thursday and the wedding on the Friday. But our route home involved a stop in Antwerp with a cargo of grain, on a schedule that admitted for no unforeseen delays whatsoever. Pa Findlay had booked a huge marquee to be erected in the garden of their home for the reception. The same marquee was required the following week for Troon Races; in the event of the wedding being postponed the marquee would have to be dismantled, taken off to Troon and brought back again, which would prove a very expensive operation indeed. Everything possible had to be done to ensure that I arrived in time.

We did not, in the event, arrive in Antwerp until Monday and I knew full well that there was insufficient time to discharge our cargo and still be sure of getting me back to London in time. There was, however, a kindly Dutch agent in Antwerp who, appraised of my predicament, decided that he would ring the General Manager of the Canadian Pacific, who was housed in the Liver Building in Liverpool, and get permission for me to leave the ship and fly home to meet my deadline. I accompanied him to the office from where he telephoned the G.M., one Captain Stewart, who had a reputation for never allowing any personal circumstance to interfere with an officer's duty (the story was that the day his wife died he undertook a routine visit to a ship in port). I felt that my chances were slim indeed. I was horrified when the agent spoke to Captain Stewart in his very good – but perhaps not entirely accurate – English:

'Ah,' he began. 'I have a problem here. I have Mr Gillett, who is Second Officer of the *Beaverglen*. Mr Gillett has got to get married on Friday.'

My God, I thought, it sounds as if Libby is in the family way!

Perhaps because he was a Scot himself, and perhaps because he happened to be in a good mood, Captain Stewart – who had not, apparently, taken the Dutch agent's explanation the wrong way – consented, and I was permitted to sign off the very next day. I caught the train to Brussels and thence to London where I arrived late on Tuesday afternoon. I had time to collect my thoughts and be ready the following day to catch the 11.40 night sleeper to Glasgow, accompanied by my father (Mother, sadly, was prevented from attending the wedding by ill health) and my cousin Judy Gillett who was to be a bridesmaid. We arrived in Glasgow on Thursday morning,

Our Wedding Day.

in time for the rehearsal and later, a stag party for me with Libby's brother John and the best man, one Anthony Dring, who was a Lieutenant in the Royal Navy and a friend of mine from Pangbourne. The next day, Friday, we were married in Paisley Abbey – a beautiful building boasting the longest nave in Europe (people used to quip that they always thought that was me!). The church was packed, mostly with Libby's friends and relatives, many of whom had never set eyes on me before. I was very brown, at the time, so much so that several might have thought she was marrying someone of foreign extraction! The service was conducted by Mr Rogan and all went well, then it was then back to the house for the reception. We had hidden our 'going away' car – the family Hillman I had driven before – nearby but saboteurs had found us out and our suitcases had been stuffed with confetti. However, away we went, leaving the party in full swing, to spend our first night at the Lockerbie House Hotel.

Our honeymoon was to be very fragmented. I had leave fed to me for only four days at a time, which made it impossible to plan ahead. One was not, in any case, permitted to stay at any hotel for longer than four days then without having to produce ration books, which would have been complicated. We resolved this by deciding to set off on a tour of England, aiming for the West Country for as long as my leave would allow; not entirely satisfactory but quite good fun. From Lockerbie our route took us to the Lakes (the Old England Hotel on Lake Windermere) then down to the Cotswolds for three days in Broadway. We then returned to London to visit my mother and collect some belongings and my car, leaving the Hillman for young John to collect and return to Scotland. My parents were now living in the Normandy Hotel in Knightsbridge, (where my father was on the board) since my mother had begun to find the steep stairs at Fairholt Street too much for her. This left the house free for our use. My mother had fully intended to persuade my father to give us the house as a wedding present, but he proved very Victorian on this principle and demanded that we find something for ourselves. However, some four years later, during which time we had lived in the house anyway, she used an inheritance to buy the property from him herself and was able to give it to us then.

After a few hours in London for lunch and dinner we continued on our way, this time to Windsor and the Old House Hotel, and then the following day to Exmouth. From there our journey took us to Cornwall, and here we remained for five days, including one night at the St. Ives Bay Hotel, which was owned by friends of the Findlays, and where Libby, having spent some time on a hotel course there, was well known to many of the staff (her expertise on hotel management was to come in very useful in later years when we travelled around the world). Our route back took us along the north coast of Cornwall and Devon, through Somerset (a stop in Cheddar and a visit to the Gorge and the Caves) and thence to the New Forest (visits to relatives).

We then returned to London and our new home. We did begin a certain amount of house-hunting but my mother, who was determined we should stay in Fairholt Street, always made very discouraging noises and in the end this activity was abandoned. I am not sure how we would have paid for a house, anyway, given my salary at the time of £800 per year – supplemented only by a few shares and a monthly allowance of £20 from my father.

I was called back to work on 21st October. Prior to this I had taken Libby down to show her around Pangbourne, where things had changed little from my day – it was still the rather meagre portion of bread and scrape for tea, if you were lucky. I recall Libby casting a critical eye at the routine which was pinned on the board, commencing with the rigours of pre-dawn reveille. She was clearly unimpressed.

'No son of mine,' she declared, 'will ever come here.'

In fact they both did, but that is another story.

I was off to sea again by 3rd November, the first of many times that I was to bid farewell to Libby as my wife. It was via Antwerp to Montreal, just before the St. Lawrence was closed for the winter and I was home on 23rd December for what was to be an extended period ashore whilst I pursued my studies.

We went to Scotland to spend our first Christmas there. The family had again just moved, to Busby House in the village of that name, which was back nearer towards Glasgow. Although the property did not boast quite as much land as the previous abode it was a pleasant, well-appointed house with a stream running through the grounds. The usual preparations were afoot and a very merry time was had by all throughout the festive season. After Christmas Libby and I journeyed south; I was to commence my R.N.R. training on 4th January.

Chapter 11

Our first benefit from my training with the R.N.R. was a decent length of time ashore. Some of those who serve in the Navy itself end up spending the better part of their time ashore, of course, but in the Merchant service that is never the case. One is only of use to one's company when at sea and time ashore is very limited indeed. It was agreed that while I was training Libby and I would, where possible, stay in small hotels together near where I was to be based.

We found one such hotel in Southsea, only a stone's throw from Portsmouth; it was homely and comfortable and remarkably cheap, and it served well for my first divisional course at H.M.S. *Nelson*. I had the car with me, and drove into Portsmouth every morning from the hotel, returning to my wife in the evenings. This course lasted for two weeks and provided a general introduction to the Navy, including familiarisation with Naval disciplinary procedures. Following this was a week at H.M.S. *Phoenix*, the Damage Control School, also in Portsmouth. Here we learned about fire-fighting, blocking up shell holes and other such repair work. This was very much a 'hands on' course during which we spent a great deal of time wearing oilskins and leaping into swimming pools which had been set alight. A dummy section of a cruiser was used, in which they created every conceivable kind of disaster, with water pouring into the sides and fires breaking out all over the place. Then came three weeks at H.M.S. *Mercury*, the Royal Navy's Signal School at East Meon, where we worked intensively on visual signalling, R.T. procedure and flags, with a certain amount of code work, too. This was interesting but perhaps not quite as much fun as other, more active courses. They also had a rather curious system of giving orders when one was marching. Instead of demanding that you 'Halt' or whatever, commands were given as signals. On the command 'Speed Sugar' we all had to raise our hands on the air; when the officer then said 'Executive' we all put our hands down and halted. It was supposed to instil in us a sense of manoeuvring as a fleet but we found it all somewhat childish. From the *Mercury* we moved to H.M.S. *Dryad*, the Navy's Navigation School.

Not to learn navigation, since we were all well skilled already in that department, but to familiarise ourselves with the Navy's sophisticated plotting equipment. This was rather fun, although the Commanding Officer of *Dryad* turned out to be something of a fitness fanatic who made us all do P.T. on the parade ground every morning before we started work. Shades of Pangbourne there!

From here we moved on to the 'hard stuff', for a spell in Chatham (again Libby and I were lucky to find an excellent little hotel nearby) for a six-week gunnery course. To quote the Directing Officer, who introduced the course, 'You will have to steam. You *will* steam!' We were kept hard at it, not only learning about gunnery but also parade training, which meant doubling everywhere and keeping everything as neat as a pin. I enjoyed parade training, for which we wore battledress and gaiters and huge boots and crashed about all over the place. From here it was then on to the relatively civilised H.M.S. *Vernon* back in Portsmouth for mine and torpedo training. The course was a four-week one, with two weeks in H.M.S. *Vernon* and two in H.M.S. *Osprey* in Portland where live sea exercises took place. Libby and I returned to our little hotel in Southsea for the Portsmouth stint and when we moved to Portland some of us were billeted in the Royal Breakwater Hotel where Libby and I were able to stay together. The bar served a very good and extremely potent scrumpy and the hotel also boasted a small west country skittle alley, where wooden balls were rolled across planks to wooden skittles. Not terribly sophisticated but the forerunner, of course, of today's ten-pin bowling. We had great fun there and it was a good place to finish off our course, with real exercises at sea which brought the whole thing into focus. There was one other married officer on the course, which meant that Libby had some female company for a change. On Sundays we would drive out into the countryside and visit local beauty spots such as Lulworth Cove.

The course had lasted for seventeen weeks in all, by the end of which time all of the officers knew one another well. We came from various shipping companies, large and small, and there were one or two I knew already from Pangbourne. We were a happy band, if all somewhat long in the tooth to be Sub Lieutenants, but such is naval hierarchy; one was not permitted in at any higher rank without a Master Mariner's certificate. The course came to an end on 5th May and we all returned to our various homes and shipping companies. In my case it was back to the *Beaverglen* and I was off to sea only five days later, leaving my wife at home once again to look after things. I was not home again until 3rd June; the first of three round trips to Montreal before I had completed the requisite sea time to be eligible for the Master's Certificate.

Before I settled down to the course at Sir John Cass, Libby and I felt that we owed it to ourselves to have a proper honeymoon, having been rather short-changed the first time. The summer in England had been a poor one and we also felt we deserved some sunshine. After a brief visit to Scotland, therefore, we set off from Dover on a great adventure. It must be remembered that this was well before the days of package holidays and organised tours. We had no great plans other than to motor south through France until we found some sun.

This we did, arriving each afternoon at some suitable town and finding a reasonable local hotel for the night. We would rarely eat in the hotel but would investigate the town for a small restaurant in keeping with our taste and the constraints of our purse. The following morning we would purchase supplies for the day and set off, picnicking for lunch and repeating the process the following night. We lived simply and frugally – but we were young, and in love, and it did not really matter much at all. Having set off from Boulogne (where the car was slung out from the ferry in a net, unlike today's roll-on, roll-off procedure) our journey took us via Rouen and other small towns until we eventually arrived, four days later, at the Mediterranean, reaching Monte Carlo on 12th August. The roads through France were fairly empty and other English cars few and far between. I would infuriate Libby by becoming very excited whenever we spotted another 'G.B.' plate, waving my arms in the air and shrieking 'Anglais! Anglais!' In the country villages we saw some extraordinary looking vehicles – rusty old Renaults with bow fronts and radiators tied on with string. I did all of the driving, which became quite hairy once we reached the foothills of the Pyrenees with all its hairpin bends and switchbacks. But at last we were in sight of the Med. Cannes was our first port of call, but there were no vacancies in any of the hotels. A similar tale confronted us in Nice, so eventually we wound up in Monte Carlo where we found a room for one night before having to move on to another hotel – the Monte Carlo Palace – where we remained for a further five days. We spent a very relaxing time, swimming in the warm sea during the day and soaking up the sun; dining out at small restaurants each night and whiling away evenings at the Casino.

Having come down on the western side of France we decided our return trip should be on the other side and headed to Grenoble for the start of the journey north. By the time we arrived, it was rather late in the day. Unfortunately every hotel in town was fully booked and we decided, therefore, to sleep in the car. A few miles to the north of the town we drew off the road into a convenient looking field, where we switched off the headlights, tucked ourselves up in travelling rugs and settled down for a rather uncomfortable night's rest. It was not until the next day that we discovered it had been at that particular spot that a British family had been murdered only a few months previously. Had we known in advance, I am not sure we would have slept quite so easily!

A couple of days later, we began to have a spot of bother with the car. An unhealthy-sounding noise was coming from the front nearside wheel and I suspected that one of the bearings had gone. With still quite a long way to go, I knew that the problem had to be addressed then and there. It was a Saturday, we were in the middle of the French countryside and I did not feel particularly hopeful, knowing that in England one would be hard-pressed to find anywhere open. However, in a small town I stumbled across a workshop built into an archway where I tried to explain my problem to the old boy inside. He spoke no English at all and I had some difficulty when it came to describing roller bearings in French, but with sign language and pictures I managed to get the message across. We got the car in and he proceeded to remove the wheel – with some difficulty – which enabled him to see exactly the full extent of *le problème*. He turned to me and explained that he would have to go and fetch something, before making off on his bicycle. I did not think for one moment that there would be any chance of finding any spare parts, but he returned some fifteen minutes later bearing an oxyacetylene tank on his back. He then sat down and proceeded to braze, from a small piece of brass, a perfect bush-type bearing. The whole process lasted for about three hours; with nowhere else to go we stayed and watched the proceedings and were gradually joined by a fascinated group of children, drawn no doubt by the unusual spectacle of our English car. Eventually the old boy finished; he replaced the wheel and, cautioning me to take care, charged me some ridiculously low price for the service. I must say I was very impressed indeed; this had been a delightful display of the sort of inventive resilience one finds among such people. The bearing caused no further trouble and stayed in

103

place until I eventually got rid of the car some years later. I could not help thinking that had I been in England, in similar circumstances, I would never have had found anyone prepared to hand craft a bearing; no doubt they would have had to send away for the right part, I would have been charged hundreds of pounds for the job and it would probably have taken a fortnight.

We continued north, stopping at Fontainebleu to look at Napoleon's palace and then to Paris for two days, where we did the sights before returning to Boulogne and the crossing for home. Before boarding, we found ourselves with just enough money to purchase a bar of Toblerone chocolate. We had had a marvellous time and made up fully for the rather fragmented honeymoon we had had earlier – although we managed to use this as an excuse for several other 'honeymoons' throughout our married life!

It was time to get back to work and to Sir John Cass to embark on the final stage of my professional qualifications. I realised how right I had been to get married first, given the opportunity that the course provided for staying at home. I was even toying with the idea of extending my stay still further by sitting for my Extra Master's Certificate – not a necessary qualification unless one intended becoming an examiner or a ship's surveyor – but nevertheless an excuse not to have to return to sea for a while.

On 9th November I celebrated my 26th birthday. This still coincided with the Lord Mayor's Show and an evening banquet in Guildhall. My mother was not feeling particularly well and was unable to attend. One of the Sheriffs that year, Sir Dennis Truscott had four daughters, whom he wanted to bring along to the banquet. Knowing that my father had a spare place, it was agreed to swap me for a daughter (my father would have been unable to take me himself since I was a man) and I was to attend as a guest of Sir Dennis. It was the first time I had been to a Lord Mayor's Banquet: little did I know then how many more I would be attending in the years to come!

On 12th November the written exams commenced. They did not cause me too much trouble but I was beginning to feel increasingly concerned at the prospect of my oral. Not so much with regard to the questions that might be asked, but rather on account of the examiner himself. I had discovered from one of the ushers that Captain Lewis, the Senior Examiner of Masters and Mates in London who would have usually done the job, was away at some conference or other. He was to be replaced, in the event, by a Captain Glass. Captain Glass and I had recently met. It was on a return to London a few months before and he had been down to the docks to check operations, scrutinising in particular the arrangements for carrying the grain which, as I have explained previously, are subject to strict regulations. He was not satisfied that the shifting boards we had in place were high enough – they needed to be two feet clear of the surface of the grain. As Second Officer I was officer of the day; the cargo officer was there too and we had a slight *contretemps* over the issue, with my fellow officer and I arguing that the grain had not settled as much as anticipated on the voyage (one took this into account when loading). Captain Glass disagreed with us and, although he took no action, we were given a warning. It was this man who was now to take my oral examination. I felt absolutely sure he would haze me on the grain regulations and therefore spent the weekend before swotting these regulations – which were very complex – until I knew them backwards, forwards and inside out. When I stepped into the examination room I recognised him at once, but Captain Glass showed no flicker of recognition towards me at all. Perhaps my luck was in. He then proceeded to grill me for one and a half hours, during which time he asked me questions on everything I had ever been taught – including obscure details from the second and first mate's certificates. But never, *never* a question on the grain regulations.

Eventually, the questions came to an end.

'Right,' he said, moving across to the desk. Now came the moment of truth. A form was placed on the desk, to the side of which were placed a blue pencil and a red pencil. One knew immediately whether or not one had passed according to the colour of the pencil selected by the examiner to mark the form: blue if you had passed, red if you had failed and needed to re-sit or, even worse, had to make up more sea time. Before selecting his pencil, he glanced up at me and said:

'We've met before, haven't we?'

'Yes, Sir, ' I replied.

'Yes,' he said slowly. 'I thought we had. It was some ... er ... some disagreement, I believe, over the grain regulations, was it not?'

'Yes, Sir', I replied.

'I expect you know them now,' he concluded. And picked up the blue pencil.

He had been playing with me the entire time. But did I care? At last, I was a Master Mariner!

Chapter 12

On 27th November I resumed my studies, this time for my Extra Master's Certificate. I had informed the company of my intention and was given their approval – not that they had to pay me for the time. This meant a bit of belt-tightening for Libby and me, but we were living for free in Fairholt Street (it did not yet belong to us but my mother was still working on it) and we were fairly economical in our spending for the duration.

Christmas and New Year were once again spent in Scotland. We had a hard winter that year and the roads were fairly treacherous on the way up, but we arrived safely and enjoyed the customary festivities and celebrations. We were due to return to London on 3rd January. However, conditions had deteriorated further over the Christmas period. We had to drive with chains on and it took us nearly seven hours to get as far as Penrith. The next morning we managed to get going and to reach Leeds, where we stayed with Libby's Uncle Douglas for the night. The roads improved gradually as we moved south but it still took us another seven hours or so to get back to London – a journey of three days in all.

It was 6th February that year that King George VI died and on the 8th I went to the Royal Exchange to hear the proclamation read. The following week I queued for two hours to see the King lying in state in Westminster Hall and the following day Libby and I watched the funeral procession as it passed through Hyde Park. It was a very sad occasion indeed; he had been a good, if unexpected king – forced in to the position after the abdication of his brother. Perhaps, as a nation, we were fortunate to have been saved from having Edward VIII as our king – no doubt he would have altered the course of our country's history considerably. One's heart went out to the young Princess Elizabeth, so recently married and now thrust into a position of such responsibility. One knew, however, that she had been well trained by her father to take on the mantle and as a nation I think we were looking forward to this new period in our history.

Easter came early in April 1952 and Libby and I went to Scotland –

in a new car. Back in '49, when I had exchanged the Hillman for the Standard coupé, I had placed an order for an Armstrong Sidley Hurricane, a large drop-head coupé, with a deposit of £50. In those days it took five or six years to get a new car and I was confident that I would have been able to pay for it by the time it arrived. In the event I was notified that it would be ready for delivery in April 1952, at which time of course I could not afford it. However, John Findlay generously offered to take over the order. Although he did not drive himself, he owned an entire stable of cars which I suspect the young John had persuaded him to acquire. This was to add to his collection and we were delighted to have the opportunity to drive north in it.

We returned to London by train and it was back to school once more. I had really not expected to pass the Extra Master Mariner's Certificate at the first sitting; very few people indeed succeeded in passing Parts I, and II and the orals first time around. Part I of the examination was chiefly mathematical and Part II more practical, covering subjects such as chart making, meteorology, oceanography and economic geography. You were allowed to hold any Part that you passed for three years. I struggled with Part I but would have like to have passed Part II. However, the exams came round at the beginning of July and lasted for two weeks. Predictably I did not pass Part I, but neither did I get enough marks to pass Part II. I did, however, pass the oral examination which was taken by Captain Lewis this time. At that point I decided that it was not really worthwhile continuing with the course; it was really for academics rather than practical seamen and I would far rather be respected for being one of the latter rather than one of the former.

My studying time was therefore over and I was to report to the company for my next appointment. Just before this, on 24th June, I was back at Guildhall to see my father elected as Sheriff for the City of London for the year. Two Sheriffs are elected: one aldermanic and the other the lay sheriff. This was a further rung on the ladder towards the post of Lord Mayor and an important step, therefore, for my father. The election was by a show of hands, although given that there were only two candidates there was no contest, exactly. Nevertheless it was an impressive ceremony, followed by a majestic procession out of the hall to the accompaniment of fanfares from the state trumpeters of the Household Cavalry. They did not assume office immediately but were appointed 'sheriffs elect' until they commenced their duties formally the following September.

Chapter 13

On 3rd August 1952 I joined the *Empress of Scotland* in Liverpool as Second Officer. This *Empress* was now the flagship of the Canadian Pacific fleet. She had been built as the *Empress of Japan*, just over 26,000 tons gross, and had been launched at Fairfields in 1929. She was a fine ship, promptly re-named as soon as Japan entered the war, and the *Empress of Scotland* she remained until the company sold her to a German line and she became a cruise ship. She was a miniature version and prototype of the 42,000 ton *Empress of Britain* launched in 1931 (sunk off the North of Ireland during the war) and held the (unofficial) 'blue ribbon' of the Pacific for the fastest voyage from Vancouver to Yokohama. I was to serve under Captain Duggan, who had been in command of the *Beavercove* and was thus known to me. The Staff Commander (who had responsibility for running the ship, whilst the Captain supervised the navigation) was Bill Maine, and under him was the Chief Officer (head of department) and under him the First, Second, Third, Fourth and Fifth Officers who all kept watch. As Second Officer, I shared the 12-4 watch with the Fifth Officer and was responsible for the life-saving equipment and boat stations.

The summer months were spent on the regular North Atlantic run with our passage to Montreal via Gourock and Quebec. We would leave Liverpool, having embarked our passengers, go up to the Clyde to embark more passengers from Scotland and from there sail to Quebec to disembark and then on to Montreal, with the process being reversed en route home. The passage at sea lasted for five days. During the winter there were insufficient passengers to justify the North Atlantic run and therefore we would cruise the West Indies from New York. One of the plusses on this ship was the indoor heated swimming pool which I would make use of in the afternoons. We deck officers and radio officers used to eat in the First Class dining room, although we had a table of our own, whilst the Captain and others would share tables with the passengers, as did the Doctor and the Purser. The menus were always of a first class standard, and we ate very well indeed.

The Empress of Scotland.

The Empress of Canada.

The main disadvantage was the quick turnaround in port. Libby would come up to Liverpool to see me, briefly, and we would stay in a small hotel, since no wives were permitted on board overnight. The company had very strict regulations on the question of wives, who were not permitted to travel with their husbands even if they had purchased a ticket for the passage. These rules were relaxed shortly after I left, but had been enforced after the experience of the *Empress of Ireland* which had been sunk in a collision in the St. Lawrence River in 1912 with great loss of life, many of those serving on board having been blood relatives. It was felt that in the event of disaster an officer might have divided loyalties if his wife were on board. 'I should hope so too!' was the comment from Libby, who did not approve of these rules, but thus were we bound.

On 29th September my father took office but as I was in the middle of the Atlantic I was unable to attend the swearing in ceremony and the Sheriff's Breakfast which followed. I was also to miss the Lord Mayor's Banquet although on this occasion Libby was able to attend as my father's guest. We arrived in Liverpool on 15th November when I had a spot of leave and was able to return to London whilst the ship was re-fitted for winter cruising. Cruising accommodation differed somewhat from that of the passenger ship, with all space being accessible to both first and tourist class passengers, who were only differentiated according to the size and decor of their cabins. On the North Atlantic crossing, various spaces and rooms within the ship were designated 'First Class Only'. An outdoor swimming pool was also fitted and we carried two extra launches for carrying passengers ashore.

After a welcome few weeks at home in London I returned on 15th December and we moved the ship from Liverpool to Southampton, from where our first cruise was due to start. We sailed to Gibraltar on the 18th, and thence to Bridgetown, Barbados, where we arrived on the 29th, having spent Christmas at sea. From Bridgetown, where we had one full day, we commenced 'island hopping', first of all visiting Curaçao, where the passengers disembarked for shopping and where the Williamstown jeweller's, in particular, did very well indeed. On New Year's Eve we departed for Kingston, Jamaica, where we remained for three days, and from there to Port of Spain, Trinidad, from thence back across the North Atlantic to Funchal in Madeira. Here, however, we encountered problems. A strong gale was blowing and port was closed. We lay off and waited until the following day but to no avail, and we were thus forced to abandon this stop and head for home, arriving back in Southampton on 19th January.

Cruising was certainly more fun than the North Atlantic run had been, with a constant round of entertainment and activities to keep the passengers amused, including fancy dress parties and, on one occasion, a 'country fair' that we ran with various stalls and side shows in aid of seamen's charities. As deck officers we did not indulge in this side of the ship's life too much but since the majority of passengers were of the elderly 'blue rinse' brigade we were not missing out on too much!

Libby came down to Southampton while we were in but it was not long before we set off again, this time to Cherbourg to collect passengers for a rough crossing to Halifax, and thence to New York. From here we started the routine American run. The cruise, then, was very much designed for the American market with the more ports of call you could squeeze in, the better. The leisurely tenor of our first cruise became a thing of the past, as we stopped for only a few hours at a time at each island before we were off again to the next. Not very relaxing for the crew, nor, indeed (one would have thought) for the passengers. One example follows . . .

We sailed from New York at 11.00 p.m. on 30th January; our first stop was at St. Thomas in the Virgin Islands on 3rd February where we arrived at 7.00 a.m. We sailed again at midnight and arrived in Trinidad at 8.00 a.m.; sailed again at 1.00 p.m. and then to Venezuela; another day there and then on to Caracas; the next day, a relaxing day at sea! Next stop, Christobel, and then another day at sea before arriving at Havana at 8.00 a.m. where we *almost* stayed overnight, sailing again at 4.00 a.m. (this was Cuba pre-Castro, and life ashore was fairly wild and unruly). From Havana it was back to New York, where we arrived on 16th February at 1.30 p.m. We drew breath, changed the linen, re-stocked the ship and were off again on the 18th.

And so it continued. The ports varied a little but the routine was essentially the same. Two days turnaround in New York and a whistle stop tour of the islands, always arriving early in the morning and leaving in the evening, and providing very little time for visitors to sample the night life. But they seemed to manage all right. It was hard work, with no time at all to see the sights ashore; I am able to list a string of places in the world I have been to but never actually set foot in!

One incident in Port of Spain that occurred on one of these cruises I believe provides an insight into the opinion that is held of sailors throughout the world. Deciding that we had the chance to get ashore for a couple of hours, the third officer and I changed out of our uniforms, climbed into a boat with the passengers and duly landed. On arrival we were ushered through a customs shed and then emerged to be confronted by a stream of taxi drivers clamouring for business from the wealthy cruise passengers. Not interested in the tours they had on offer, we both set off on foot down the road, only to be followed by their insistent pestering. I realised that because we were in mufti, they must be under the impression that we were passengers. I turned on them and said firmly, 'Look, we are *not* rich passengers. We are members of the crew. We do *not* want a taxi.'

Instant smiles of recognition spread across their faces.

'Ah!' they said, with clear understanding, 'You want a *woman!*'

I think they eventually got the message that they were not going to get any sales in that department, either, and eventually they left us alone.

Finally we sailed for England, returning to Liverpool on 3rd April. What relief! I had a few days leave and then joined the *Beaverburn*. My rank: Chief Officer.

Chapter 14

My promotion to the *Beaverburn* meant my first step out of watch keeping and on to more executive duties. As I have mentioned previously, along with the *Beaverford*, the *Beaverburn* was an ex-ministry cargo ship, similar to the other *Beavers* but without goal-posts, and able to carry up to twelve passengers.

We sailed from London on 17th April, directly *en route* to Montreal. My duties were quite different, with watch keeping exchanged for responsibility for the loading of cargo, the ship's stability and the use of ballast, the running of the deck department (the boatswain reported to me), inspection of the hatches and the crew accommodation. It was a 'walkabout' job with a fair amount of paperwork involved as well. I rather enjoyed it, and would, on my perambulations, take a degree of personal pride in the ship's appearance, rather as if she had been my own personal yacht.

On the outward journey some time was spent preparing seamen for their Lifeboat Certificate which they took in Montreal (they all passed). Then, in Canada, we were to embark a rather unusual cargo. The Royal Canadian Mounted Police horses were to be shipped over to England to take part in the Coronation Parade. This entailed using the upper 'tween deck abaft the accommodation which had to be rigged out with stalls. We embarked twelve Mounties, including a Staff Sergeant, who were going to take care of the animals. The usual method of transporting horses was in narrow padded stalls, but these police horses were V.I.P.s – they would need to be exercised and kept clean throughout the journey. We had a very smooth crossing and every day the horses were taken out by a Mountie – two horses to a man and with half their number being taken out at any one time. They were paraded around the square of the hatch whilst the rest of the team mucked out, slinging soiled bedding over the side and laying fresh straw before the horses were put back in again. In the evening the Staff Sergeant would come round to each horse individually to 'kiss them goodnight', patting them and feeding them carrots. A Mountie was on duty on the deck with horses all of the time, day and night. They were indeed treated well. On 12th May when they were discharged, the Mounties rode them proudly through the streets of London to display them on the way to their barracks in Knightsbridge.

My leave that time was marred by a very sad event. Libby's mother Florence had not been well for some time, continually plagued by her weak heart. On the Saturday following my return home she passed away, at the very young age of 49. Despite her poor health it came as a great shock to the family, and Libby went up to join them in Scotland, together with Dorothy Anne who came up from Cheltenham. The funeral was on the Tuesday. Sadly my duties prevented me from attending in person and since Libby stayed on in Scotland to help her father sort out affairs afterwards, I did not see much of her at all on that occasion.

We sailed for Montreal again, via Antwerp, arriving in Canada on 1st June. On the 2nd, we dressed the ship in preparation for Coronation Day and had celebratory drinks before lunch. Although unable to be at the ceremony in person, we were able to see the film of the event which was flown out to the Commonwealth countries the very next day. On12th June the Queen attended a special luncheon at Guildhall in her honour and after lunch, she knighted both my father and the lay Sheriff within Guildhall itself. Father would have normally expected a knighthood at the end of his Shrievalty (the following September) in a ceremony at the palace along with a queue of others, so this was indeed a very special occasion. I received the news in a radiogram sent to the ship; all rather exciting and very pleasing indeed for my father.

After three voyages in the *Beaverburn* I returned to London at the end of July and took over as Chief Officer of the *Beaverlake*, in which I was to make one more voyage before returning to London to await appointment for my R.N.R. training. I had applied to do one year in the Royal Navy on sea-going R.N.R. service, being obliged to undertake a nine-month and a three-month period before I could be rise to the rank of Lieutenant and subsequently be promoted to Lieutenant Commander. I thought that I might as well do the whole lot together and thus applied for the year. One ulterior motive behind my application was that it was a way of avoiding another season or two of cruising the West Indies; my appointment would mean working a more or less regular 9.00 to 4.00 day in a Home Fleet destroyer, probably based in Portsmouth, or Chatham, or somewhere, with the odd weekend off and holiday at Christmas and Easter: all in all, I imagined, a fairly civilised option.

I was, therefore, somewhat nonplussed when the official brown envelope arrived and within it a letter, couched in the sort of language that might have been more appropriate to the era of Captain Hornblower ('You are hereby required and requested to repair on board H.M.S. *Flamingo...*') which continued: 'You are to catch Flight No...to...Malta'. *Malta!* This was most unexpected and not part of the game plan at all. Libby was equally surprised and disappointed. 'Not to worry,' I reassured her 'It may well turn out for the best. We can take a flat in Malta; I can return each evening, be home at weekends and there will sun all the year round!'

Thus it was that I set off to fulfil my other requirement, which was to report to Queen Anne's Mansions for my first T.A.B. inoculation. On my way back I thought I might just drop in to the Admiral Commanding Reserves' office and find out a little more about my forthcoming appointment. I duly introduced myself to a Lieutenant in the office there, and explained who I was, and that I had been appointed for training to H.M.S. *Flamingo*, which, I assumed, was a bird class frigate stationed in the Mediterranean. 'Oh no,' came the hasty reply. 'No, no. She's not part of the Mediterranean Fleet. She's merely at Malta working up after a major refit. She belongs to the Persian Gulf squadron.'

'Where?' I asked, not quite believing what I was hearing.

'The Persian Gulf'

'But surely... surely they don't ship reserves east of Suez in peace time?'

My cunning plan was beginning to collapse before my eyes.

'Oh, well... this is a special case. The Captain has requested an extra officer. As you know there has been trouble in Abafan... Your name came up, I'm afraid.' I subsequently found out that the Second Sea Lord had appointed an additional R.N. officer as well, so there were two extra. Not that that was of any help under the present circumstances.

'It seems an awfully long way to go...' An element of doubt was creeping in.

'Oh, you'll enjoy it out there! She's an independent ship, bags of watch-keeping!'

I drew myself up to my full height.

'I am nearly twenty-eight and hold a Master's Certificate. I have been watch-keeping all my life. I did not come into the Navy to learn how to be a watch keeper!'

'Oh well,' he said cheerfully, 'If you don't feel you're getting any value out of it let us know and we'll see what we can do.'

I knew full well that this was an entirely spurious remark. The Persian Gulf was a forgotten legion; it took six months to order a pot of paint, never mind a replacement officer.

'What about . . . er . . . wives?' I enquired hesitantly.

'No wives allowed on the station,' came the swift reply.

It was a difficult journey home. The T.A.B. was beginning to take effect, making me feel as if I had a bout of 'flu coming on. And I had to report to my young wife that not only was I not going to be in the home fleet, but that I was, in fact, going to be away for a year. Cruising in the West Indies for three or four months in the winter now began to take on an altogether different complexion. However, there was nothing to be done.

I had a period of time in between leaving the *Beaverlake* and awaiting orders from the Admiralty. We decided that it was time for another honeymoon and set off for the Scottish Highlands, again, as in France, travelling 'on spec.', with no forward planning. We left Glasgow on 12th September and spent our first night at the Netty Bridge Hotel, on our way across to the east coast. From there we headed north for John O'Groats and then south to Ullapool, stopping for one night at each. The following day we were travelling across a remote moorland road when a car came in sight in the opposite direction. The road was narrow – little more than a single track – and I pulled across to provide room for the oncoming vehicle to pass. Unfortunately the manoeuvre was somewhat over-enthusiastic and we slipped into the drainage ditch at the side of the road. We were completely stuck and I held out little hope of assistance in this wild and isolated location. However, someone must have been on our side! Within minutes, a tractor had appeared, attached itself to us and we were safely pulled from our predicament. We proceeded on our way to Mallaig and the white sands, which we saw at their best in glorious sunshine. It was then on to Oban via Glencoe. My only comment on Glencoe is this: if the MacDonalds chose to live in that particular part of the world then they deserved to be massacred: dark lowering clouds and hills made the place seem gloomy and threatening and not at all beautiful. We returned to Busby House on 18th September via Inverary and the Gairloch having had a very pleasant week and feeling that we had 'done' Scotland. The trip was made complete on our third wedding anniversary which we spent sight-seeing in Edinburgh, before returning the following day to London to await instructions.

The cynical among my readers might consider that I had so far done pretty well in ensuring the maximum time possible ashore. I am aware that I seem to be relating constantly tales of holidays and times spent at home. I can only offer by way of excuse that I have refrained from boring my readers with the mundane hours, days, weeks and months spent at sea, and that times at home with Libby were precious indeed. However, should you be seeking any sort of come-uppance for me, then look no further. I was about to enter one of the most challenging periods of my life.

Chapter 15

At the crack of dawn on 29th October Libby drove me to Euston to say farewell. It is hard to describe how miserable and unhappy we both felt. Euston was an assembly point for the party travelling together; we were bussed to an airport to fly out to Malta. Others in the group were naval ratings joining or re-joining their ships and there were also one or two wives with children presumably on their way to join husbands somewhere where they *were* allowed.

Just after 5.00 p.m. local time I found myself aboard H.M.S. *Flamingo*. I was greeted warmly by my new brethren who, apart from the Chief Engineer and the Gunner, were all younger than me. I was told afterwards by the Gunner and the Doctor, who were ashore when I was having my welcoming pink gin but called in to see me on their return, that comment was made along the lines of, 'Have you seen the new Sub? Bald as a badger and covered in medals!'

Before this time, the R.N.R. and the R.N.V.R. had worn distinctive stripes (they were referred to as the 'wavy navy' as a result). However, in a fit of economical zeal it had been decided that this was no longer to be the case; that stripes would all be straight but that the R.N.R. would only be distinguishable from the little 'R' inside the executive curl. Both the R.N.R. and the R.N.V.R. would also now be referred to as R.N.R., with professionals and volunteers distinguished according to different 'Lists' (we were List One). With my stripes therefore appearing the same as naval stripes I believe that several of the crew mistook me for a branch officer (one who had risen from the lower deck) which seemed to be the only explanation for one as old as I was being in the rank of Sub Lieutenant. (I was actually to be promoted during the course of my time in H.M.S. *Flamingo*.)

The ship had had a major re-fit at Chatham and had come out to Malta to 'work up' before joining the two other frigates which together formed the Persian Gulf Squadron, based in Bahrain. We were fairly busy over the next couple of weeks, taking part in exercises, firing guns, landing landing parties and generally getting ourselves into trim. There was one particular element of training which we had to undergo: we did not carry any marines and therefore if we needed to land any party to assist the civil power we had to form a body of our own men trained in the use of weapons and basic strategic operations. We had two platoons, one of which was commanded by the Second Lieutenant; I was designated as platoon commander of the other. Each platoon was sent off for five days to the Royal Marine Commandos Training School to the north of the island. The first platoon were already undergoing this training when I arrived on the scene and returned a few days later, many of them sporting broken ankles, sprained backs and what have you after the rigours of the assault course. The captain displayed extreme annoyance and expressed the view that exposure to such dangerous activity was quite unnecessary for a sailor. When it came to my platoon's turn to visit the training school, he took me to one side. 'Look,' he said, 'You are not to allow our men to do the assault course'. I assented.

On the third day of our training, my merry band and I were duly shown the assault course and given a demonstration by some very powerful Marines who rushed over the ropes and ramps in no time.

'Right. We'll let you have a go in slow time.'

I warned my men on pain of death not to break anything – otherwise it would be my head on the block – and off we went.

The assault course had clearly been designed by psychiatrists determined to reveal every weakness, inhibition and fear known to man. With my tendency to vertigo I was, at times, really quite terrified. But we all got through safely and lived to tell the tale. 'Right. Tomorrow we'll do it properly'. This meant at full speed, with packs and carrying rifles. Having climbed and scrambled over all the walls and ramps and such like, one then had to run 100 yards and fire ten rounds at targets. I remembered all too well my captain's warning, but there was no way I was going to approach a Sergeant of the Royal Marines and explain that we sailors had been told not to join in these games as our captain thought they were too rough for us. Again I had to exhort my men to take care and, with the exception of one sprained ankle, we got through the thing without too much self-damage. As we returned to our ship we saw the captain standing at the brow scrutinising us to ensure that none of his precious lambs had been hurt. The men managed successfully to shield the petty officer with the ankle from the captain's gaze as he limped on board and nothing further was said.

Sub-Lieutenant Gillett leading a landing party on Malta.

The rest of our training was fun, if at times giving some cause for concern. I often felt like the Duke of Wellington who was rumoured to have said of his men: 'I do not know if they will frighten the enemy – but my God, they frighten me!' Watching some inept Sri Lankan steward wielding a sub machine gun one never knew quite where the bullets were going; throwing hand grenades was equally disturbing and one diced with death regularly as the men would pull out the pin and throw the grenade about three yards away. It was a case of 'Everybody down!... Quick!!' I shall not forget that in a hurry. But we were all passed out as fit for shore landing, ready for anything the Gulf might throw at us.

I assimilated the naval routine fairly easily, with my training and my experience at Pangbourne both coming in useful. What surprised me was an element of laxity by comparison with the tight ship run by the Canadian Pacific, where many of the officers were of the old

120

school and ran their ships as rigorously as any warship. The current Navy of the 1950s was not the same Navy of, say, 1939 that I had read about in books and seen in films. I recall the coxswain coming up to me one day, having noted my sense of disapproval, 'Well sir,' he said. 'Must apologise. Of course the Navy's not quite what it was, sir.'

'Yes, ' I agreed, 'Things do seem to be rather slack.' I had been alerted to this state of affairs on my second day. Despite the fact that I was considerably older than he was and had probably been doing the job for longer, I was given the job of acting assistant to the Navigating Officer – I suspect for want of anything better to give me at the time. We were on the bridge as we departed from Malta, with all hands lined up on deck as we slid out of the harbour. The men were fallen out and the Yeoman of Signals came up to me, saluted and said, 'Excuse me sir, but – permission to smoke?' I looked at him with the same expression I might have used for one who had asked if they might spend a penny in St. Paul's. No man serving on a cargo ship would ever have dreamed of asking for permission to smoke on the bridge and although one might have sneaked a quick puff on one's pipe if one was alone on the watch, one always made sure that one was *never* caught. It just wasn't done. Clearly the Yeoman considered his request a reasonable one and I turned to the Navigator to check this out. 'Oh, yes,' he said. 'Once we're out of harbour, provided they ask permission, that's O.K.'. I turned, feeling rather aghast at this, and said to the Yeoman, 'Yes, well...er...carry on smoking!' And so they did, puffing away whether they were at the wheel, or manning radar positions, or whatever. Everyone was at it. This seemed to be very much the case with a number of things; clearly the Navy was not all spit and polish as once it had been. More of this anon.

It was certainly interesting, and provided me with a number of new opportunities which I would not otherwise have had. The Navy was certainly better at letting people 'have a go' than the Merchant service, where one was only permitted to do a certain task once one had been promoted to it. I can never recall being asked if we would care to handle the ship in any way, for example. You never let go an anchor until you became Chief Officer, when at last you were able to stand on the fo'c's'le head and then that was your job and it was expected that you knew how to do it.

One evening, after a day's gunnery exercise, we came to Marshlock Bay and anchored there for the night, ready to resume exercises the next morning. Also at anchor was an anti-submarine frigate, H.M.S.

Roebuck. We had not been anchored long before a signal was sent across: R.P.C (request pleasure of company) wardroom to wardroom. We were rather anxious, thinking that these might be the sort of people who dressed for dinner, which we never bothered to do outside the Grand Harbour. We signalled back W.M.P. (with much pleasure) and the query 'What are you wearing?' Back came the reply, 'Vacant expressions'. Deciding that we could give as good as we got we decided to repay the humour and before we went over undertook a bit of jacket-swapping. Our First Lieutenant stayed as he was, but the Chief (who looked very young for his age) swapped with an R.N.V.R. (Sub Lieutenant E currently on national service). I swapped with the Third Lieutenant who acted as Gunnery Officer (and was in fact the extra R.N. officer that the captain had acquired following his request). The Navigator swapped his uniform with the Doctor and also borrowed a pair of my spectacles. The Gunner had to remain on board as officer of the day but the Second Lieutenant borrowed his jacket.

We went across, were duly received and introduced, and sat down for pre-dinner drinks. Quite naturally, each one of their officers tried to pick his opposite number from *Flamingo*. The unfortunate Lieutenant Mason, who had swapped with me, found himself sitting next to a Chief Officer from the Orient Line, who was also R.N.R. 'serving time'. He recalled enough of his conversations with me about the Canadian Pacific to be able to talk with reasonable intelligence but was having to field some fairly precise questions from the Orient Line man. I got stuck with the T.A.S. (torpedo and anti-submarine) officer from *Roebuck* who kept trying to blind me with science and fired questions about our own equipment, a subject about which I really had no clue whatsoever. I think they were all beginning to find us a bit dim. But most amusing of all was the sight of the *Roebuck* Midshipman, who was doing his national service, settle down with our Navigator and, assuming he was talking to the Doctor, begin telling him how he had been allowed to take the ship out of the Grand Harbour and instructing him in the finer points of navigation. Our Doctor, posing as the Navigator, was struggling somewhat with their own Navigator.

We sustained our pretence for about three quarters of an hour, by which time we were all wearing rather thin. Our First Lieutenant (acting as himself) was keeping a watchful eye on proceedings and realising that by now they assumed that we were all completely barmy he stood up and began: 'Er...I feel I must tell you, chaps. We have been playing a little bit of a joke here. We will now put on our proper jackets. '

Solemnly we re-exchanged jackets until everyone was restored to their rightful uniform. The joke was taken well as the light dawned upon our counterparts but the poor Midshipman who had been trying to teach our Navigator how to navigate fled in embarrassment! The rest of the evening was most congenial and enjoyed by all present.

On reflection, I am not sure that this incident could have occurred in the Merchant service, where the relationship between officers tends to be rather more rigidly compartmentalised. Our larger and more comfortable cabins meant that each officer would retire there, rather than to a common wardroom which in the navy was used communally by all officers to eat, drink and spend time together, regardless of rank.

Three weeks after I joined, *Flamingo* was considered to be worked up sufficiently and was cleared to proceed to her station in the Persian Gulf. Having obtained permission from the Captain to 'grow', I commenced cultivating my very first (and last) beard, along with several others who were also taking the opportunity of the long stretch ahead to grow uninterrupted (one was not permitted to go ashore until one's beard was fully grown). In fact in the hot weather we were to experience a beard makes life a great deal more comfortable – it is nature's 'air-conditioning'; you perspire into your beard, the wind blows through it, evaporation takes place and there is a cooling effect. It also denies the possibility of 'razor rash' in the sun. The worst place to grow a beard would be in the sub-zero temperatures of the Arctic – nothing could be more uncomfortable than a frozen beard!

Our first port of call was to be Port Said. On our voyage there, an incident occurred which was to establish a pattern for the future. The Navy have different watch systems from the Merchant service, using what is referred to as the 'dog watch'; this means splitting the afternoon 4-8 watch into two, first dog and second dog watch, which allows a rotation in the sequence. This is, of course, quite unlike the fixed watch routine favoured by the Merchant service. Also unlike the Merchant service, the navy keeps a superfluous number of watch keepers on board with various specialisations, and a navigator responsible round the clock for navigating (in the Merchant service

H.M.S. Flamingo.

the navigation was undertaken by the watch keeper). In suitable weather during the dogwatch it was 'hands to bathe'; the ship was stopped, a boat lowered and those who wanted were permitted a swim. I was officer of the watch on the bridge with the Navigator when this exercise first took place. When the bathe was over and everyone was back on board, the Captain turned round to me and asked for our course to Port Said. I knew full well what it was since we had been steering the course before we stopped for the bathing exercise. I gave my reply and off we went. The following day the Sub Lieutenant R.N.V.R. – the engineer Jimmy Morris, who was keeping his watches down in the engine room as part of his training, asked me if I knew what was being said down in the stokers' mess. 'No?' came my reply.

'Oh,' he said. 'The word is that after we stopped 'hands to bathe' yesterday, neither the Captain nor the Navigator knew the way to Port Said and had to send for the Merchant Navy Officer (as I was known on the lower deck, apparently) to tell them.'

So rumours begin. I was to live with this myth, which formed the basis for many others, for the rest of my time on board. I rather suspect the Yeoman of Signals was the source of these fabrications. He was intrigued by the process of navigation by the stars and when I was on the bridge with him at night I would gradually teach him the names of all of the various constellations – a subject drilled into me as a cadet when I would have to know the name of a new star or constellation every night and be quizzed frequently on the subject by the Officer of the Watch, who would come up to me, bark 'What's that star?' and expect an immediate response. To this day I am familiar with the patterns of the night sky and can name most of the visible constellations. However, those in the Navy, which boasts an array of sophisticated equipment for night-time navigating, are not required to have this degree of knowledge and I rather think the Yeoman considered me to be blessed with mystical powers. His sense of awe permeated through to the engine room and I was the talk of the lower deck! As my story unfolds, it will become apparent that this P.R. grapevine continued to work for me throughout my time on the ship, becoming worse, if anything (or better, I suppose I might say myself) as each story built upon the next and the myth steadily grew.

The Red Sea was its usual hot and humid self. We arrived at Aden nine days after leaving Malta, greeted there with the news that on our way up to the Persian Gulf we were to search for a pirate dhow. The incident had in fact taken place at the entrance to the Gulf, near Muscat, when an Indian dhow had been in collision with another and the pirates, on board the 'rammer', boarded the Indian ship and took her over. The crew were placed in a boat and pushed out to sea, the pirates continuing on their merry way in their newly-captured prize. The aggrieved crew landed and proceeded to Muscat where they complained to the Sultan. Because that part of the coast was under British protection the British government was duly informed and the Navy were given the task of intercepting the pirates and bringing them to justice. H.M.S. *Flamingo* just happened to be the most convenient vessel around to do the job. Our orders were to embark an interpreter to accompany us and to try and intercept the pirates as they sailed down the Arabian coast, very probably heading for Zanzibar. Not, as you may well imagine, a very easy task. At that time of year there were literally hundreds of thousands of dhows coming down from the Gulf to the African coast and to the untrained eye one dhow looks very much like another. We had ourselves a needle in a haystack situation, to be sure. However, orders were orders. Various conferences were held in Aden prior to our departure, including with the R.A.F. who might have been able to offer support from the air.

Before sailing, we embarked our Somali seamen. This practice was a hangover from days of yore when it was thought that the white man was unable to work out in the midday sun; hardly surprising given

125

uniforms which covered them from head to toe and veritably encouraged prickly heat and sunstroke. Living in rather more enlightened times, we wore only shorts and sandals (no shirts, no stockings) and caps when at sea. Those with more sensitive skin were permitted to wear a shirt, or were given jobs below deck. But the Somalis were nevertheless still embarked to work on deck. There were sixteen of them in all, together with a tindal, or petty officer in charge who was also the religious leader of their tribe and who kept them in line with a strict disciplinary regime. However, they were all good fellows and mixed in very well with the ship's company which was, in itself, diverse in terms of make up. Because *Flamingo* was a Devonport ship she recruited her crews from that division, that is to say from the West Coast of Britain. We therefore had men from the Hebrides, from Ulster, from the West Coast of Scotland, Liverpool, Wales and of course Somerset, Devon and Cornwall, who were not only diverse in origin but also embraced between them a number of different religions (Methodists, United Reform, C. of E.). With these were mixed in Goanese and Sri Lankan stewards and cooks (Catholics and Buddhists) and finally the Somalis who were all Mohammedan. They had their own mess deck; the Goanese and Sri Lankans shared. At one end of this particular deck one found a small Buddhist shrine with a can of incense continuously burning in front of it and, at the other end, a figurine of the Virgin Mary with a red candle burning in front of *her*. But they all seemed to get on extraordinarily well, with no sign of any racial tension or religious conflict. Apart, that is, from one incident which may as well be related here. A member of the British crew (for fun, so he later said) threw a pig's trotter into the Somalis' mess deck; they emerged as if plagued by a swarm of bees. Not only was this a great insult to them but it also immediately rendered the place unclean and they refused to go back in again until the tindal had uttered a few appropriate prayers and pronounced it purified.

After thirty-six hours in Aden away we sailed, on the lookout for our pirate dhow. Our method of investigation was as follows: any dhow seen during the day was immediately approached; our interpreter would rush up and shout to them in Arabic and demand they identify themselves and if he received a satisfactory answer we moved on to the next one. At night they tended to anchor in some of the bays along the South Arabian coast, in which case we would swoop in and blaze them with searchlights and, having woken them all up our interpreter would repeat the process. Not entirely satisfactory but really the best we could do under the circumstances. We called in at various places on the way up the coast, where British residents (and, in one case, a British Intelligence Officer with his faithful Arab bodyguard) would emerge to provide the latest information. None of it any use at all since no one knew anything anyway. It was not until we arrived at the Sultan of Muscat's Summer Palace at Salala that we gained some real hard intelligence and we gathered that the pirates had been found. They were at anchor, our informant told us, some 100 miles further back the way we had come. We retraced our steps immediately; arrived in darkness at the small inlet where we had been told they were at anchor and pulled in fairly close. With searchlight we were able to identify them and a boarding party was sent across, headed by the First Lieutenant with an armed crew behind him to take possession. On board only two people were found. They claimed to be 'ship keepers' and explained that the real crew were ashore. It transpired that the pair was, in fact, the Captain and the Mate. They were at once placed under arrest, as were the rest of the crew on their return to the ship and all were kept there overnight under guard. There was no trouble of any description; these were not storybook pirates with eye patches and cutlasses between their teeth but rather inept hi-jackers. However, the incident was reported by the BBC and in the press in a way that rather inferred they had offered resistance and which conjured up images of decks swimming with blood and courageous acts of heroism on the part of the British officers involved. Indeed the BBC version had the pirates being surprised in their bunks – in itself a fairly surprising account since there was not a bunk to be found on the whole ship.

Our next dilemma was what to do with them. It was quite a way back to Aden but Plan A was for the First Lieutenant and myself, with a 'prize crew' to sail the errant vessel back. I was all for this; it seemed to me the stuff of books to be sailing our prize valiantly home and I was eager to have a go at sailing a dhow. However, it was decided that it would be more rational to tow her back to Aden. Daylight came, a tow was arranged and the Captain and the Mate were kept on board *Flamingo* while the rest were kept on the dhow under armed guard. We travelled at about eight knots back towards Aden. On the first day we lowered a whaler and the Doctor and First Lieutenant went on board to ensure all was well with our charges. The following day the Captain sent me to accompany the Doctor, with orders to check their cargo and give an assessment of its contents. No romantic contraband

– just dates, I'm afraid. However, I went on board with the Doctor and had a good look round. I must say my observations led me to feel immense relief that we had not, after all, been permitted to sail her back to Aden as originally planned. She was riddled with every sort of vermin you might care to name. The crew themselves were also a diseased looking lot. There was no accommodation; they all slept on deck and the 'heads' consisted of a box over the side with a hole in it. As soon as I was back on board *Flamingo* I promptly had a bath, liberally sprinkled with Dettol.

Fortunately the weather was good for most of the way and we had a clear run back. The pirates were delivered up to the hands of British justice and I heard no more of their fate although I imagine the captain and the mate would have received fairly hefty custodial sentences. We stayed for only twenty-four hours in Aden before heading on our way once again, hoping this time to reach our station at Bahrain. The troopship *Empire Clyde* happened to be in Aden at this time. Word had obviously spread about our exploits and we were also sporting, rather jauntily, a home-made Jolly Roger under a white ensign. The Royal Scots who were on board the *Clyde* en route to Korea all gave us a loud cheer before we left and sent their band round us in a motor boat playing excerpts from 'The Pirates of Penzance', 'Hearts of Oak' and 'Auld Lang Syne' – a wonderful gesture.

Chapter 16

Six days out from Aden, on Tuesday 15th December, we arrived at
our anchorage off Bahrain: we were at last on station. There were
no fewer than eighteen letters awaiting me here, which meant a fair
amount of reading to catch up on home news. After fuelling at the oil
jetty we proceeded to our mooring buoy. There was only one other
ship in the anchorage; a U.S. Navy converted seaplane carrier who
carried a one star Admiral. At that time she was the American
presence in the Persian Gulf. The following day we had an official
visit from the Senior Naval Officer, Persian Gulf (short title:
S.N.O.P.G.), one Captain Webb. The officers were lined up with
swords and introduced one by one by our own captain. When he
came to me, he reeled off all sorts of 'guff' about my being a Master
Mariner and a Chief Officer to which S.N.O.P.G. responded, 'And
what are you doing *here*?'. Tempted though I was to reply, 'Well, sir, I
was always rather too fond of the bottle', I refrained.

The next two days were taken up with visits by our captain to the
political Resident who returned the complement and was given a
fifteen-gun salute; the next day it was the turn of the political Agent
(only entitled to eleven guns and no guard). Such to-ing and fro-ing is
all very much part of Naval routine when arriving in port and
especially when arriving at a home station.

Headquarters ashore in the Persian Gulf was H.M.S. *Jufair*, which
consisted of administrative buildings, a wardroom, a swimming pool,
NAAFI, some stores and the residence for the Senior Naval Officer
(S.N.O.P.G.), the resident Naval Officer and the Secretariat. It was
connected by a jetty to the bay where the ships of the Squadron lay at
buoys when 'in port'. There were three frigates in the Gulf: *Wren*, *Wild
Goose* and *Flamingo*. They did not operate as a fleet but were all
independent ships and seldom worked together unless they were on a
specific exercise; it was very unlikely that more than one, or perhaps
two at most, would be at the moorings at any one time and there was
always a frigate sculling around the Gulf either on inspection or on
patrol somewhere.

At that time the whole of the north of Arabia, from Muscat through to Kuwait was known as the Trucial Oman; an area consisting of a series of sheikhdoms, the largest being Oman itself, all under British protection. It was our job to guard them against any 'nastiness' that might occur, patrolling the area regularly. We were actually part of the Far Eastern fleet which meant that support could be given if required.

The term 'frigate' is somewhat confusing nowadays; when I was young it was reasonably simple, with battleships, cruisers, destroyers and frigates, all easily distinguishable by size and armaments. Nowadays frigates can be bigger and more heavily armed than some cruisers. However, our Bird Class frigates had been developed during the war for convoy duties and were not terribly sophisticated; we carried depth charges and ahead-throwing weapons (hedgehogs) for dealing with submarines. We had three twin four inch mountings for six four inch guns; some of the original fittings had been removed to create more space on board to provide accommodation for the occasional V.I.P. or for entertaining by the captain.

The ship's displacement was just over 1700 tons; she was 300' long, with a 37' beam and they drew an average 10'. Large enough to be useful, but also small enough to get in to coastal areas. For the intense heat of the summer months there was a very rudimentary sort of air conditioning on board, consisting of strategically sited chilled vanes in a box on the mess decks, with a large fan behind them, blowing the air across the vanes to try and keep the temperature down. Unlike conventional air conditioning systems this did not actually filter or wash the air; it merely circulated around the mess deck cold air thick with the aroma of sweaty sailor's feet. Far from ideal, but better than nothing. At this time of year, coming up to Christmas, it was of course quite cold; on entering the Gulf we had changed from our whites back into our blue uniforms, and when on watch at night one was even glad of a duffle coat, for it could get really quite chilly.

We were due to go to Kuwait for Christmas and on 22nd December we slipped our buoy and proceeded north westwards, arriving the following morning. Hospitality was much to fore from the ex-patriate British oil community, who were most generous in laying on buses to take the lads ashore for duty free shopping and numerous trips to oilfields – I have to confess that one oilfield looks very much like another and by the end of our stay in the Gulf we were all rather sick of the sight of them. There were football matches, and dances at their club ashore. Christmas Day was spent on board in traditional Naval form: the officers went down to the mess deck and served the crew their Christmas lunch. We had all bought light-hearted presents for one another in Bahrain and had our own Christmas dinner in the wardroom. The following day not only brought hangovers but also a fit of despondency at not being home, particularly among those of us who were married (the First Lieutenant, the Chief, the Gunner and myself) and who did not feel much like going ashore and dancing.

On 27th, a Sunday, we did what the Navy does rather well: we threw a party on board for the British and American children from the ex-patriate community. The officers dressed as pirates and all guests were stamped with a skull and crossbones on their wrists as they boarded. We had a load of small toys as presents, and armed with squeakers and funny hats these children swarmed all over the ship, climbing over Bofors mountings and the like in a scene reminiscent of a Giles' cartoon. They were given tea down on the mess decks and then shown a film, where the young 11-12 year old Americans (rather more advanced for their years than their innocent British counterparts) took their chance once the lights had gone down and could be seen snogging in the back rows, which rather alarmed those supervising the show. But no one was sick, or injured, and a good time was had by all. They eventually piled off the ship and we breathed a sigh of relief – it had been an exhausting experience. All good P.R., however, and a way of saying thank you to the parents who had been so good to us whilst we were in port.

On New Year's Eve a fancy dress party was given by the Political Agent ashore, attended by the Captain and some of the officers. Poor old Gillett was officer of the patrol which meant I had to dress in my gaiters and sword belt and proceed ashore with my full patrol party consisting of a petty officer and about eight hands, also in white gaiters, to keep order whilst the rest of the hands celebrated in the NAAFI canteen as only sailors know how. The event was high-spirited but nothing untoward occurred and we managed to clear the bar of ratings by twenty minutes past midnight and of chief and petty officers by a quarter to one. The revellers staggered along the jetty and climbed into the motorised dhow and other craft which we used as tenders to transport people to and from the shore. The Americans had a jeep which they kept ashore; their patrols looked rather like snowdrops with their white steel helmets and long white sticks which were used freely and often. The American ships were dry, which meant that when they did go ashore both officers and men would ' feel the effects' rather more rapidly than the British whose immunity was developed by their daily tot of rum.

On New Year's Day we landed a guard and fell them in the Residency ashore, where the ruler of Bahrain was to be entertained. He was received with military honours, inspected the guard and then mingled with us at a garden party in the Residency garden, but of course the ruler of Bahrain being a strict Muslim no alcohol was served whilst he was there. We all stood around dutifully sipping glasses of orange juice and waiting for him to go. Which he did, eventually. Almost as one the orange juice was shot into the flower beds and waiters appeared with real drink which was gratefully quaffed by all the non-Muslims present.

The presence of all three frigates at Bahrain was too good an opportunity to miss and on 2nd January we proceeded to sea to carry out various exercises as a formed body. We finished the day by passing mail between the three frigates, (two at a time) and then dispersed, towards evening, ready for a night exercise which consisted of a night 'encounter', where one of the frigates disappeared into the night and had to be picked up on radar and illuminated with star shell. Once the exercise was over we all went our various ways, we heading for Umm Said on the eastern edge of the north tip of the Odeid peninsular. From Umm Said we managed a bit of sailing, and in on the afternoon of 4th January held yet another children's party, although Umm Said was a much smaller oil community than Kuwait and we only had seventeen children, who were given a tour of the ship and allowed to ride on the guns and suchlike. They were much better behaved than the lot from Kuwait, generally conducting themselves with more decorum. There were only about forty expatriate families in total at Umm Said; they had their own club, which we visited, meeting most of the community and inviting them back on board for a film. The oil company also had some 16' sailing boats, and they invited us to join in one of their races. We provided two crews; I went with Lieutenant Mason in one and we raced over a four mile triangular course, and were pleased when our boat won.

We left Umm Said and returned to Bahrain to fuel for our long leg down to Colombo. Perhaps I should explain here that the ships would go down to Colombo in turn, at approximately six monthly intervals, partly for a re-fit and partly to give the grew a spell out of the Persian Gulf, which in summer was particularly welcome. This was our first trip down, and I was kept busy preparing for the re-fit which would take place when we arrived, followed by an inspection by the C-in-C. This *should* have been the job of the First Lieutenant, but he was rapidly getting into a somewhat unstable condition as a result of too many trips to the bar. His chances of lasting beyond our arrival in Sri Lanka were becoming slimmer and the Captain had him marked down for the 'chop'. We did get a chance in Bahrain to receive some mail, but there seemed to be no logic or sequence to this at all. It was now 7th January and I was getting letters dated 22nd December and others dated 2nd January. The rather idiosyncratic sequence of communication meant that one would often be reading correspondence which assumed knowledge of events related in previous letters which one had not received, and it could all become rather confusing. Reading between the lines of these rather haphazard communications I ascertained that my grandfather had died, although I could not make out exactly when this had happened. He was 94, so it was not unexpected and he had had a good innings, managing to remain alert and as bright as a button right to the end. He used to paint watercolours from life when younger, and would often copy paintings from portfolios. We would always receive Christmas calendars with pictures that he had painted, which were exquisitely executed and which I keep to this day. I managed to dash off letters to my father and my Aunt Frances who had been looking after him, before our departure.

We cleared the Persian Gulf and headed through the Gulf of Oman and on into the Indian Ocean. This was to be our longest sea passage for some considerable time. As we passed out of the Persian Gulf we logged 10,000 miles since leaving Chatham. Nine days at sea brought us to Colombo. Our time had been spent carrying out dogwatch exercises of various sorts every day, such as man overboard, firing off flares and the like, and the nine days passed quickly. The Navy at that time had recently started using quick method tables for taking sights, devised during the war for aircraft, developed by the United States Navy and now adopted by ours. These replaced the method I had been brought up with, and comprised several large volumes of pre-computed figures for various bands of latitude throughout the world. This meant you could work out sights much more quickly, although the volumes did take some getting used to. The Navigator was using them all the time, to try and familiarise himself with the system. I tried them but found it took far too long and reverted to my old tried and tested methods which actually meant that I was getting my calculations out faster than he was. As the Navigator grew more practised, however, he gradually caught up and was able to work out his sights at the same speed as me. Came the day his perseverance paid off and he was faster than I was. This fired me to have another go and see whether I should not be able to master these things. I realised that when I returned to the North Atlantic it was unlikely that the company would have bought all volumes and I would be able to get by on one volume only. I switched back and found that, with more practice, the easier it became, until once more I was level pegging with the Navigator. This did mean that my time spent with the Navy had provided me with one new skill, which I am sure I would not otherwise have acquired. Our dear friend the Yeoman of Signals was of course greatly impressed by my accomplishment and the myth of the Merchant Navigator was further enhanced.

We arrived at Colombo where we waited in harbour before going into dry dock. We had to clear the ship of everyone except a duty part: a number of seaman, and a duty officer who stayed on board just to keep an eye on things. The others were billeted on shore – the officers in hotels around Colombo and the ratings in prescribed accommodation. One of the things they were supposed to be doing during this period was a musketry course; I believe they did go off into the country and engage in a bit of rifle shooting, but it really was just a means of keeping them occupied until the ship was out of dry dock and we could prepare for inspection. I was billeted in the Bristol Hotel, a fairly Victorian sort of place, with saloon-type doors on the bedrooms and large rotating fans. It was fairly basic and the restaurant was not up to much; what finally put me off was when I was sitting having my dinner one evening and a large rat ran across the floor, disappeared under the table and my feet and was then followed by another. I decided that a move was in order, and took myself off to the more salubrious environment of the Great Oriental Hotel (G.O.H. as it was known).

The First Lieutenant was finally sent home by the Captain, having had one binge too many, which meant that I was kept particularly busy whilst we awaited a replacement. On to me devolved all the seamanship side of the First Lieutenant's normal duties, while the Second Lieutenant was given responsibility for all the disciplinary procedures. I became at the same time the mate of the Upper Deck, the Mess Deck Officer and the Shipwright Officer and it was I who, at both watches of the hands in the morning, would decide the duties that the seamen would perform; it was I who crawled through the double bottoms and the deep tanks and tested rivets, and generally undertook all the shipwrighting, and I was the one who wrote the daily orders, subject to the approval of the Second Lieutenant. I moved into the First Lieutenant's cabin, having been sharing before. The Mess Deck Officer's duties meant looking after the interior of the ship, keeping it clean and looking after re-decoration, etc. All in all it was rather like being back as Chief Officer of a *Beaver* again. I still kept a watch, of course, and it all meant that as we were about to go into a re-fit situation I was doubly busy. However, I was accustomed to dry-docking ships and although I was not learning anything new I felt that I was really able to pull my weight.

There was opportunity to do a bit of sightseeing on shore. The Navy provided recreational transport and we would explore some of the local sights, whilst one of the evening attractions was the local night club – a large hangar of a building open at the sides where there was dancing and a floor show to watch. The principal attraction was an Egyptian belly dancer, reputed to be King Farouk's favourite, who was not only performing at the local night club but also had the next room to us in the G.O.H. She was, however, chaperoned carefully by an older lady – presumably her mother or an aunt, who kept a careful watch over her charge. Whilst we were here, the wardroom numbers were augmented by the arrival of a midshipman R.N.V.R on national service, one Jimmy Roe, who was put into my care. I was responsible for generally overseeing his training; young Jimmy did not have a berth but slung his hammock outside our cabin.

We spent ten days in the dry dock having our bottom inspected and painted. Whilst there, we busied ourselves arranging the cable, testing and marking it; I had the hands working flat out on the upper deck doing the painting in preparation for the inspection. When I took over the First Lieutenant's duties and checked up on the stores, I was horrified to find that we were going to be desperately short of paint – particularly white paint. It would seem that neither of the last two First Lieutenants (the first had been dismissed for incompetence prior the second's dismissal for an over-indulgence in alcohol) had kept a check on the stores. This was a problem; we were the Forgotten Legion and any supplies could take months to arrive. We managed to procure some Silverene (a type of silver undercoat) from a merchant ship, but it was impossible to lay our hands on any white or any other useful colour, and in the end we were reduced to mixing those colours that we did have. We mixed blue with yellow chromate to produce some green for the dados and the mess decks and when, at the end of the day, we came out of dry dock and painted the hull, we found that we had just enough to cover the starboard side and round the counter and up to the break in the quarter deck on the port side. However, we did not have sufficient to do anything about the port bow and back aft of the quarterdeck. It all looked rather like a stage scene: spick and span one side only and rather like a cardboard cut out. We scrubbed the other side and cleaned it as best we could but it still looked rather lacking. However, there was nothing we could do. When the time came for the Admiral's inspection, I had tipped off the coxswain on his launch that on no account was he to approach on the port side; this he adhered to. When the Admiral left, having been throughout the ship and inspected the mess decks and every other corner, the coxswain skilfully manoeuvred him back down the starboard side and, thankfully, he did not set eyes on the port side at all. Afterwards he sent word that he had been very pleased with what he had seen. I wonder to this day whether this signal was tongue in cheek and whether he had realised all along that something rather fishy was going on. However, the captain, too, was very pleased with the way things had been organised. I had driven the men pretty hard, but everyone seemed impressed with this, given the lack of interest that had been displayed by their erstwhile First Lieutenant. The myth of the Merchant officer was enhanced yet again! We did not, incidentally, acquire any more paint until our return to Bahrain.

There was one further incident in Colombo which served to enhance my mystique beyond all bounds. When we came out of the dry dock we were lying to anchors for'ard and wired up to a buoy aft. I was on duty one evening, with another ten sailors or so on board. We received a weather forecast saying that there was a gale blowing up, and I thought it wise to check our moorings. The stern moorings were rather slack, which gave me some cause for concern, and I thought we should heave it in a bit. Unlike a *Beaver*, a frigate did not have any power aft. The Navy in those days was used to heaving and hauling; with the number of guns on board and the corresponding number of men, they could well afford to have chaps heaving on ropes. I called all the hands on deck and announced that we would have to heave the wire in. This would be done using a 'stopper' – a length of a chain and a rope to take the weight of the wire. The instruction was given to the petty officer, who turned to the nearest able seaman and relayed the command. The men stood by as the command came to 'Heave!'. They all heaved, but nothing happened. The stopper did not grip the wire at all. The petty officer continued with his command to the leading seaman to affix the stopper. I knew exactly what would happen. Despite the fact that this was an approved stopper as shown in the Admiralty Manual, it was not the sort that we used in the Merchant service, either for doing the same sort of job or for holding a wire while you were making it fast. I did not, however, deem it wise to interfere at this stage. But the same thing happened again. The command came to 'Heave!', The men heaved and the stopper just slid up the wire. By this time the Petty Officer was clearly becoming irritated, whilst his lads were losing face in front of a Merchant Navy officer. So *he* put the stopper on. Again I felt powerless to interfere, although of course the performance was repeated once more. At that point I thought I might tactfully intervene. 'We don't seem to be getting very far with this,' I offered. 'Er... now let me just try one thing. There is another approved stopper that might be used. Let's just try that one and see if it works.'

They watched while I put on the other sort of stopper, handed the rope to the men, and the Petty Officer gave the command once again to 'Heave!'. Of course the wire came in like a dream, with no slipping, and we tightened it and made it fast. This tale went round the ship faster than greased lightning and I cannot tell you what that did for the ever-increasing myth of the Merchant Navy Officer!

Chapter 17

It was at last all over and time to return to the Persian Gulf. On Tuesday 11th February we said our farewells to the city of Colombo and with some of us, at least, rested and refreshed, we started on our way back north. We had one extra hand, in addition to the midshipman who had joined us. The Reverend Emlyn Williams was taking a passage to the Gulf where he was going to do a stint in each of the ships. The padre was berthed in my former cabin – a fairly large cabin with room for three berths. However, he was forced to share this space with the crypto machine, which meant that if any coded messages were coming through, one's sleep could be severely disturbed. It was a large contraption – the British version of the Enigma machine – and it was like having a typewriter or telex machine working in your cabin. One other passenger who joined us on this voyage was a beautiful Siamese cat belonging to friends of the engineering sub-lieutenant. Unwilling to leave the cat to the mercy of their Sri Lankan houseboy when they returned to England they asked if we would mind taking it in our care for the duration of their leave. Pio Toy was duly embarked and for some reason decided that it was more fun to sleep in my cabin than in the three berth. He would either sleep curled up at my feet on my bunk, or I would make it a bunk of its own from a drawer. It was, at first, very much a wardroom cat, dining in the wardroom and proving itself a very good sea cat. At one stage, however, it decided to transfer to the mess decks, much to the delight of the sailors who willingly adopted it as their own. It took a turn for the worse at one time and became quite poorly, and it was duly taken into the sick bay by the ship's doctor, whilst the sailors tip-toed about in order that it would not be disturbed. A daily bulletin was issued on the state of the cat's health, in much the same manner as it might be from Buckingham Palace were the Sovereign to be ill. Much to the relief of all, the cat recovered and stayed with us until our next trip to Sri Lanka when it was returned to its grateful owners.

Sailors are by nature a soft touch when it comes to animals. A case in point occurred in the Gulf when locals approached the ship in dug out canoes carrying live turtles which they tried to sell to us (to eat, of course). The sailors would buy the turtles and then duly take them across to the other side of the ship where they would then release them back into their element. Presumably the poor creatures would then be caught once more only to be sold again, in an endless cycle. We were also, on one occasion, given a present of a goat by a Sheikh. This flop-eared rather pathetic looking specimen stood bleating on board; the sailors were immediately all over it and would have kept it, no doubt, as a pet – but the Captain wisely passed the creature on to the Somalis who knew just what to do with it. It was strung up by its hind legs on the spot; its throat was cut and the ship was soon filled with the aroma of cooking meat. The British crew all took photographs of the event, with mutterings of 'Bastards!' under their breath as they did so.

We were, meanwhile, re-tracing our steps back up to the Persian Gulf. The weather was as bad as I had seen it since my arrival and our Midshipman, Jimmy, visibly turned a delicate shade of green. He was sharing the watch with me and I tried furiously to keep him preoccupied with various jobs to try and take his mind off the state of his stomach. We met the Wren on the way down to Colombo to have her re-fit. As on the way out, dog watch exercises were carried out daily and on one occasion we dropped a couple of buoys with flags on them and we would each in turn have a go at picking them up. On 18th February we passed through the so-called 'Gates of Hell' – the very tip of the peninsula which almost seals off the entrance to the Persian Gulf. We anchored in a little bay where ashore there was a disused wartime naval station, manned by a caretaker, which was serviced by visiting warships from the Gulf Squadron. We called to check that all was in order before proceeding on our way the following day.

Saturday 20th saw us back off the oil jetty at Sitra where we stopped for fuel and to collect our mail. I had over a dozen letters waiting for me but Libby was helpfully numbering all of hers so I could read them in the correct sequence. Then it was back to our buoy. The next day I landed at the earliest opportunity to assess the paint situation at the store. It was not terribly helpful: all of the drums were pretty rusty and two of them had actually burst. There was one drum of 'Exterior White' which proved, upon opening, to be a very creamy colour which was not what we were looking for at all. However, orders were sent for more and we did in fact acquire enough there and then to finish painting the port side of the ship which had never been done in Colombo. At last the ship looked presentable from both sides rather from the starboard side only.

The swimming pool at the base which had been closed for cleaning was now re-filled and I took the opportunity to purchase a snorkel, mask and flippers. Thus equipped, I took myself off for some practice runs in the pool. My intention was to explore the coral reefs, which I hoped to do as soon as I got the chance; having read Hans and Lotte Hasse's book on diving in the Red Sea I was eager to give it a go.

A new passenger embarked whilst we were at Bahrain – one Hammond Innes, the well-known writer. He was a cousin of the captain's wife and had permission to accompany us for a couple of weeks because he was researching a book on the oil business and the Persian Gulf.

Come 1st March we were off on our travels again, this time to the island of Jasda Daz, an uninhabited island just to the east of the Qatar peninsular, used for bombardment practice. We were intending to bombard on the day we arrived but had to postpone activity because there were several dhows anchored nearby and one or two people on the island itself. To let off steam we let off a couple of depth charges for good measure, and then lowered the boats to see if we had caught any fish in the process; when we had let off depth charges or undertaken Hedgehog exercises off Malta we had invariably managed to kill or stun several fish in the vicinity. On this occasion we were not very lucky – we killed only about five catfish, but we did use this rather heavy-handed method of fishing on other occasions.

On March 8th we slipped and proceeded on our next expedition which was to take us to the south east coast of Arabia, out of the Gulf and part way towards Aden, where there was going to be a landing to establish a new oilfield. *Wild Goose* accompanied us, although I am uncertain as to why it was considered necessary for two frigates to support the landing. I can only suppose that this was a precaution in case anyone else attempted to lay claim to the patch, or 'muscle in' on the act. Some of the boundaries between sheikhdoms were somewhat arbitrary, and our purpose in being there was, after all, to offer British protection. Whatever the reason, orders were orders, and that is where we were heading. We stopped at Khor Kuwai on the way to replenish the Naval station there and landed some drums of paraffin and other supplies that they needed. I also took the opportunity whilst we were there to do some 'live' snorkelling for the first time. I had purchased (very cheaply) a small spear gun from the NAAFI; it was fired by a kind of trident powered by elastic, rather like an underwater catapult, and was rather a fearsome looking thing.

Our next stop was around the corner at Muscat, the capital of Oman, where we embarked Consul General Major Chauncey, who was to accompany us for the rest of the journey. We were also due to pick up the Sultan from his summer palace at Salala and we did not, therefore, stay long in Muscat, but the glimpse we had of it was enough to reveal quite an amazing place, filled with old forts and other medieval buildings; one almost expected to see a body swinging from a gibbet on the battlements. Muscat is bordered by steep cliffs on either side, onto which the names of past warships had been daubed in white paint – some dating back to the last century.

We continued on our way, doing exercises en route as was our wont. Next stop was Salala, where we were to go and fetch the Sultan. As usual, the job fell to me. Being older than many of the others I carried a few more medals, which always looked better on state occasions. I was also a sort of 'spare hand' which meant I was often called upon to undertake all sorts of tasks. There was a saying in the wardroom at the time: 'Earthquake in Guatemala – send Gillett'. Not that I minded, in any way, as it often proved rather fun to do the jobs that were not run of the mill. So off I went in our motor cutter to meet the Sultan. The heavy surf meant that we were unable to go in, and the Sultan came out to meet us in his state 'surf boat', and transferred aboard. A twenty-one gun salute was fired, and then we came alongside to put him on board, where he received a guard presenting arms on the quarter deck. I was unsure as to what to do at this point, but decided it would be best to follow passenger ship routine (always follow them up when ascending the side of the ship in case of accident). The Sultan was quite a short man, and wore flowing robes. I had visions of an awkward diplomatic incident should he trip over, and therefore dutifully came up just behind him. He stepped off the platform at the top onto the quarterdeck where bugles sounded and the men stood ready with the royal salute. Unable to hover halfway, I stepped off the platform too. Of course I towered above the Sultan, and it rather looked as though I was receiving the royal salute rather than the man himself; the captain was not best pleased and asked me afterwards what the hell I thought I was doing coming up at the same time as the Sultan – I did my best to explain that I only had his safety at heart!

The Sultan was accompanied by a team of armed bodyguards who were provided with accommodation on the gun deck for their two nights on board. The Sultan himself slept in the Captain's cabin and the Captain moved into his sea cabin. We set off on the final leg of our journey to Duqqam, where we rendezvoused with the L.C.T. and did a little beach survey for them. They duly beached and we supplied what appeared to be most of our crew to discharge oil drums and equipment. Having stayed there for three days we then returned to Salala to land the Sultan. We anchored and I took the Sultan and his retinue to the surf boat in the motor cutter; he left with a royal salute from our guard and we lay off for another twenty-one gun salute. I waited, on instruction, for his Treasurer who was sent out with a gift for the crew. This was a sack of silver dollars – still used in Oman today – with enough for four each for the officers and two each for the members of the crew. Before leaving the Sultan had also given the Captain an Arabian-style silver coffee pot (interestingly enough hallmarked by Mappin & Webb) and we in turn had presented the Sultan with a ship's plaque, suitably polished and mounted. All in all I think his time with us went well and he seemed happy enough.

From Salala we headed north for Masira, an island where the R.A.F. had a station. Here I was able to spend a fascinating afternoon snorkelling on the coral, with some spectacular sights of shoals of colourful fish darting in the warm blue green water. I was able to swim right amongst them without them even seeming to notice.

Hammond Innes was due to leave the ship, and we held a dinner for him in the wardroom that evening. We had just got to our liqueurs when the wind suddenly got up and almost without warning was blowing at Force 8; all hands were needed to get the awnings off her. She was beginning to drag, so we weighed anchor and proceeded further out. Unfortunately there was no chance to recover the boats: we had a whaler on the boom aft and the large motor cutter and the 16' motorboat were both lying from the starboard boom. We steamed slowly towing them with us; the whaler survived and was subsequently recovered when we anchored further out, but the motor cutter was not so lucky and she capsized on the way. We spent until 4.00 a.m. trying to secure her but she kept dropping back and capsizing again. She had lost her canopy, and her buoyancy tanks went floating off and eventually we just lashed her up as best we could to stop her from sinking altogether. We had to wait until daylight until we could tackle her again. We managed to bring her from under the falls and I went down into her with my mask on. Once down I succeeded in getting down into the cockpit where I found the after chain slings which I was able to shackle on under the water so we could hook on the after fall. We then carefully hoisted until the gunnels appeared and then attached a pump to pump her out; eventually the water cleared – it was dreadfully oily and slippery – and I was steadying myself with my hand on the after fall. Suddenly I felt the two smaller fingers of my left hand being drawn into the block as she was being hoisted; I yelled loudly with the pain as I felt my fingers being pulled into the block. Fortunately everyone was paying attention and the hoisting stopped immediately; they slackened her off a little and I was able to pull my fingers out. A couple of seconds later and no doubt I could have lost those fingers, if not my whole hand. I gather from those who saw the incident that the pain was evident from the expression on my face. I was pulled up on a fender and sent immediately down to the sick bay, where it was revealed that happily no bones were broken and I had only suffered bruising. However I was covered from head to toe in a mixture of oil and salt water, which had got into my hair and my beard, and the doc. proceeded to put me in a bath with plenty of detergent and helped me to clean up with a scrubbing brush. My mask had saved this unpleasant muck from getting into my mouth or nose, thank goodness. I have a photograph as a memento, which Hammond Innes himself had taken of me as I stood on the accommodation ladder, black from head to foot!

The cutter was at last back on board and in the chocks, but was an absolute write-off and we would need to replace her in due course. The 16' motorboat, being that much lighter, had suffered a little external damage but was all right.

Hammond Innes now left us and we received orders to proceed to Aden where the L.C.T. that had been used in Duqqan was in dry dock with a damaged rudder. I suppose they wanted us to escort her back when she was repaired. So on the Sunday to Aden we proceeded. On the Wednesday, I received a rather curious telegram. Addressed to Lieutenant Gillett it read HEARTIEST CONGRATULATIONS LOVE MOTHER AND FATHER. All was to be revealed the following Saturday, when the C.W. list appeared with my promotion in it. It was backdated to 16th August 1953, which meant that I had actually been a Lieutenant for quite some time without even knowing it! I could only assume that my promotion to Lieutenant had been gazetted and

Returning after my dive – photo by Hammond Innes.

that my parents had seen this in the paper. Several of my contemporaries on the R.N.R. course had been similarly promoted.

I already had my stripes prepared in anticipation that this would occur at some stage so I hoisted them up. As I did the rounds on the mess-deck at the first dog watch, with the hands standing stiffly to attention, I could not help noticing the whispers and goggling eyes as I passed by and my new stripes were noticed. Since we were at sea there was unfortunately to be no 'wetting' of my stripes at that time.

Chapter 18

We only stayed for three hours in Aden before returning to the oilfield, escorting the L.C.T., once again having to provide most of our crew to help discharge her. We sailed for the Gulf on Monday 29th March; just in time as a sand storm was blowing up. These would play hell with my beautiful paintwork, with particles of sand blown at high speed acting like sandpaper on the painted surfaces. However, we arrived back safely and anchored in Khor Kolia on 31st March, where I was able to a little more 'snorting'. I had not yet succeeded in shooting a fish; as I soon discovered, you had to go very close, practically having to lay the harpoon against the fish before firing, since the line travelled so slowly that any fish was well away before the spear reached its target if you were any distance away from it at all. No doubt it would have been different with a compressed air harpoon, but I felt my catapult-like contraption made it more exciting, in a way – you really had to stalk your prey carefully and get up close. It was also fairer on the fish.

The next day we were off again and back to our home port at Bahrain, arriving on Friday 2nd April. There, waiting for us, was a new First Lieutenant: – one Lieutenant Commander P.R. Fitzgerald D.S.C., R.N. He had been a Sub-mariner, and proved himself quite a different kettle of fish from his predecessor. His arrival meant of course that I had to bid farewell to my pleasant single cabin which I had vacated the night before in anticipation, and I went back to join the padre and the Sub E in my old cabin. However, the new man was delighted with the set-up that he found when he arrived and sought not to interfere with it too much; it seemed to him as if he were the Commander of a cruiser, where he would have had an additional First Lieutenant beneath him. And so I remained Mate of the Upper Deck and Officer of the Mess Decks and Shipwright Officer, while he took over the disciplinary duties from the Second Lieutenant David Ridley. The next day was spent in showing him round the ship; we were joined by the First Lieutenant from *Wild Goose* since they were off down for their re-fit and he was looking for some tips as to how we had dealt with our mess decks and suchlike. The afternoon was spent in the pool with my gun, getting in a little more practice with my underwater target skills using a piece of wood.

The following night saw me as Officer of the Patrol once again. It not being New Year's Eve or anything I was not anticipating much trouble, and all was, indeed, quiet in the canteen. Until, that is, one of our skates (the naval term for a second class citizen, as far as behaviour is concerned) became very difficult and the Petty Officer of the Patrol was forced to thump him. In so doing the back of his hand met with the other chap's teeth and he sustained a rather nasty gash which we had to bind up. The man had to be manhandled to the jetty where unfortunately we ran into Captain Webb (SNOPG) who was on the warpath about the number of boats lying around the jetty. However, we managed to get the chap back on board where the doctor proceeded to stitch up the Petty Officer's hand – a horrible sight to watch.

The 7th April saw us slip underway for Basra – a regular port of call for ships on duty in the Gulf but a place I had not yet visited. The R.A.F. had a base there with a refrigerated cold store, which supplied us with beef and other perishable foodstuffs. We entered the Shat-al-Arab, which is the river leading up to Basra, on the Thursday. In those days, before Saddam Hussein, Iraq was fairly quiescent. There were a number of British bases there, with the R.A.F. in particular having a strong presence. It was alongside their jetty that we berthed. As we passed Ashar on our journey up river we saluted the sovereign state of Iraq with a twenty-one gun salute. This used to be returned from the shore by elements of the Iraqi Army using ancient field guns. Whereas our salute was terribly smart and efficient, with five seconds between each gun on the dot, theirs went off in random fashion, with Bang! – long pause – Bang! Bang! – another ten seconds – another Bang!... It was always something of a worry that a live round might come whizzing past as one was never sure that they had checked the guns first. I always got the job (again by virtue of my medals) of standing on the quarterdeck where the accommodation ladder would have been (had it been over the side) and saluting when this whole procedure was taking place. The trouble was that with the port saluting gun just over my head, bits of wadding would come out upon firing and drift down not only all over my nice white uniform but also attaching themselves to my beard. By the time the whole thing was over I was somewhat grubby, and had to pick bits of wadding out of my beard. One of 'Gillett the Extra Hand's' many duties.

Basra. Not a city of particular beauty or one which I might seek to visit on my holidays (even if that were possible nowadays, which of course it isn't). The people we met there were possibly the worst of their breed – ex-patriate Brits. whom we used to refer to as 'faggots', who treated their native servants with unnecessary imperiousness (the sort of people who would never have had servants at home) and who just loved to entertain. The arrival of a British warship meant endless parties and obligatory reciprocal visits on board, which became rather a bind in the end. I can recall officers in the wardroom falling over themselves to volunteer to be officer of the day so they could stay on board and not have to attend yet another of the ghastly parties. And this was just our first trip – with the promise of plenty more in the offing! One blessing was that there were no oilfields to look at, but nevertheless there was not much of note there at all. One other unpleasant facet was the number of somewhat unsavoury objects which would come down the river – I recall dead cows floating past with their legs in the air, together with all kinds of rubbish and detritus which would collect along the side of the ship and prove very difficult to clear away. It was hot and it was sticky and . . . well, enough said of Basra.

On Easter Monday, 19th April, we sailed at 0800 hrs for Kuwait. Two days later we landed a guard for the ruler's inspection at the Residency, it being the Queen's birthday. This was followed by the usual firing of twenty-one gun salutes and a garden party. We then sailed again for Sitra, Bahrain, making a brief call there to collect mail and our paint which had at last arrived and for which I was profoundly grateful as an inspection by S.N.O.P.G. was almost upon us. We had been doing practice exercises on the journey in anticipation. After leaving Sitra we proceed to Khor Kolia where I took my platoon on a successful landing exercise following which I had time to go and do a bit of snorkelling with my spear gun. I actually shot a fish this time. The only trouble is that when one is underwater these things can look quite a reasonable size; on surfacing with the thing on the end of your harpoon you discover that they are really quite small. I also saw a shark on this occasion but he cannot have liked the look of me much as he buzzed off pretty quickly in the opposite direction. Although I had read at length about what to do in the event of a confrontation with a shark – either biffing them on the nose of shrieking at them through one's mouthpiece was supposed to do the trick – I was never sure whether the sharks had read the books and whether *they* knew what they were supposed to do. However, no trouble this time and I was spared the ordeal of having to find out.

The next day (26th April) we were once again all hands practising various drills, pointing the ship, laying out anchors and taking part in all sorts of exercises in anticipation of the inspection. That afternoon we took the motor cutter away and dropped some quarter pound charges, which produced a vast amount of fish, either stunned or killed, floating to the surface. These were duly collected in waste paper baskets to supplement the diet of those in the messdecks and the wardroom for another day or two. Not, it must be admitted, a terribly environmentally-friendly way of killing fish but not a practice which we indulged in to excess. The following day was another busy day of preparation; *Wild Goose* arrived with some mail and we lined up ready for the exercises which were going to take place. After breakfast on the 28th some departmental inspecting officers boarded from *Wild Goose* and commenced their inspection of various parts of the ship – the opening round of the inspection that was to take place over the next few days. I had a final conference and we received the signal to 'splice the main brace' to celebrate the fact that the Queen was passing through the East Indies station on her world tour, which meant that all hands had an extra tot. This proved rather too much for one of the A.B.s who was promptly sick on the mess deck just as I made my rounds before turning in. Rather unfortunate, but he must have had what are known as 'sippers' from his mates to produce such an effect – either that or he had a very weak head. I must say that the ship was in pristine condition – not a rope out of place, spanking new paint and only a quick rub on the brass needed to bring her up to last minute perfection for tomorrow. All turned in early ready for the Big Day, Friday 30th April. 'All hands' was at 4.30 in the morning and we fell in at 5 o'clock. Divisional officers took charge of their parts of the ship for a final polish up; I was dividing my time between the mess decks and the upper deck. We had breakfast at 7.00 and a last look round at 8.15. The Senior Naval Officer arrived at 9.00 and was received by a Sergeant's Guard; I was doing my usual Officer of the Day duty, sword and medals at the head of the gangway. With no division of my own I then trailed the inspection party with the Senior Staff Officer, Operations who was picking men our for kit inspection. Once the inspection was over we moved to the upper decks; I kept just ahead and out of sight of the inspecting party, watching out for last minute permutations and getting reports of what he was looking for, and then popped down to the mess decks and did the same there. It was very thorough but he was quite pleased with what he saw. He went everywhere, then came aft, inspected the kits and the books and left at noon. We had time for a quick lunch before preparing for general drills. He boarded again at 1415 and we commenced drills; we fired rockets, pointed ship, sent off a landing party, signal party and devolution party; cooks rowed round boats and stokers, too. It was all over within the hour – but what a packed hour! We did very well and after a cup of tea I went with the captain to the beach to do a bit of 'snorting'. When I was coming back to the boat I stood on a bit of porcupine coral which cut my big toe; back on board the doctor tried to remove the bits of quill but they just crumpled to powder. He dressed them to remove any poison and I limped away. The effects lasted for some weeks afterwards, and it was rather painful.

The following day we went to sea for our sea exercises. Once we were clear, 'war' began. Minefields, submarines, air attacks, damage below, steering gear breakdowns and casualties. I was made a casualty during an air attack and was bundled into a Neil Robertson stretcher and borne by Somalis down to sick bay. This is the sort of stretcher into which one is lashed, and rendered completely immobile. To get me down from the bridge meant going down two vertical ladders; the Somalis were chattering away as if it were all great fun but I have to say I was not quite so sure, particularly when they happily took me down the ladder head first which was more than a little worrying. Had I been dropped I would have landed straight on my head and that would without doubt have been the end of Gillett. However, I arrived safely at the sick bay where I found the First Lieutenant who had fallen down the bridge ladder (not as part of an exercise) and damaged his elbow. I was very shortly informed that I was fit again for exercise and it was back to battle. Another unscheduled incident in the midst of it all was when one of our leading seamen developed appendicitis and we had to send a whaler over to fetch *Wild Goose's* doctor for a second opinion. His condition confirmed, that was the end of the exercise and we went back with our patient to Bahrain.

On 5th May we were back at Mena in Kuwait where a rather embarrassing incident occurred. Someone must have switched the navigation lights on at sunset without my noticing. The Captain did notice and, even worse, the lights were spotted by a Merchant ship who sent a signal across saying 'Your slip is showing'. Caught out by my 'brother cloth', so to speak.

On 7th May, still at Kuwait, a few of the officers, a couple of the hands and the coxswain were driven in to the Cumberland Yacht Club and we had a couple of races in X Boats and Seagulls. There was not a great deal of wind but it was very nice indeed to do some sailing again, as opportunities had been few and far between since the start of my commission. That evening we entertained some of our local hosts back in the wardroom with a very good party – the ex-pats. here were a far more civilised lot than their counterparts in Basra. I note from the journal I kept at the time that once our guests had departed I was feeling in splendid form and helped to 'tidy up' the bar by drinking four Drambuies, three Crème de Menthes, two Cointreaux and a brandy in rapid succession, following which I turned in feeling fine. I also note from the same volume that I awoke at 8.00 a.m. the next morning still feeling fine and consumed a hearty breakfast. I conceded to feeling a little tired later on that morning and took a nap from 11.00 to 12.30 which restored my energies sufficiently for the afternoon's activity: another children's party, with all the customary entertaining of the local 'brat pack'. They arrived in two boatloads at 2.30 p.m. and we went through the Christmas procedure all over again. On this occasion the upper age limit had been restricted to eight, so there was not quite so much 'dialogue' between the sexes. All were returned happy and safe to their families, with none having been squashed, killed or worse and we cleaned up ourselves – washing off the burnt cork that had been used to enhance our pirate kit – in time for the Political Advisor's party at 6.30 p.m. that evening. After the main party we were taken in hand by various guests who took us to their respective homes to a number of private dinner parties. How much more pleasant it was to spend time in Kuwait than it was in Basra!

We sailed on 9th May and our next destination was to be new territory: Khor el Ama. This was the base for an American oil company, although it was a very new development and there were no buildings as such – only an L.S.T. on board which most people lived. The oilfield itself was some way inland and was reached by driving in trucks. The populace consisted mostly of oil company Texans who were able to consume large quantities of whiskey in a very short space of time. We entertained them on board and they invited us to see a film and have a meal. Their food was flown out – as were all their supplies – from the U.S., if not daily, then certainly at very regular intervals, and the table was laden with a rich variety of American foodstuffs. We were taken out to the oilfield which we dutifully admired, making all the right expressions of interest and heaving a sigh of relief when the tour was over and we were able to return once more to the air conditioning. We departed on 11th May laden with gifts, including delicacies such as tinned oysters and anchovies from their copious stores.

Within twenty-four hours we were back at our buoy in Bahrain. I went ashore in the afternoon and had a swim in the pool. It was, by then, very warm indeed – an enervating 90 degrees. I must say that my stay in the Gulf rather spoilt me for swimming in cold water around our own islands – or anywhere else in the world, for that matter; I found I no longer cared for plunging into cold water having had the experience of swimming at leisure for several hours without ever getting chilled.

The next day the officers went off in one of the whalers to do a training run for our forthcoming Regatta. That evening we entertained the Staff Officer, Operations and the Secretary's wife, who came off for dinner in the mess. They left at about 11.00 p.m. and then, I regret to say (it sounds as if I am becoming an alcoholic), the doctor and I sat down and drank a bottle of Drambuie between us in the course of putting the world to rights. I took three Dispirin before turning in that night, which seemed to have the right effect, for I was away at 6.30 a.m. the following morning in the whaler again for a bit more Regatta practice. The afternoon saw a lovely sail in the dinghy with Jimmy Morris; it was blowing quite hard, with plenty of spray – but of course this was hot spray, which made it very pleasant indeed.

The next day our call was 5.30 and we were out again to train. I had not done so much pulling since my days at Pangbourne, but most of the muscles still seemed to be there in one form or another. There came another evening of putting the world to rights, this time with the First Lieutenant and the doctor, and another bottle of Drambuie was put away. We retired to bed at 3 o'clock in the morning, only to get up again at 5.30. With the weather now bitingly hot we were in 'tropical routine': early morning calls, but an early finish at lunchtime and the afternoon was free, since by then it was far too hot to do anything.

Monday 17th May saw an early breakfast in preparation for the decathlon, which started with whaler pulling at 0800 hrs. It was a half-mile course, with each providing four crews, raced two by two in four races. *Wild Goose* won the first two by a hair's breadth and then came our team. Our wardroom crew, which pulled against a ship's company crew from *Wild Goose*, beat the opposition by half a length amid terrific applause. We led all the way, despite the fact that the chief jumped his oar from its crutch during the racing start and was not pulling for the first few strokes. Next came our Somalis, who beat *Wild Goose*, making the event a draw. Jimmy Morris and I should have raced in the dinghy next, but it was too rough and blowing too hard, so in the end only the whalers raced. Here our coxswain only lost to the Engineer Officer of Goose by half a length over a three-mile course. We landed to watch the hockey and soccer and cheer the lads: here again we were defeated, 1-0 in the hockey and 3-1 at soccer. After lunch there was tennis, 2-2 shooting, cross country, tug of war, medley relay, water polo and water relay. All we won was the 2-2 shooting. Mrs Webb (S.N.O.P.G.'s wife) presented the cup to *Wild Goose* at the swimming pool.

The next day (18th May) passed peacefully enough. We were storing ship during the morning and everyone took the opportunity to replace energies expended the previous day whenever they could. We had an R.P.C. out to *Wild Goose* and some of their wardroom members came over for drinks in the early evening. We entertained with some of the goodies from the American 'oily boys' we had been given the week before. We then had a dinner in the wardroom, which the Captain attended; he retired fairly early – and it was then that 'The Night of the Long Knives' commenced.

David Heath, the Gunner, had had a beard for as long as I had known him. He was due to go home in a few days' time and, knowing that his wife would not approve of his growth, slipped out at the end of the meal to his cabin and shaved it off. It is an extraordinary thing, but if you have always known a man with a beard and he loses it, he is almost unrecognisable. Any criminal considering using a beard as a disguise would be well advised to grow it first, commit the crime and *then* shave it off, since it is much easier to identify a man with a beard if you happen to have known him without one, than it is in the reverse. Anyway, the Gunner returned to the wardroom and we all gasped at this clean-shaven and rather pale face. It must be explained, at this juncture, that there existed among those who had not succeeded in growing beards (some, of course, did not actually want to but there were those who had tried and failed) a certain amount of jealousy towards those whose facial hair was by now respectably thick and bushy. I turned to Jimmy Morris who sat beside me, sporting a very nice beard indeed, just as the cry went up: 'Let's get the beards!' Jimmy was borne aloft and pushed, resisting, into a chair, where his growth was mauled with scissors and knives until it was so chewed that his only option was to shave off the whole thing. They then turned to me, and I was pushed, likewise, into a chair. The First Lieutenant handed the Midshipman a pair of scissors, with the instruction: 'Midshipman, cut off that beard!' Of course I was this man's mentor, and I believe he was quite frightened of me. 'You touch one hair of this beard', I roared, 'and your life will not be worth living!' The Midshipman havered and looked again at the First Lieutenant who repeated his command. 'Cut off that beard!' He turned back to me, who continued to threaten him. Finally, caught between two stools, he took a half-hearted snip at the pointed end of my beard and fled from the wardroom. By that time, I myself had consumed sufficient quantities of alcohol to weaken my better judgement. I went back to my cabin and looked in the mirror to assess the damage, which was not, I must confess, irreparable – had I waited a week or so I could have grown in the missing bit. Of course what I should have done was to return to the wardroom and incite the scissor-wielders to get the next bearded man. Instead, foolishly, I returned and announced loftily: 'It's nothing. I shall soon grow this back again...' The next thing I knew I was down in a chair and my growth was attacked from all sides, leaving such a mutilation that, like Jimmy, I had no option but to shave off the remnants. That was the end of the beard, which I had had since we left Malta. I had intended to keep it and come home with it to surprise my wife, but perhaps in the end it was just as well I didn't. In my next letter home I came clean and told her all about my beard; I received a very shirty letter in reply from Libby who wrote 'To think that for all these months I have carried a mental picture of you as the reasonably handsome man that I married – while all the time you were looking like some sort of goat'. I really felt quite hurt – but I have not tried to grow a beard again since.

The next morning I awoke 'surprisingly fit but very shorn'. I had to shave, which came as a bit of a shock, having not had to do so for six months, to the day. A shocking bore. I hardly recognised myself and it was rather curious walking about the mess decks where some of the men thought that I was a new officer. Opinions differed: some said I looked younger without it, some said I seemed older; some better, some worse. My only regret is that I do not have a really good photograph of it. Still, there it was, gone.

After three very pleasant days at Umm Said, where we had gone for our second visit, we sailed again for the dreaded Basra, where we arrived on the 26th May. Noon temperature was 99o in the shade, with a very strong, hot wind blowing, which was to persist for some time with little relief. We gave the customary salute to the sovereign state of Iraq on our way up the river. The usual bits of wadding came floating around my ears from our gun and again came the intermittent and irregular return from the Iraqis and their version of the twenty-one gun salute. It was back to our usual berth and the usual boom we had to rig to divert the unpleasantries that were constantly floating down the river – and the usual invitations from the local population. The First Lieutenant reminded us in no uncertain terms that we were obliged to go and do our social duty and compiled a careful roster, which ensured that everyone took his turn. There was to be no escape. I was finding that tropical routine, although appropriate to the weather conditions, played havoc with the maintenance and upkeep in the appearance of the ship. However, we made full use of having a jetty with fresh water alongside us and landed all the awnings which were rigorously scrubbed when the opportunity arose. The R.A.F. sent their D.D.T. sprayer on board and gave us a good going over: the mosquitoes were rife here and we had been taking preventative measures for some time.

Saturday 5th June saw us back at Khor Kolia, where we landed our old damaged motor cutter. I towed her ashore in the small motorboat and we beached her above the high water mark at the inboard end of the jetty. We then collected a replacement and took it back on board. Quite a lot of work was needed to bring her up to scratch but at least she was not going to sink on us.

Chapter 19

On Wednesday 9th June the Captain called me to his cabin and I learned that I was to be that I was to be the Naval Liaison Officer in L.C.T. *Afri* – a landing craft which was leased to an oil company at Umm Said from the Navy, on the condition that the Navy could have her back for up to eighty days in the year if she was required for operational purposes. That time had now come. Geophysicists from the oil company Aramco, supported by units of the Saudi Arabian army, had been carrying out an illicit survey in a portion of the peninsula that belonged to the Sultanate of Qatar. Representations had been made to the Foreign Office and Churchill, the Prime Minister at the time, had instructed the Admiralty that the intruders were to be sent packing. 'Operation Cactus' was to take place, and we were to embark a squadron of Trucial Oman levies – Arab troops who had served in the levies and had been allowed to keep their rifles to serve if required – and land them at various points in the desert at the base of the peninsular so that they could go and investigate. No shots to be fired unless we were shot at ourselves, but quietly to advise the intruders to leave. The 'Earthquake in Guatemala – send Gillett' principle applied and I was selected for this out of line operation to shore.

On 11th June, having fuelled at the fuel jetty, we proceeded to Umm Said where we were going to pick up the L.C.T. On the Sunday there was a conference ashore about Operation Cactus, attended by Staff Officer, Operations and representatives of the army, the local Marine Superintendent and Terry Stamp, the Captain of the *Afri*. We ironed out most of the minor points and set some tentative times for beaching. I spent the afternoon packing and writing letters, leaving to go aboard *Afri* at 18.00 hrs. She was delayed in sailing due to high winds and it was 20.00 hrs before I went off in the motor launch and boarded her as she passed. She had a cargo of petrol and oil in drums, and some vehicles. Once clear of the channel we had dinner in the cabin below the bridge. It was very nicely fitted out, with air conditioning units at each end, radio, etc. Terry Stamp normally had

Afri.

his wife with him, and the youngest of his five children, but they had been sent ashore for the duration of this particular operation. I was sleeping in a camp bed in the cabin; very comfortable it was, too! Watch keeping was done by the two mates – both Bahrainis. The only member of the crew who actually spoke English with any degree of fluency was the Chief Engineer, who was an Indian. The rest of the crew spoke none at all. On the next day (Monday) I rose at the very civilised hour of 9 o'clock, showered and had breakfast and we went to pick up the buoyed Channel. We only had use of magnetic compasses and a trident log – no radar or sounding machine; no sextant; not even a barometer. But she seemed to find her way about. We headed for Ras Zubbaya and found the army already in camp, although we had not expected them until the next morning. There were three British officers: a Major Johnson in charge together with two Captains and they all joined us on board for a drink before dinner. At 22.10 we started to discharge our cargo, which was completed at 3.00 a.m. At 9 o'clock we started to load the vehicles. There were fifteen in all: five Land Rovers and ten trucks, together with a water bowser and drums of petrol. There were three British N.C.O.s and 61 Arab levies. I made a radio check with the R.T. to Michael Tudor Craig on board *Flamingo* and we retracted to 12.55 to start the trip to our landing beach. The weather was very nasty, with low visibility, thirty-knot wind and a short sea. As soon as we cleared the Channel we were smacking into it and taking some spray. *Afri* shook like an aspen leaf. The army were rather concerned about the spray affecting their engines but there was nothing we could do about it other than spread tarpaulins, which we did. Trying to get some sleep after lunch was nigh on impossible: it was like being over the bogeys on a British Railways train travelling at speed on a particularly bad piece of line. We came up to *Flamingo* at 17.00 and got a weather report. We spoke again at 21.00, including a rude signal, which made reference to it 'always being calm in the Persian Gulf'. The wind had eased a little by 24.00 and as we were then off Jaz Zirko we decided to risk a bow sea and turned W.S.W. to make a shorter passage.

The following day I rose at 7.45 after a peaceful night to find the wind had reduced to about 18-20 knots, with a lower sea. We passed Jaz Dalmah at 06.30 and headed west. The weather moderated as the morning proceeded and by noon was perfect. At 12.55 we beached on the Odeid peninsular and a reccie party landed on foot to survey the terrain. It returned to inform us that we had better beach about half a mile further east as the beach we were on would not permit a dry landing with a vehicle. We retracted and anchored off and at 15.15 Major Johnson landed by boat with a small party and set up an H.Q. with radio transmitter ashore. At 18.00 we beached *Afri* at the new beach, which proved excellent. The army disembarked but left five one-ton trucks on board as they did not think the ground suitable for them. They set up their base camp and we retracted at 1900 hours as we did not wish to dry out. We anchored about two cables off the beach where Terry Stamp and I tried fishing from the boat, but with no joy. Routine chats with *Flamingo* continued at odd hours until 21.00 and I turned in at 22.30, well ready for a 'zizz'.

Thursday 17th June I was up at 08.00 and landed by boat to see how the army had fared. They had had a good night and had just sent out two patrols in Land Rovers. I spoke with *Flamingo* and agreed that we should steam up and down the coast for about ten miles in either direction. Something fell out of a passing aircraft whist we were thus engaged, which was thought might be a message for us; we picked it up but it turned out to be a letter to an airman from a girlfriend, which we decided we would post on to him once the operation was over. We re-anchored off the camp at 14.15 having sighted several likely beaches. After lunch Terry and I went off to some nearby rocks. He tried again to fish (unsuccessfully) while I 'snorted'. I shot two small fish and a 6lb rock cod. I did hit one other rock cod but he managed to escape, swimming off with a torn side after being hit by the harpoon. I returned to keep my 17.00 schedule and at 18.15 we beached and let the army re-fill their water bowser. It had been a good day, and they had covered a lot of the peninsular. They had found plenty of tracks but no signs of life ashore. We discussed the possibility of returning to Umm Said for replenishment the following evening. We unbeached and anchored at 19.35. I had some difficulty in raising *Flamingo* which resulted in fairly terse comment: one was supposed to be able to raise them at any time, in case of emergency.

Friday 18th June I was up at 06.55, feeling freezing cold. The air conditioning was far too efficient! After contacting *Flamingo* I proceeded ashore to meet Major Johnson and iron out our communications worries. I managed to speak to *Flamingo* on the army set and then returned to *Afri*. I spoke to the T.C. at 09.00, *Flamingo* was by now underway which meant that my signals were going through to the bridge. I landed at 10.45 and paced out the beach dimensions, (having no better measuring device) and snorkelled over the approach area for obstructions, but found none. I returned on board at 13.15 (the outboard having broken down) which meant that I was a little late for my 13.00 call. At 15.00 we tried to beach but could not make it, so went off on a broad sweep and ran in again at 17.30. This time we made it, with a little pushing. The tides here seemed to be the same as those at Umm Said. The army topped up with water once more, and moved their remaining five trucks. They came aboard for a beer and left at 19.00. We unbeached at 19.05 and set course for Umm Said; no difficulty was experienced from shoals although strong southerly set delayed our arrival until 22.00. We spent an hour trying to raise Umm Said for berthing instructions and eventually received orders to berth on the jetty, which we did at 22.25. Terry went off home to his wife and I turned in after a shower.

The following day, Saturday 19th, I went ashore to borrow some surveying gear from the oil company, without which it was quite impossible for me to do a proper chart, which I had been commissioned to undertake whilst I was taking part in this operation. I was able to borrow a surveying sextant and a steel measuring tape and I bought some more film for my camera so that I could take pictures of the profiles of the beach and the land. I discovered whilst I was ashore that Terry Stamp would not be coming back with us – leaving me as the only white man on board. The one advantage was that I got the Captain's bed! I should point out that the L.C.T. was beautifully equipped; as living accommodation for the Captain and his wife there was a big double bed, fridges, radios and what have you. I even had an Arab servant to look after me, who brought me my meals and cooked the fish that I caught. Foodstuffs were flown out for the oil company, and I had a choice of about three different kinds of cereal for breakfast, with fresh orange juice and all other trimmings. I did feel rather sorry for the army chaps in their tents, eating Arabian cooked eggs off tin plates while I was living in the lap of luxury. I had also brought with me a bottle of gin and some beer from *Flamingo* and when the lads came on board I was able to entertain them quite lavishly. They were quite clearly made aware of the differences between being a soldier and being a sailor: sailors will carry with them their creature comforts wherever possible, whilst the army are more prone to taking pot luck and living off their wits and the land. Still, there it was: they had chosen their profession and I had chosen mine.

In the afternoon we left Umm Said and returned to our beach head. We brought the water bowser on board to fill it up from our tanks and then retracted for the night. In the morning I went ashore to see how the soldiers were getting on, to find that they had a problem: one of the levies was ill and running a very high temperature. We raised *Flamingo* on the army R.T. set and got hold of the doctor. By describing symptoms to him carefully, he was able to offer a diagnosis over the radio and surmised that the man had probably got pneumonia. His temperature was by this time over 104° and he was really quite feverish. The situation was quite worrying, not least because the Trucial Oman levies might well have taken it amiss if one of their own had suffered at the hands of the white doctor. It had been known for them to shoot their officers on occasion, and I always carried with me a Webley .38 as a precaution. However, the chap responded to the radio treatment prescribed, and thankfully his temperature dropped. It occurred to me that it was just as well it had not been appendicitis or something similar, as we could have been in considerable difficulty.

Now fully equipped with all the apparatus necessary for surveying, I was able to embark on this task. I built a cairn of rocks as a datum point; my first job was then to produce my base line, which I was going to run along the beach, from which to measure my angles. I had nobody to help me other than one of the Arab crew; although he had no English he looked reasonably intelligent and willing. I needed him to stand at the cairn and hold the end of the measuring tape whilst I walked away unrolling it and thus measured my base line. I indicated with sign language what he was to do, handed him the end of the tape at the cairn and away I went, unreeling the steel measuring tape as I went. When I had proceeded a few yards I stopped and looked behind, only to see the man dutifully following me, still holding on to the other end of the tape. I took him back to the cairn and again indicated that he was stay put. The message seemed to hit home second time around and I succeeded at last in getting my base line measured. I had chosen suitable points on the beach and built smaller cairns (it would have been unreasonable to expect any more of the crew to be capable of standing still as measuring posts) and all I intended to do was to shoot sextant angles along my baseline to various points and then be able to get triangulations. Thus the rest of the day passed, while the army were off on patrols in their trucks. On subsequent days I took soundings from the ship's lifeboat (the only boat we had) armed with a hand lead along various lines along the bay. The afternoons were often spent sleeping. It was terribly hot, even speaking as one who likes the sun and the heat and who does not burn (I just get browner and browner). I was in fact doing all of my surveying clad only in a pair of bathing trunks and sandals, the sand being too hot to stand on in bare feet. No hat or any protective wear and as far as I can recall not even any sun cream. After a little snooze I would then go out snorkelling whilst the Arabs fished from the side of the boat; from time to time I would surface, much to their amazement, with a fish impaled on the end of my harpoon. The coral there was spectacular, and the fish glittering and colourful. No doubt they had never encountered a human before and did not perceive my being in the water as any kind of threat. It was possible to swim through whole shoals of fish which flicked past, quite oblivious to my presence. I saw a few sharks, which did not seem to bother me and the only things that did give me slight cause for concern were the barracuda. They are indeed rather evil looking specimens although I am not sure that even they would attack unless severely provoked. On one occasion I spotted a shoal lying below me, and flippered rather gingerly away from them looking back over my shoulder from time to time in gesture equivalent to a fighter pilot's 'Messerschmitt's twitch' during the war; in my case it was 'barracuda twitch', just to check whether or not I was being followed.

Once a day, generally in the evening, I would beach so that the army could refill the bowser with water. Those who came on board would be able to cool off in my air conditioning and have a cold beer before returning ashore. I was in regular contact with *Flamingo* at all times. Reports were now coming in from the patrols of evidence of seismic activity, although no sightings of people. We never did, in fact, encounter 'the enemy', I am glad to say, who must have been long gone. Presumably they had got wind of the fact that we were coming to chase them out, and vanished in good time. So happily no diplomatic incidents ensued.

One rather amusing incident occurred when I was making one of my morning calls to *Flamingo*. The radio set aboard the L.C.T. had been playing up a bit, although I was always able to use the army set as a back up. This had happened the previous evening; I was not sure of the cause but assumed it was to do with adverse atmospheric conditions. That morning, however, I went up to the bridge to make my morning call. It seemed to be working, this time, but there was a terrible smell coming from the transmitter. On taking off the front, I discovered a rat inside – very dead and decomposing. It must have been there for at least a day. I assume that it had been munching on a tasty piece of insulated wire until I pressed the transmission button, when it would have been immediately electrocuted. The set did not seem to have suffered unduly.

My survey was proceeding very nicely. As well as my measurements and soundings I also had to chart a beach gradient. After ten days the soldiers felt that they had completed their patrols sufficiently and it was decided that it was time to break camp and leave, which we did on Friday 25th June. At 5.00 a.m., having embarked all the vehicles and broken camp the evening before, we proceeded on our way back to land our troops at Ras Zubbaya, which we reached that evening. I was returning with the convoy to Dubai, where I was going to be met by H.M.S. *Flamingo*. At half past midnight we formed up the vehicles, and I travelled in a Land Rover with one of the captains. The vehicle did not have a glass windshield – which must have been fine during the hot days, but of course at night the desert became very cold, and I was grateful for the blankets around my shoulders and over my knees. We proceeded on our bumpy ride across the desert, our vehicle bringing up the rear in case of any breakdown. In fact we broke down ourselves, with a burst tyre, at one point, which we had to stop and repair. We arrived at Dubai at 8 o'clock in the morning where I bade farewell to my merry compatriots and reported to the Political Agent. He had in fact been asked by an old school friend of mine from Pangbourne to 'keep an eye out' for me and offered hospitality which was gratefully received – a good bath and breakfast – while I waited for a dhow to take me out to re-join *Flamingo*. I was there in time for lunch and able to relate in full my adventures.

One of the rather pleasant things that I discovered was that although I had been living in considerable luxury on board my L.C.T. (far better than my shared accommodation on board *Flamingo*) my time spent with her actually entitled me to 'hard lying' money for being in a sub-standard ship, which amounted to some 4/- a day!

Once back I had to settle down and actually produce a chart from all the sketches and information I had collected during my survey. The only reason I felt I could do this with any degree of competence was from my studies for my Extra Master's Examination. Although I had not acquired the certificate I had actually done the work, which included chart-making. I completed this over the next few days and was able to inscribe proudly at the top: 'Part of the Odeid Peninsula Surveyed By Lieutenant R.D.P. Gillett R.N.R. of H.M.S. *Flamingo*' together with the appropriate date. I felt right up there with Captain Cook! Although not actually able to name any features after myself, I did label the bay Tol Bay (Trucial Oman Levies). The finished work was sent off to the Admiralty and, as an operational chart, it then became a confidential chart with its own confidential chart number. When they printed it they gave me a copy, which I still have to this day. I was rather heartened by the fact that all the charts in that part of the world had things written on them like 'the coastline is *believed* to be 3 miles further east/west' etc. The terrain was also liable to alter quite considerably due to sandstorm effects and the place could easily look quite different, so any discrepancies in my chart might quickly be covered up. However, it had certainly been fun to do and far from routine. And without doubt I would never have had the opportunity to do anything quite like that in my Merchant Service career.

Chapter 20

On Tuesday 29th June I was back at our buoy and normal home port routine began again. The U.S. Navy were changing vessels at the time and replacing the *Ducksberry Bay* with the *Valcour*. On the Thursday we received Admiral Henderson, their senior representative in the Persian Gulf. It was at the time that the U.S. Navy had re-introduced the wearing of swords by officers. Up until then we always felt on official occasions that we were upstaging them somewhat, as we were always decked out in sword and medals but they were not. I believe that they had stopped the carrying of swords during the war, but now it had been reinstated, and this was the first time we received one of their officers on board dressed in sword and medals just like us. Ever ones for one-upmanship, however, I also carried a telescope under my left arm as well as my sword. The R.N. always had to keep one step ahead!

News came of trouble ashore. A mob had, it appeared, stormed the police fort in an attempt to liberate some members of their particular religious party who had been incarcerated therein. A punch-up had taken place some days previously, when two Mohammedan sects had had some sort of argument; fists flew and the police were called. As I understand it, the members of the ruling sect had been sentenced to seven days' imprisonment, whilst the other lot were given seven years. Not unnaturally, this miscarriage of justice left them feeling rather peeved and this was why they were now rallying against the police fort. The police panicked in response, some shooting took place and four people were killed, which of course only served to inflame the situation. As Platoon Commander I was given notice that my platoon might have to land in order to protect the base or to restore order. Shore leave was stopped and we were all briefed. That evening, with typical British phlegm, and despite the fact that we might be called to duty, we held a dinner party in the wardroom to celebrate David Ridley's 26th birthday, Jimmy Morris's imminent departure and my recent return. It was a very good party; the Captain was present and we played 'wardroom games' afterwards, all retiring to bed at 1 o'clock in the morning. Needless to say we were up again at 6.00, when the Captain cleared the lower deck and explained to the ship's company what all the trouble ashore was about. Later that afternoon a signal came through indicating that both Platoons would be required to land at first light the next day, to guard the Agency. We all packed our kit bags and filled our water bottles in preparation. By 11.30 that evening we had received another signal, changing the order to only one platoon, at one hour's notice. We all relaxed again and went to bed.

On Tuesday 6th July we sailed again, this time to Doha, where we arrived late on in the day. The following day the Captain, the Navigator and myself were invited to make an official call on the Sheikh of Doha. I rather feared that we would be subjected to a coussi – an Arab feast where one was liable to have a sheep's eye popped into one's mouth. In the event the message came off to say that the call was cancelled and we had to sail at once back to Bahrain since it seemed likely that the previous trouble was about to break out again. We arrived back that evening, but by the next day things had quietened down and all the panic was over. Apparently a re-trial had been ordered and this had eased the situation. We had had banners all prepared with 'Disperse – or we fire' written across them (or at least, that was what we had been told they said; written in Arabic they could have said virtually anything and we would have been none the wiser). Anyway, this was the nearest I got to taking part in any exercise or drill as learnt in Malta – which is probably just as well.

The next few days were spent in routine matters in Bahrain, with a fair amount of partying involved as this was to be our last visit before we went off for our second stint to Sri Lanka. We were to rendezvous there with the East Indies Fleet and take part in some exercises, which would mean that we would not be back in the Persian Gulf for some time. I had my usual stint as Officer of the Patrol one night, which passed without particular incident. We duly left on Friday 16th July to proceed to Basra, which we were to visit prior to sailing down to Colombo. We berthed at our usual jetty and commenced the usual round of socialising with the 'faggots' who were, if anything, even more 'faggotty' than on the last two occasions. They insisted on entertaining night after night; fortunate indeed was he whose lot fell to be Officer of the Day and who did not have to endure all this entertaining.

We did not leave again until Tuesday 27th July, making a brief call at Sitra to take on our last mail and to fuel before leaving for Sri Lanka. The passage from the Gulf down to Trincomalee, on the far side of the island, was 'in the teeth'; we were heading in a south easterly direction right towards the south west monsoon, which meant that we rolled considerably all the way down. Not a particularly comfortable voyage, but otherwise uneventful. We put the Midshipman through his navigation exams; I thought that I had drummed a lot of my knowledge into him but clearly not all of it had stuck, his biggest howler being when asked in an oral chart work exam what the little alphabetic citations were alongside of the soundings his suggestion that they might be the initials of the surveyor (they were, of course, references to the surface of the bottom, sand, gravel etc.). Somehow I felt that I had failed in my teaching role, although it is hard when you have being doing something all your life to be critical of one who has just had a normal education and probably did not want to make a career of the sea, anyway.

On Friday 6th August we anchored in the early morning in a little bay to the south of Trincomalee to have a final look at the ship and make sure she was spick and span. The First Lieutenant and I went around the ship and the whaler; given the fairly rough passage we had had on the way down she did not seem too bad. We put the finishing touches to her with a bit of last minute painting, just to ensure that we would not let ourselves down before the Fleet. We weighed at 12.45 and proceeded to Trinco., arriving on the dot at 19.00 (our e.t.a.) The Officer of the Guard boarded us (I was Officer of the Day and had to wear full Number 10s until midnight). On the Saturday we shifted to our buoy, next astern of the flagship H.M.S. *Ceylon*. General panic all morning with saluting of the flag and the arrival of various other ships – there were to be six frigates and four destroyers of both the Indian and Pakistani navies, who would not play with one another but who were quite happy to play with the R.N. C-in-C of *Ceylon* was to take charge of affairs. Our Captain called on the C-in-C., one Vice-Admiral Norris, who returned the call that evening. He was received with due pomp and spoke to the ship's company on the quarterdeck. We were rather disappointed that he did not comment on the ship's appearance, having worked so hard on it the previous day.

With so many ships coming together for our forthcoming exercises, the opportunity was taken to hold a Fleet Board

Examination for those wishing to qualify as Leading Seamen. A signal to this effect went out and the 'old myth' emerged again. The signal announced that examining in gunnery, parade training: Lieutenant (G), R.N., examining in signals: a communications Lieutenant, R.N.; examining in elementary navigation: another Lieutenant (N) R.N.; examining in boat-handling, seamanship and rigging: Lieutenant R.D.P. Gillett R.N.R. This apparently struck terror in the Fleet – a real sailor examining in seamanship! I was never to live down this eternal myth.

On the third day, we began the examinations. I was taking them out in the whaler and throughout one morning they were given one hour each in charge of their whaler with a crew from *Loch Alvie*, one of the Loch class frigates. The candidates themselves were all from our ship. They also had to do an eye splice in wire, which they were permitted to do in their own time, rather than in front of me. However, they brought to me these 'votive offerings' as it were: beautiful examples of wire splicing as if laying them at the feet of the gods. I am sure I could not have executed such fine examples myself, but pretended to look at them very critically before I passed them. They were not quite so good in the whalers. It was curious that whenever Jimmy Morris and I had gone sailing and had requested a volunteer crew it always seemed to be the stokers who wanted to go sailing. Had these chaps availed themselves a little more of the opportunity for practice, they may well have fared better in these examinations. The next day we actually had them sitting in front of us, asking them questions germane to our own particular disciplines and specialisations. It was, I must say, quite comprehensive, and the ones who passed certainly deserved their 'killicks'.

There was slight excitement that evening: without any warning the C-in-C ordered a crash 'Darken Ship', which meant that all the ships in the Fleet had to completely obscure all lighting – an exercise watched keenly, no doubt, by the assessors on board the flagship. I am pleased to say that *Flamingo* got a 'Well Done' from the flagship.

The next few days proved to be a busy time. There were boats with Senior Officers and Admirals whizzing to and fro, keeping the Officers of the Day and the Watch on their toes; visits to and fro various ships and never a dull moment, although we did occasionally get ashore in the afternoons to have a swim in the bay nearby. I could now fully appreciate the difference between being an independent ship as oppose to being part of the Fleet. We were used to doing our own thing and in our own time; here one was subject constantly to evolutionary exercises.

Although, somewhere along the line, it had been indicated to me that I should be leaving for home whilst we were down in Trincomalee, I had heard no further of this. On Monday 16th August I went ashore to see if I could be further enlightened, to discover that I was actually booked to return home on the troopship *Dilwara* on 19th August. Someone had obviously forgotten to tell me! I had not been expecting to depart quite as quickly, so I had to return on board smartly and prepare people for my imminent departure. I would have to take the train across to Colombo to join the ship, and time was now getting short! There was not even time to organise a farewell party, but that evening a small affair was laid on in the wardroom, commencing at 6.30 p.m. A liberal amount of pre-prandial drinking took place, and over dinner the Captain and First Lieutenant made some nice speeches. I was presented with a little pot labelled: Raspberry Jam (With Wooden Pips) – a reference to my comments in the mess book over the year wherein I had complained about the 'wooden pips' in the jam. The crew had made a huge cat o' nine tails to be passed over to me by the officers – no doubt a comment on the way I drove them hard as Officer of the upper deck and the mess deck. After dinner there was a little game playing; the Captain retired fairly early, as was his wont and then commenced the 'Drinking of the 'Buie': following my earlier experiences of cleaning up the bar they decided that I should be seen out best by consuming, on my own, a whole bottle of Drambuie. The Midshipman was provided with a little thistle glass and a bottle, poured me a glass and handed it to me. Falling in with the game, I started a series of jocular toasts, each time knocking the glass of Drambuie down my throat and holding it out with the command: 'Midshipman. My glass!' whereupon it was refilled and I toasted again. The bottle amounted to 22 glasses, after which I was still on my feet. But then I made the mistake of sitting down. I virtually passed out, and four of them got hold of me and carried me aft to my cabin. I recall very little about the journey, although it was reported to me the following morning by one who had overheard the kerfuffle that as we neared my cabin the comment came 'Careful – don't drop him!' Thus I went out.

The following morning I awoke at about 7.15 feeling extremely ill. I managed to stagger up to the heads where I was violently sick, and fell back into my bunk. The doctor was summoned and gave me bicarbonate of soda but I was unable to keep this down at all. I think the doc. was beginning to get quite worried about me, fearing a possible case of alcoholic poisoning. We were supposed to be going out on exercises that morning, although since I was leaving the ship that afternoon my absence was justified (although rather than packing and preparing I was actually lying prostrate on my bunk, being intermittently sick!). By 2.00 p.m. I felt well enough to crawl out of my pit. The wardroom steward supplied me with a 'horse's neck' – a brandy and ginger ale – to help revive me, which I managed to swallow and keep down and which seemed to help. I had hoped to spend the forenoon saying goodbye to all those I had worked with but this was by now out of the question. The Captain saw me and gave me an excellent 'flimsy' as it is called, with the promise of a good S206 (a fuller report on my competence as an officer). Although I never saw this, I did hear in time that the report had been very good indeed. When I actually left at 16.30, quite a crowd gathered to see me off and I left to the cheers of many of the ship's company. I had formed strong relationships aboard *Flamingo* and my departure was a sad occasion indeed.

I was billeted overnight at the H.Q. ashore, to catch a train the following day to Colombo. There were four Midshipmen also on their way home sharing this temporary accommodation. The First Lieutenant, the doctor and David Ridley came ashore and we all went to the Surgeon Commander's house for a party in the evening. By 7.00 that evening I was beginning to feel back to normal; a couple of dry martinis and I was back on form!

The following morning I was up at 7.00 a.m. and went with the Midshipmen to collect our baggage and board the train. It was a night sleeper but unfortunately the accommodation comprised only a four-berth sleeper, for five of us. The Midshipmen drew lots and one slept on the baggage.

We reported in at Colombo the following morning and cleared customs. With a little time to kill before we embarked we went to the Grand Oriental Hotel (fond memories) and I had there the full treatment: shampoo, hair cut, shave, wash and brush up, which I certainly felt that I needed after a night bouncing across Sri Lanka on the train. I purchased a few souvenirs in town and visited Witeway Laidlaws, a company which had large stores in Colombo and other sites in the East and of which my father was the then chairman. The manager sent a cable for me to advise Libby and my parents that I was about to embark on the homeward voyage.

We embarked at 11.00 a.m. and I found that I had been allocated a cabin with two others: one R.A.F. officer and one army Captain who were to be my travelling companions on the way home. The ship was very smart; my experience of troopships had of course been during wartime, but this B.I. ship was a dedicated peacetime troopship and had thus been purpose-built. The journey itself proved fairly dull, for me – I dislike being a passenger in a ship where I am not permitted to do anything, although it was a good rest and I whiled away the hours sunning myself and reading Agatha Christies. I would sleep in the afternoons and in the evenings there was a certain amount of entertainment, including a cinema, or card games. Most of the troops embarked on board were National Servicemen returning to be de-mobbed or troops returning for discharge – she had come from Korea and had collected men in Singapore and Malaysia, before Colombo. Next stop was Aden, then Port Said, and then home. Amongst the passengers was a delightful lady – the retiring matron of the Royal Naval Hospital and Trincomalee, called Kay Greenwood, who quite often sat down with us for drinks in the evening. One evening she leaned over to me and in a very sweet voice said: 'I believe, Mr Gillett, that you do a very good trick of drinking a whole bottle of Drambuie – I should love to see you do that!' Just shows how impossible it is to have secrets in the Navy. I was horrified at the prospect and explained very firmly that I rather felt I would never touch a drop of Drambuie ever again after the experience of my farewell party; to this day even the smell of it is enough to remind me how ghastly I felt the next morning, and I declined her kind offer to purchase a bottle for me. We did play one rather good game called 'Seven, Fourteen, Twenty One' – the first to throw the seventh ace with poker dice ordered a drink (a mixture of drinks, in fact); the one who threw the fourteenth ace had to pay for it and the unfortunate who threw the twenty-first ace had to drink the ghastly concoction. By the time we had finished playing the bar was closed so the forfeit had to be postponed until the next day. I got caught with having to drink a gin/brandy/port/crème de menthe mixture – which actually did not taste too bad. I followed it quickly with a pint of beer and a couple of pink gins to show there was no ill feeling. When it was my turn to select the drink, I chose a Drambuie/Cointreau and Orange Curaçao mix.

Having sailed from Colombo on 20th August we passed through

the Straits of Gibraltar and turned north for home on September 7th, at which point we went into blues, for the first time in a very long while. It seemed quite strange. We actually docked in Southampton at 4.30 on the afternoon of 10th September, although we were not to disembark until the next day. Formalities were soon dealt with and I was allowed to proceed to a sort of guarded 'pen' which they had on the dockside, where Libby and I were at last reunited after 318 days apart. We were permitted half an hour together before the next day, when I was fully disembarked, cleared customs and after five minutes was free to go. Libby was there with the car and took me back to the Hotel Lyndhurst. Needless to say, it was a very joyous reunion. By the evening, we were back home at our little house in Fairholt Street. It was, at last, all over.

Looking back on it now, although I still feel that it was an inordinate amount of time to be apart from one another, nevertheless we survived it. Certainly in my case I was kept so busy whilst I was out there in the Gulf that I never had time to dwell too much on the situation. I kept my journal so that I could describe everything to Libby, and we had written diligently to one another throughout the whole period. And professionally, it had been a marvellous experience; I had learnt a lot, met a lot of nice people, had done many things I would not otherwise have done, and discovered some of the ways of the Navy. I can recall that much of my time on watch was spent dispelling the myths that were rife among Navy men about the Merchant Service, such as better pay, overtime etc. I would point out the number of allowances in the Navy which compensated for the lower pay and also the fact that employment did not cease once ashore, unlike the Merchant Service where payment ceased until one was aboard ship once more. I also clarified the overtime myth – pointing out that we were under strict constraints about the amount of overtime and even as a Chief Officer I had to fully justify every minute of any overtime I spent. In the Navy one was always given time off in lieu if extra hours were worked. I also referred to the different ways the two services were treated in port: when a Merchant man gets into harbour, apart perhaps from the 'Missions To Seamen' venues, he is on his own, whereas the Navy are met, bussed about on trips and tours, entertained and have a number of services at their disposal. They have a pension to look forward to, welfare for their families, get flown home on compassionate leave if necessary... no way can the men complain that they have a rough deal! I am not sure whether I was fully believed, but it was nevertheless an interesting comparative study.

Although I was now home, my year's training had not quite finished. The Admiralty calculated that I was due 31 days' leave but at the end of that I had to stand by for further orders, and report to another ship to complete my year.

When we got back from Southampton we spent twelve days in London, meeting my parents and Libby's father who came down a couple of times on business, and generally picking up on normal life once more. I was still looking fairly black from the sun. We celebrated my return with a party for twenty and then the next day (our fourth wedding anniversary) invited a small number of people around. I reported to the Admiralty and they intimated that my next appointment would be to a Fleet minesweeper, H.M.S. *Cockatrice*, and that orders would follow in due course.

Chapter 21

On 24th September, Libby and I drove up to Busby House in Scotland. We were able to use one of my father-in-law's cars from his 'stable': a Vanguard, which Stella had driven down to London. We spent one night at Busby House and then proceeded to 'Erins'. This was a large, turreted, baronial home of a place, which my father-in-law had purchased, fully furnished, the previous year.

Inside, the house was extraordinarily comfortable. It had ten bedrooms, a lovely drawing room, a large dining room and a full-sized billiard table in the billiard room. There was also a gunroom which doubled as a smoking room. It was an ideal house for a large family, and a perfect place for a country house party. It was somewhat isolated: the nearest human habitation apart from the lodge at the end of the drive (occupied by one Archie, the gardener-cum-handyman) was about four or five miles away. There was a kitchen garden at the back of the house, masses of rhododendrons and acres of woodland surrounding the house. Beyond that were the moors, guarded by a deer fence. The upper windows of the house afforded marvellous views across Loch Fyne.

We were staying there together with my father-in-law, another married couple who were guests of his, and my brother-in-law John and his wife Elspeth with their young daughter. The weather was good. John had with him a telescopic-sighted .22 rifle and on our first day he and I climbed across the deer fence onto the moors. I had always been led to believe that one stalked deer by crawling stealthily for hours on end through the undergrowth; however, all of a sudden one just appeared on a hill, not very far away from where we were standing. Before you could say Jack Robinson, John had drawn a bead on the animal with his telescopic sight and shot it clear through the head. We were then faced with the problem of getting it back to the house. There were some ponies belonging to the estate, which were grazing some way off, and we toyed with the idea of using one these but dismissed this notion realising that we would have wasted far too much time trying to catch the thing. John had with him a fairly large clasp knife and knowing that we had to try and reduce the weight of the carcass in order to carry it down, he set to with this instrument. We began by removing the head, not without some difficulty, I might add. He then contemplated skinning and disembowelling it, but decided against this as we needed to preserve its legs to hold on to. The difficulty, clearly, was going to be getting it over the deer fence. To lighten the load still further he slit it open and we removed what had been its lunch – a quantity of undigested grass – and off we went, carrying the creature by its legs between us. When we reached the fence, it was evident that the only option was to throw the thing over. With three heaves we managed to throw it over the fence, and then clamber after it ourselves. Then we had to take it down through the woods, which was a bit of a scramble, but eventually we arrived with it at the stables where we hung it up and proceeded to peer inside. Such was our scant knowledge of anatomy that we were not at all certain which bits to cut out and dispose of, and which to keep. Happily, however, Archie appeared with a companion and we were able to hand over to the professionals who knew exactly what they were doing. We decided to try the venison as fresh meat, rather than hanging it for a length of time as is customary. In my opinion it was far tastier and more succulent, too.

This was really the full extent of our shooting expeditions. John and his wife left to go back to Glasgow with the rest of the party, leaving Libby and me on our own to enjoy another honeymoon and together we spent many happy hours taking out the boat and fishing for mackerel on the loch. I would row, whilst Libby dealt with the spinners over the stern. The fish were in plentiful supply and practically gave themselves up to us, and we always took home a good catch. Seals would appear in the loch, small, whiskered, round heads bobbing out of the water to snort at us for taking away their food supply.

We drove down to Tarbet in the car on a couple of occasions, but on the whole our days were spent on the loch and our evenings attempting to master the art of snooker on the big billiard table. After a week spent relaxing in this way we returned to Busby House, packed and the next day took the night sleeper down to London where my orders were waiting for me from the Admiralty. I was to join H.M.S. *Cockatrice*, an Algerine fleet sweeper that was lying at Port Edgar, near Edinburgh. It was back up to Scotland, where I took the train on 10th

October, reporting on board for further training – although in fact I only had two weeks left to do.

Autumn in the North Sea was certainly a sharp contrast to the Persian Gulf. *Cockatrice* was part of the Fourth Mine Sweeping Squadron and together with the other sweepers we were off for exercises. I had never done any minesweeping before, although it had been one of the things I had hoped to learn during my time with the Navy. Not that I was particularly interested in minesweeping, but it was something different from ploughing to and fro across the North Atlantic and was also a good lesson in station keeping. You are really kept on your toes at all times when doing a sweep. We played around at this for three days, and then proceeded further north to Invergordon, where we were to have our annual Regatta. On arrival, on 14th October, I took the bus to Inverness and then the train to Glasgow and met up with Libby at Busby House, then returned to Invergordon three days later in the car, where we checked in to the Royal Hotel, as there was no need for me to live on board. Libby was in fact the only wife in the whole Squadron at the Regatta, so they made a bit of a mascot of her during our stay. The next three days were spent in practising for the Regatta which took place on the Friday 22nd October. This also happened to be Libby's 28th birthday. I am glad to say that *Cockatrice* won all the events and thus we had cause for great celebration in the wardroom. Libby was there too, and presented them with small pink elephant which she had made out of felt. It was promptly christened Libby and made into a wardroom trophy, sitting on a wooden plinth at mess dinners and the like. I am not sure that the elephant made it to the Naval Trophy Store when *Cockatrice* was de-commissioned, but she certainly remained in the wardroom throughout many years of service. To recover from the Regatta celebrations we had a 'black velvet' party (a concoction of Guinness and champagne), which also marked my departure from my stint on board.

We drove back down to Glasgow and then took the night sleeper once more back down to London. My year in the Navy was now over, although my contact with H.M.S. *Cockatrice* had not quite ended: she came down to Chatham for a re-fit shortly afterwards. We had made great friends with the First Lieutenant, one Mike Garnett, who was still on the ship, and were invited down to visit. Dodo was staying with us at the time so we all drove down to Chatham and had dinner on board, followed by a game of poker which went on long into the night. This was, one must recall, before the days of breathalysers or strict drink/drive regulations and I drove back up to London afterwards, but crossing Blackheath we were stopped by the police. Feeling extremely anxious with regard to the quantities of alcohol I had consumed, I prepared myself for questioning. They asked me several routine questions about the car and then apologised for disturbing me but they had been looking for a stolen vehicle with a similar number plate. It was with immense relief that we finally arrived back at Fairholt Street! The evening had meant the final farewell to H.M.S. *Cockatrice* and to the Navy, although we were to keep in touch from that time onwards with Mike Garnett.

It was now time to think about returning to the Canadian Pacific. On 8th November I joined the *Beaverglen* as Chief Officer, back once more on my home stamping ground. Quite significantly, on Sunday 14th November we went to have tea with my mother and father and they presented us with the title deeds of Number 4, Fairholt Street; my mother had at last persuaded my father to do what she had always wanted him to do and give us the house as a wedding present (as previously indicated, she had virtually bought the house off him in order to do so). I have always considered myself very fortunate indeed, never having had to face the ties of a mortgage which most young couples have to face. Libby and I were able to start out our life with a house of our very own, and no financial outlay. Since we had moved in, in 1945, the value of the property had increased several times over and we knew that we were sitting on a marvellous investment. We both loved the house and had gradually been making it our own since first moving in there together. It felt very comfortable indeed to know that it was now fully our own.

Chapter 22

On 17th November I was off to sea again. We sailed for Montreal on the usual trans-Atlantic route, which had changed very little since I had left. The temperatures were of course considerably different from the Gulf; winter was approaching and this was the last voyage of the season before the St. Lawrence froze over. Before I was married, I had often mused that it would be rather fun to be stuck in Montreal for the winter (as had been known) but it was now the last thing I desired, particularly having been away for a year. However, I was safely back in London by the 22nd December, just in time for Christmas at home which was a treat indeed.

After Christmas, I was in to Assistant-Marine-Superintendent-mode, relieving ship's officers as they came in to enable them to go on leave and looking after the ships whilst they were in port. At that time of year many of them we going in to dry dock for re-fitting and I would go and supervise day by day, moving on to the next *Beaver* as she came in. The 28th November saw me reporting to the *Beaverburn*, to oversee her re-fit and dry-docking. By New Year she was done and I went to the *Mapledell* – this was in fact the same ship as the *Beaverdell*, mentioned earlier. Two of the *Beavers* had been taken out to the Pacific, partly to revive the company's trans-Pacific service and had been re-christened *Mapledell* and *Maplecove* to distinguish them from their sisters in the Atlantic fleet. The next to come in was the *Beaverburn* and I undertook a similar exercise with her. These were of course all ships that I had sailed in before. The task in hand was therefore not unduly taxing and it was very nice to have a shore appointment for a while. I was also able to put into practice some of my shipwrighting skills when supervising the re-fits. However, the call came on 20th January; I was ordered to Liverpool to join the *Empress of Australia* – not the same ship that I had sailed in during the war; this was in fact a French line ship, the *Degrasse*, which the company had purchased to cover their North Atlantic passenger trade after the loss of the *Duchess of Richmond/Empress of Canada*, which had caught fire and had been destroyed in Gladstone Dock in 1952, and whilst their new ships, The *Empress of Britain* and The *Empress of England* were being built. This French ship was quite elderly and, to my mind, a bit of a fire trap. But nevertheless better than nothing. She was lying in Liverpool, where I joined her as Second Officer. We sailed on 26th January for St. John's, New Brunswick. The weather was atrocious: gales and more gales and (unusually for a passenger ship) we were actually hove to for three hours on 31st January, following which it snowed for two days. We arrived at St. John's on 4th February and I returned again to Liverpool, where she was to go into dry dock. Libby came up to Liverpool for the duration of dry-docking, and then we returned together to London at the end of the month. I was then back to the *Maplecove* as Chief Officer and joined her on 17th March.

It was at this time that it was confirmed that Libby was 'in the family way'; the doctors announced that our first-born was expected in September. I think we had both agreed on my return home that we were ready to start a family and no doubt our excitement at being reunited had borne fruit!

I sailed on 2nd March for St. John's once more – and once more we had gales all the way. Such was the North Atlantic. In the summer: fog and ice, in the winter: gales, gales and more gales – westerlies, to boot, which meant right on the nose. Home via Antwerp on 12th April, to sail again on the 26th. Spring had arrived and we were to be first ship up river to Montreal that year. This was always considered a significant point in the calendar – akin to seeing the first swallow heralding the approach of summer – and tradition had it that the captain of the first ship up the St. Lawrence received a gold-headed cane and a silk hat as a trophy. We were certainly in with a chance on this run. As we came south of Newfoundland we ran into pack ice. This was navigable, and one could break it up by steaming into it (not that this did much for the paintwork along the waterline). But you could not stop. The ice would crack and be pushed aside but would close again in your wake and to avoid the propeller being caught in the ice it was imperative to keep going. The terrain was often populated by seals, who would sit on the ice and look askance at the ship or plop into the water as you passed by. Once in the river, the ice was broken up but there were no buoys – these having all been removed for the winter – only withies protruding from the water which indicated where the buoys would have been for navigation purposes. We were, indeed, the first in that particular year, arriving in Montreal on 6th May. We came back via Antwerp.

Being a Londoner, I found I always got on well with the Cockney crews. They were a cheeky lot, much given to *bons mots* and great good humour. They also never bore a grudge and they respected their own art form – if you responded in like manner they were always fully appreciative. I can recall two examples of such encounters. One occurred on the fo'c's'le head, when an out of line remark from a particularly cheeky crew member was met with equal wit from me. The other crewmen who had been egging him on quickly acceded the point and the chap was put in his place. The second incident occurred as we were about to leave Antwerp. It was foggy in the river and we were waiting for the pilot to come on board. The men were all gathered around the accommodation ladder, waiting to hear whether or not we were to sail. The crew were still on their day routine, as in port. As soon as we sailed and reverted to sea routine, overtime was due to be paid to those not on watch. It is a known fact that every sailor likes overtime and every Company Marine Superintendent does not, and it was the job of every Chief Officer to make sure that his overtime bill at the end of a voyage was kept to the absolute minimum. I was obviously keen to keep the men on a day routine situation, so that they would not start accruing overtime. If the Captain decided he was going to sail we would want to go to stations, with half the crew for'ard, half the crew aft to let go of the ropes all at once. If the decision was not to sail we would just stay as we were. My best interests were to keep them standing ready and in sight; if they were to disperse they would take no end of time getting ready and preparing, having cups of tea and the like should the call come. The men knew that the pilot was on board, discussing the situation with the Captain. I was standing on the deck above them, looking down. One of the better spoken men came forward, looked up at me and said: ''Ere, Mister Mate – Are we on stations or aren't we?' This was of course the question that I did not want to answer. Had I said 'Yes', they would have all gone on to stations at once, which would have to be paid if we did not go; if I said 'No' I would lose them. I said nothing. He looked at me with a pained expression on his face. 'Oh say something Mister Mate – even if it's only bollocks!' I can't quite recall what came next, although it was probably something along the lines of 'all right then – bollocks!' But I suppose this is the kind of incident at which some officers may well have taken offence. In my mind, their sense of frustration was justified, to some extent, and I could not have taken umbrage at their words. The Liverpudlian crew were quite a different kettle of fish. Far less outspoken, they were more likely to harbour a grudge without saying anything. I had a strong affection for the Cockneys and their up front manner.

If we were coming in to London, and were due to arrive at a reasonable hour, Libby would often come and meet me off the ship. She would stand on the jetty, and the sailors, who of course did not know who she was, would often wolf-whistle and shout apprecia-tively (being sailors) on catching sight of this pretty girl waiting for the ship. I would not say anything, not wishing to spoil the fun. On one particular occasion there was one among the men who *did* know who she was. ''Ere!' he called to his fellow crew. 'Better watch it. That's the mate's missus, that is!' They all shut up instantly, and were immediately occupied pulling ropes and what have you, trying not to catch my eye. Not that I minded. In fact, I rather thought it was a compliment. But give me a Cockney crew any day. Half of them may have been in prison at one time or another, but as far as I was concerned they were the salt of the earth – the sort of chaps that would bring you a cup of tea just when you needed it most, or who would come to your aid immediately if there was any trouble in a foreign port. They would pinch anything that wasn't nailed down, but would never steal from their own.

We arrived at Southend on 27th May and had to anchor for two days because of a dock strike in London. Although we were found a berth after two days, the strike itself went on. And on ... and on. This was all very well for me, since I was at home. But not so good for those stuck outside, or for the ship owners. But nevertheless, a gift from the gods! We were not even allowed to do much on board, such as painting, since that was all undertaken by shoremen. Our cargo had not been discharged, so we were unable to load anything else. I was at home for a very long time and it was not until 4th July that the strike was eventually over, to sail once again on 9th July, destination Montreal.

We sailed from Montreal to Quebec on 24th July and once there we embarked a rather special passenger – in the form of a baby moose. It is quite common practice for zoos throughout the world to exchange young animals in order to broaden their stock. It so happened that the Quebec zoo had a baby moose, rescued when its mother had been shot. They were sending this infant across to Whipsnade, in exchange, I believe, for some baby camels. A man came down from

179

Feeding my baby moose.

the zoo with a large box, some 5' long, 4' high, and 3' deep. Inside was a small animal, about the size of an Alsatian dog. I went down on the jetty to inspect this cargo and was introduced to it by the French Canadian keeper.

''Ere is ze baby moose!'

'Is it going to stay in its box all the way across the Atlantic?' I enquired, rather anxious at the prospect.

'It eez OK. Only a small hanimal'

'But won't it get rather smelly and dirty in there?'

He shrugged. I now felt decidedly perturbed and sent the stevedores off for twelve sacks of sawdust for a start.

'What does it eat?' I enquired, my anxiety now growing.

He shrugged again. 'It eez not weaned'.

'You mean it's not taking solids?'

'It eez very small hanimal. Taken from its mother. You 'ave to feed it with a baby bottle. Hevery four 'ours.' He gesticulated to the case, alongside of which was a box containing several tins of Carnation milk, together with an American style quart glass milk bottle with a large rubber teat. Hevery four 'ours. You mix the milk 50/50 with warm water and you feed 'im with zee bottle.'

'And is he likely to take solids during the course of the journey?'

Again a shrug. 'You can try if you like. Zere eez some cattle cake 'ere. But I think 'e will not take it.'

I clearly was not going to get much change out of this chap, who did not seem to be particularly interested in the welfare of the creature at all. We had the case taken on board and put up on the boat deck, where my cabin was situated. Just for'ard of my cabin was an office with a door out on to the deck, with a screen just outside of the door to provide protection from the weather. This is where we put him, so that I was able to keep an eye on him at regular intervals. I got the carpenter to construct a decent-sized pen (about 12' square) so that we could let him out if the weather was not too rough.

We set off on the voyage home, and my nursing duties began in earnest – I would feed him with his baby's bottle every four hours. This was no trouble during the day and in fact several of the crew would take turns at the feeding routine. The moose became quite a ship's pet. But night feeds were solely my responsibility. I would be woken by his piteous bleating at midnight and four in the morning – he had come to know exactly when his feeds were due and would start crying for his milk about half an hour beforehand. Another problem was the rate at which he consumed the milk, guzzling it down at once at a terrific rate. I would try to withhold the bottle to give him some air – I had vague notions about having to wind babies and wondered if the same principle applied. But he did not seem too bothered and within a day or so had clearly come to regard me as his mother. My office had a door out on to the deck with a fly screen on a spring catch. We had a smooth crossing, for once, and whilst I was working away in my office he would come in, pushing the fly screen open with his nose and then come up to me for a stroke and a bit of a chat. He was very sweet – not particularly good-looking but nevertheless like all baby animals very endearing. As I have said, the crew took to him immediately and made a great fuss of him. He never did get weaned but lived the life of Riley. He was kept spotlessly clean and we groomed him regularly. Before he was due to be collected by the keeper from Whipsnade on our arrival, we lavished on him all the attention of a pony being prepared for a gymkhana, giving him an extra scrubbing so that his coat gleamed and even polishing his little hooves. Apart from tying a pink ribbon around his neck, he was prepared as if for a show. The keeper was astonished, never having seen an animal in such peak condition. I assured him that had we followed the instructions we had been given, he would not look anything like this, and possibly might not be alive at all.

'How are we to get him off?' he enquired.

'No problem,' I assured him. 'I shall walk down the gangway onto the quay and he'll follow'. Which he did, of course, like a dog at my heels. He then went placidly into his little wooden house and was taken off to Whipsnade. I did ask the keeper whether it was an advantage to have the animals hand-reared in this way and in fact was told that it was not always a good thing. It would mean that the creatures had no inherent fear of man and when they grew bigger, would often not be aware of their own strength. If our moose weighed two tons when he was fully-grown and nuzzled one or trod on one's toe he could do considerable damage! Whipsnade were in fact very pleased indeed with the way in which their cargo had been handled and Libby and I received a personal invitation from the director to look round the zoo and see 'Mickey' in his new home. (The name derived from the story about the Scotsman staying in Canada with a friend; they saw a moose in the woods and the Scotsman said: 'Och, what's tha?' and his friend replied, 'That's a moose.' 'Well if that's a moose, I dinna want to see a rat!'). We took up the invitation and were taken around in the director's Land Rover. Mickey was in quarantine still but we went to his pen and when I called him he came trotting across at once to have his nose scratched. I had rather hoped with my level of expertise confirmed that I would have responsibility for the baby camels that were being exchanged, but it was not to be – they must have gone on another ship. We did have baby bears on one trip, however, and a memorable cargo of one hundred canaries from Antwerp on one occasion. Sadly Mickey did not survive in captivity and died a couple of years later.

Well . . . from one baby to another. The next voyage to and from Montreal passed without incident. But when I sailed for the subsequent voyage on 20th September, Libby was within weeks of being delivered of our first-born. She very gallantly drove me down to the ship, as usual – despite being heavily pregnant she could still get under the wheel. In those days the road leading down to the docks was still cobbled, and Libby claims that it was the bouncing over these cobbles which brought things on a bit. She went into the nursing home in Queens Gate on 22nd September and Nicholas, our elder son, was born in the wee small hours of Saturday 24th, some two to three weeks before he was expected. I had hoped to be at home, but this was not to be. He was a big lad, and poor Libby had quite a hard time, having to have 24 stitches afterwards, but recuperated quickly and all was well. Not so, however, with the procedure for letting me know the news. We had organised a code between ourselves, having decided on names beforehand, and Libby was merely going to send me a telegram with the appropriate name. However, I managed to live through Saturday, Sunday and most of Monday without being aware of the fact that I was actually a father and it was not until about 5.00 p.m. on Monday evening that the radio operator advised me that there was a message for me. The message read 'Nicholas and I doing well, Love Libby'. Very economical. Of course I assumed that he had been born that day and immediately radioed back flowers and messages of goodwill. However when I arrived in Montreal, on 30th September, there was a telegram awaiting me from my father telling me that Nicholas had actually been born on the Saturday. Apparently my parents had visited Libby on the Saturday and my father had offered to send the telegram to the ship on Libby's behalf. However, he had sent it straight to Montreal. Libby told me afterwards that she felt the nurses were regarding her rather suspiciously when three days passed with no word whatsoever from the father. She had eventually asked her brother-in-law to send a second telegram, correctly addressed to the ship at sea on this occasion.

She returned home with Nicholas on 8th October, which was the day I sailed from Montreal. The first time I set eyes on my son was on 15th October, when he was already nearly one month old. I had some leave due, however, and handed over the *Maplecove* on 21st October in order to spend some time in London learning at first hand how to be a father and doing a little decorating of the house when not engaged in my paternal duties. On 5th November I accompanied my father to the consecration of the new addition to the Merchant Navy Memorial on Tower Hill, which commemorated those lost in the Second World War. It was built round a garden, on the walls of which were the bronze plaques with the names of the ships that had been sunk and the names of the officers and crew that had been killed. The next day was Remembrance Sunday (this having been moved, at that time, from the eleventh to the first Sunday in November) and I went to lay the wreath on behalf of the Canadian Pacific at that memorial.

After my brief introduction to parenthood I got a ship again on 8th November, when I was appointed Chief Officer of the *Beaverlake*. We sailed on Monday 14th via Antwerp for Montreal. Again we left it pretty close to the closure of the St. Lawrence before our departure from Montreal, leaving on Wednesday 7th December, by which time the ice had formed across the dock. A couple of days previously I had been out to stay with friends at Sennerville, to the west of the city, where the lake was frozen solid enough for us to skate on. In the winter months, children in Montreal would skate in the streets. No wonder they were so good at ice hockey.

On that occasion we returned to Liverpool, where we docked on 17th December. I came down early by train to London in time for Nicholas's christening in the afternoon of Sunday 18th at Holy Trinity, Brompton. My parents gave a party afterwards at the Rembrandt Hotel, where they were now staying. I returned to Liverpool on the Monday and we came round to London on the following Thursday, to our normal berth in the Royal Albert Dock. I handed over the ship there. Although I was not to sail in a *Beaver* again after that time, I had not quite finished my service with them, since after another very pleasant Christmas at home I was back to my Marine Superintendent duties once more, passing ships through their re-fits as they came in. This kept me occupied until the end of January, when I was appointed to go to Scotland to stand by the final fitting out of the brand new *Empress of Britain*, which was now nearing completion in Fairfields Yard on the Clyde. This was a marvellous opportunity because it meant I could live at home with Libby and we all went up to Scotland to live at Busby House, from where I was able to drive to the yard every day to oversee the preparation of the ship. I was appointed as Second Officer, and therefore my particular interest lay in the lifesaving and fire-fighting equipment which was being installed. To be present at the final fitting out meant that you knew your way around the ship completely, a fact which was to prove on one occasion not long after, a Very Good Thing.

Chapter 23

Libby, Nicholas and I all travelled north to Glasgow by train overnight. I reported to the yard (using one of the numerous Findlay cars) and for the next four weeks lived the life of a commuter, travelling in every morning and returning at teatime, which meant that Libby and I lived something of a more normal married life, albeit in Scotland. It was very pleasant indeed. I would go down to the yard in a variety of cars from Pa Findlay's stable. The Armstrong Sidley Hurricane which he had bought off me had now been exchanged for a more up to date Armstrong Sidley Sapphire saloon – a lovely car, which made me look very grand. In fact, I looked so grand on one occasion that I turned up at the yard that some stroppy Glasgow workers let down the tyres. On some days I would take the Vauxhall Wyvern, or if I felt in dashing mood I would take the TR2 – a little green sports car which attracted great interest from the kids who would refer to it as the 'wee green racer'. We stayed in Glasgow until Tuesday 28th February, when I actually joined the ship. We sailed the next day from the yard and on March 1st and the following day we spent out in the lower Clyde doing our trials: speed trials, crash stops, turning circles and the like.

Not being required once the ship was in dry dock I slipped back up to Glasgow for a couple of days before returning. We then proceeded to the Isle of Arran and Ailsa Craig to commence our trials, which took place over the next four days. We did everything from crash stops and turning circles to general exercises with various manoeuvres to produce data and check all our gear. There was, I recall, one incident of note. She was full of all kinds of fail-safe devices and at one point during our speed trials the engines proceeded to shut themselves down. She stopped, and the entire engine room automatically closed down. This had happened as a result of some minor fault or other and was easily remedied, although it was necessary to wait until the shut-down process was complete before they could flash up the boilers and start again. Apart from this one small hiccup all went well and she proved to be a beautiful ship. She

The Empress of Britain.

was the first of our Fleet and the first ship I had sailed in to be fitted with stabilisers. These are retractable fins which act like two little wings and which respond to the motion of the ship when she rolls. To test them it was, of course, necessary to make the ship roll and then ascertain how well the roll was corrected.

She had a sister ship being built on the Tyne – the *Empress of England*. Empresses had traditionally been three-funnelled ships and the Duchesses two-funnelled. Unlike her predecessors, however, the *Empress of Britain* had a single funnel. It was now practice to paint the house flag on the funnels, which those of us of the old school found somewhat excessive, particularly on ships with more than one funnel. She had been launched by H.M. the Queen on 22nd June 1955 and was now ready to enter into service. Not as big as her forbear, she was, nevertheless, 26,000 tons gross, with twin-screw geared turbines producing a cruising speed of 20 knots. She carried 1050 passengers: on North Atlantic runs this meant 900 tourist passengers, which was the trend those days, and 150 first class passengers. On cruises, the system was more akin to that of a hotel, with cabins being sold individually according to their position. The crew numbered 450 and she boasted all mod-cons. She was fully air-conditioned – unlike her predecessors who carried only a system of ventilators which blew air out at people – and fitted with all the latest navigational equipment. All in all, really quite a dream boat.

After we had finished our trials, we returned to Glasgow where we went into the King George V dock and remained there for the last remaining details of fitting out and vital storing. I was back to living ashore in Busby House and coming down the ship each day. On 28th March all must have been complete. Fairfields (the yard which had done the work) held a cocktail party on board to which Libby was invited. The following day we sailed to Liverpool, where we remained until 9th April when we started on our 'shakedown' cruise. This was a 'jolly', sailing from Liverpool to Southampton with V.I.P.s on board – regular customers, the press and anyone else to whom we wished to show off our new ship were all treated to a very boozy party. We arrived in Southampton on Tuesday 10th and on the Thursday we sailed back to Liverpool with some of the same crowd and some additions. This shakedown provided time for last minute fine-tuning as well as allowing the stewards time to find their way around the ship before we eventually started on our maiden voyage proper.

We finally embarked on 20th April for Montreal. I already had one maiden voyage under my belt, on the *Beavercove*, but being a cargo ship this had not felt quite so significant. To make a maiden voyage in a transatlantic passenger liner inevitably evoked memories of *Titanic*, although happily in our case all went well, despite the fact that almost at once we ran into gales. However, they moderated after a bit and by the time we reached the Canadian side we were back into the habitual fog. We arrived at Quebec on 25th April and then proceeded to Montreal the next day. Lots of whoopee in both places to show off the new ship, with parties on board. I dressed up in my best uniform and stood by the gangway to greet all the V.I.P.s as they trooped aboard to admire our gleaming white new ship. We were on a regular routine now once more so sailed the following week back to Liverpool. I went home, then, on the boat train. Libby met me in London and I was able to have a few days off before I had to return.

It was on this return that I found myself promoted: Slim Miller, the First Officer, was in hospital and I had been given his job – a fairly rapid rise, since I had only made one voyage as Second Officer. It meant a change of watch and a change of cabin but otherwise things were much the same. We were off once more on 11th May, again to Montreal, and back on the regular run passing the same seagulls sitting on the same iceberg, travelling in the same direction every three weeks, much like a glorified ferry service. I did sometimes manage to get away for a few days, to Senerville to the west of Montreal where I would stay with the Cumyns' – whose father had been a business friend of my father. They had children varying from just adult to late teens and there were usually several folk around. There would be tennis to be played in the summer months and the refreshing air made a change from the heat and humidity of Montreal. Then it would be back on board on the Monday to prepare to sail on the Tuesday. From Liverpool I would generally catch the boat train down to London, have a few days respite and then turn around again to Liverpool.

On 30th July I had arrived in Liverpool and travelled to London as usual, but was summoned to return the next day to find that I had been promoted to Chief Officer. I cannot now recall why, although I assume that Slim Miller was back in hospital once more. This meant three straight stripes and more responsibilities, being now in charge of the deck department. I no longer kept a watch, and had a table of my own in the First Class dining room, with passengers to entertain at meal times. One of these passengers I was to get to know very well: Mr John Gilroy, the artist, a very good portrait painter who had painted many members of the Royal Family, but whose greatest claim to fame was that he designed the artwork for the 'My Goodness – My Guinness!' advertisements. He was eventually to paint my portrait, too. Up until this point I had had no occasion to have memorable contact with the passengers any more than an engine driver might have with the passengers on his train. Now I was in a position to meet them at first hand – and very nice they turned out to be.

My first voyage as Chief Officer passed without incident. We changed Captains in Liverpool. Captain Keay had been my first captain on the *Empress of Britain* and I had served under him in cargo ships for some time. He had been desperately in love with my mother-in-law when, as a young officer, he had met her when she had been sailing in the ships, and he had even come north on a train when she eventually married father-in-law in a last attempt to stop the wedding! I suspect that this was one reason why he had always had rather a soft spot for me. He was a very fine seaman: a quiet and gentle man who as a young boy had lived in Ireland and had lost both parents and a sister who had been shot by Fenians when they burst in upon the family home. He himself had escaped by hiding under a table but had witnessed his family being shot before his eyes.

Captain Keay was relieved by Captain Bell for a voyage so that he could take his leave ... and off we set once more.

By the time we arrived back in Liverpool I myself was due for leave. The Chief Officer had by this time recovered sufficiently to take up his job once more and I proceeded on three weeks' leave, which in effect meant a whole voyage off and proved a very substantial slice of holiday. Libby and I had decided that it was about time that we had a new car. Our old Standard 12 – that of the brass bushed nearside front wheel – had really reached its last days and was unfit for human consumption. We got £110 for it as a trade in for a second hand Ford Zephyr Mark I drop-head coupé, cream coloured, with a red roof: spiffing! It had only done 9,000 miles (or so the clock said). It was 1954 vintage and we paid the princely sum of £185 for it. It was the first car that I had with a gear lever on the steering column; it boasted a six-cylinder engine and was in all respects a very fine vehicle. We could open the roof, which we liked, and which was even more useful with a youngster, as Nicholas was still in his carry cot stage and it meant that we were able to open the roof, sit the carry cot across the back seat and then close it up again – all very convenient.

Then we headed for Frinton, where my parents still had the house, although they had by this time finished their summer stay and were back in town. We took over the house and spent a pleasant ten days, even managing to swim, although after the pleasures of the Persian Gulf I found it hard to do anything much more than dip my big toe in to the North Sea in September! After a very relaxing holiday we then returned to London, and all too soon my three weeks were over and it was back to Liverpool. Here I arrived on Thursday 4th October in time to sign on and take on, once more, my role as First Officer. This was to last until 6th December, which meant a final three trips as Navigator. At the end of the November voyage I had another dose of leave, and on my return from that spell I found myself once again as Chief Officer, a post I was to hold permanently until the following March.

The *Empress of Scotland* was doing the West Indies cruises in the winter time, but the *Empress of Britain* was kept on the St. John, New Brunswick run, as it was now felt that there was a need for a passenger service. Here in St. John we encountered something of a problem. We were embarking passengers for the home run and the shell doors in the ship's side were of course open where the gangways came in. It was bitterly cold outside – about twelve degrees below – and the air conditioning, which not only kept the ship cool but also enabled the ship to be heated in cold weather, started to fail, being unable to cope with the rush of cold air coming in. We finally had to stop embarking the passengers and close up the doors to allow the system to claw its way back to a reasonable temperature. The air conditioning system was elaborate and idiosyncratic at the best of times, often taking several voyages to 'settle in' and maintain a controlled temperature. Passengers would always be complaining that it was either too hot or too cold and the engineers were kept constantly on their toes. On this occasion the passengers were kept waiting for a couple of hours in a rather inhospitable shed as we tried our best to get the temperature up on board.

The home run was not much fun, either. Gales, gales, gales every day and our brand new stabilisers were kept fully employed. We arrived in Liverpool on 24th December and by catching the midnight train for Glasgow I was able (just) to make Christmas Day at Busby House, where Libby and Nicholas were already installed. I got in at 8.30 a.m. on Christmas morning to be met by Libby in the car, and thus just managed to squeeze in another family Christmas. I had to return to Liverpool on the Thursday to attend to my duties but managed to escape the following day and spend the next two days in Scotland before returning to Liverpool overnight on 31st (missing Hogmanay) to sail on 1st January 1957 back to St. John, New Brunswick. By the time we returned home on 18th January Libby and Nicholas had gone back to London. All too short a time at home and back to the ship on 22nd for gales, gales, gales. The North Atlantic is not a place for much fun in the wee small months of the year!

I was now well settled in to my Chief Officer's role. Having been there at the start, when the ship was being built, I also felt I knew the *Empress of Britain* better than any ship I had sailed in before. Later on in the year, in March, an incident occurred which meant that this level of knowledge was to pay off. We had arrived back in Liverpool and went into re-fit for a general overhaul. On one day the staff Chief Engineer was with an assistant in the CO_2 room down on the working deck doing some testing and inspection. This room contained rows of large bottles containing CO_2 gas. A smoke detecting system was in operation on board, linking this room and the bridge. It sucked air out of the holds and the engine room, into a glass cabinet. If there was any smoke it would immediately be evident, alarms would buzz and it would be possible to detect from which compartment the smoke was coming. Then by opening the appropriate valves from the control room, it was possible to release CO_2 from some of the bottles and smother the fire. It was also possible, by pulling one particular lever, to release *all* the gas from *all* the bottles into one compartment at once, should the fire be particularly bad. On this particular occasion, the staff Chief Engineer had gone in to the CO_2 room wearing a boiler suit with a belt which, instead of being properly buckled at the front was fixed in a loop at the back. He bent down to look at something and in so doing caught the belt of his boiler suit in the vital lever which released all the gas. All the valves opened at once and the resulting pressure (with no valves open to the holds) meant that the joints began to leak and the entire room filled at once with CO_2 gas in a sort of white fog. The Chief Engineer and his assistant came whizzing out. I was on the scene, having supervised this part of the fire installation when I was Second Officer, and the fire brigade (which after the fire on the *Empress of Canada* earlier on had special arrangements with a direct line from the ship to the Fire Station at Bootle) came haring down and it was not long before the alleyway was full of firemen. They donned breathing apparatus ready to go in, but clearly did not have much idea of what they were looking for or where they were going. Because of my prior knowledge of the ship, however, I knew where there was a valve which it was possible to open to release all of the gas up the funnel. So I too donned breathing apparatus and entered the compartment followed by a couple of firemen holding on to my waist. I felt my way around the room until I found the right valve, was able to open it and thus release all the pressure and direct the gas up the funnel. With the best will in the world no fireman would have been able to locate this valve – and thus it was proved that it can certainly pay off to know one's ship. I made sure on any other ship that I was in that I could find this particular valve in the dark!

As part of the overhaul drill, it was necessary for the ship to be fumigated; every living creature had to be off the ship, she was sealed down and gas was pumped through, a fairly regular procedure which was ostensibly to get rid of the rats and other vermin. I was personally convinced that the rats could be seen following us down the gangplank with their little sea bags over their shoulders ready to return on board once it was over, but never mind...

I used the opportunity to nip down to London for a night. Back in Liverpool we dry docked her for a couple of days for final inspection and I was back to London again on Friday 15th, returning on the Sunday. This time Libby came with me (minus Nicholas) and we drove back up to Liverpool and stayed in the St. Winifred Hotel in Bootle, which was conveniently near to the ship. We enjoyed a few jaunts from here, visiting Libby's godmother Auntie Marion in Chester on one day. She too had been a Canadian Pacific 'candy kid' in the 1920s and had married a Purser (she it was who had been staying with the family in Glasgow on the occasion of my first, memorable visit). After this enjoyable break together we drove back to London and I then travelled north once more. On my arrival in Liverpool I was informed by Captain Burns, the General Manager of Canadian Pacific, that I was to be appointed to the *Empress of Scotland* as Staff Commander. I had had an inkling of this from Slim Miller, whom I had relieved as Chief Officer and who was now Staff Commander of the *Empress of Britain*, so when I was summoned to the Liver Building and was told what was in store for me, I was not taken altogether by surprise. I have to say I felt rather lukewarm about the idea. The *Empress of Britain* was, I felt, very much my ship. I had been in at the birth and had worked my way through the ranks of Second Officer, First Officer and now Chief Officer with her. The idea of being a Staff Commander did not really 'turn me on' at that stage in my career – I had always said that if I could miss out a step on my way up the ladder, then this was the step that I would choose to forego. As Staff Commander most of one's duties were with the passengers and did not involve much seamanship. I still, rather ignorantly, regarded passengers as no more than self-embarking freight and whilst I was quite happy to drive them safely from A to B, I really did not want to have anything further to do with them. However, this was, on the other hand, a considerable promotion – a brass hat job and with the flagship of the Fleet. Captain Burns informed me that Captain Keay was also being transferred to the *Empress of Scotland*, and in all likelihood he had asked for me to join him as his Staff Commander because he felt I could fill in the social side which he chose to avoid wherever possible.

It was a challenge and, in addition to everything else, I knew that I was going to face a difficult situation: the Chief Officer currently serving on the *Empress of Scotland*, a Canadian, was at least twenty years older than I was. He would obviously be expecting the job himself, and would find it very hard having to take orders from a young whippersnapper like me. I was at the time only 31, and extraordinarily young for such responsibility – as far as I knew it was the youngest ever appointment to this rank. However, it was a situation I knew I could not avoid and it would have been churlish to turn it down.

Chapter 24

So with some reluctance I left the *Empress of Britain*. I spent the next two days handing over to my relief, Godfrey Palmer, who had arrived in the *Empress of France*, and then went home for a little embarkation leave (we managed a trip to Frinton) before joining the *Empress of Scotland* on her return from the West Indies. The job took some settling in to, not least because of the Chief Officer felt, as I suspected, affronted and had offered his resignation when I was promoted above him. Eventually he was persuaded to stay and it was promised that he would be moved elsewhere after one more voyage. He remained, but reluctantly. I had a chat with him, explaining my own feeling of embarrassment but suggesting that we both had a job to do and assuring him that I would not interfere with his if he did not interfere with mine. In fact after a few days he mellowed somewhat and things settled down.

I was familiar with the ship, of course, having sailed with her before on cruises and suchlike and there were no problems in that respect. I had also had my table as Chief Officer on the *Empress of Britain* and was accustomed to that procedure. In other respects, however, routine was very different. We made rounds every day with heads of departments, inspecting the accommodation in the cabins, and one was required to join the passengers' evening entertainment. I admit that I found, to my surprise, that I quite enjoyed myself. It was certainly different and I was not engaged in much 'sailorising', but at least I was at sea and the passengers were on the whole good company. They were a mixed lot, of course: Brits who were emigrating for the first time to start a new life in Canada; service people going to take up appointments; business people who travelled regularly to and fro (many of whom were Canadians) and also Americans who were taking the 'scenic route' home. Unlike the new purpose-built *Empress of Britain*, the *Empress of Scotland* was a pre-war vessel with much more space and accommodation allocated to first class passengers. Tourist passengers (who numbered some 500) only had one lounge and their deck space was also somewhat limited, whereas the first class (some 450) had a sitting room, bar, card room, a ballroom for dancing, and the whole of the boat deck and most of the promenade deck for perambulations. This strong social divide had been broken down in the new post-war ships, which had one communal ballroom for all passengers and a cinema open to both, reflecting the new more popular approach to sea travel. The entertainment on offer was never terribly exciting – after dinner bingo followed by dancing (first class one night, tourists the next with the orchestra moving from one to the other) and did not compare with the style of entertainment enjoyed by cruise passengers. I suppose we were halfway between eras at that time. Over the next few months we began to 'step up' the entertainment, as air travel was now becoming increasingly popular and more reliable. It was what I refer to as the third battle of the Atlantic, with all passenger companies fighting to retain their numbers. Of course in the end the air won, and passenger traffic across the Atlantic became a thing of the past. However, we were at that particular time in the business of encouraging passengers, and therefore set about making the whole thing much more fun, with entertainment more akin to the 'Butlins holiday-camp' style of a cruise. It soon became apparent that the chap responsible for much of this had to be the Staff Commander. On cruises we carried a Cruise Director, responsible not only for managing shore visits for passengers but also for passengers' entertainment on board. There was no such person on the North Atlantic runs, but the only person with the wherewithal and authority was myself. There were advantages, of course, to the Second in Command taking an interest and being seen to watch out for the comfort of the passengers; his personal intervention set a good example, particularly to junior officers. Developing a relationship and gaining respect from passengers would also bode well in the event of disaster, when the passengers would need to be instructed clearly as to procedure. Much of the effort which went in to keeping them happy was in actual fact a subliminal attempt to prepare them to accept my command when it might become necessary. This was particularly true of American passengers who on the whole would not readily accept authority and discipline as their British counterparts might. Being young was also a great advantage: I could happily dance the night away and still be chirpy in the morning. If one was around when dances were over, one could also ease the transition to bed and prevent any disturbance or noise that might otherwise disturb other sleeping passengers. I was on a fast learning curve, and I worked hard to justify my promotion. I had a feeling that the company had deliberately sent Captain Keay and myself to the *Empress of Scotland* as a good team. He found any excuse to avoid being at table with the passengers and relied on me to keep socialising and ensure that they were all kept happy. We were both, I think, somewhat surprised to find ourselves on board following time spent on the *Empress of Britain*; the *Empress of Scotland* was beginning to show her age and did not compare favourably with the new ship. Our journey also differed somewhat. From Liverpool we did not go straight to Montreal but went first to Greenock on the Clyde to embark Scottish passengers, calling there again en route home. It was nice for me, since Libby would come across if she was staying in Scotland and would sometimes lunch at my table with the passengers before we sailed. Coming in she would join us for breakfast. As we pulled out of the Clyde she would drive the car to Clock Point and flash her headlights at us as we passed. When the ship was in port I had virtually no duties at all and was I free to get away to London after a voyage report to the Liver Building, and could maximise my time at home. Likewise in Canada I could confidently spend a full weekend with the Cumyns.

One of the compensations of being a large passenger ship was that we had an indoor swimming pool. Part of my daily routine was to go down at about 5 o'clock for a good swim before changing for dinner; we had always had the facility on the *Empress of Britain*, but now I regularly had the time to fit in a swim. The dancing provided good exercise too – I always made a point of trying to 'get things going' on the dance floor as part of my developing relationships with the passengers. It was important never to favour any one set, of course, and I had a sort of mental rule that if I had a dance with a pretty girl (of which there were precious few) I would give myself a penance of three old dears to push round the floor afterwards. In the bar I had a self-imposed rule of tomato juice when at sea, not wanting to set a poor example to the junior officers or to my passengers.

My table I reckoned to be a better one than the Captain's table, which naturally attracted the worst kind of snob. Mine was always more fun, and I always picked my guests with great care. We were given a list of V.I.P.s on any particular voyage but I chose largely to ignore this and would collect my own list and invite them as one might to a private dinner party. The longer I did the job, the more

Staff Commander on board the Empress of Scotland, *receiving a book from the Commonwealth Youth Movement.*

regular clientele I developed, with passengers who would request that they join my ship and whom I got to know quite well. I kept a log with notes on each guest, such as 'crashing bore', 'never again' or 'great fun' which proved a useful aid. The trouble was with so many voyages it was difficult to remember who everyone was. I would stand at the gangway as they boarded, with the Chief Deck Steward alongside me, and he was always able to fill me in with information on names and suchlike if I had temporarily forgotten, so that by the time they reached the top of the gangway I was able to pump their hands enthusiastically, say how nice it was to see them again and would they care to join me at my table? We were always the last in and last out, and always the table that made the most noise. The food was out of this world, akin to eating at the Savoy, and I was encouraged by the head waiter to order special food for one's guests. His crêpes suzettes were a performance in themselves, with flaming dishes at the side of the table and a team of acolytes hovering to hand him various implements to complete his creation. His name was Hartley and I confess I used to rag him a bit. He was once told by a passenger that he made better crêpes suzettes than they did at the Savoy. He would come and see me at lunchtime to find out whether I had any special requests for that evening's menu, and I would ask him which of his 'flaming puds' he was going to produce that evening. Poor Mr Hartley would cringe visibly at the thought of his delicate creations being referred to in this brutal manner. With all this high living at sea, I was always eager, once home, for a bit of plain home cooking, rather than the repeated diet of lobster thermidore and Chateaubriand to which I was subjected. I certainly needed my daily swim and regular dancing to keep my weight down! This I managed to do, still wearing the same uniform in my early thirties as I had worn when I was seventeen. This did not last into middle age, I regret to say.

There were various things that I believed in that I introduced: one was better communication. As we went up the St. Lawrence I would get on to the blower and broadcast points of interest to anyone who cared to listen. This was not excessive – I did not want to sound like a river boat going up the Thames – but I was aware that there were people on board who had never been up the St. Lawrence before and who might never do so again and who would have missed the several features had they not been pointed out. They seemed to appreciate it. 'Tell them all the time' was my motto, particularly in the event of delays. On one of our homeward voyages we were delayed because of the ice. Everyone could see the ice and could understand why we had slowed down. We were due to arrive in the Clyde on the Monday but it soon became apparent that we were going to cut out the visit to the Clyde and go straight to Liverpool to arrive on time, with a special train being laid on to take the Clyde passengers up to Scotland. Captain Keay was not on board on that particular voyage, but I went to the relief Captain and suggested that we had to inform the passengers at once. One has to remember that it was not just a case of being mildly inconvenient for the passengers that they were not going to disembark at the Clyde, but that they also had relatives and friends coming from all over Scotland to meet them at Greenock; some, indeed, may well have been away from home for many years. If we were to delay telling them of the re-arrangements it would probably be too late to do anything about it; were we to explain now, they would still have time to radio home to those who were due to meet them. But I was unable to persuade the captain to take this course of action: 'No, no,' came the reply. 'We'll wait and tell them on Sunday.' I tried to explain, but the anticipation of a riot on the part of the passengers on hearing the news meant that they delayed informing them for as long as possible. It was Sunday evening before the news broke, and then there nearly *was* a riot, with angry Scotsmen threatening the pursers. I tried to elicit the support of the passengers bound for Liverpool, whose potential delayed arrival time had been averted by our change in course. The incident was certainly a great lesson in P.R.: always keep the passengers informed if there is a possibility of trouble. If it doesn't happen, then you're laughing, if it does, then forewarned is forearmed. This is something that has not happened in various marine disasters, where passenger ships have caught fire or have had to be abandoned. In order not to frighten the passengers, those in command have delayed in calling them to the lifeboats in case it might cause a panic, and the result has been even greater panic and, in some cases, the loss of life. I am sure that had I been allowed to broadcast the information about our change of course as soon as it had been decided, in an appropriately conciliatory and understanding manner, then we would have had much less trouble.

The 'stepping up' of passenger entertainment on our North Atlantic service to a standard more akin to cruises had, of course, to be commensurate with the prevailing weather conditions. However, over the next few years we improved our entertainment facilities quite considerably. This included the introduction of a series of activities for children, who would very quickly get bored with the ship and would start to run about and annoy. Providing distractions for them not only made life easier for other passengers but also endeared one to their parents. I would take the children off their hands for an hour every morning, for a period of activities, which varied over a three-day period. The first day comprised indoor games (party style games such as passing an orange under your chin, or games of dice with forfeits); this was followed the next day with outdoor sports on the promenade deck (these included sack races, wheelbarrow races and egg and spoon races). I would organise these games as 'Uncle Robin' with a team of junior pursers, both male and female, to ensure all was well. The third day was a bit of a risk, as this took the form of a treasure hunt. The children were given a list of items they were to collect and bring back to me – all harmless, small items such as a paper clip or a book of matches – with a prize for the first one home. Although I did try to organise the list to include things they could collect without disturbing the other passengers too much, and although it never required them to find their way to the engine room or suchlike, they were nevertheless swarming excitedly about the ship. However, most passengers seemed to be very sympathetic to the fact that activities were provided to keep the children amused, in particular the young mums who were at last able to relax, leaving young Willy and his grubby little sister to be looked after by me. Again, I feel it was of benefit for a senior officer to be seen to be taking an interest in the welfare of the younger passengers, rather than just being seen as a figure of authority.

Another activity popular with passengers was a tour of the bridge, which took place twice a day – once before lunch and then again at about 4.00 p.m. We could manage a party of about fifty, again if the weather was favourable, and they were able to peer into the radar, learn how the ship was driven, find out about safety mechanisms and generally see how things were done. It was another good chance to develop strong relations with the passengers and I was the only officer free to be able to undertake the task. I cannot claim responsibility for all of these innovations, which were also happening on other ships with other Staff Commanders, but I suspect that as the young one, I approached the prospect with more enthusiasm and more imagination. Some of the more senior (in years) would perhaps not have been quite so keen as I on the idea of getting down on all fours to play bears with the younger passengers.

In the evenings, in addition to the usual dances, we introduced a highly successful night of 'community singing'. This appealed, in particular, to the elderly passengers, who would fill the Empress Room. The orchestra would play and although I cannot sing terribly well I would endeavour to lead them in rousing choruses of 'Old Macdonald Had a Farm' and 'She'll be Coming Round the Mountain'. On one trip the Chief Officer, who happened to be a good pianist, would lead a hymn singing session on a Sunday evening, which again proved immensely popular.

Other forms of amusement included a cinema, dancing, and bingo. We tried fancy dress but this was often problematic as there was a limit to the costumes people could rustle up. However, we did have more success with fancy hats. One highly popular sport was 'horse racing'. This had been successfully tried and tested on the cruises and was now introduced on the North Atlantic run. The race was undertaken by girls, with six girls to a race. Each girl held the end of a line of binding tape, some 12 feet long, in one hand and was given a pair of curved nail scissors. When the race began, the girls had to cut up the length of the binding tape with the scissors and the first to reach the post at the end was the winner. Should they, in their excitement and haste, cut the tape completely, then they were considered to have 'fallen' and were out of the race. Betting took place, and each girl was given a name ('Hungover by double gin out of late night' is one that springs to mind) and an owner, which could be either an individual or a syndicate. There were five races and the winners were then auctioned and the money raised for the auction then became the selling plate. It was all great fun – and guess who used to be the Commentator, Master of Ceremonies and Auctioneer? I would rise to the occasion by dressing up – sporting a moustache that made me look rather like Raymond Glendenning, with a grey top hat, thick horn-rimmed spectacles and raincoat, completing the get-up with a pair of binoculars around my neck. This activity took up an evening and took the place of dancing, on occasion.

Similarly I used to compère fancy dress parades, always dressing up myself 'pour encourager les autres'. I am sure some of my older colleagues felt that such frivolity was beneath their dignity but not only did I enjoy myself thoroughly, I also held fast to the belief that it was necessary to come down off one's high horse and show willing if

Leading by example. In fancy dress on board the Empress of Scotland.

you want other people to join in. It certainly worked, in my experience.

On Sundays we always had a church service, taken by the Captain, or by the Staff Commander if the Captain was unavailable. It would not have made any difference if we had had the Archbishop of Canterbury or Cardinal Hume on board: it was a function that was always carried out by the ship's senior officers as a non-denominational, ecumenical service. Sometimes the Captain and Staff Commander would split the job in two, rather like vicar and curate, with the Chief Officer or perhaps one of the other officers reading the lesson. I used to enjoy this too, and it was always very popular with the passengers. Other than this, Sunday was always a bit of a day of rest as far as entertainment was concerned, except for the hymn singing mentioned earlier which we introduced in the evening and which seemed to strike the right note.

On other days of the week, at 11 o'clock each morning, the Chief Officer, Chief Engineer, Chief Steward and Purser, Second Steward and myself would meet on the main square and set off on the tour of inspection of the ship. Each deck that had passenger accommodation and the crew's galleys down below were inspected by this team every day. We would split the job between the decks and swap decks every day, so that in the course of the voyage you would cover all the ship, from top to bottom. We were pretty damn thorough about this task, going into all of the cabins (not, of course, if they were occupied), literally running our fingers along the top of ledges and suchlike to ensure that the cabin was always in first class condition. The inspection would also cover all the store rooms, where enough food was stored to feed over 1400 people for a week or a fortnight: I particularly recall the sight of little rows of haggises (haggi??) sitting there all plump and round and awaiting Burns' Night, in addition to the great sides of beef and the like which hung in the cold stores. In the First Class accommodation, passengers were afforded the cream of the stewards and stewardesses as well as the top waiters. This was what I would describe as real old English butler service: the allowance, on the *Empresses*, for each First Class passenger, was *twelve* clean towels a day: if you washed your hands after breakfast and then went up on deck, there would be a fresh towel in its place by the time you returned. In the evening (this was still a time when people would change for dinner) *his* dinner jacket, shirt etc. were all laid out ready; *her* dress (ironed, if necessary) would be laid out on her bed in preparation. You could ring a bell at any time of the day or night and arrange a cocktail party in your cabin, with special little eats laid on for you. They were very proud of their tradition of service; some of the stewards had been doing the job for many, many years and many of the passengers would return time and again. Before embarkation we used to do an inspection, for which the stewards would have been up before dawn, preparing the cabins for the passengers' arrival. As an inspecting officer I found that it was necessary to do the job as thoroughly as possible; the stewards would seem almost unhappy unless you turned up a piece of dirt somewhere or asked why something wasn't straight. One developed a certain 'sixth sense', rather like Customs Officers, I suppose, and would be able to spot immediately if something was not quite right as soon as I had entered a cabin. In the dining rooms, the First Class waiters were excellent. The Captain's steward (or 'tiger', as he was called) looked after his table, and my steward looked after mine, and these were the only tables they looked after. I always got excellent service, since they knew full well that their fate was in my hands when it came to tipping. They could take an order for ten people without ever writing it down, and you could be sure that when the food arrived, everybody got exactly what they wanted. This service extended to breakfast (although several passengers would not attend) and they would remember every detail of the various instructions for cooked eggs, or texture of toast, without ever having to be told twice. They really were the cream of their profession and it was a joy to be served by them.

This type of service is something that will never come back again. Those last three years that I spent at sea were almost in the twilight of the North Atlantic passenger runs. Although there are still a few ships today offering such voyages, most now spend the majority of the time cruising. All our stewards and waiters then were British, brought up in the tradition of service that characterised the nation, and never to be replaced.

Come September I found that I had three-week spell of leave due to me. I went off down to London and relaxed, needless to say, after the constant grind, enjoying some plain home cooking after the luxurious fare that I was subject to daily. Amongst other things Libby was an excellent cook, and I wanted for nothing when I was at home. Not being a complete old meany, I would take her out for dinner, too. It was during that holiday that our doctor confirmed that Libby was once more 'in the family way', and that Number Two was due to arrive sometime in May. We could only hope that perhaps this time I would be at home for the birth. Of course these days most fathers expect to be 'in at the kill', so to speak (rather an inappropriate expression, perhaps) but it was not so for a sailor at that time.

My leave was as usual over all too soon and I was back in Liverpool to re-join the *Empress of Scotland*. I was to have two more voyages in this ship and then, when she came in in December to prepare for her West Indies cruising, I signed off her and came back for another Christmas at home. The *Empress of Scotland* was in fact to be sold fairly shortly, to become the Hanseatic of the Hamburg Line, where she lost one of her funnels and was completely re-fitted out. For the Canadian Pacific, the *Empress of England* was now ready to go into service.

Chapter 25

This was an ideal opportunity for me to help the company by 'getting out of the way', being the most junior Staff Commander and now without a ship, and an appropriate time to get in some more R.N.R. service, which would keep me busy during the winter months. I knew there were plans afoot to have a Staff Commander in the *Empress of France*, which had not happened before, but meanwhile I applied to do the long, tactical course in the Navy. This took place at Woolwich and it was there that the big tactical trainer was situated. It has subsequently moved, and its permanent home is now in H.M.S. *Dryad*, just outside Portsmouth in Hampshire. As this is where the Navigation School is sited it does seem a more appropriate location, although at that time there was not sufficient room for it.

It was a very sophisticated piece of kit, with a series of simulators which had been built to train people in the skills of general wartime tactics. It consisted of a series of cubicles, each equipped like the Operations Room of a warship and each representing a different type of ship. Once in the cubicle, you had complete control. There was a big plotting table, where a wren plotter was provided; there were communications; there was a wheel and revolution counter so that you could steer courses and alter the speed of your 'ship'; and there were radar displays aplenty – in fact all the paraphernalia you would expect to find in a warship. All this information passed through a controlling console and was displayed on a large screen where the 'battles' were displayed in full. We played convoy games, torpedo attacks, and coastal convoys. We played with ships that already existed, and we also looked into the future with ships that we did not yet actually have but which were planned, to see where they might slot in to the general picture. Whatever you did in your cubicle was not only relayed to the screen outside, where it would be assessed by the controlling staff, but also interacted with the other cubicles: in other words if you were in a submarine and you stuck your periscope up, that periscope would show up on the radar of one of the other cubicles if they were ships within range. Remembering that radar can be detected at twice the range at which it can itself detect, it was important either to keep your radars off to avoid detection, or switch them on for a brief scout around in the hope that no one would detect you whilst you did so. It was just like real life, with one notable exception. In order to speed up the process, it was possible for the control to go to 'four times action speed', which meant that if you were travelling at, say, twenty knots, it would be translated into eighty knots and you would whizz across the screen at speed. This would be in order to bring you rather more quickly to the next 'incident' which would be fed into the arena by the controlling staff. Communications were radio-telephone (R.T.) and again, just as in real life, you were able to speak only to those who were within range. If anyone used the wrong procedure it would be blocked, and of course if you did start transmitting when you were supposed to be observing radio silence, then the enemy could pounce at once. It was a marvellous piece of computerised equipment which was used not only for training purposes but also as a mean of analysing battles past, present and yet to come. I was one of the very few R.N.R.s on the course, which included people of various ranks, amongst whom were some very senior Captains, who had been behind desks and the Admiralty and were about to go to sea again. Every day, within our cubicle team, we would share out the various jobs: someone would take command, someone would take the role of Navigator and someone else would look after the radar, etc. Some of these old boys were a bit out of date with their phonetic alphabet, which had been changed several times since the last war (primarily to make it more useful for foreigners and for use by N.A.T.O. and suchlike). On many an occasion they would pick up a microphone to make some sort of broadcast with the old 'Able Baker' rather than the new 'Alpha Bravo', which would immediately be blocked by the strict control. This would result in flared tempers and cries of 'Well what the bloody hell is 'A' nowadays anyway?'

It was, all in all, a fascinating course, which certainly kept me busy and amused during the winter months, with the added advantage that I could spend time at home. Whether or not it would prove useful rather depended on whether there was to be another war or not, but it did at least sharpen up my plotting skills. The course lasted ten weeks and a little time after that, on 31st March, I went to join the *Empress of France* as Staff Commander.

There were a few notable differences from my last appointment.

For a start, this was a new appointment for this ship, and there was no accommodation available. This they overcame in two ways: there was some shuffling among the normal Deck Officers' accommodation, the Fourth Officer was moved to another cabin and everyone moved around, with the First Officer giving up his cabin to be the Staff Commander's sea cabin. It was not a very large cabin, and certainly did not compare to the palatial space of the *Empress of Scotland*, where I had enjoyed *en suite* facilities and room enough to entertain. I was also allocated a First Class cabin on A Deck, should I find it necessary to be down below. In actual fact I found this rather inconvenient, being situated miles away from the Bridge and the other officers, and only used it on rare occasions. Otherwise, my duties were much the same. Given that I was the first to hold the post, I was able to stamp my personality more on this ship than on ones that were used to having a Staff Commander.

On our return to Liverpool from our second voyage, it was pretty well 'launching time' for our sprog number two. I came down to London on the Wednesday and Libby gallantly met me by car at the station. At 2.00 a.m. the next morning she announced that things were starting, and I drove her at once to the nursing home. Nothing actually happened then, nor did it happen the next day. I was due to leave on the midnight train from Euston, but our doctor swore that it would all be over by then. I thus spent the entire day in the nursing home, waiting with bated breath. My vigil continued throughout the evening, but by 11.30 p.m. the doctor finally admitted that nothing was going to happen, and then drove me in his car to Euston! Number two son, Christopher, literally popped out at 1 o'clock the following afternoon, by which time I was on board and embarking passengers. Libby was able to speak to me on the telephone; both were doing fine. I had missed the birth but at least this time I had actually been aware of the event as soon as it happened.

I did not actually see Christopher until my return home, but I had three weeks leave due and was then able to spend time getting to know (as far as is possible with a baby) my second son. We had at one time thought that it would be rather nice to have one of each – a boy and a girl – but Nicholas had been such a success that we were quite content to have another boy, and it would obviously make life easier later on in terms of accommodation in a small house. I spent the entire three weeks in London, and much of my time was spent painting things, either in the garden or in the house, and of course

The Empress of France.

taking out the various members of my family for airings in the park. It all went too soon and I was back on Thursday 26th June to Liverpool and Staff Commandering.

Whilst in Montreal on my next trip, I was invited to stay with some friends at Nolton, south of the city, where I was taken out riding. I had not sat on a horse since 1939 (we are now in 1958) and, although I knew what ought to be happening and how it should all work, I found rather disconcertingly that nothing that I wanted was there – I had no grip in my knees at all and I was in the rather embarrassing position of having no control, so that when we moved into a canter I found myself having to hold onto the pommel of the saddle with one hand to prevent myself from falling off. My friends were happily leaping over five barred gates, but there was no way I was going to attempt jumping anything at this stage. Clearly the muscles you use as a sailor are not those you need to ride a horse! I have to say I was not to try this in Canada again – although I did get on a horse once more when on holiday in Spain.

Life on board the *Empress of France* was much the same as on other ships, with a similar routine for the trans-Atlantic runs. She was still of course of the 'old school', with relatively cramped tourist accommodation and rather more generous First Class quarters. I was

209

With Captain Keay, as Staff Commander of the Empress of France.

Nicholas and Christopher.

used to her sister ship, the *Duchess of Richmond*, in which I had sailed during the war and found that, with the exception of an additional radar, nothing much had changed. The end of October saw me back in London for another dose of leave and, on 8th November, we went to Guildhall to see father installed as Lord Mayor of London – the day before my 33rd birthday. On Monday, 10th November, it was the Lord Mayor's Show. We took Nicholas, who joined Libby and me on the Mansion House balcony, although this was not really good enough for Nicholas who wanted to know why he could not travel in the golden coach with his grandfather. In the evening, we attended the Lord Mayor's banquet at the Guildhall. Traditionally, of course, Lord Mayor's Day was 9th November, but as this had fallen on a Sunday it had been transferred to the following day. This was the last time that the Show was to take place anywhere near 9th November, since it was decided (as with Armistice Day) to move it to a Saturday in November to make it easier for the traffic. It slightly lessened the significance of my birthday but was on the whole a good move, and did allow more children to come and see the Show.

Mother and Father were now installed in the Mansion House, which was very nice for them. At the time it did not occur to me at all that one day I might find myself as occupant, too, since I still thought, at this time, that I was going to be a sailor all my life.

That week was a very busy one. On the Wednesday we christened young Christopher; this was rather late in the day, since he was now nearly six months old, but we had held him back because we had wanted him to be christened from the Mansion House by my father's chaplain. The only difficulty was that he was to wear the family christening robe, which every Gillett had been christened in since time immemorial, and he was getting rather on the tubby side for it. With a few minor adjustments, however, we managed to squeeze him into it and he was duly christened. One of his godfathers was, in fact, Sir Rupert de la Bere, who had been Lord Mayor when my father was Sheriff.

Chapter 26

On the13th, I caught the train back to Liverpool to join the *Empress of England* as Staff Commander. She was very similar to the *Empress of Britain* so there were no problems finding my way about her. For the first time I was now able to enjoy the full glory of a proper Staff Commander's accommodation on a new ship. Basically the Captain and the Staff Commander lived underneath the Bridge, one deck above the rest of the officers. It boasted a very large day cabin and a separate night cabin, *en suite* bath a shower and separate loo. The Captain's tiger and mine shared a cabin on the same deck and were at our immediate beck and call and we had our own little bit of deck outside where we could sunbathe. The Captain was Captain Bell, whom I had sailed with before in the *Beaverlake*; he was, I think, somewhat wary of my approach to entertaining the passengers – probably due to the fact that the house magazine had published an article about my antics, complete with photographs with me dressed up as a pirate and in my auctioneer's rig. Whether he was a little envious of the rapport I am not sure, but I decided to play it fairly cool to begin with. Eventually he came round and did not seem to object too much, although I still think he suspected me of being on some sort of ego trip and engaged in an attempt to steal the Captain's thunder. However, he enjoyed meeting his passengers and was certainly not a recluse. We got on reasonably well, and with one of my best chums, David Jevons, as Chief Officer, we were a good team. We made one voyage to Montreal before the St. Lawrence was closed for the season, and it was then time to prepare for cruising. This year there was to be no escape. The plus side was that with no duties involved in the preparation I was able to come home for the whole of December, which happily meant yet another Christmas at home. Libby and I held the first of our Christmas parties for friends and neighbours, which were to become a Fairholt Street tradition in future years. Quite how we managed to get so many people into the house I am not sure, but by folding up an antique table and pushing it to one side we actually managed some dancing in the dining room and hall. My 'holiday' did not, alas, extend to the New Year and on Tuesday 30th December it was back to Liverpool and ready for the off.

On 2nd January 1959 we sailed from Liverpool to St. John, New Brunswick, where we disembarked passengers bound for Canada and embarked some Canadians joining us for the cruise. We then went on down to New York to collect the bulk of our cruise passengers, sailing at 11 o'clock in the morning on Wednesday 14th January. The first thing we always did on leaving New York was to hold a boat drill for the passengers. Broadcasts were made and everyone was sent up to the Promenade Deck for lifeboat drill. The doors were opened and the lifeboats lowered from the boat deck above so that the passengers could see where they should go. When the bulk of the passengers were British they seemed to accept this routine and the philosophy of women and children first (a bequest from the days of the Crimean War when the troopship *Birkenhead* was wrecked off the south coast of Africa; the troops all lined up and stood to attention whilst their wives and children were put into the boats. The men all perished with the ship.) They would dutifully line up with their lifejackets on (most being able to tie reef knots; the others being shown how) and with wives and children in the front row. I have to say this did seem to me now to be rather unnecessary: the rule about women and children had been introduced because it hailed from a time when there might not have been sufficient lifeboats for all; now there was room enough for everyone it seemed faintly ridiculous to put children in first, followed by the women and last of all the men, who would not then have been able to row. However, our boats did not require rowing, since they used what was known as Fleming gear – propellers that were manually rotated by a series of levers on alternate sides, which could be used by passengers of any shape or size. However, the Brits clung dutifully to the tradition and lined up in ordered fashion with women and children at the front. However, with the American passengers (who comprised some 75%) it was rather a different story. They did not really comprehend the concept of queuing and had to be sorted out by the crew into some semblance of order, and invariably assisted with their lifejackets. Then, having got them all sorted out in one direction and moved down the line to help the next lot, the first would then break rank and move all over the place, leaning over the side with ciné cameras and what have you, and then had to be shoved back into line again! I knew, from conversations with American passengers on the regular North Atlantic run, that the general feeling about British ships was that they were safe, but not much fun; people travelled in British ships (and aircraft, for that matter) for safety, but in Italian or Greek ships for fun. We were stuffy, but safe. I had learned to play on this, and once the junior officers had sorted everyone out and they were all standing in the right place, I would walk down the line, looking very authoritarian in full uniform complete with brass hat and, somewhere in the middle, I would stop and use my Chatham parade ground voice to bellow at them 'Do you all understand what you have to do? It's really quite simple. When you hear that horrible noise from the sirens, you come up here with your lifejacket and stand exactly where we have put you today. You will get into the boats, the boats will be lowered . . . and then we shall all row home.' At which point a few giggles and laughs would erupt – this touch of humour at the end seemed to do the trick and make me seem a more human figure. This was stage one in the masterplan to 'get them on my side': it was vital during the first three days of the voyage, before we had actually got anywhere, that I had got them into a position whereby if I was to give them orders and instructions there was a fighting chance that they would actually carry them out, because they respected me, liked me or whatever. So all kinds of little things were done to project the right image. At most of our ports of call, we were too big to get alongside and they would have to go ashore in boats (supplemented by shore tenders). They would all want to go first, none of them understood queuing and it was therefore essential that they were in a malleable mood so that I could restore some sort of order: the sort of state whereby I could have gone up to an American senator trying to pull rank and say to him with a nudge 'Come on now, Senator, I know you're just trying to get ahead so you can get ashore and find all the women!' at which his wife might roar with laughter, prod him and say 'Oh honey, y'hear what the Commander is saying?'. If such a remark had gone down the wrong way I would of course have been in dreadful trouble and it was therefore crucial that I felt confident enough to be able to joke with them and jolly them into waiting their turn.

We carried a Cruise Director who job it was to organise the shore parties and the entertainment on board. During the first three days, they would give talks on each port of call and I would get up and explain the routine with the boats, so there was plenty of opportunity for contact. There were also dances, at which I worked hard, really M.C.-ing the thing to make sure that they knew who I was. It worked, on the whole, and when they saw that you were trying to be helpful, rather than merely bossy, they were on your side. One great advantage was the great British accent, which immediately endeared me to the majority of Americans. They would approach and say 'Say something, Commander!' at which I would look puzzled and ask what it was in particular they wanted me to say. But I could say anything at all, and they would go away happy. Probably the most contrived thing I did in my campaign to win them over took place later on, when we got down into the warm weather. On a day when we were at sea, between islands, we would hold aquatic sports in the outside swimming pool. We had a swimming instructor who ran these sports, but I would be there in overall charge. There would be activities such as two people astride a greasy pole, hitting one another with pillows until one fell in; diving for spoons and other fun activities (the pool was not big enough for races) with a large spectator element. As part of my attempt to be a 'regular guy' (which I believe meant that as far as the Americans were concerned you were generally considered to be OK, not too stuffy and able to take a joke) I devised a scheme whereby at the end of Aquatic Sports, when I had made my formal closing remarks, I would be pushed in full uniform into the swimming pool. This was staged by one of the junior officers who would approach some of the younger passengers beforehand and get them to ask a friend to do the deed – but without letting on that it had been suggested, so that the person pushing would not know that *I* knew. I would wear an old uniform, with an old pair of epaulettes and a pair of white plimsolls, and an old brass hat, which I kept especially for the purpose. This was always a roaring success; those doing the pushing would inevitably tip off their feat of devilment to their chums who would come along armed with cameras; I would go flying into the pool and emerge shaking my fists in fake anger (but sufficiently fake that people would realise I was not going to close the pool for the rest of the voyage) and I was reminded of the joke at every possible opportunity for the remainder of the voyage (the question 'Y'all still wet, Commander?' did wear a little thin, but the resulting P.R. was certainly worth it). In a way (and without wanting to sound disparaging to any American readers) the American passengers were rather like children, not prepared to be bossed about but gently encouraged to do exactly what you wanted them to do. This was particularly true when they returned from their shore visits having indulged rather heavily in the local rum, and would want to engage in noisy parties or open the bars once back on board. I would stand there as they boarded, dressed in my full white regalia, with a telescope under my arm to make it look even more impressive, and look sternly at them as they greeted me with 'Hi Robin! C'mon up and a have a drink!' I would bark at them to get along, and off they went, giggling, to bed – just like naughty children.

Our routine on the cruise was generally to arrive in port at 7 o'clock in the morning and then leave again in the late evening. Passengers would go on shore where taxis and buses were laid on to take them on tours, or they could shop or what have you. We did not interfere but were on hand to offer guidance should they require it. Whether at the end they remembered all the places they had seen was uncertain: it was rather like the bus tours of Europe which offered 13 countries in 14 days (the 'it's Thursday, it must be Brussels' syndrome). Our first port of call was San Juan; from there we went on to La Guaira, the main port of Venezuela; then it was Curaçao by 7 o'clock the next morning, sailing again at 6.00 a.m. The next day was a whole day at sea (time for Aquatic Sports!). When not ashore, the passengers would need to be kept amused the whole time, and in addition to our water sports we had a Floor Show, for the evenings, as well a variety of galas, fancy dress, and even an Olde Englishe Fayre out on deck with games and prizes. The entrance fee would be donated to the Missions for Seamen, and we always succeeded in raising a respectable sum. From Curaçao we progressed to Panama; the next day was the Fayre; next day the Fancy Dress – and then we arrived in Havana. Things here had changed considerably from my last visit in 1952, when I was with the *Empress of Scotland*. Then, of course, it was under a dictatorship, but by this time the Castro revolution had taken place. It was, however, still at a time before things had turned sour with the United States (pre Bay of Pigs) and we were still visiting. Havana was our last port of call and one of the few places they stayed a little longer; having arrived at about 11 o'clock in the morning we then stayed until 4 o'clock the following afternoon, which provided the passengers with an opportunity to sample some of the night life for which Havana was well known. It was curious to see the place again; Castro having arrived with his young bands of bearded men (boys, rather) who were in evidence all over the city and who were at pains to give the visitors a good time. One of the most evident changes was when Customs and Immigration boarded. In days gone by a strict hierarchy of bribery had operated, with drink

217

and cigarettes changing hands as a matter of course in order to get the passengers on shore, but now they were accompanied by these young 'soldiers' (automatic weapons left at the bottom of the gangway) and one could visibly see the Customs and Immigration officials pleading with their eyes to the Purser not to hand over anything: had they been spotted accepting bribes it would immediately have meant the chop for them. Havana was always rather a strain for me and my staff since the passengers would inevitably get hopelessly drunk whilst ashore and dealing them when they came back on board required a certain amount of tact and diplomacy. Eventually, however, they would all be tucked up and out of the way, the pontoons hoisted and we could all breathe a sigh of relief as we headed north for New York.

At the end of each cruising season I would always receive a supply of Havana cigars which I would put to one side and which would last me for the rest of the cruising season. The captain and I would, on occasion, go ashore and visit some of the places where the passengers would be spending money and would not be averse to accepting the occasional gift on the assurance that our passengers would then patronise their shop.

Back to New York, where we did not stay for long; just time to disembark our passengers, send linen ashore to be washed and clean up the ship ready to embark the next lot... then we were off again, with the same drill and the same smiles on our faces. After that first voyage, we docked at New York at 3.00 p.m. on the Wednesday, had disembarked the passengers by 3.30 and sailed again on the Friday, for a slightly different trip in terms of ports but in all other respects very much the same. This time we started at St. Thomas in the Virgin Islands, sailed from there at 2 o'clock in the morning and had arrived in Martinique by 7 o'clock the next day; left at 7 o'clock in the evening to arrive at Bridgetown, Barbados at 7 o'clock in the morning again; sailed again at 7.00 p.m. and then – thank goodness – a day at sea. The boat routines were run by the junior officers. We carried a Sixth Officer for cruising, and the Third, Fourth, Fifth and Sixth Officers all drove the ships' launches. We had two special launches for cruising, in addition to our own two motor lifeboats and then we had back-up from the chartered boats from the shore. When I was a junior officer I used to find this rather fun, since I love driving boats but whilst the Second and First Officer kept anchor watch on the Bridge, the Staff Commander and Chief Officer controlled the movement of passengers into and out of the boats. This was a bit of a chore, but it had to be done, since the Americans were liable to slap great insurance claims upon the company if anything were to go wrong, such as a slip on the boat, either real or imagined – unlike the Brits who would be given a dusting down and say no more about it. Lawyers would be practically waiting for the American passengers as they disembarked, salivating and rubbing their hands together, and wanting to know if there had been any accidents. In order to disembark the passengers had to climb down the accommodation ladder onto a pontoon, which would then be lowered down to the boat, and they then had to be handed in. The quartermasters did the actual handling of them, although occasionally if the weather looked a bit dodgy I used to go down myself and help the blue rinses in or out of their boats. If something had gone wrong, and someone had slipped or, worse still, fallen in, there would have been hell to pay if a senior officer had not been present. On their return to the ship they would be laden with endless amounts of rubbish and I am sure that they would vie with one another to see who could spend the most. They would lay out their wares on the tables in the smoking room, itemising each piece and telling the gathered audience how much each one had cost. If we ever had bum boats alongside – something we tried to avoid if at all possible – they would buy with equal abandon, and in Haiti they came back with items such as bongo drums made out of uncured skin or small pieces of native wooden furniture which would be crawling with termites. Quite a lot of it was just left behind, in the end, but they just *had* to buy whilst they were there and the natives were certainly wise to the power of the almighty dollar.

To return to this particular voyage, our stop at Bridgetown and a day at sea was followed by a call to La Guaira again, in Venezuela, and then Curaçao again, another day at sea and then Christobel, another day at sea, and then Kingston, Jamaica, and then to my least favourite place which was Port au Prince, in Haiti. I have never seen a country that looked quite so inhospitable; Papa Doc was in power at the time and there was a brooding sense of evil about the place. I went ashore once, to have a look around and found it a very spooky place indeed. In fact I was almost shot on that occasion; some of our passengers had met up with a Haitian Air Force officer and they got drinking and arrived back late. They wanted to bring their new friend on board to give him a drink but the ship was ready and waiting to depart and it would have been impossible. So we had to refuse him, at which he unbuttoned his holster, pulled out his revolver and started waving it about. I managed to persuade the passengers to get on board, and calmed him down sufficiently to get him back in his boat and return to shore. Not a nice place.

Havana was then our last stop before the return to New York. Again we were there only for a day before leaving once more for the next cruise. A slight variation here: we went to St. Thomas, first off and then to Grenada, which was lovely. Here we had something of an incident; some passengers disembarked for the town, and then we had other boats leaving for a beach a little further down the coast with a bathing club. I went in one of these boats to ensure all was well, and on our return to the ship the engine broke down. We carried an engineer on board the whole time but a fuel blockage meant that we could not get the thing started. The tide was beginning to set us away from the ship, which was anchored off, and for the first time in my life I had cause to send off a distress flare, which I recall singed all the hair on my arm as I did so! The few passengers on board all thought it was frightfully exciting. Fortunately the Officer of the Watch was keeping an eye out and spotted us, and another boat was sent to tow us back. I was most relieved, as I was beginning to have visions of us floating off helplessly down the coast.

However all was well, and we were soon on our way to La Guaira. I took the opportunity whilst here to visit Caracas, the capital of Venezuela, which was a fascinating place, where grand modern architecture and fine boulevards lay cheek by jowl with squalid shanty towns. We were soon off again, to Curaçao and Christobel. Here the passengers would get a trip down by car or by bus to the other end of the Panama Canal. Kingston, Jamaica; Port au Prince; Havana and back once more to New York. There was time for one more 'quickie' two days later, which took us to St. Thomas, La Guaira, Curaçao, Christabol and Havana. And that was it, as far as that season's cruising was concerned. It was go, go, go all the time, and although I suppose had the advantage of being in the sun I did not get much sleep. I stuck rigidly to my no drinking rule whilst at sea, although when back in New York for a couple of days I would let my hair down a bit. Some of the passengers even invited us ashore and we would be taken to theatre or some such, by way of a thank you. We sailed from New York for England and home on Easter Monday. Three days out, we received a distress call from a small German freighter, which was carrying a sick crew member on board. We rendezvoused, lowered one our boats with the doctor on board and then took on board the patient, to take him back for hospital treatment. We arrived back in Liverpool on 6th April and proceeded to dry dock, for a routine annual re-fit ready for the North Atlantic once more. We had a cruise conference the next day with management to discuss the success or otherwise of the cruises and make suggestions for the future. I was given an award by the company for my idea of a questionnaire to be given to all passengers asking them their views on the entertainment on offer. I believe I got £25 for this, although in fact the questionnaires did prove very useful to me and enabled me to ascertain exactly what we were doing right and what we were doing wrong. Also, subliminally, it gave the passengers the chance to get off their chest any particular grouse they might have had. Another lesson in communications: always best to lance the boil, rather than letting it fester!

I was down in London in time to attend the Easter Banquet at the Mansion House. I had not, up until now, seen very much at all of my father's Mayoralty, having been away so much. I was, however, able to attend this function which was given for the Diplomatic Corps. Libby had, meanwhile, been doing quite a lot, because my mother did not enjoy very good health. Libby would stand in as 'Lady Mayoress' little realising that she was to go around the course again in years to come. However, it was to come in very useful indeed having had the opportunity for a 'dummy run', as it were. It was indeed good to be home once more in the bosom of my expanding family, with young Christopher by now sitting up and taking notice and Nicholas running around and chatting on quite happily.

By 16th April I was back in Liverpool and we were off on our North Atlantic drill once more, with swimming pool removed and dry-docking over. We went up to the Clyde, which we had taken over from the *Empress of Scotland* and then to Montreal, back once more on the 'ferryboat run'. On my next visit home for my blessed two days, I went to *Wellington*, the sloop lying at Temple Stairs, which was the Livery Hall of the Honourable Company of Master Mariners, for an interview there with a view to becoming a Member of the Honourable Company. By the time I was back in Montreal once more, the weather was beginning to hot up, and I spent a relaxing weekend with the Cumyns in Sennerville, well out of the way. There were two more voyages to Montreal to be had, and then, the next time I was in London, I hit the Bishop's Banquet at the Mansion House. This was the annual banquet that the Lord Mayor made for the Bishops and Archbishops of the Anglican Communion and it was certainly a bit of a bonus being able to attend.

And then back once again to Montreal, finally signing off the *Empress of England* on 7th July, when I was due some well-earned leave. My first week was spent in London, when young Nicholas made his first stage appearance, at the Adelphi (he was now three, going on four). He used to attend Miss Ballentyne's Dancing Academy just off Sloane Street, and was ushered onto stage as a Chelsea Pensioner with several other young hopefuls. This was, in fact, something that both he and his younger brother were to make a habit of (stage appearances, that is) in later life. After a week in London we went down to Frinton, which was most pleasant. We spent most of the time on the beach, and Libby and I even managed a dance at the Tennis Club on the Saturday night. We had by this time started on a series of *au pair* girls, who followed one another in quick succession but were all very good. The first two were Austrian, and then we had two or three Germans, two French, one Italian and two Spanish throughout the course of the boys' childhood. They lived with us as one of the family and proved a great help, coming on holiday with us and generally speaking being like big sisters to those boys.

Chapter 27

I returned to London by train on 22nd July, leaving Libby and the boys down in Frinton, and spent my first night at the Mansion House before catching the 8.30 train to Liverpool in the morning. It was now time to change ship, back once more to the *Empress of France* for my last stint as Staff Commander in her. We sailed on the Friday as usual – she did not go to the Clyde, now, but in all other respects the routine was the same. On my return home after that first voyage I went up to Glasgow, the *au pair* having flown up with Nicholas and Libby having driven with young Christopher and all meeting together at Busby House.

On my next voyage across the Atlantic we undertook another rescue at sea, this time taking a sick seaman off a small cargo ship (all very amusing for the passengers who were at the ready with their cameras) and bringing him on board. A couple of voyages later, during my home visit on 24th September, a party was held at the Mansion House to celebrate Nicholas's fourth birthday. About fifty children were in attendance, with a conjuror and all the usual trappings. It was a great success and a memorable occasion to be held in such auspicious surroundings.

It was in Montreal on our next voyage that we were to be specially chartered by the Canadian Ministry of Defence. We did not embark any passengers at all in Montreal, but went down to Quebec to embark Canadian troops on their way out to serve in Germany – it was almost like being a troopship back in the war once more. We took them to Rotterdam, where we arrived on 13th October, and sailed again straight back to Quebec with returning troops. This was one of the few times that I actually had time to go ashore at Quebec, which impressed me greatly. It is, of course, terribly French, and is dominated by the large Château Frontenac which is a big Canadian Pacific hotel. We sailed once again to Rotterdam with more troops, only making a diversion this time to land a sick passenger at St. John's, Newfoundland. My parents had both been to Rotterdam in the August of that year on a return visit to the Burgermeister who had previously been to London. On my visit this time the Burgermeister entertained me to dinner at the Châlet Suisse, where I spent a very pleasant evening in the company of him and his wife. It was then back to Quebec for a final troop run, before heading on up to Montreal. Here I was to learn the news that my father had now been created a Baronet, which was an excuse to hold what by brother officers referred to as a 'Sir' party. However, I am not sure that the prospect of my one day becoming Sir Robin Gillett meant that they treated me with any more respect than usual (or any less, for that matter). I discovered an interesting myth that was circulating in the Canadian Pacific, which I believe stemmed both from the knowledge that my father was Lord Mayor and from my background, which differed somewhat from the norm. I think they found it difficult to understand why I had opted for a career at sea, given the opportunities I had for gainful employment ashore, and they invented the tale that I was actually there for my health. It seemed beyond them to believe that I was actually at sea because I happened to enjoy it! I had been completely oblivious to this until I was having coffee with one Chief Officer one morning who happened to mention it in passing, and enquired further after my health. This came as a complete surprise to me, but it was also clearly something of a surprise to him when I explained that I was with the Canadian Pacific because I had always wanted very much to 'do my own thing' and prove to myself that I could have a career in a field that was completely alien to my predecessors. I can actually remember feeling quite annoyed with my father on one occasion when, out of sheer generosity of spirit, he invited the General Manager of Canadian Pacific to the Lord Mayor's Banquet. I felt quite offended and concerned that it might be seen as an attempt to influence my career, although I am sure at that stage it made no difference whatsoever. My reaction did, however, indicate my strength of feeling on the matter and my concern that I should be seen to be making my own way in life.

I took some more leave in November, prior to joining the *Empress of Britain*. This afforded me a very pleasant stint at home with my family, and on 22nd December we threw another of our 'young folks' parties, with twenty-six people at No. 4, Fairholt Street. I recall the occasion well. I was given Libby's permission to join my old friend Christopher Rawton, who was working for a firm of stockbrokers in the city, for his firm's Christmas do at lunchtime, whilst she and the *au pair* prepared for the party at home that evening. I had assumed it would be a fairly straightforward lunch but it turned out to be a pretty boozy affair, with a very good Christmas meal followed by ample supplies of port. Christopher's father-in-law, who was also there, then suggested that we move on to the pub across the road, where he bought another bottle of port which we saw off before returning to Christopher's office. By this time we were not feeling much pain, and it was getting fairly late – about 6 o'clock in the evening. Christopher telephoned his wife and asked her to phone Libby to let her know that we were running late but were now on our way. She refused, saying that I could damn well ring Libby myself! This I did and then we made our way back to Fairholt Street. I can recall climbing into a taxi, where I think Christopher fell asleep across my lap, clutching a pot of hyacinths which he had bought as a peace offering for Libby. When the taxi arrived at our house, we staggered out and were greeted by Libby, clearly not amused. I shall never forget the sight of Christopher sliding his pot of flowers gracefully across the parquet flooring! Christopher then departed and I was left to face Libby's wrath myself. I felt absolutely ghastly and took myself off upstairs to lie down. I took plenty of Alka Seltzer and washed my face thoroughly but I have to say I had not felt quite this bad since leaving H.M.S. *Flamingo*. The first guests were due to arrive at 7.30 p.m. By the time the front door bell rang I had managed to change into my dinner jacket. Looking quite green I slithered downstairs to greet them, with noticeably slurred tones. I have to say I did not much enjoy that party until I picked up again at around midnight. A night to remember, as they say.

I was fortunate enough that year to have both Christmas and New Year at home. On New Year's Eve our next door neighbours, Tony and Valerie Boydon held a fancy dress party to which we were invited. Just before midnight the *au pair* knocked at the door to say that there had been a telephone call from Scotland. Father-in-law was very ill and it was feared he might not live for long. We left the party hurriedly. Libby decided to fly up to Scotland as soon as possible and I booked her a flight for Saturday 2nd. That morning we heard the news that he had died in the small hours. I flew up with Libby, having warned my company and requested an extension of my leave. It was all terribly sad. We joined the rest of the family: Libby's sister Stella and her husband Richard, my brother in law John and his wife and Dorothy Anne who was a student at Glasgow

University and was living at home at Busby House. On the Tuesday the funeral was held at Paisley. Reluctantly I caught the train at 6.50 that evening to Liverpool and joined the *Empress of Britain* as Staff Commander at 2.30 a.m. the following morning. It transpired that I was coming down with the 'flu, and had to retire to my bunk under doctor's orders, which meant that I really did not contribute much at all to the voyage to St. John, New Brunswick. I surfaced again once we arrived there, but during the time that I had been lying in my bed of sickness, I had been reading a book on Lloyd's of London which had been loaned to me by the captain. I studied this with great interest, for it was now that my mind was turning more and more towards the possibility of leaving the sea. There were two strong reasons at that time for my change of heart. Firstly, I was getting increasingly fed up with the constant separation from my family, having been married for nearly ten years but having spent very little of that time with my wife. The boys would be growing up all too quickly and before I knew it would be away at boarding school, when I would see them even less. Secondly, I could see that despite all our efforts the passenger service was gradually going to be eased off the North Atlantic and, if we existed at all, it would be more frequent cruises. The company was beginning to expand into bulk carriers and tankers and I really could not envisage myself driving one of those all the way around the world with a Philippino crew: this was not what I had gone to sea to do. Libby had always said that I must not on any account leave the sea unless I found something that I wanted to do. It would not be enough to leave merely on her account, as in all likelihood I would spend the rest of my life blaming her and she would also feel very guilty. Having read the book on Lloyd's, it occurred to me that marine insurance might well be an area I could find of interest. I filed this away for the moment in my head, but resolved to explore possibilities further.

The cruise followed much the same formula as the year before, only with a slight change of itinerary. Havana had now been dropped from the list and we called at Nassau instead, but otherwise the routine was much the same – as were the passengers. One difference on this run was that Captain Dobson was excessively social and loved being with his passengers. This was all very well, although I recall one incident when on a North Atlantic run. We had been struggling through the fog all day and come the evening he called me up onto the bridge and asked me to hold the fort while he attended to his passengers at dinner. So I was left driving the ship through thick fog, while he went off to enjoy himself. He did not return until midnight, having spent time dancing the night away. He took one look at the weather and, deciding that it had improved enough, announced that he would now go to bed. I felt rather put out, at the time. However, on the whole he was good company, and with no fog in the West Indies no such incident occurred there. I mentioned to him my notion of Lloyd's and he expressed an interest in my thoughts on the subject. Other than this, I put the idea on the back burner until we had finished our cruising season.

One point of interest on this cruise: one of our passengers who embarked at Liverpool and remained on board for the whole season was George Formby, who was travelling with his wife, Beryl. He had been very ill, and it had been recommended that he take a sea trip to aid his recovery. They took the best suite on A Deck and remained with us for the duration, often taking a spot as part of the floor show in the evenings, with Beryl standing in the wings making sure that he did not overdo it! They were a delightful couple; he was a great raconteur and I can remember when I went ashore with them to Spritzer and Firman, the big jewellers in Williamstad. He wanted to buy a gift for Beryl, and was looking for a necklace to match a ruby and diamond brooch that she had. We were ushered into the manager's office, where he explained what he was after. An acolyte was sent off and brought in a beautiful piece of jewellery cushioned on black velvet, for Beryl to view. I was hoping very much that she would like the necklace, since it must have had a hefty price tag and a sale would elevate my standing with the manager even more. I myself had my eye on a couple of aquamarine earrings for Libby and was hoping for a good price. However, Beryl was not to be persuaded.

Another of George Formby's passions was collecting watches (he also collected Rolls Royces) and he asked to see some watches to hand out as presents to various members of the crew. He purchased a number of these, and then asked to see a rather unpleasant gold painted telephone that served as a gimmicky cigarette box: when you dialled, a cigarette was ejected from its insides, and a cigarette lighter was cunningly concealed in the earpiece. It also doubled as a musical box. I thought it a hideous thing, but George was fascinated, and took half a dozen. He then turned to me and said 'Would you like one, Robin?' I could hardly refuse but muttered something about there being no need to buy me a present. However, he would not take no for an answer and I dutifully carried the thing with me, presenting it to Libby on my arrival home with the words, 'Look what George Formby bought me!' Libby was unimpressed and refused to have the thing in the house, so it eventually ended up in my office.

We arrived back in the U.K. on Wednesday 23rd March and, as in the previous year, we went into dry dock. A post-cruise conference was held the next day and then I was able to get away and join my wife and family. I was in London until 7th April, before returning to Liverpool to recommence the regular ferryboat runs. During my time in London I took the opportunity to visit Lloyd's with Christopher Rawson's brother Sam, who showed me around. By this time I was pretty well convinced that this was something I would look into more deeply. I discussed my ideas with Libby, who was encouraging. I knew that I would have to start with a firm of brokers, although it was really the underwriting side of things that was of interest to me. After five years I would be able to become a working Name at Lloyds, which was where I wanted to be. It would mean starting all over again, and of course I could not expect a decent salary at the outset. As Staff Commander I was earning £1800 (not much by today's standards, but at that time a pretty decent salary – even a captain earned only £2500 a year!).

We to and fro-ed in the usual way – the two *Empresses*, both the *England* and the *Britain*, were doing the run now. It was nice to be back in the *Empress of Britain*, which I considered to be 'my' ship. By this time I had built up a regular clientele of seasoned travellers, who would choose their ship according to the personnel on board, which was always flattering, the only difficulty being that with so many passengers passing through, it was rather problematic keeping track of them all. With ten people at your table on every trip, it meant twenty people every three weeks. As soon as one lot were off and another lot arrived, the first would tend to fade from the memory. They would then re-appear, and fully expect you to remember them in the way that they, of course, remembered you. People used to ring up from Heathrow with greetings such as 'Hi Robin! Remember me?' and you used to have to think frantically to try and recall who on earth they were. I was even stopped in the street, on occasion, by ex-passengers who would recognise me. I would try and make myself learn the names of every single one of the 150 First Class passengers on every trip, so that as I bade farewell to them as they made their way down the gangway I could refer to them by name. Then of course I would have to clear all of them from my memory bank to get the next lot memorised.

Chapter 28

I suppose that there were many at that time of my generation who were leaving the sea for the same reasons that I was; wanting their home life but also realising that the career upon which they had embarked was going to change radically, if not pack up altogether. There were others, therefore, looking out for a job ashore, and we were all much like puppies in a shop window waiting to be adopted. At least three of my contemporaries had already been lured away with good offers, one going to the States and two to Canada, by employers who had seen them at work and felt confident in their abilities as prospective employees. Much the same thing happened to me. Crossing the Atlantic to Canada on one voyage in June was a married couple – a Mr Kingsbury and his wife. He was a Director of firm of Lloyd's Brokers and they were on their way to visit the firm's Montreal office. The Captain mentioned to them the fact that I had an expressed an interest in Lloyd's and during the rest of the voyage Mr Kingsbury made it his business to get to know me pretty well. On my return to London, Libby told me that there had been a telephone call from a Mr Kingsbury who would like me to get in touch with him the next time I was back in London. I telephoned, and was invited round to their office in the Minories for a chat. I discovered that although they were not looking for someone in the marine market, they were looking for an administrator and were about to embark on a round of consultancy with Urwick, Orr and Partners who had insisted that they must appoint someone to implement such recommendations as they accepted.

As with other important decisions in my life, swift action was required. My last life-shaping decision had been to join the Canadian Pacific, when I had given no thought to a career with the Merchant service. This time I had, of course, been reflecting for some while on the pros and cons of staying at sea, and wondering what I might do when I came ashore. Within a very short space of time I had resolved my course of action, knowing full well that such an opportunity might not come along again very quickly, if at all. The job satisfied my three criteria: it brought be ashore and offered the prospect of home life; it secured me in a job which was not likely to disappear as I feared my sea-going career might do in the next few years; and it was something that I felt I could do because all the training I had had at sea in terms of man management would prove ideal preparation for this position. With hindsight I was to discover that it was, in fact, a far better job than I might have hoped for had I gone into the marine insurance side of things. To be offered proper training to re-orientate myself was also a marvellous opportunity which might not be repeated.

I accepted in principle and duly wrote to the Canadian Pacific announcing my intention to leave the sea at the end of the subsequent voyage. On my next visit to Montreal I said my goodbyes to all my friends in Canada. We returned to Liverpool on 19th July, to find that there was a seamen's strike in progress. Amongst other things, I had been Treasurer of the ship's Sports and Social Club. All members of the committee of this said club were Communists, and fully signed up members of the Seamen's Union. When I once asked why it was they wielded so much power, I was told that it was because they were the only ones who ever bothered to turn out to the meetings. The same principle applied in the Social Club; it was always the extreme left who turned out to organise and run things. When the time came for me to leave the ship, they were all on strike. Nevertheless they all wanted to make a presentation to me and had subscribed to buy me a cocktail shaker. So a little deputation of them came up to my cabin, shuffling from foot to foot in uncharacteristic fashion and looking quite embarrassed. In my position as Staff Commander I was obviously the 'enemy', but they still seemed to like me and wanted to wish me well in my new job.

All three *Empresses* were now lined up awaiting developments and it was not until about a week later that they managed to find some sort of scratch crew to get things moving. However, this was my problem no longer. I said goodbye to all my friends, and had a lengthy interview with Captain Burns in his office in the Liver Building, who sought to dissuade me from the action I was about to take. It was almost seventeen years to the day that I had joined the company, and he outlined the promising career that might lie ahead, saying that I would get command within a year and stressing how hard it could be for sailors going ashore and how much of a shock it might be. However, his words could not deflect me from my decision.

When he saw that he was not succeeding, he then did a very generous thing for which I have always remembered the company. Many a ship-owner in similar circumstances would have quite categorically shown one the door with the order never to return, but far from that Captain Burns said, 'Look, we don't want to lose you, but it's your life and you must make that decision. But if you do find that it doesn't work out and you wish to come back, within a year, we shall pick up your pension scheme and your seniority and you will be welcome.' I managed to retain a very friendly relationship with them despite the fact that when my year's leave of absence was up I wrote to them to let them know that I was very happy in my new life and would not be returning to the sea.

My farewells over, I came down to London to begin my life as what some people would call a 'normal human being'. I had further meetings with Urwick Orr, the consultants and with Mr Kingsbury. The consultancy was to spread throughout the firm from top to bottom, in an attempt to shake it up and bring it kicking and screaming into the twentieth century. The procedure would take a year, and I was to be working with the consultant who was put in to do it, at the same time learning what made the firm tick. The next course at Slough did not commence until the beginning of September, so I had some 'de-mob' time to get settled into my shore state.

If I were to ask the question now, did I make the right decision? the answer would be an unqualified 'yes'. My predictions as to the future of the North Atlantic passenger trade came true all too soon, and within ten years of my leaving the Canadian Pacific had no passenger ships left at all. The *Empress of Canada*, which was slightly bigger than the others, was nearing completion when I left, and came into service but did not last very long. She and the other two were sold off to other flags and other companies, and the Canadian Pacific flagged out the remainder of its fleet to Bermuda. The company still existed in the form of the Canadian Pacific Railway, and the newly formed Canadian Pacific Airlines, although long train journeys were now being superseded by air travel.

Did I feel I had wasted my time? The answer would be an unqualified 'no'. The Navy that I had thought that I wanted to join no longer existed and I think that in the end I had the best of both worlds. The Merchant Service had certainly taught me more that would prove of use to me in later life than the Navy might ever have done, particularly in terms of dealing with people and customers as well as staff. I think I learned an enormous amount at sea, and gained responsibility very early on. Where else did one see one's superior at first hand under considerable stress and be able to learn from them at such close quarters. One learned to make decisions rapidly, at a very young age, which would inevitably stand one in good stead. Were I to have my time again now, I would not go back, however, since it would not be the same at all. I had been privileged to serve in the 'golden era' of trans-Atlantic travel, and I had seen something that will never be replaced.

I was also very fortunate in that I had not had to go around cap in hand searching for gainful employment. Libby need feel no guilt and I was happy in the knowledge that I was doing a job to which I was suited. The only person who had any doubts at all might have been my mother, who clung to the belief that I had thrown my career away. My only regret, perhaps, was that I never got command. But then had I waited for that, I probably would never have done all the other things in my life that I subsequently did. I think that I had learned enough of the responsibility without every having to take on the mantle and a captaincy would not have meant any more time off than I had had before, to spend with the family. It may well have completed my career, but then cadet to Staff Commander did not seem bad at all, to me.

The separation from my home and family had been a long one. For many years now, I had been serving full time, which meant no weekends off, and long, long periods of time away from loved ones. I think that sailors generally need a very understanding, and very good wife, prepared to be alone and strong enough to deal with all sorts of matters: financial, bringing up the children; deal with crises and make decisions without consultation. Nicholas was now of an age when he was beginning to question my absence, and could only partially understand why I could only be at home very occasionally. Now this was all to change. Gone were the days when I had to go and peep in to observe two little sleeping bodies as I left to catch the train to Liverpool to be away for yet another three weeks. There were to be many compensations to life ashore, but perhaps you really have to experience the other first in order to fully appreciate those compensations and not take life for granted.

Part Two

Chapter 1

Well, the fish was out of the water, hopefully not flopping about in its last throes on the beach, but in its new amphibious mode and prepared to take on the new challenges of the man. My life so far appeared to have fallen into approximately seventeen-year periods: the first growing up, the second at sea. Little did I think that this, the third, would see me achieve the highest civic office in the land.

As my course at the Urwick Management Centre at Slough did not commence until the beginning of September, Libby and I and the two boys took ourselves off to Frinton to enjoy a very happy holiday. This was punctuated by a brief return to London when Nicholas developed tonsillitis and had to go into hospital to have his tonsils and adenoids removed. I should point out at this juncture that we had always tried to avoid abbreviating either of the boys' names. We took Nicholas at first to the local doctor, who squatted beside him and said, encouragingly, 'Well, Nick old boy lets have a look at your throat,' whereupon his patient drew himself up to his full height and said with great dignity 'My name is Nicholas!' This peremptory interlude apart, all went well and we were soon able to return to the seaside.

On the 19th September it was off to Slough to start my course. We were accommodated at the Old House Hotel at Windsor from whence I drove to Slough each day and home each weekend, Friday afternoon to Monday morning. More time at home than between voyages at sea! There were twenty-five of us on the course, six being consultants under training, the rest from clients' firms like me. We were all from the middle management range and aged between about 35 to 40. The pace was pretty intensive with a considerable amount of homework and syndicate problem solving. Lectures were from permanent staff, working consultants and specialists visiting from outside. There was a retired Air Commodore amongst the trainee consultants with whom I chummed up as a fellow ex-serviceman. We had no difficulty with the man-management subjects but had to concentrate much more deeply with the accountancy, linear programme and similar subjects. We were both somewhat horrified at the lack of knowledge amongst some of the client students on personnel-type subjects which we took for granted and could tell by the sort of questions they asked what little experience they had had outside their specialist fields – no wonder the country was riddled with strikes!

The main course finished after six weeks and I stayed on for a further four to do the O & M course undertaken by all the consultants. This would prove very important in the job that I had to do assisting our appointed consultant when back in the firm, and I learnt techniques that I had never used before. Upon starting the course I was being paid £1300 per annum. I had been receiving £1750 as Staff Commander, but had fully expected to drop somewhat on starting a new career, and I soon made up the slack in the first few years. These figures look derisory nowadays but of course they are not compatible due to inflation. Looking at my expenses book for 1960, I see six gallons of petrol cost me £1.7s.9d. The Evening Standard cost me 1d and my lunch but £1 including a beer at 5/-.

The 28th November saw me enter the hallowed halls – my first day at work at the offices of Bevington, Vaizey and Foster. The consultant who was there already was one Bill Massey, with whom I was to work for the next six months. My father, who was perhaps somewhat outdated in his dress and who always insisted in wearing a morning coat and a white slip on his waistcoat for any board meeting he was taking, generally believed that those who worked in the city should look the part. He insisted on buying me a bowler hat – an item of dress which I had never possessed before – and also a rather nice dark grey overcoat with a black velvet collar similar to his own, for which he paid. Thus kitted out, and with my rolled umbrella and my new briefcase, I looked really quite the city gent as I entered upon my new career. How different from today when one never sees a morning coat except at Ascot or a funeral or an occasional city function. One is more likely to meet people walking the city streets in anoraks and sneakers these days, rather than the blue pinstripe suit such as I had underneath my overcoat. However, having been used to wearing a uniform for the last seventeen years of my life, dressing smartly was no bad thing as far as I was concerned.

The firm of Bevington, Vaizey and Foster was housed appropriately in Bevington House, a new office block built post-war in the Minories on the eastern edge of the city. It was five floors above the ground and was mainly open plan, with offices for the Directors only. It was an L-shape and as such not a very easy space for planning, with an awful lot of wasted space. The furniture, which was somewhat antiquated, had been brought from other offices during the war. The firm had been bombed out of one office in Fenchurch Street and existed in two 'make-do's' until they got their new building. The furniture was largely wooden for the typists or steel for the general clerks – only the Directors had fine pedestal antique desks to work from. There were approximately four hundred members of staff within the building, which was the totality of the organisation. The ground floor was largely occupied by a motor syndicate at Lloyd's, the Lion syndicate, and shared with the post room. Below them, in the basement, were a garage, the stationery stores and suchlike. The first floor housed the non-marine, and fire and accident department, the second floor had the Claims and Marine departments and a small sub-company doing business with North America and another one doing business with the Far East. On the third floor were the boardroom, the chairman's office and secretariat and the re-insurance department. On the fourth floor was the North American department (we did a lot of business with North America) and on the top floor were the accounts and policy departments. Bill Massey and myself were given a small office on the fifth floor, with a desk each. I rather amazed the 'Queen Bee', one Miss Lancefield, who was head of female personnel, by asking her for a typewriter. At sea I had always been used to doing my own typing – on a passenger ship the Purser's office might provide senior officers with a typing facility if they needed it, but it was certainly not an option in cargo ships – and I used to carry around a portable typewriter of my own in much the same way as I would carry round my sextant. One was expected to type any correspondence to head office, and it was therefore a necessary tool of my trade. I also found it a great time-saver; you were far less likely to be verbose and issue memos all over the place if you had to type them yourself, and you would either handwrite the instruction or ring somebody up, which saved a great deal of time and effort – something I was very keen on with my O & M training. Needless to say there was some surprise when I asked for a typewriter at the office. Anyway it was duly delivered and everyone was happy. We did not spend a lot of time in the office of course, as most of our time was spent out and about round the firm.

Christmas was fast approaching and I discovered that a Christmas review was to be put on by the staff – largely an opportunity to make fun of the Directors. The form was rather like that of the school play; it took place not far away, in the church hall of St. Olaf's, just off Seething Lane. I don't think I actually participated in it that year but I was quickly to be sucked in and found myself either writing material for it or doing little sketches. We also had a Christmas party for the children of the staff. This took place in the St. Bride's Institute, which was the largest room we could hire. Tea and buns were provided by some of the more elderly ladies of the staff and one willing member of staff would dress up as Father Christmas. Everyone got a present and we always hired a conjurer to entertain the children, and played games with them. I became involved very quickly by dint of my rich experience of this kind of thing in my role as Staff Commander on passenger ships. My own two boys were old enough by now to come along too and join in the fun.

Christmas festivities apart, the main thrust of our work was now underway. Bill Massey had worked out a plan for us to proceed with our investigations and one of our first tasks was to investigate the Fire and Accident department. We strongly suspected that: (a) their methods were somewhat archaic, and that they were doing things in a rather expensive 'Rolls Royce' way just for ordinary small customers and that (b) the firm was actually losing quite a lot of money by doing business at a loss. One of our remits was to ensure that the firm was profitable. Even if it might be the case now, nobody on the Board actually knew whether they could be *more* profitable or not. There was a degree of complacency that existed; Directors were quite happy to look at the balance sheet and congratulate themselves on making a profit, without appreciating that this profit could in fact be greatly increased by pruning out some of the unprofitable business. To some, indeed, such a view was an anathema: they considered that we were there to serve the public, never mind the cost. Nobody, in fact, knew just how much money was lost, because nobody actually knew how much it cost to do the business. This, then, was one of our prime tasks: to discover just how much the process of renewing a fire and accident insurance policy actually cost the firm and how much we got out of it. It was quite a mammoth job since there was no way of doing it other than carrying out sampling. We would have to find out, for example, just how many cover notes typists typed in a day, or a week, or a year or whatever and thus work out how much it cost to do that side of it; then find out who the document went to, who else dealt with it and look at what they were paid and how much of their time was attributable, and then ascertain whether the system could be improved. My job was to go round and sit down with everybody working in the department and get them to explain to me just what they did and what their function was and why they thought they did it that way. However, because they had been brought up man and boy to do their own particular job in a particular way, it was very difficult to get them to agree that what they were doing was a waste of time. They had invariably been told as a lad that that was how the job was done. It was as if the shadows of long-dead former managers were looking over their shoulders remonstrating, 'That's not the way I've told you to do it!' But we managed to engage them with a little bit of sympathetic chatting and also a degree of flattery provoked by our interest – after all, no one had actually bothered to ask them before *why* they did their job in a certain way, and to have some fairly senior person in the organisation come round and seek their advice, immediately made their job seem more appealing. However, it was a long, slow task. I used to draw flow charts in my notebook as I went along, rather like plumbing diagrams, which recorded where a document was going, where it had come from, where it moved, what was done to it when it was received, whom it was passed on to and that sort of thing. This diagram could then be analysed to see how many short cuts there might be and which part of the procedure might be superfluous. Wasted time correlated directly to wasted money.

So that was how my time was spent during my first few months with the firm. It was fascinating and immensely useful, because by the time I had gone through the procedure right the way through the firm I probably I knew more about the nuts and bolts of the firm's business than most people. This helped me a great deal later when I was to take on personnel, since I knew exactly what everyone's job was and what they did and when asked to recruit somebody I had a very clear idea as to what they would be expected to do and what was required of them.

Analysing the typing was quite a job because I had to assess the workload of every typist. The firm was forward-looking enough to have a typing pool, with lots of secretaries working for everybody. There was a 'queen bee' with twelve girls under her who allocated the work and ensured that everyone was kept busy. The completed typing was then fed back to the appropriate department. When we needed to look at their workload, every girl took an extra carbon copy of each document they typed. This sample was given to Bill Massey and myself, and then by finding how many lines of type there were we were able to work out the typing speed of each of the girls. It provided a fairly accurate estimate of how long it took to do a particular job and if you could time it, you could cost it – which we did. Having computed all our figures, we finally ascertained that the commercial business undertaken by the Fire and Accident department was fine; there was a lot of work involved but with big premiums the returns were good. However, 75% of their business was not with big commercial properties but was small domestic business – to which they would apply the same principles. The result was that it lost money. We worked out that the cheapest way you could do any piece of business, in the manner in which it was conducted, was £3/10s (as it was in those days). They even brokered it at Lloyd's, treating a policy for a small domestic residence in the same way they would a large factory premises. It should be pointed out that this practice was not uncommon and ours was by no means the only firm working this way.

When we finally presented these figures to Management (we reported as we went along at the end of each particular exercise) the reaction was varied: some were horrified and others just didn't believe it. And they seemed to think that the solution was to get more business: 'If we do more, then we shall make more money.' We tried to explain that the reverse was true. 'You'll lose more money; you won't make any more because it's going to cost us more. It's not as if we are a sausage making machine where if we make lots more of the thing it will be cheaper by the dozen. If you use a Rolls Royce system for the simplest things it will never pay. '

Fortunately the Chairman himself, who initiated the investigation, was determined to drag the firm – kicking and screaming if need be – into the twentieth century. His word was final.

We were Lloyd's brokers of course and placed a lot of our business with Lloyd's, but we also did business with the insurance companies as a lot of brokers do. The Eagle Star was quite a large customer as far as fire and accident was concerned. We approached them and they agreed to take all this little business off us, for which they would pay us a commission. They put it on to their computers (which we were really not big enough to have, at that time) which enabled them to do the work in a very quick, cheap way. Although the insurance retained its value, the process was more efficient and much more cost-effective. Eagle Star were happy to have the work, and we were happy to have the commission.

There was a further nonsense within the firm, which made the situation worse. To encourage the staff, they were given fifty per cent of the brokerage that we earned from any new business that they introduced. The net result of this incentive was that all kinds of rubbish was being introduced – insured items such as old Aunt Aggie's sewing machine and Uncle Jack's bicycle, on which the premium alone, never mind the brokerage, was small. We might, for example, get five shillings a brokerage on a particular case. Half of this would then have to be given to the staff member who had introduced the business, so we were left with half a crown for a job, which had cost us £3/10s to do. And we were actually encouraging this! The staff were quite happy of course. They didn't have to pay the costs and they pocketed half a crown, which was then lost to the firm. The practice was stopped and a limit imposed which meant that the brokerage for any new business had to be above a certain figure to merit the incentive payment.

We also looked at the system that produced all the paperwork, to see if there were easier ways of doing it. We knew that insurance companies were more streamlined – using computers or other highly mechanised systems to produce renewal notices and that sort of thing. So we devised a scheme whereby an offset litho master was produced for each type of document, with the information that was common to each document reproduced – rather than originating a new document every time the bell struck, as it were, which was the current practice. So when you wanted more copies, for instance of a cover note or a renewal notice, you just ran the master through the machine and filled in the gaps appropriately. Even doing it that way we only brought the cost down to about fifty pence from about seventy-five pence. It didn't save a lot of money but saved a lot on typing time. This meant that we needed to introduce the machinery to undertake this work. I hunted around to find out how it was done. In the printing room, where there were two girls, we installed an offset litho machine and got the process underway. Another benefit of having such a machine was that we could now also print our own stationery.

I was to be seen in those days always dashing around with my white lab coat that I wore around the office, which marked me down as an efficiency 'expert'. I remember one day going into the

Chairman's office with two pieces of paper, one that I had just printed on the offset litho machine myself, and inviting him to guess which of them had been printed by the firm's outside printers and which had been produced in-house. I'm glad to say that the one he chose was the one I had just printed which looked better than the one that had been printed outside at a cost! From that point we went into the printing business. These little changes were happening all the time. As we went through each department various things were mopped up: the filing system, for example, was converted from drawer files (dangerous when open) to lateral filing. These cabinets also acted as a kind of partition and provided a useful dual purpose.

They were already (I am glad to say) using Grundig tape audio machines for the audio typists although I did switch them to a sheet type, which were easier to pass around. Another common practice – in all the departments – were cumbersome 'failsafe' procedures. Such a mechanism is usually installed because once upon a time the Chairman might have asked for a particular piece of paper, which couldn't be found; to avoid such a mistake happening again an elaborate, foolproof system was put in place for all eternity. I always used to quote the story about the Tsar of Russia. When visiting some small town he had got very upset to discover that there was no train available to take him on to his next port of call. From that time onwards, right up until the revolution, an engine was kept in a siding, with a full crew and with steam raised ready, even though they was the very remotest possibility that the Tsar would ever visit the town again.

This was just the sort of attitude that prevailed within our firm, and it was evident in the use of Registers within each department. These were great expensive ledger-type books bound in leather. In most departments there was an old boy whose job was to register all the documents that came into the department and then, when they had finished with them, register them out again. It was a job that he had done, I suspect, since he was a lad. There were obviously various documents that moved about between the departments, for instance the slips that were taken away from the brokers from Lloyd's, and then were brought back to us, and then went up to the Policy department with the necessary papers where they were looked at them and then sent back down the department to be sent off to the client. Every time the document came into the department it was registered in, and every time it left the department it was registered out, with a time and a date on it. I enquired of one of the chaps who was doing this. 'What's this book you're filling in? 'Ah,' came the knowledgeable reply, 'This is the final register, it records when we send the final documents to the client'.

'And what purpose does that serve?' was my next question.

Evidently satisfied, he said 'Ah well we've got it down – we know it's gone, we know we've sent it off'.

So I said, 'All right – so it doesn't arrive. Say the dog ate it on the mat or the postman put it in the wrong letter box – the client hasn't got his cover note, his renewal is due – what are you going to do about it?'

The reply was 'Well we sent it, we can prove we sent it'.

I said, 'Yes I know we can prove we sent it, but he hasn't got it, he is the one who is on risk and he wants it'.

'Well', he said, 'He'll ring us up or write to us to say that he hasn't got it'.

'And what do you do then?' I said.

'Well we type out another one and send him that'.

'I suppose you register that one out as well?' I quipped, adding, 'And how often does this happen, how often does someone complain?'

Confidently he claimed, 'Very rarely! You see we've got the system'.

I said 'But the system doesn't actually get the document to the customer and the customer wants it, the customer needs it, he hasn't got it and what do you do? You do another one – so why don't you wait until he hasn't got it, and then tells you. He's not going to be impressed by you saying that you have sent it to him – he'll just want to know why it hasn't arrived. And he's the customer'.

'O, well . . . couldn't possibly get rid of this. Old so-and-so, he was very keen on the book, you know . . . ' And so on, and so on. They even registered each document amongst themselves. When a piece of paper went up to the Policy department, it was formally registered out to the Policy department who then registered it back again. It was a fine example of yardarm clearing, which cost both time and money and was not actually very efficient. And for the number of times it went wrong it would have been cheaper to buy the person their own insurance. Happily I was able to persuade them to get rid of some of the registers.

The mail was another area for concern. In the Marine department only the Directors opened the mail, insisting that all post came up un-opened onto their desks. In most departments it would at least be sliced open in the post-room before being distributed throughout the building but no, in the Marine department the two Directors sat there opposite one another with their letter openers opening the mail whilst about an hour of the department's time was wasted because nobody could get on with their work. Then the Directors actually wrote in a book themselves that they had received it, before parcelling it out to the appropriate recipients. And at the end of the day (and only the Directors were able to sign the letters, once typed), they logged the post out again. It's a wonder they didn't actually put the letters in the envelopes and stick the stamps on themselves!

Little things like this were happening all over the place. The essence of my job was really to ask fundamental questions about the nature of each man's work – it was no more that any intelligent human being with a questioning mind might reasonably do. I needed to know: why are you doing this job? What is the object of the exercise and, more importantly, what would happen if you didn't do it? Often the only reason given was that it had always been done this way. And there it was. And this kind of attitude prevailed in a hundred offices in the city. It certainly couldn't be afforded in this day and age.

We then proceeded to tackle the actual layout of the offices themselves. Unfortunately they had moved in without taking proper advice and had slapped up lots of partitions here, there and everywhere, without any thought given to the flow of work and paper throughout the offices. So I had a real go at that and reorganised it. Another of our major projects was the Accounting department. You will recall that I had run away to sea to avoid becoming a Chartered Accountant – I certainly did not aspire to accountancy by any stretch of the imagination. But once again it was a question of methodology, and finding out the easiest and quickest route to obtain the best results and the sort of returns you want. As in all other departments, there was no statistical information available; they did not know where their money came from and they did not know how much of it they threw away. The bookkeeping was done on national accounting bookkeeping machines. I don't suppose there are many still around or that many of my readers will remember them. They were like huge typewriters, which produced ledger cards, spreadsheets and what have you. These machines did not actually do any calculations – those were all done by the comptometer operator. A comptometer, a machine which has now vanished from the scene, looked rather like an adding machine but it had umpteen rows of buttons. The comptometer operators were worth their salt in the market and were very expensive. However, they could bang away on these things with about six figures at once, calculating premium and brokerage and suchlike. The results of these were fed to the people doing the book-keeping who again were a highly qualified rare breed and therefore expensive. The system did not actually produce any by-products, but just produced the accounts. We certainly could not afford a computer; these were the days when computers were huge machines, which took up acres of space in their own air-conditioned rooms and worked on valves and things like that. Even the calculators were large; the calculators on people's desks were hand driven. However, we thought that a punch card system would supply a lot of the information that we required. If you punched a statistical code into the card you could feed in information about the sort of business it was and where it had come from and then with your sorting machine you could sort the cards into the appropriate order and print out a list of your sources of premium or whatever, and in an instant get an overview of management statistics. When we eventually decided on a machine and we put in a punch card system, I went round to the managers and explained enthusiastically that now we had this marvellous machine we should be able to tell them much more about their business and where it was coming from and whether it was practicable or not. 'What statistics do you require?' I enquired.

They looked at me blankly. Clearly they did not know the answer as nobody had asked them such a question before. Why would they want to know such information? In the end I had to do it for them. Piece by piece I explained to them the kind of information that I thought they ought to know, and showed them how their people could feed in a certain code for each piece of information so that ultimately we could 'force feed' them with the answers and they would be able to see where they were going. But it was an uphill struggle. The Accounts department were very conservative in their views and reluctant to change. I recruited a team internally, not wanting to get in people from outside the firm, consisting of a comptometer operator, a girl who worked in the policy department, someone from the accounts department and a couple of typists. We all went off on a course – myself included, together with the assistant I had recruited by then from the accounts department, and we all learnt how to embrace the new technology. Those were the days of plug boards, and machines which, whilst not exactly steam driven, chuntered away to get their data and results. Speed was nothing compared to the instantaneous results of computers, but nevertheless, it was better by far than spending five weeks at the job, which is what it would take when sampling.

We were coming now to the middle of the next year when the consultant was going to finish. My role was then to remain behind and implement the recommendations that had been made. The consultants had in fact made one or two recommendations which affected the very top positions in the firm, suggesting that we ought to have a Managing Director to ease the burden carried by the chairman, who was acting as both Managing Director and Chairman and trying to run the underwriting agency as well. Personnel, at that stage, was being handled by the Company Secretary who was really far too busy to do that as well as his other duties. He was also supposed to be looking after the underwriting agency. The result was that none of the jobs were being done as well as they should be and recruiting was pretty haphazard. We were alright on the girls' side because the Queen Bee took care of them, but male recruitment was mainly left to the Company Secretary or individuals. This area was high on our list of priorities and it was agreed that it would be one of the things I would take over when we settled down.

Another aspect of working life at the firm was the attitude of office workers to 'manual labour'. I found it difficult to tolerate their attitude that such work was beneath them. If desks needed to be shifted, for example, or the office needed re-organising, they would expect somebody to come and do it for them. So it was a great surprise when they found me rolling up my sleeves, picking up the end of a desk and saying, 'Get hold of the other end and we'll move this down here'. It was simply the way I had always worked. Quite often I would come in at the weekend and persuade the clerical workers to do likewise. We would get paid overtime and in the end they found that they actually rather enjoyed it. It was a bit of fun throwing your furniture about! This was not something that I had learnt from the Management Centre, but had brought with me from my sea-going days, and also inherited from my father who used to be like that as well. He had been at one time, amongst many other roles, the chairman of Whiteley's the big store in Bayswater. On stocktaking day he would go up there himself and help, and was actually seen heaving blankets or what have you about. The staff were highly delighted that their Chairman was not standing aloof from them but seen to be one of them. Such an attitude was great for staff morale, and I think it is a trait that I have inherited from him. I really cannot stand people just standing back and thinking 'Well I'm just too superior to lift that up!' Working alongside the staff in this way helped me to settle in, as well. I was, after all, a stranger in their midst, and a certain mystique surrounded my job and some of the things I did. Basically I believe that most people just want to be noticed, want you to take an interest in them. If you were helpful and did not talk down to them or tell them what to do, but instead suggested as an equal 'Come on, let's do it this way – because this is better isn't it?' you were much more likely to have them on your side.

The process continued throughout the firm. We had changed the accounting system. We had put in our own printing; we had sorted out the renewal system. I did suffer a little bit from those who assumed that I thought that mechanisation was the answer to all our problems. One or two of our directors seemed to become mechanisation freaks. Without really understanding the concepts, they would eagerly produce newspaper cuttings about some marvellous new machine or something some firm had done and suggest that we acquire this thing. I was always at great pains to point out to them that mechanisation was not necessarily the solution; some things are actually more economic when done manually. Of course it certainly looked more impressive – a great spreadsheet with holes down the side emerging from a computer – but the process involved a girl having to punch holes in a card from a source document which then had to go to another girl who re-punched or checked those holes with her machine (a verifier) to make sure that the first girl had got the holes in the right place, then they were passed through a sorting machine which put them all into some sort of order, then you put them on to a printer which whirred out sheets and sheets of continuous stationery with the answer on. My job was to look at it and say well I can do that for you and it will cost you X amount of money in equipment and maintenance and people's time. At the moment all this is being done for you by 'old Joe' who sits in the corner and produces the answers just as satisfactorily but just doesn't look modern. We certainly could not afford to invest large amounts of money in modern gadgetry just because it made a lot of noise and apparently did the job for you. It was important to know that mechanisation would actually save us money. The early 1960s was a period of very slow change, compared with the pace of change today. In some cases we were waiting for the machine we needed to be invented. This was no excuse for spending lots of money and rushing into mechanisation just for its own sake.

However, there is no doubt that it was an interesting era to be in. Equipment was being developed, however slowly, and the minds of those at work were changing. When I joined the firm we had two sorts of copier: one was a thermafax which used to make copies fairly quickly on to a rather nasty brown paper by some sort of heat process. The only trouble was that if you left your paper on the radiator by mistake the whole thing turned black and was lost forever. The others were various forms of photocopier, which often resulted in the hanging of pieces of wet paper around the print room on a clothes line with clothes pegs whilst they dried off. This was expensive and slow until Rank Xerox arrived on the scene and you could make copies *ad lib* and very fast (provided, of course, that you could keep the staff from copying their football pool coupons and things on it, as it was by no means cheap). It was very fast and efficient though and it did cut down on all the typing. Some of our girls were typing twelve carbon copies in one go; if they made a mistake they would have to peel the thing back and erase the mistake twelve times over. A photocopy of a correct original, on the other hand, did not have to be proof read again – another labour and time-saving factor.

I was responsible for giving contracts to firms who did our decorating and partitioning and suchlike. I would tell them what was wanted and they would then submit a quotation. Common practice was for the person authorising it (i.e. me) to have the whole thing re-typed, accepting the quotation. I considered this a complete waste of time, which also introduced the possibility of error. So I would photograph their original quote, and then rubber stamp the copy with 'APPROVED – PLEASE EXPEDITE', sign it and duly send it back. We then both knew for sure we were working from the same document. It seemed common sense to me, but caused great concern the first time it happened! It was the same with memos. I had a little 'test' for efficacy of a particular manager: my Memo Test. It worked thus. I would send out a Memorandum with the information that there was to be a strike the following day, and asking if there were any members of that Manager's department who might require transport. All I required was one of three answers: yes, they wanted transport and could it be arranged; no, no one required transport, or yes, there were some people affected but they would be able to sort it out themselves. The good manager would either pick up his telephone and tell me the answer, or they would scribble a response on my memo and send it back to me. The managers who *thought* they were working well would write their own memo in response to mine (or worse, have it typed): 'Reference your memo of (whatever date)...etc. etc.' My memo was filed, a copy of their answer was filed, even though the whole thing would have no relevance in the future; the memo itself would go on a journey through the building and waste a number of people's time. It was an example of the sort of practice that gradually, by grinding away, we slowly rectified.

Ours was by no means the only firm in the City operating in this way, as we were to find out later when we made our first merger. We already incorporated one or two smaller firms within our own organisation, but our first large merger came in 1967 – just when I thought we had everything running more or less on the right lines. We merged with a firm called P. Wigham Richardson, who were big in Marine insurance. They were an old family firm, as ours was. Our Marine insurance was quite small, although as I have said we were strong in North American business re-insurance and Fire and Accident, whereas P. Wigham Richardson were the reverse. It was a marriage of two minds. However, where I had thought that Bevington, Vaizey and Foster had been somewhat behind the times, it was nothing compared to P. Wigham Richardson. They inhabited a very old building behind the Baltic Exchange, where they had been for a very long time. The Chairman, George Wigham Richardson (who subsequently became Sir George Wigham Richardson when his elder brother died) ran the operation rather like a Victorian iron master. He was The Boss; the board were very much under his control and his word was law. Their attitude towards the staff was positively Dickensian; the Christmas bonus was handed out to forelock-tugging minions who would write and thank him graciously afterwards; they had a canteen (we had a luncheon voucher system) housed in their basement where many hours were pleasantly wasted; they had no dictating machines but everyone still used shorthand which was then becoming one of the most expensive ways of operating and, worse still, every individual manager had his own typist who would only type for one person; if the typist happened to be sick or unwell they would hire in a temporary at great expense, not considering whether or not the girl had any work to do. With our typing pool system we very rarely needed temps, unless there happened to be a 'flu epidemic. There was a certain amount of upheaval as we moved some of our people with them and some of theirs came over to our offices. I was of course, regarded with complete mistrust. However, we took things slowly, and showed by example rather than imposing a new regime all at once. With dictating machines, for instance, we sat two managers in one office together. The Wighams chap still had his secretary sitting with him taking his dictation and would then have to wait some while before it came back to him. Our chap, on the other hand, spoke briefly into his machine, the tape was whisked away and the results were with him sometimes before lunch to sign. It was not long before their men saw the results of our own system and were asking us for a dictating machine of their own.

Another subject which crept into my life once I had taken on Personnel was the question of salaries. In Bevingtons a salary review was undertaken every year, before Christmas, when the salary committee (consisting of two or three of the main Board Directors) would sit around the Board table to discuss the recommendations of the managers of the various departments for their staff. It was a fairly arbitrary process and might well depend on whether the Directors concerned had had a good lunch or not. No advice was given to the managers about current market rates on which their recommendations should be based. I changed this. I went round and visited each manager, having introduced a salary scale, which I kept up to date by keeping an eye on published information and was thus able to discuss each recommendation with them. Between us we managed to iron out discrepancies, ensuring that the chaps we wanted to keep were rewarded accordingly. I would join the manager in their representation to the Board and could thus support and justify any queries that were raised. When we joined forces with Wighams, I approached one of the Directors to ask which manager I needed to talk to in order to discuss the impending salary review. He was aghast. 'Talk to a manager? What would you want to do that for? Managers don't know how much their staff are being paid!' Pay was determined only at the very highest level, with the secretary to the Chairman keeping a watchful eye to ensure that no one would be getting anywhere near her own salary. It was certainly a battle, but I did in the end succeed in breaking down some of the archaic attitudes that prevailed, if only by pointing out that if they continued to operate such a system they would soon be without any staff at all. It was quite dispiriting, having spent seven years on Bevington, Vaizey and Foster, having to start all over again with this lot. However, we just about kicked them into shape!

When the two companies merged, they went public – very nice for the Directors who owned the company but fatal, in a way, from the firm's point of view. The famous Jim Slater was on the lookout. He already had a firm of brokers and they had bought Rose Thompson in order to get into Lloyd's. He was now keen to buy us – which, indeed, he did. It was an unhappy time for the firm. Slater appointed a Managing Director to undertake a hatchet job, brought new whizz kids on to the board and basically commenced a process of asset-stripping. We were in fact already planning to decant some of our staff and I had spent some time looking around the country for a suitable location. We had found a site in Barking, which was convenient since many of our staff lived that way out of the City and there were excellent rail links. The Wigham office was sold off under the new regime and we proceeded to build a new office there. Jobs were shuffled under the new regime; some were dispensed with and some went of their own accord. I, too, suffered. I was sent for by the new Managing Director and was instructed to prune down my staff. I was asked what role my assistant played, and I explained that he was there to oversee the punch-card system being computerised, and also to act as my stand-in. By that time I had become an Alderman and had to spend time sitting on the Bench; the Shrievalty was also approaching which would mean being away from the firm for almost a year. The M.D. quizzed me further on my civic duties. When I asked whether or not he approved, he quickly affirmed that he was all for it, as long as they were not expected to pay. My salary was sliced by a third and I was stripped of my two directorships. In addition I was not permitted to replace my secretary who was due to leave shortly as she was expecting a baby. If I wished to pursue my civic career I would have to accept their terms and I was given that evening to consider my options. I recall my secretary being so annoyed she threatened to go and kick his headlights in! However, I went home to Libby and explained what was happening. I thought we would probably survive; my civic career looked promising and I had become an underwriting member of Lloyd's and, on balance, it seemed worthwhile continuing with the firm. I went in the next day and informed them of my decision. They were quite happy and, to be fair, within a couple of years they had relented somewhat and I think had come round to the view that there might well be some advantages to the firm in having one of their number in civic office. In fact the new regime did not last long; Slater also happened to have an insurance company, and the fact that they had a brokers as well was regarded with some suspicion. Business was thus being lost and we were sold on to Jimmy Goldsmith (or Sir James Goldsmith, as he was to become). His management style was quite different; the Managing Director left and the atmosphere was altogether more pleasant. Goldsmith had in his stable the brokers Polands and we were given the choice of merging – although no pressure was put upon us to do so. We did, in fact, merge and became Wigham Poland. The Barking office had been put on hold during all of the upheaval but was now continued and 600 of our staff moved down there, keeping Bevington House and a small office to the rear as our London base. The policy and claims departments and all the typists moved to Barking; we introduced a system of flexible working hours for them there.

The 1970s saw considerable advances. We acquired our first computer and a computer staff. Charles Buckingham, from Polands, who had been their administrator, took over the whole administration side of things and I stuck with Personnel. One of the outcomes of the Slater-Walker era had been to dispense with central recruiting and get the managers to recruit for themselves. It was given that managers did not end up with the people they wanted and would be better off interviewing for positions themselves. I saw this as a complete waste of management time and in fact my staff and I continued to recruit 'on the side' for them. We did not, in point of fact, actually appoint ourselves, but would undertake the process of advertising and initial screening, so that managers were presented with a shortlist of suitable applicants for a particular post. I had also started a graduate training scheme, which was also stopped in the Slater-Walker era; their policy was one of 'poaching' people who had been trained elsewhere.

Chapter 2

Having left the sea and embarked on what some people might refer to as a 'normal' life in the City meant that I had the opportunity of following in my father's footsteps, at least in his civic career. The City, its history and its unique form of government had always fascinated me and I was now in a position to contribute to this living history myself. Quite early on in my land-based career I had set my sights on becoming elected a member of the Common Council – the 'lower house', one might call it, of which the membership was elected from the twenty five wards of the City. Each ward of the City had a ward club to which local residents and business people could belong. Club members would indulge in various civic activities, and the clubs themselves were really the breeding ground for potential members of the Common Council. I had a bit of problem in so far as my office was situated in the ward of Portsoken on the eastern edge of the City, but the family ward (the one which my father had represented for so long as a Common Councilman and of which he was now the Alderman) was the ward of Bassishaw which was the area to the eastern side and to the north of Guildhall. In order to back myself both ways, I decided to join both ward clubs with the idea that I could stand for Common Council when a vacancy occurred in either – although my preference would of course have been Bassishaw. I was duly elected to the committee of both clubs. Portsoken was traditionally the Jewish ward of the city, with many of the big warehouses sited in the area. Six Common Council members were returned for their ward, five always being of the Jewish persuasion, but one position was always reserved for a Gentile. It was this position that I had my sights set upon. In 1963, a vacancy came up in Bassishaw. The ward club secretary, Gordon Wixley, had been waiting for such an opportunity and went for the job. Having put my name down as a candidate, I withdrew it just before the elections; such a move sufficed to indicate one's intentions of standing next time around. I succeeded Gordon Wixley as secretary for the ward club and thus became very heavily involved in the ward. It was not a terribly onerous task but did mean that I became well known within the ward. We had an annual lunch attended by the Lord Mayor, and one of my duties was to prepare the seating plan for the occasion. An important task indeed as we were also known as the 'chartered accountants' ward, and several accountants and their guests would always be in attendance and needing to sit with the right people. I would prepare my plan with care and just have it right when inevitably the telephone would ring the night before and I would be told of a further three guests who would have to be slotted in, which would mean re-scrambling the whole thing. In Portsoken I was also doing fairly well, and coming up to being Vice Chairman of the ward club. In 1965 another vacancy occurred in Bassishaw and this time I stood for election. I was duly elected and thus sat in Council with my father. He had been a Councilman from 1930-1948, and the Alderman thereafter. It was a proud moment indeed to join the Council for what was jokingly referred to as the 'Gillett pocket borough'. I had absolutely no serious thought at that time of aspiring to follow him to the position of Lord Mayor; it did not seem at all feasible to have two Lord Mayors in two generations of the same family and anyway I had a new career to pursue and a family to educate. Perhaps, one day, I would become Chief Commoner or even a Lay Sheriff, but that was really as far as my ambition went at that stage.

My introduction to the Common Council was fairly easy, in the sense that everyone knew who I was. The difficulty lay in the fact that everybody assumed that having been born to it, as it were, I was not in need of help or advice and whereas any ordinary new member would have been shown the ropes, I found that more senior members, who had been around for a couple of years or so, would come and ask *me* for advice on occasion! Bassishaw only returned four Councilmen, which meant that there were four committees on which to serve. One of these was the Civil Defence committee, which was still in existence in those days. The country was divided into regions for Civil Defence purposes, with the regional directors invariably being Admirals, Generals and Air Marshalls – retired, high-ranking servicemen. Frequent conferences were held in various parts of the country, to which the Chairman of the Civil Defence Committee in the City was always a delegate. It so happened that at the end of 1966 (my first full year), the then Chairman of the committee, who was a T.A. man, was wanting to retire and they were looking for a replacement. Civil Defence was never a terribly popular committee, not being as interesting as Planning or Finance, or suchlike. In my capacity as a previously serving officer, the committee looked to me and asked if I would stand for the chair. According to committee rules, you were not eligible to stand for chair unless you had served for two years – or *part* of a year. This meant that my brief two and half months at the end of 1965 counted, for the purpose, as a full year, and that I was eligible for the post. It was pretty well unheard of for a committee member to take the chair after such a brief spell of time but there seemed to be no objections raised, and thus I found myself at the beginning of 1967 as the Chairman of a Corporation Committee. It was all very exciting, and I think stood me in good stead because it was not until one reached the position of Chairman that one really had the opportunity to get to know the Corporation staff, and had a much closer association than when confined to the back benches. I was determined to kick the committee into life, in much the same way, I suppose, as I was doing at my firm. I therefore tried to make our meetings as interesting as possible, acquiring films from the Home Office to show and thus lighten the tone somewhat. The result was that the committee became rather more popular than it had been before. At conferences I also stuck my neck out. The conferences were addressed by Ministers, who reflected the mood in the country at the time that questioned the need for Civil Defence at all: if the bomb was going to drop we would all be dead anyway so why bother? seemed to be the prevailing *zeitgeist*. I forcefully refuted such doubts and argued that there was a strong need to increase public awareness and show the films that had been made for the purpose, before the need necessarily arose. My analogy was to point out that we did not wait until the storm was breaking to have lifeboat drill at sea, but rather at the start of the voyage so that everyone would know what to do if things started to go wrong. Needless to say, my voice fell on deaf ears.

At the end of my first year, there was a strategic review of Civil Defence and it was decided that instead of the 'four minute warning' prescribed at the time, there would be a four-week warning. Based on this decision, all the Radiac equipment around the country was withdrawn and Civil Defence centres closed down. Civil Defence found itself in a 'stand by' situation despite my own strong views against such a move. The following year I was re-elected, but this year marked the end of Civil Defence. All units throughout the country were disbanded and volunteers throughout the land who had been trained to deal with civil emergencies received a formal letter politely thanking them for their time but informing they were no longer required. The only vestige remaining was the Planning Officer in local government whose duty was to make contingency plans for civil defence. In the city, as well as in boroughs throughout the land, the Civil Defence Headquarters, established to ensure that the country would still be run after a nuclear attack, were all put into mothballs and in our case the Civil Defence Officer became a part time post. The Civil Defence Committee also became surplus to requirements and we were merged into the General Purposes Committee. Thus my chairmanship came to an end. However, it had been a very good experience and had whetted my appetite. In my defence against our 'hatchet' Managing Director who complained that I wasted the firm's time in the pursuit of my civic activities, I would argue that, to the contrary, my activities were part and parcel of management development and that not only was my chairmanship excellent experience, but it also enabled me to meet people from other walks of life, and from other firms, with whom I might discuss problems and broaden my ideas. My firm may have been happy to have paid for me to train on some specified course; within the Corporation I was gaining excellent training at no cost at all other than a few hours of my time.

In 1969 a new Magistrates Courts Act was brought in. There was a Labour Government in power at the time and the then Lord Chancellor lowered the retirement age for Magistrates. Originally an unlimited age, it had been reduced to 75 and was now to be reduced to 70 in yearly steps. This particularly affected the City, because the Magistracy in the City of London was supplied entirely by the Aldermen who were *ex officio* magistrates sitting on their own – one at the Guildhall, one at the Mansion House – every day, a custom which had been in existence since time immemorial. Since Aldermen were elected for life many were already over the age of 75 and therefore excluded; now with the age limit being reduced again many more would be precluded from sitting. It was feared that if nothing were done the Lord Chancellor would abolish the right of Aldermen to sit as magistrates altogether (which would have affected the position of the Lord Mayor, as the Chief Magistrate) and put lay magistrates in instead. A Commission of the Peace was appointed for the City and by 1970 we were to have three on the Bench instead of one, as on any other Bench in the land. Six senior Aldermen would keep their positions as Chairmen of a bench, but the others would be elected by a Magistrates Courts meeting as elsewhere. Sometime before this, the Aldermen had agreed that if they were unable to sit on the bench they would step down and this meant that, despite the Charter, the more elderly Aldermen were all having to go. Suddenly we found ourselves in the position of needing quite a lot of new Aldermen. In our ward my father, who had thoroughly enjoyed his magistrate's duties and was still very active, now had to depart, leaving a vacancy to be filled. My three fellow members turned to me and suggested I stand for election. I protested that I had not had any particular aspirations in that direction, neither did I think that I could afford it. Becoming an Alderman was the first step on the ladder which would lead eventually to Sheriff and Lord Mayor and such a commitment at this early stage in my career, with two still at school, seemed rather too much. They argued that my father would surely support me in such a move, but I rather suspected that my father, whose views on such matters were somewhat Victorian, had in mind somebody else. He would feel that I was too young, with a new career and besides, he was extremely anti-nepotism and would not dream of using his position to push me forward. However, the deputy of the ward, John Newson-Smith, offered to go and see my father. After initially offering the reasons I had put forward myself against standing, my father eventually came round and said that if the Court of Aldermen accepted me, then he would support me. This meant that I would have to go and see the senior Alderman, as one did in those days, to test the ground and find out if I was likely to be vetoed. My fellow members were very encouraging, and took me up to the H.A.C. for lunch and filled me with beer, and finally I relented and said I would visit the senior Alderman; any resistance and I would happily stop there. Not that I did not want to become an Alderman; indeed I found the prospect very attractive, but I had not thought of it before now, and was not entirely sure that such a step was right for me at this stage.

So off I set to see the senior Alderman, Sir George Cullum Welch, to ask him to take soundings from the court of Aldermen and find out if I would be acceptable. This all came at a time prior to the first merger at the firm. The chairman, George Vaizey, was very keen on the city and was very supportive. The soundings were duly taken and it came back that I would be acceptable to the Court of Aldermen. The Lord

Mayor of the day, Sir Charles Trinder, would seek consultation with any ward members whose ward was offering a candidate for the position of Alderman, to ensure that the candidate was acceptable to them. John Newson-Smith happened to be away, but I accompanied the other two members when they went up to see the Lord Mayor. He began by asking George Hunt if he would have the candidate. The reply came: 'No'. He then asked Gordon Wixley if he was happy with the candidate. 'No', came the reply once more. Then he turned to me and said, 'And what about you, Robin? Do you want him?'

'You ask me a very awkward question, Lord Mayor, ' I replied, 'Because I *am* the candidate.'

'That's not what I was told,' said the Lord Mayor.

The whole meeting had to be adjourned at once. It turned out that he had been under the impression that someone else was standing – the candidate my father had first put forward. We left and returned the next day, to go through the whole procedure once more, only this time he asked the other members if they were happy for me to stand. I was duly elected, first by the ward and finally admitted to the Court of Aldermen on 18th March 1969. Two days later I took my seat on the dais for my first Common Council meeting as an Alderman. It was customary for the Lord Mayor of the day to give a luncheon subsequent to the election for the new Alderman and his wife. This took place at the Mansion House, with other guests comprising the other Aldermen and their wives, the object of the exercise being for them to have their first look at what they had got. The Lord Mayor would make a welcoming speech and the new Alderman was required to stand and say something about himself by way of introduction to his new brethren. I made a bit of a black out of this, I'm afraid. The old 'ready wit' proving itself alive and well, I decided to borrow a little story I had first heard from the Captain of H.M.S. *Vernon*, when I was serving with the R.N.R. Addressing my new brethren, I began by saying that I sincerely hoped that, once they had learned a little bit more about me, they would not repeat the words of the Sultan who, on returning to Constantinople and finding half his harem in the family way, reprimanded his chief eunuch with the words, 'Abdul, you're obviously not cut out for this job.' Some of the younger men present laughed appreciatively. Some of the more elderly wives, however, looked rather po-faced. Nothing was ever said, even by my father who was present as a guest. However, I found out later that the Lord Mayor's secretary warned all subsequent junior Aldermen not to 'do as Robin Gillett had done'. Of course they were never told what I had done, although I was able to enlighten them eventually.

And so I settled down to perform my Aldermanic duties, which were somewhat more onerous than those of a Common Councilman, despite the fact that I had been serving on six committees. I also started my training, such as it was in those days, for the bench. I had no particular worries about administering summary justice, which I had been accustomed to doing in the R.N.R. The system in those days (it is now much more sophisticated) was that you received a certain amount of instruction from the Chief Clerk and were given various books to read, and then sat alongside, observing one of your senior brethren who was sitting in the Guildhall justice room. He would explain after handing out a sentence why he had done so; you had to sit in on six of these and then you were free to go solo. I had recently completed my six when, one afternoon at my office, I received a call from the Chief Clerk to say that Sir Peter Studd, the Alderman on duty the next day, had gone down with 'flu. As I had finished my training, would I come and take over? He assured me that the list for the day was very straightforward and that he would be there to assist if needed.

The following day I duly set off, to sit for the first time as a magistrate on my own on the bench in the old Guildhall Justice Room. This has since been pulled down to make way for a new west wing, but at that time it was a very Dickensian-looking place, with tall pews at the front, and if you half-closed your eyes you could almost see the Peelers sitting there waiting to give evidence. A large stable clock on the far wall slowly ticked away the minutes and the hours. I arrived at ten o'clock, to receive my instructions for the day and to sign any warrants (proceedings did not commence until 10.30). The Clerk sat with me and went through the day's list.

'I know I told you that there were no problems', he began, 'But something has cropped up overnight.'

Oh fine! I thought. Just what I need on my very first day. As I approached the court I was aware of the 'red collar men', the ushers of the court (who of course knew my father well) eyeing me carefully. 'Here comes the lad – let's see how he does!' However, I believe that I conducted myself well and the day's proceedings passed without any real difficulty. I even sent a man to jail, for sending a brick through a plate glass window (criminal damage). I have to say that he more or less indicated that if he were not sent to jail he would probably do the same thing again; no doubt he was eager to get inside and out of the cold – but thus I passed my first custodial sentence. I could feel the red collar men look at one another with glances that said, 'The lad'll be alright – chip off the old block there!' My father had been a very strict magistrate; he would reprimand a defendant if they so much as leaned against the side of the dock with the words: 'Are you tired or something? Stand up and take your hands out of your pocket!' or if they were chewing gum it was 'Haven't you finished your breakfast yet? Take that stuff out of your mouth!' But he was a very fair magistrate, and a popular one too, and when he retired the Clerks and the police (there was no Crown Prosecution Service then) presented him with an engraved Shaeffer pen.

Such was my baptism of fire. I was to see twenty-six years as a magistrate and enjoyed it immensely, feeling that it was perhaps one of the most important things that an Alderman did and felt it an immense privilege to sit there on my own. When the new magistrates were introduced towards the end of the year and we sat as one of three, I rather felt that in some ways this diminished one's powers of concentration. Sitting on one's own, with a man in front of you, certainly focussed the mind. With three of us and the opportunity to discuss the case between ourselves, I felt that I could be persuaded against my own reasoning. I actually felt that I dispensed better justice on my own, listening to the voice of my own conscience. It was certainly quicker, with no retiring to consider the case. You had to 'think on your feet', particularly when, having decided on the fate of a particular defendant, you then heard the mitigating circum- stances of his background (dying wife, six children to feed, the only breadwinner – that sort of thing) and quickly had to re-think a more suitable sentence.

The local government of the city was largely in the hands of the Common Council. Although we sat on a raised dais in our distinctive red robes, the court of Aldermen was not exactly a Senate, and did not have separate voting powers. We attended the same meetings and voted on the same debates and with 130 council members and only 26 of us we could easily be outvoted. The only difference was that Council men were up for election every year and we were there for life.

In addition to sitting in the Magistrates Courts, we also did Quarter Sessions, where we sat with a senior Alderman at the Old Bailey, hearing cases that had been referred from the magistrates. Two juniors, the senior Alderman and the recorder would listen to such cases, although this was also subsequently changed when the Crown Court system was introduced and the recorder assisted by two magistrates would sit in on the cases. A further duty at the Old Bailey was to put the judges in. We were on daily rota to see the judges into their courts, assisted by the Sheriff on duty. You had lunch there with the judges and then put them in their courts again for the afternoon. It was possible to stay and listen to the case if you so wished; at the Old Bailey the middle seat in the court was always reserved for the Lord Mayor as the first named in the Commission (all Aldermen were judges named in the Commission – that is to say, judges at the Old Bailey). The judge would sit in the seat to the right; if the Alderman wished to stay he would sit in the Lord Mayor's chair and the Sheriff would sit on the left. I think I only once exercised my right, out of interest, but usually was far too busy at the firm to spend a whole day in court.

The other duty we performed (also to disappear in 1972) was to take jurors Ballot Day. Before each session when the jurors had been chosen from the voting lists, they had the right to appear at the Old Bailey, either to ask for a deferral, or to request a short service, or indeed to be dismissed from jury service altogether. Despite the fact that this took up a whole morning I used to find this quite interesting. Having been introduced by the recorder in Court Number One, you sat in your scarlet robe listening to the jurors' varied excuses – and they certainly came up with some most extraordinary tales. It was almost worth it just to be called 'Your Lordship' for a morning, rather than the mere 'Your Worship' as in the Magistrates Court. I would try my best to excuse those who would clearly be seriously inconvenienced – people, for example, who were self-employed such as window cleaners or those who ran a small business and would lose out financially if they were to sit on a long jury service. Others were obviously just trying to get out of it because they were too bloody idle to sit on jury service. To these I gave short shrift and made them serve. I recall one man who worked as a chef in a directors' dining room in the city. He produced a letter from his Managing Director who said that he could not possibly spare him for jury service; they were in the habit of entertaining important foreign clients and he was quite indispensable. I asked the chap how he felt about this himself and whether he had any objections to serving on the jury.

'No, ' he replied, 'I would be quite happy to serve.'

'Well,' I said, 'Tell me, in this important directors' dining room of yours, what happens when you are sick, or when you go on holiday? What do they do about it then?'

'Oh – they get a substitute chef in,' came the response.

I said, 'Well, they can get a substitute chef in while you serve on the jury!'

He seemed quite happy with the outcome, although I shall never know what the Managing Director thought. An example of one of the feebler excuses with which I was presented. Another man, from IBM, said that he could not possibly serve on the jury as he was in the middle of some umpteen-pound deal on some computer he was selling and could not be spared. I said, 'You mean to tell me that a firm the size of IBM is going to lose a sale because you are serving on the jury? You could well be sick or something? They must surely have someone they can put in to conclude the sale on your behalf!' I made him serve as well. I recall my father telling me that one day as he was travelling up on the train from Frinton, when he was doing a similar thing, he happened to share a compartment with some chap bemoaning the fact that he had to go up to the Old Bailey. He had been called for jury service, but felt he could not waste his time doing such a thing. 'I've got two jolly good excuses why I can't serve,' he confided to my father. Of course when he arrived at the Old Bailey who should be sitting up there on the bench but my father. His fellow passenger at least had the good sense not to try on either of his excuses, and agreed to serve. Often those with legitimate medical reasons would whisper their condition, not wishing it to be heard in court that they were incontinent, or whatever. However, provided a valid doctor's certificate was produced, such cases would be excused.

Of course nowadays the function is a clerical one and Aldermen are no longer required for the job, but I did find it one of the more interesting aspects of my post. In my mind it is the duty of every citizen in the land to take part in jury service, and it is certainly no good complaining about the leniency of today's jurors if one is not prepared oneself to take an active part.

Whilst on the subject, I must confess to one bit of inadvertent judicial humour. It occurred on day when I was sitting in the Mansion House; I was in the chair with two wingers either side. The man standing before us had been an accountant with a small firm in the city. After defrauding the firm of a considerable sum of money he had disappeared to Europe and then to the United States and Canada where he had lived off his ill-gotten gains, and found himself a job. However, pricked by a guilty conscience he eventually returned like the prodigal son to the UK and gave himself up to the police, confessing all. His Counsel advised that he was already paying back the money he had stolen from the firm from his current earnings. We decided, in the end, to defer sentence, which meant that we would see him again in six months to ensure that he was maintaining his payments. We suggested a rate of payments at £20 a week, but his Counsel came back and argued that £20 a week would be rather more than he could afford – could we make it £15? I consulted with my two wingers and we were all of the opinion that it ought to be £20.

I addressed the defendant. 'You must realise, Mr —, that there is an element of punishment in this and we feel that you can afford £20 a week, which you must therefore pay.' I did not hear myself say what followed, but was not allowed to forget it afterwards. 'You may find it hard, and you may have to pinch a bit, but you must try.' Meaning, of course, *pinch* as in save. Both my wingers looked at me in astonishment and there was a suppressed titter around the court. I had not realised that I used the colloquialism in quite the wrong context. We had always been told to avoid using lengthy speeches when sentencing, as you were bound to trip up sooner or later, and even the judges at the Old Bailey confessed that from time to time they had done so. But advising a defendant to pinch? As far as I am able to recall, that was, I hope, the only real boo-boo I made.

During the last twelve years as a magistrate I was Chairman of the Lord Chancellor's Advisory Committee for the City Magistracy. This involved selecting new magistrates for the City Bench for appointment. Having been in the personnel business myself I found this a fascinating procedure, and an important one too, for the Lord Chancellor relied heavily upon his Advisory Committees to select suitable candidates – not only to provide a spread of backgrounds in terms of ethnic origin and work experience to the bench, but also to test one's own gut feeling towards the suitability of any candidate. In addition to interviewing them and scrutinising CVs, we also used to have a mock 'sentencing' exercise with the candidates, really to pull out any woolliness of thought, or bias or extreme opinion they might have. This was done by giving the candidate two cases to read – real cases, and not necessarily straightforward. The candidate would then be invited to come in and sit with two magistrates to discuss the case and the sort of sentence they might deem appropriate (they were given guidance as to what sort of sentences were available to them). The magistrates who were retiring with the candidate were deliberately chosen to play act: one as a tough 'hawk' and one as a more soothing 'dove'. As Chairman I would sit in on this procedure and invite the candidate to retire with the two magistrates to decide upon sentence. The hawk would be primed to swoop in at once with comments such as 'Far too much of this sort of thing going on! Do you realise that Marks & Spencer's (assuming a shoplifting case) lost x million pounds last year due to this sort of thing? It must be stamped on from a great height!' etc. etc. And he would advocate a custodial sentence or some swingeing fine. The candidate would then be invited to comment, at which the dove would come cooing in, remonstrating against such a harsh judgement and suggest a mild period of probation or community service or some such. Again the candidate was invited to comment. All of this proved a far better way of finding out what they really thought than an interview situation might do. One of the things we sought was a clearly thought out opinion: those who were never asked to sit were the ones who agreed with both. I found the exercise a most useful tool and one which I believe resulted in a very good Bench.

Apart from the normal Common Counsel duties – sitting on the various committees of the corporation – Aldermen also had various other outside duties to perform. We were all, for instance, governors of Christ's Hospital and King Edward's School Whitley, which was the Bridewell Foundation. These were split half and half between us and I did Bridewell. The City had been highly involved in the foundation of both and still maintained an interest – particularly in the schools, which were the modern reflection of the original charity. I was also a governor of my old school, Pangbourne, and I found it very valuable to be able to compare notes, particularly as King Edward's, Whitley was co-ed (250 boys, 250 girls). I was quite convinced that we should eventually move to co-education at Pangbourne, too. Apart from the advantages of having both sexes educated together, which to my mind provides a far more well-rounded experience, there is also the great inconvenience faced by parents having a son and a daughter away at different boarding schools, with different holiday dates, school plays, sports and that kind of thing to attend. Co-ed schools also provide an only child, who has no other opportunity to experience the relationship of a brother or sister, with a ready-made 'family'. I also recall the inconvenience of the school play itself, when as an all-boys institution staging a production of *H.M.S. Pinafore* we would have to resort to using the junior boys dressed up in wigs to play the female roles. Nowadays Pangbourne takes in girls, who are certainly an asset to the place, although many traditionalists took a lot of convincing before the doors of the school were opened to the female sex.

My duties as an Alderman were therefore not only an asset to my managerial duties at work, but also provided me with the opportunity to contribute in some way to society. There were numerous other charities that we looked after, and all in all the work proved much more fulfilling than the work on the Council had been. One was also being groomed, in a sense, for stardom, in so far as every Alderman was a potential Lord Mayor, although the route was by no means automatic. There were some who tried to cut down on their Aldermanic duties, with the reasoning that it interfered with either their work or social life; my own view was that if that was the attitude, then they should not have joined in the first place. It was all or nothing, a way of life and a total commitment.

Chapter 3

The next rung on the civic ladder was that of the Shrievalty. The office of Sheriff dates back to the reign of Henry II, when the citizens of London were granted the right to elect two Sheriffs. This differed from the appointment of Sheriffs elsewhere in the country, who were all chosen by the Sovereign. The population of London had obviously always been a rather stroppy lot, unhappy with kings just appointing people over them, and they had wanted a say in the matter, which Henry II had fortunately given to them. These two Sheriffs had originally represented the county of London (a county in its own right) and the county of Middlesex, and this persisted right up until the abolition of Middlesex as a shrieval county in 1888. After this time, both became Sheriffs of the City. Sheriffs throughout the land were the King's Officers: they served as tax collector, law enforcer and general regent for the shire over which they ruled (the word sheriff is derived from 'shire rieve'). There were other 'town Sheriffs' in some cities, whose writ differed somewhat; they were appointed locally and they were not quite of the same calibre as the two Sheriffs of the City. Although not appointed by the sovereign, city Sheriffs who were more akin to the county Sheriffs (who now called themselves High Sheriffs). The Sheriffs of the City were elected by members of the Livery Companies, of which there are one hundred, embracing some 24,000 Liverymen. Each year, in Common Hall, the Liverymen gather to elect the two City Sheriffs on Midsummer Day. The Sheriffs, duly elected, commence their appointments on the day before Michaelmas Day. It is customary to elect one Alderman and one lay Sheriff. Occasionally two Aldermen are elected, although the Court of Aldermen itself only nominates one candidate. The traditional means of election was by a show of hands, although nowadays a postal ballot is permitted, if necessary (that is, if there are more than two candidates). Sometimes the process is contentious; sometimes it is not, depending on who is standing. However, the Shrievalty is an essential step for any Alderman wishing to be considered for the Mayoralty – although it matters not whether he has served as an aldermanic Sheriff or a lay Sheriff. The idea dates back centuries, when it was deemed that the Shrievalty determined the suitability of a potential Lord Mayor. The route is by no means an automatic one, however, and many fall by the wayside, either voluntarily or by persuasion. There can, of course, be many reasons why some don't make it to the final office and it may well be due to extraneous factors such as family or work commitments. The lay Sheriff does not have to be a member of the Common Council, and the role is not related to local government.

I steadily climbed the ladder until I was nominated for the Shrievalty by the Court of Aldermen for the year 1973-4. I was lucky in so far as there was no contest that year and my fellow Sheriff and I were spared the nausea of a poll. The other candidate was a chap called Tony Hart, an architect by profession and a Liveryman (of the Inn Holders Company). On Midsummer Day in 1973 we were elected in Common Hall to become the Sheriffs of the City for the year ensuing.

As Sheriffs elect we had no duties to perform (although I had my customary aldermanic duties to maintain), until we took office on 28th September. Just prior to this we were both given our Shrieval chains – the badge of office for the Sheriff which comprises three gold chains meeting in the city arms at the front, from which is suspended the Sheriff's own personal 'badge', usually his own coat of arms and the smaller shields showing his Livery Company and interests. Each chain is quite individual, although invariably gold. My father gave me his chain, which he had worn as Sheriff in 1953 and which had in turn belonged to a previous Sheriff in 1932. It was indeed a beautiful chain – fourteen feet of 18 carat gold, with faceted links, which glittered in the light. However, I had my own badge made for me, declining to borrow my father's even though we shared the same coat of arms. A rather sad tale surrounds this: I wanted to have my father's badge encapsulated in an acrylic glass block, rather like a paper weight, so that eventually I might pass it on to one of my sons and the other son could then have my own badge. The outline of my badge was a ship's wheel, suspended by two dolphins with emerald eyes, from the city badge where the chains met in front, with my coat of arms in the middle and various others round the outside: Trinity House, my Livery Company and the R.N.R. amongst them. Traditionally the chains are given by public subscription, by the Liverymen in one's own company and by others who are invited to subscribe. Since I already had my chain, most of my money went on the badge, which had to be 18 carat gold to match the quality of the chain. Tradition also has it that your lady receives a brooch, supposedly bought with the money left over. Libby's brooch was a city shield in diamonds with the St. George's Cross made out in rubies, surmounted by the naval crown, also in diamonds. These are presented in one of the Livery Halls – in my case on board *Wellington*, whilst Tony Hart's was presented in the Barber Surgeon's Hall. At the same time I had planned to present my father, who was there, with his own badge for his lifetime keeping. I had given Asprey's my father's badge, to have it encapsulated in glass as planned. Asprey's then sent it away, but unfortunately it was lost and never seen again. All I had was the insurance money. I never told my father this, and he seemed happy enough that I was to have his fine chain.

The chain presentation was followed by our admission, when we went on 28th September to Guildhall, dressed in our court dress, and were formally sworn in. Our chains were hung about our necks by the outgoing Sheriffs and then we proceeded to the Sheriffs' Breakfast, which in our case was taking place in Plaisterers' Hall – the first time that the new Hall had been used for such an occasion. The Sheriffs' Breakfast was something akin to a wedding breakfast, I suppose, and was lunch, rather than breakfast. The recorder proposed the outgoing Sheriffs and the Bishop of London proposed the incoming Sheriffs. We both spoke and then, unusually, we went back to the Old Bailey and changed out of our glad rags into our 'going away' clothes (even more like a wedding!) and took off in our Rolls Royces to Heathrow, to fly out to Brussels, where we were to join the Lord Mayor (Lord Mais) and Lady Mayoress.

In Brussels the airline succeeded in losing our baggage, temporarily, but we were reunited with it at our hotel at 1.30 the following morning. The next two days, which happened to be the weekend, were spent in various civic duties: we inspected the Pikemen of the H.A.C. in the city square; opened a Euro exhibition and on the Sunday we went out to a château for a lunch party for about eighty people. We returned to London on the Monday to embark on civic duties at home. The overseas visit had been all very exciting and certainly got us into our roles straightaway. The Sheriffs have no corporate duties, unlike Aldermen, but really serve as aides to the Lord Mayor. Their main task is to look after the Old Bailey (one has to be on duty there each day) and to attend the Lord Mayor on civic duties at home and abroad. The Sheriffs take office on the day before the election of the Lord Mayor (Michaelmas Day). This means serving for six weeks with the outgoing Lord Mayor, before the new Lord Mayor takes office on the first Saturday in November. In our case we had Lord Mais at the start and then Sir Hugh Wontner took over and we served with him until the time came for us to hand over in September 1974. I could not have wished for two better Lord Mayors to serve. Different in their backgrounds and ways – Raymond Mais was very much the soldier and ran things along rather military lines, whilst Sir Hugh was Chairman of the Savoy Group and not militaristic at all – but two excellent men.

There are a couple of residential flats at the Old Bailey for use by the two Sheriffs. However, because Libby and I lived in London ourselves we did not make use of the bedroom accommodation unless we had had a particularly late night or if I happened to be there on my own. But we would return to the Old Bailey after one of our nightly Livery banquets to change out of our finery. Our chauffeur lived at the Irish Embassy, (just behind what was then St. George's Hospital and is now the Lansdowne Hotel) where his wife was housekeeper, and he would take us in our car as far as there, and I would drive the last stretch to Fairholt Street. In the past, Sheriffs had provided their own Rolls Royces, but by the time we were in office the corporation had seen fit to provide the cars. However, we still had to provide our own chauffeurs. This was not a problem for Tony Hart, who had his own firm's chauffeur, but I inherited my predecessor's man, who unfortunately had to leave half way through my term of office. This meant employing a new one, and the very young-looking son-in-law of one of the Lord Mayor's chauffeurs took on the job. We were given an allowance for the car and the chauffeur but did have to pay them ourselves, which proved very unsatisfactory, since it meant they had no continuity of employment. My chauffeur had no way of knowing whether my successor was going to employ him or not. Whilst in office, I struck a blow for the freedom of the Shrievalty and arranged for the Court of Aldermen to change the rules. The chauffeurs thus became employees of the Corporation and could enjoy various benefits, such as pension schemes, as well as security of employment. It also saved worry for us, since if the chauffeur was off sick it was up to us to find a temporary replacement, which all proved rather expensive and inconvenient.

Thus I was set to embark on my year as Sheriff. An interesting and rewarding year lay ahead, and I will return to my tales of the Shrievalty in a later chapter. Life at home, meanwhile, was changing fast.

Chapter 4

Back in 1961, life on the domestic front was beginning to settle down. Gradually I was getting used to my role as a father at home, going for walks in the park with the boys and being a part of their everyday life, which I greatly appreciated. At the beginning of the summer term, Nicholas started at Wagners School, Queensgate. This was a pre-prep school (although in some cases boys stayed there until they reached public school age), and its main 'rival' in the area was Hill House. Before this time, Nicholas and Christopher had both attended a Montessori school housed in a building in the church gardens behind Holy Trinity, Brompton, which offered the basics and was really a sort of pre-school playgroup.

In the June of that year my old chum Christopher Rawson was elected a lay Sheriff. He put me on to his Sheriff's committee, responsible for organising various bits of the Lord Mayor's show and banquet, which provided me with a little taste of that side of civic life, and a foretaste of things to come! By dint of the fact that I was serving on the committee, Libby and I were invited to the Lord Mayor's banquet that year (not our first, of course).

In the late summer of '61, Libby and I had our first proper holiday abroad together. Leaving the boys and their *au pair* with Libby's sister Stella and her family, who now lived just outside Colchester, we joined Christopher and Rosemary, with Rosemary's brother and father, at a villa in Cala d'Or in Majorca for three weeks. The place was remarkably cheap and the price included a Spanish housekeeper who looked after us all. We flew out on the 2nd September, enjoyed three weeks of glorious weather and good food, and had a marvellous time.

My parents still had the house at Frinton, which we often made use of for family holidays. I always felt it was healthy for the boys to get out of town and enjoy the fresh air of the country. Libby would often take the boys down at Easter and during the summer we would all go down there once my parents had taken their early summer holiday and returned to London. In 1962, we were all at Frinton for Easter – a holiday made memorable by the fact that the boys and I all came down with German Measles. Not a very serious complaint; we spent much of the time in bed but soon recovered and were able to benefit from the bracing air on the sea front.

We were having trouble, that year, with some developers in Knightsbridge, who were buying up property and converting former homes into offices. Our corner of Knightsbridge was pleasantly residential – almost village-like, in parts – and the last thing we wanted was for it to be turned into another Mayfair. We had already successfully opposed a change of use for a building in Montpelier Walk, just at the end of our street, which had been used by Harrods as a store for banqueting furniture and was to be converted into meeting rooms. No sooner had we done that than Westminster City Council announced that they were going to move Basil Street Fire Station, to make room for a vast new development on the corner of Sloane Street and Knightsbridge. The new fire station would occupy the entire length of Cheval Place, from Montpelier Street through to Montpelier Walk. It was to be the largest fire station in London and would have completely ruined the neighbourhood. We knew that we would have to get ourselves organised, locally, if we were to resist this sort of encroachment. A meeting was held at Bonhams, the auctioneers at the end of Cheval Place (who obviously had a vested interest as a compulsory purchase order loomed) and the so-called 'Knightsbridge Association' was born. We were to have a proper committee and a subscription in order to start accruing some funds. We elected a Chairman and a Treasurer, and Libby offered to take on the post of Secretary, a job she embraced with characteristic enthusiasm. For the next ten years our dining room was to look more like an office, with typewriters and papers scattered all over the place. However, it all proved very worthwhile, and it also meant that we got to know everybody in the locality; Libby was unable to walk down the street without people stopping to chat. The association was run on a shoestring but over the years has grown to become a highly organised machine. Westminster City Council appreciated that it could be used to their advantage and that they could save wasting time with planning applications by consulting us prior to any planning committee meeting, rather than have to take things to appeal *after* a decision had been made. Indeed, so pleased were they, that they asked us to extend the boundaries in subsequent years, and now the Association encompasses the area along the north of the Brompton

Road, up to the Albert Hall and Queensgate and almost to the borders of Kensington and Chelsea. It was all great fun and I would contribute by taking photographs of the various streets and buildings for them, thus recording the existing area before any development, and at the same time indulging my hobby.

But I digress. Also in June 1962 I took the Freedom of the City. I thought that this was something I could do by patrimony (that is, because my father was a Freeman before I was born I could automatically claim Freedom at the age of 21). The other routes were by redemption – that is, you paid a fine (having been proposed and seconded by two Liverymen) – or by apprenticeship – becoming apprenticed to a Livery company and then claiming freedom through the company. I had not been apprenticed, but consulted with my father as to the date he took his Freedom. I was sure that this had been prior to my birth, since he had been so keen on his civic career. 'No', he replied. 'No, I don't think it was. I think you were born *before* I took the Freedom.' This meant I had to pay my dues (£12) in order to get the Freedom of the City. Subsequently however, after my father's death, I was going through his effects and came upon his Certificate of Freedom. It was dated 1921 – four years before I was born! So I could have claimed patrimony after all. The Chamberlain, however, was unsympathetic and would not let me have my twelve quid back.

In July my mother, who had never enjoyed very good health, had a heart attack and was admitted to the Royal Masonic Hospital. I went to visit her a couple of days later but only a week after my visit she had a second heart attack and died. I spent a great deal of time with my father, supporting him through all the organisation that had to be gone through and the preparations for the funeral. In some ways it was a blessed release; she had suffered a great deal through her life and, although loath to complain, had never been terribly happy. Her relationship with Libby had been somewhat strained, which I suppose goes back to my being an only child. My mother was always very possessive, although she tried hard not to be, and although she was all for it when I got engaged, she could often be fairly beastly towards Libby, implying that she failed to feed me properly and suchlike. She would telephone and announce that she had observed that 'Robin is looking a bit peaky – he had better come out and have a *proper* dinner with us'. Not a move likely to improve relations. When I was abroad in the Gulf for a year, I had hoped that she would treat Libby rather more kindly. Libby was certainly very good to her, taking her out for drives in the car and spending time with her, but if she so much as hinted that she might be missing me she received absolutely no sympathy at all, but was subjected instead to lectures from my mother about wives in *her* day having to cope whilst their husbands went off to run the Empire. When I was at home I would be in deep trouble if I did not telephone my mother at least every other day; any longer and my father would be put on the line, with the implication that I had done wrong to neglect them. And when on the telephone, she would go on relentlessly, for half an hour at a time – I could happily abandon the telephone and leave her rabbiting on, just returning to mutter the occasional affirmative every so often. I would get letters, too, pages and pages of diatribe about my level of neglect and lack of concern for them. It was terribly sad, really, and thus probably a relief not only for her but also for my father when she died. Libby was down in Frinton with the children, but I went to the cremation on 2 August and brought my father down to Frinton to stay with us afterwards.

On 17th August, Libby's youngest sister Dodo got married to a senior lecturer in chemistry at Glasgow University. They were the last of the family to stay on in Scotland, where Dodo had embarked on a career of social service work. The reception was held at brother-in-law John's house in Moscow in Ayrshire. I attended the Lord Mayor's banquet again that year (beginning to make a habit of it already). Sir Ralph Perring was the Lord Mayor at the time; he had been aldermanic Sheriff for my father, hence the invitation. And we wound up the year by becoming the proud owners of another car. The first Ford Zephyr had just about run into the ground and I replaced it with a (second hand) Ford Zephyr Mark II, a dark blue drop head coupé and one of the nicest looking cars in that range.

The following year, 1963, began with my election at the AGM to be the Honorary Secretary of the Bassishaw Ward Club. On 23rd January I was admitted as a Liveryman of the Honourable Company of Master Mariners. Because they wanted to get their name on my Freedom Certificate I was obliged to go and pay some more money to have an endorsement.

We had a very cold winter, that year. The Serpentine froze solid and I remember taking the boys for a walk across it. In Fairholt Street cars lay buried beneath mounds of snow and all movement became very difficult. Traffic on the main roads kept going but pavements and roads were awash with brown mush and sludge. Snow in town is really not much fun. I cannot recall anything quite as bad since, so perhaps we are due for another hard snap soon.

Although I had left the sea I was allowed to stay on the R.N.R. list for one year, and in March I went on another R.N.R. course for two weeks – a general refresher course for promotion to Lieutenant Commander. This was followed by another course the following year, once I had received a dormant appointment as a Coastal Convoy Commodore (designate). I had to go on a Coastal Convoy Commodore's course, which meant one week in Greenwich and one week in Portsmouth. I was the only R.N.R. on the course (the rest were all bowler-hatted R.N.s who had come up from the Navy). A dormant appointment meant that you had no further training to do but you were given a rail warrant and in the event of crisis you would be expected to rush to the nearest train station and head for Invergordon, commandeer the nicest looking trawler you could find as your flagship and then await further orders.

Christopher had by now joined his elder brother at Wagners, and in 1964 Nicholas embarked upon his career at Prep. School. Way back in 1905 my father, who had attended Highgate School for Boys, left with one of the masters, who went down to Dorset to open a Prep. School, taking with him some of the senior boys from Highgate to found it. The school, Durlston Court, was still going strong, having moved to Barton-on-Sea, just inside the New Forest. My father was very keen for his grandsons to keep up the family tradition and we all went down to visit the school. The Headmaster was good, as were the facilities and it was decided to put both boys down. That summer we saw Nicholas off at Waterloo in his new school uniform for the first time. He had a very happy time there, and was joined there by his younger brother in due course.

I had been very keen to get myself a boat again. I was eager to teach the boys to sail and to sail myself again when we were at Frinton. I found a Gull dinghy (a bit like a baby Wayfarer – just the size I wanted, manoeuvrable and ideal for trailing behind the car) for sale somewhere near Kempton Park. At that time we were attending the races fairly regularly and went up to look at the boat one time when we were there. She was in excellent condition and only cost £150 (including trailer and outboard engine). The deal was concluded and we brought her down to Frinton. That summer we were off to Morfa Nefyn on the Lleyn Peninsular to stay with the Rawsons (they had two girls, slightly younger than our boys). I drove up with Nicholas in the car, towing the boat, which we called *Tequila*, from Frinton whilst Libby brought Christopher up on the train. We had a marvellous time; Christopher (big Christopher rather than little Christopher) hired a fishing boat for himself and we all spent many happy hours out in boats together and laid lobster pots to our culinary delight.

On 30th January, 1965, with Nicholas away at school, I took Christopher with me to stand in The Strand to watch Winston Churchill's funeral procession. Fortunately, Christopher happened to be wearing his school uniform, a very distinctive blue and black cap and blazer. As we stood at the side of the street, someone from a window above us called down and asked if we would like to come and watch from there. It turned out that the chap who owned the office had been at Wagners himself and had spotted young Christopher. We thus had a grandstand view, and once the cortège had gone by, we gave our thanks and left, arriving home in time to see the service at St. Paul's on the television.

On 6th July, disaster struck. Christopher had been playing with friends in Kingston House South (some people called Furno – the boy was at Wagners with Christopher). The boys had been playing on a piece of equipment that was something of a cross between a see-saw and a roundabout, which spun round but also went up and down. Christopher lost his hold, shot off it and landed on his right elbow and fractured the joint in three places. He was taken by ambulance to St. George's and then transferred to Westminster. I heard the news from Libby when I got back from the City; I saw on the X-ray the severity of the damage and there was some debate as to whether the arm should be cut open to operate. The surgeon, who was very good, believed he might be able to manipulate the bones back into place, which he managed to do in two stages, successfully. Christopher was encased in plaster from his shoulder to his wrist; it healed very well, despite some misgivings from the hospital that he might have trouble with it in later life or that it might be shorter than his other arm, although now in his forties he does experience some stiffness. At the time, he took the whole thing in his stride and indeed rather revelled in the attention. Because it was a slightly unusual case, the surgeon would wheel in strings of students to examine the elbow and he thoroughly enjoyed holding court.

We managed to tweak him out for our summer holiday that year, which was spent once again at Morfa Nefyn. We travelled as before, by train and car, and Christopher spent the holiday seemingly untroubled by his arm, running around as normal and having great fun in the boat.

1965 was a significant year in so far as I signed up to be a working Name – a member of Lloyd's. Since I was employed in the business, I had to place a deposit of only £12,000, which was supplied by my father on my behalf. As an underwriting member of Lloyd's I was able to augment my meagre income somewhat. At the time of joining, we were in a loss situation, along with many other syndicates. Hurricane Betsy had just swept through the southern states of America, causing lots of expensive damage and Lloyd's had been hard hit. However, this was, in fact, a very good time to join, since the situation could only improve. I made a loss in my first year but this was carried forward and after that my profits continued to rise steadily.

In November that year I was elected to the Court of Common Council, as has previously been described, and that year I attended the Lord Mayor's banquet – this time in my own right!

In 1966 a new company was formed within my firm: Bevington, Vaizey and Foster (Services) Ltd, of which I became a Director. As a service company, but a subsidiary of the larger firm, this provided a commission for Directors based on the profit of the whole firm. In January I was also elected Chairman of the Bassishaw Ward Club. This was not a very onerous task; it meant chairing committee meetings, making a speech when we entertained the Lord Mayor for lunch each year and occasionally presiding over any outside events and activities that we had. It seemed rather soon, having so recently been elected to the Common Council, but the policy was to alternate Common Councilmen and ordinary members as the Chairman and since all other Councilmen had been 'used up' it happened to be my turn.

In the summer a launching ceremony was held at Chichester Marina for Christopher Rawson's new motor cruiser he had had built at Tough's Yard in the Thames. She was not all that large but fairly comfortable. He wanted to call her Lotus after the boat he used to hire when we were in Wales. This meant some difficulty when it came to registration, since there were already five Lotuses in existence, but he got round the problem by calling her *Lotus VI*, for registration purposes, and *Lotus Vi* for use. We went again to Wales that summer, with my boat, and saw the year out with the Lord Mayor's banquet, again in my own right, as a Common Councilman.

In 1967, the year I was elected Chairman of the Civil Defence

Committee, young Christopher joined his elder brother at Durlston Court. The boys got on well; although Nicholas had never shown any signs of homesickness, Christopher had always missed Nicholas when he was away and on the first night Nicholas returned to school after any spell at home young Christopher would wander downstairs, tears in his eyes, to say that he was missing his brother. Nicholas was always very protective towards his sibling and would leap to his defence if he were ever bullied.

For some reason I have always found it hard to turn down any offer of work that involves training young people. Particularly if it is to do with the sea, and particularly if it is voluntary and unpaid. Such is my inability to say 'no', I have often thought that had I been a girl I would have been pregnant by the time I was thirteen. Some might think of me as a soft touch. As a result of my connection with Civil Defence I came across a chap who, as well as being a Civil Defence instructor in the city, was also a colour sergeant at a Marine Cadet unit (sea cadets), who belonged to Sherbourne House. They owned a 45' motor fishing vessel which they kept in what was then Commercial Dock, which had been acquired for them from the M.o.D. by an old Sherbonian Commandant General, Royal Marines. The cadets were all East End lads, and unable to make use of their boat since they had no one qualified to drive her. Consequently, the local area Sea Cadet Officer had his eyes on her, claiming that he had more right to a boat than any Marines. Realising that I was a Master Mariner, this chap broached the subject with me and asked me to come down and join the unit, to save the boat from being requisitioned. He indicated that the commitment would only involve the occasional weekend, and so I agreed to go and have a look. The two officers who ran the unit were H.A.C. (Honourable Artillery Company) officers, training the cadets as a sideline. To cut a long story short, I agreed to join the unit. (Technically this should have involved joining the Sea Cadet force but as a Lieutenant Commander R.N.R. I felt I could bypass this). And so there I was. Having announced I would not take divisional duties at H.M.S. President because I wanted to spend more time with the family, I had saddled myself with a commitment which of course turned out to be far more than I had been initially led to believe, with at least one – or sometimes two – nights a week instructing the cadets in seamanship, tying knots and that sort of thing as well as taking the boat out. A right bunch of little tearaways they were, too, half of them on probation, and I would come away after an evening with them thanking God that I was not a schoolmaster in an East End school – how on earth they coped all day I have no idea. On one occasion, I was teaching a group of them how to tie a knot when I became aware of a disturbance in a corner of the room. Turning round I discovered a boy face down on the floor, his knees bent and his thumbs tied behind his ankles (a good way to tie someone up with only two inches of string). 'What on earth are you doing?' I asked, at which one lad produced a hangman's noose, which he proudly held up. 'How about that, Sir?'

They did not take kindly to classroom work, but were at their happiest when on the parade ground being shouted at by colour sergeants. They were immensely proud of their uniform and always managed to look smart. One characteristic of the area was the strength of territorial feeling; if a boy from Southwark happened to stroll across the border into Rotherhithe he was likely to get beaten up severely. The law of the jungle ruled – but more of this anon.

We went down to Frinton in July that year, at the start of the holidays. One of the boys had a project to make something, and I suggested a raft. We bought half a dozen old oil drums, some timber and some rope (no nails) and I demonstrated how to lash the drums and timber together. We even built a deck, a mast and a sail and attached a small outboard bracket at the back. The whole thing was creosoted (we managed to do ourselves and a fair sized chunk of the lawn, as well, which I don't think ever recovered) and took it down to the sea for a test. It did not sail particularly well but floated, nevertheless, and it was certainly a proud moment. We took a number of photographs of the stages of construction and also built a model (using balsa wood and the plastic canisters that films come in) and the boys won a prize at school for their efforts. Subsequently I used the same principle as an exercise for my cadets.

We went up to Wales again, later that summer. *Lotus* had been transported up there and we sailed her round the end of the Lleyn peninsula. We used to dine quite well on lobsters, although did engage in a slight fracas with the local lobster catcher who was concerned that we were encroaching on his patch.

Libby and the boys stayed at Frinton for the rest of the summer holidays, and I would join them at weekends. I had tried to commuting daily to Frinton but it was a complete waste of time since I had to get up so early and got back home so late that I barely saw anything of the family anyway. I would stay with father in his flat during the week, to keep him company.

Of course I attended the Lord Mayor's banquet, as usual, in the November of 1967, something that was from now on to be an annual event!

It was the following year when I put my raft-building skills to the test in an exercise with the cadets. The exercise involved some G.M.T.C. (the girls' side of the sea cadet corps) who took on the role of a group of scientists who had been captured by a foreign power (communist agents); they were encamped on the Isle of Wight and were to be taken off by a submarine. The job facing the lads was to rescue them. There were six cadets in all, sixteen and seventeen year olds, who were camped on the mainland. Their job was to build a raft, paddle it across the Solent and land it, whereupon they would be met by a friendly spy who would provide map references for the prisoners' camp. They then had to find their way across the Isle of Wight, raid the camp at night, rescue the scientists and bring them back to the raft and finally row them back across the Solent. I took the lads down from London in my car and we set up camp on the sea wall at Keyhaven, just up from Hurst Castle. We did not get much sleep – we seemed to be in the middle of a gull sanctuary or something and the screeching and twittering was relentless. I rose early and went out to check the weather; I had worked out the tides beforehand since it was critical that they had to cross at slack water. Looking out across the Solent I saw to my horror a mass of white sails. I had completely forgotten the round the island race which had started early. I knew that they would not take kindly to six lads attempting to cross in a homemade raft in their path. Luckily by the time the boys were ready to cross, the sailing boats had cleared, much to my relief. All went according to plan. The boys crossed safely, rescued the girls and brought them back to Yarmouth.

We were quite keen on such tests of initiative, such as taking them to the north of London and letting them find their way back home, although we had to be careful that they did not take such opportunities to fare dodge on the tubes or other such games, as they were wont to do. In fact one of the boys who was supposed to be with the group in the exercise described above had found his own way down to the Isle of Wight all the way from Waterloo, having missed our departure; he managed to evade the ticket inspector on the train, got on the ferry at Rye and then hitch-hiked across the Isle of Wight, turning up at supper to join us that evening with a broad grin on his face. It might have been illegal, but it was certainly a great show of initiative.

Christopher Rawson had taken *Lotus* across to Holland, and later that year I flew with him and his brother-in-law Richard to Ostende to collect her and bring her back home to Burham Pool. The weather was lousy, however, and we all felt rather grim, so stopped at Dunkirk the first night and then managed to get her back as far as Dover.

We did not spend any time in Wales that summer, but in August I joined Libby and the boys in Frinton, and on this occasion we did a bit of salvage work. We had returned from an excursion in *Tequila* one day, to find a rather agitated looking chap on the beach jumping up and down and pointing out to sea. His son had taken out a rubber dinghy and the engine had failed; trying to row he had lost his oar overboard and finally had decided to abandon the dinghy and swim ashore – a very foolish thing to try and do, of course. He had reached the shore safely, but now the dinghy – a brand new one – was floating away out to sea. So off we set to rescue it, much to the chap's gratitude. He came round to the house the next day and presented me with a cheque, which I promptly sent off to the R.N.L.I. It was not the first – or the last – time I was to witness such foolhardiness by those inexperienced at sea.

That year I did a bit of sailing on the backwaters with Mr Bailey, our local chemist – someone I had known all my life.

It was at the end of that year that, by virtue of the new rule regarding age, my father retired as Alderman for the ward of Bassishaw. Without making any fuss he and several contemporaries left, although not all were as quiescent about it as he was. By the end of 1969 all the 'old guard' were gone (some kicking and screaming) leaving the way clear for newer, younger blood, and it was 3rd March that year that I was elected Alderman for the ward of Bassishaw.

On the home front, Nicholas passed his Common Entrance for Pangbourne, and joined in the summer term. We were in Frinton at Easter and I took Nicholas down afterwards to join the 'family division' in Hesperus. It was the last term that Pangbourne was governed by a Captain Superintendent; they were about to change and have a headmaster, instead. Nicholas had one term under the old system, with a Director of Studies as the head of the academic staff and a Captain R.N. (retired) as the Captain Superintendent as had been the system in my day.

On 30th April that year – perhaps because of my elevation to Alderman, I am not quite sure – I was elected to the court of assistants of the Honourable Company of Master Mariners. The election took place within the whole company, so was not a 'put up job', and I became a member of the Court of Assistants, which was the governing body, under the wardens, of the Company.

On 31st May I went to Scarborough for a Civil Defence conference, which lasted three days. I recall little of the event but in all likelihood spent the time shooting my mouth off, accosting any minister who came near me with a lecture on how foolish it would be to abolish it all. However, I suspect that it was, by then, too late; our fate had been sealed.

Nicholas's godfather, General Biddle (of the Biddles of Philadelphia) came over on a visit from the U.S.A. later that year. I brought Nicholas up to meet him at the French Horn restaurant where we had a very good lunch. We went down to Pangbourne for Founders Day, and watched him marching very smartly. Then it was down to Frinton for our hols. 1969 also saw in a new car; we replaced the Mark II with a Zodiac Mark IV (skipping III). It was a huge, silver model with a great long bonnet, which housed the spare wheel in front of a six cylinder engine. It made Libby and I feel as if we must be getting old, since this was the first time we had had a saloon car, which seemed very staid after all the drop-head coupés. It cost £710 (second hand), which seems ridiculous, now.

In August I went out on an exercise with *Dorset Commando*. We sailed from Surrey Commercial Dock to Harwich, stopping off at Southend for a night (alongside Southend Pier) and then anchored off Frinton where I got off to see Libby and the boys. Then it was up to Harwich before returning via Brightlingsea and Sheerness to Gillingham. The boys returned to school at the beginning of September, and on 30th September I attended my first Sheriff's breakfast in my capacity as Alderman.

November saw another exercise with *Dorset Commando*. We took a group of H.A.C. chaps down the river at night, landed them at Denton, just beyond Gravesend, to do a night exercise fighting the 'enemy' (our marine cadets). My God, it was cold! The following day we embarked them and brought them back up the river, and I can remember my face suffering severe windburn from having to stand on the open bridge. It was all good fun, however, and I enjoyed keeping my hand in this way.

In the summer of 1970 we returned to Frinton. On this occasion I organised an expedition for the boys and Charles Furneaux, taking them to camp on Stone Point at the mouth of the Walton backwaters. We took two dinghies, towing one with all our gear, and marooned ourselves for four days, sleeping in tents at night and exploring in dinghies during the day. It was real 'Swallows and Amazons' stuff!

The Lord Mayor in 1970 was Sir Peter Studd. He happened to be a governor of Pangbourne and I succeeded in persuading him to have a marching party and the band from Pangbourne in the Lord Mayor's Show that year. Unfortunately it turned out to be one of the wettest shows in history. The rain came down in stair rods from start to finish, streams of water running down Ludgate Hill and washing over the boots of policemen who were lining the route. Nicholas was in the marching party, and so wet by the end that we had to put his uniform into the spin dryer before he could wear it to return to school that evening.

Chapter 5

It was 1970, and it was by this time that both the boys were beginning to show some signs of musical ability. They had played recorders at Wagners and both went on to learn the clarinet. It was Christopher who was particularly talented; at the age of six he played the recorder beautifully, and on the strength of this I bought him a second hand clarinet for about £25 from a music shop in the City. After his first term at Durlston Court, I asked after Christopher's progress, to which the peripatetic teacher (who happened to be the first clarinettist with the Bournemouth Symphony Orchestra) replied that he was doing very well but needed a decent clarinet.

'Believe me, it will be an investment' he assured me, even offering to get hold of one 'on the cheap' through the orchestra.

'How much will that be?' I asked.

'£108,' came the reply.

I was staggered – Christopher was only seven, after all – but allowed myself to be persuaded. When Christopher finally sold the instrument, after he was married, he got some £600 for it. In the meantime it had won him a scholarship to Pangbourne, kept his lungs going when his voice was breaking, and gained him a teaching grade so that he was able to return to the college himself to teach for a couple of terms. He had a spell as a peripatetic teacher at St. Mary's School, Ascot and played a very mean jazz clarinet as well as a strong classical repertoire. Nicholas never showed quite the same level of promise, and finally gave up the instrument after a succession of teachers who all seemed to instruct in a different manner. His forte turned out to be the mouth organ – the only instrument that Christopher could not play!

I recall one incident, printed indelibly on my mind, which occurred when Christopher was a little older. I took him into Harrods just before Christmas. In those days, the music department was housed on the second floor and we when we arrived here we found that a special Christmas demonstration was taking place. A salesman was trying to whip up enthusiasm for a small Cassio electronic organ.

A paper template had been placed over the keys to enable interested passers-by to play 'Three Blind Mice' with a degree of accuracy. Christopher was spotted by the salesman who enquired whether the little boy would like to come and try out one of his machines. Christopher was not particularly interested, but I was encouraging.

'Go on, have a go. Why don't you show them what you can do?' I suggested – not knowing myself quite what he *could* do, although I was aware that he had taught himself to play the piano. He relented at last and went over to the machine, whereupon he carefully removed the paper template from the keys, drew up his piano stool, flexed his hands together, stretched them out to shoot his cuffs in the manner of a true professional, and then proceeded to give an impeccable performance of Bach's Toccata and Fugue. The salesman's jaw dropped practically to his chest and other parents with children stopped in their tracks as Christopher happily played on. Eventually the salesman leant over and hissed in my ear, 'I think perhaps you should be going over *there*,' pointing across to where the Hammond organs were on display.

On 29th April 1970, the Reverend Basil Watson was installed as the new vicar of St. Lawrence Jewry. I had been on the panel that interviewed for the post, since it was within the remit of the General Purposes Committee. Basil Watson had been a naval padre all his life and had just retired from his post as chaplain to the Royal Naval College, Greenwich, which is where I had met him previously. He was a typically robust naval padre, what one might refer to as a 'muscular Christian' and just right for the mission which St. Lawrence Jewry had to the Corporation staff. Being a Guild Church, St. Lawrence Jewry only had services during the week. It was a popular living and there were several up for the position. When asked at the interview why he wanted the job, I recall Basil Watson's sanguine reply: 'Because there is no Mothers' Union, and no service on Sundays.' The Chairman looked rather po-faced at this response but the rest of the Committee laughed heartily. He got the job, and was subsequently to be my chaplain when I was both Sheriff and Lord Mayor. As Alderman of Bassishaw I served as his Church Warden, since the Aldermen of Cheap and Bassishaw filled the roles of Church Warden.

Whilst on matters ecclesiastical, it is worth noting that two weeks later we went down to Pangbourne, where Nicholas was confirmed in the chapel. Coincidentally the Bishop of Oxford, who was taking the Confirmation, dedicated the ship's wheel from the old clipper ship

Macquorie, which had been found in Australia. Sir Philip Devett had brought it back to Pangbourne where it was installed in front of the lectern.

The 9th June saw Libby and I at the first of what were to be many Royal Garden Parties at Buckingham Palace. It was not an occasion I felt particularly enthusiastic about – the prospect of standing about in the hot sun in a morning coat did not fill me with great excitement and once you have done it once or twice the delights of strawberry cake and iced coffee in an over-crowded tent begin to pall, rather – but Libby liked to go and we used to meet quite a lot of friends there, which was always fun.

On June 12th I was able to combine my sea cadet activities with my civic duties. The Mayor of San Francisco was on a visit to the City and I arranged to drive *Dorset Commando* from Tower Pier, where we picked him up with the Lord Mayor, Sir Lionel Denny, to Greenwich. Here I disembarked with them and we went round the Royal Naval College and the Maritime Museum before returning by car to have lunch at the Mansion House. I was back down again that evening as a guest of the Admiral President at the Ball at Greenwich, which Libby and I used to attend most years.

The end of June saw another civil defence conference at Scarborough. With both of the boys at school, Libby was now free to accompany me for the two-day conference, and we used the opportunity to call upon Libby's Auntie Pearl on the way home.

At the end of the autumn term at Durlston Court we took my father down to see Christopher who was singing the Judge in *Trial by Jury*. He was extremely good – he had sung in *The Mikado* the previous year, but this was clearly his masterpiece. I had borrowed a proper judge's wig from the Old Bailey for him, so he was well dressed for the part. The following day we went down to Pangbourne, where Christopher was to be interviewed.

We move on to March 1971. The Prince of Wales received the Freedom of the City with due pomp and ceremony in Guildhall, followed by lunch at the Mansion House. He looked so young, then, and it seems so long ago. He made a very good speech and everyone was very impressed, having been led to believe by the media that as a schoolboy and student he was not terribly bright and rather gauche. However, he refuted this image quite clearly in the space of one day and he was thereafter recognised as the intelligent and pleasant young man that he was.

Christopher succeeded in passing his Common Entrance with very good results and was also awarded Pangbourne's first ever music scholarship. He joined his elder brother at the College at the beginning of the summer term. They were both in the same division (*Hesperus*, where I had been myself). Nicholas was by then very superior and, when at home, Christopher would complain about how unpopular Nicholas was as Chief Cadet Captain of the division, throwing his weight about and giving orders. I reprimanded young Christopher, explaining that his elder brother had certain responsibilities, which he would find out about only too well in future. He did, naturally, when he became Chief Cadet Captain of the division himself in due course.

In May I was invited up to Llandudno, for a two-day conference of the Association of Civil Defence Officers. These were the only people remaining once Civil Defence had been abolished, and they invited me on the strength of my prior efforts to argue in favour of Civil Defence.

In the early part of the summer holidays, both the boys joined a school party to Switzerland, where they stayed for two weeks. On their return they joined us at Frinton, having had their first taste of overseas travel. We spent the remainder of the holiday in Frinton, before another expedition, towards the end of August, in *Dorset Commando*. I was able to take the boys with me on this occasion. There was a party of 17 cadets, plus the officers. We embarked on Friday 27th August for Portsmouth. It was very rough off Dover and many of the boys were unwell, so we decided to go in to Dover for a while, until things settled down. Christopher was already showing signs of being interested in cooking. He was one of the youngest there, but managed to impress them all in the morning by making French toast – unheard of before by these East End lads. We left that afternoon, but as we approached Beachy Head, the Engineer reported that we were losing fuel oil and we were in danger of running out. In those days there was no Marina at Eastbourne and there was nothing by way of shelter on the south coast before Beachy Head, so we decided to make for Newhaven. We rounded Beachy Head at about 1 o'clock in the morning; many of the boys were asleep and we were about two miles off Newhaven when the engine stopped. We had run out of fuel! My greatest concern that was once the tide changed we would find ourselves drifting back onto Beachy Head and I had visions of all these 'children' (as they would be referred to in the press) caught up in disaster. However, we were not in any immediate danger and all we needed was for a boat to come out from Newhaven and tow us in. I called up on the VHF to Newhaven coastguard to explain our situation. There was no response from Newhaven, but Shoreham contacted us. They cheerfully offered to send us the lifeboat, and despite my protestations (we really did not need a lifeboat – just a motor boat to tow us in) before you could say Jack Robinson there were maroons and rockets flying up from Newhaven, announcing the launch of the lifeboat. The only boy aware of what was going on was young Christopher, who bounced up on the Bridge in great excitement. The lifeboat duly appeared and took us in tow to Newhaven. So far so good. Most of the lifeboat crew were sea cadet officers themselves, and fully appreciated the predicament. However, our adventure did not pass unnoticed. We were under naval control on this exercise and had to keep them informed of our movements. The naval signal station at Fort Gillicker, off Portsmouth, had intercepted my message and he said he would report the incident to C-in-C Plymouth, whose control they were under. When we were going through the breakwater into the harbour a motorboat appeared on the scene. A man shouted up 'How many kids have you got on board?' Fearing adverse publicity, I did not reply. When we got in, the police came on board, which they were duty bound to do after the lifeboat had been called out. I asked them who the chap in the motorboat might be. They muttered about him being someone from the press, and assured me that they would deal with him. Presumably he had inside information directly from the lifeboat station so that he could always be first on the scene for a good story!

We had got in to Newhaven at six in the morning and, having filled her up with fuel, we were on our way again by 9.30 a.m. to Portsmouth, where we arrived safely without further incident later that afternoon. We then returned home by train, although the saga was not yet over. Two weeks later I went with the senior boys – about eight of them – down to Portsmouth to bring her back to London. We had a marvellous passage; the tides were with us all the way and the weather was fine and consequently we had arrived off Southend Pier by about 1.30 the next morning. There is quite a good place to anchor there and we decided to stay the night as we had the whole of the following day to finish our trip. The anchor party went forward so that I could pick my spot to anchor. I then rang astern to take the way off her, preparatory to letting go the anchor. Then I rang stop – but, unfortunately, she didn't. She was going faster and faster astern, until she started going round in circles, very fast. I was ringing down stop and the cry came back 'We can't!' Somehow something had jammed. I told them to cut off the fuel – although the problem with diesel is that this would not stop the engine immediately. The tide was now taking us nearer and nearer to the end of Southend Pier. It would not have mattered had we been the other side of the pier, or had we been stuck full ahead, but as it was we were heading for disaster. Eventually she stopped, just in time, and we swiftly got the anchor down. There was nothing further we could do that night, so decided to turn in. The next morning I went off in the 'rubber dubber' we had, to the coastguard station at the end of the pier. I asked the chap on duty whether the lifeboat engineer could come out with us and have a look. He did so, and informed us that it was a job for the dockyard – there was nothing he could do himself. I asked to borrow their telephone and called the Duty Officer at Chatham, where there was a naval dockyard. I explained our predicament to him, saying that although we were not in a naval vessel, the Admiralty did have responsibility for her. He agreed to send out the Duty Tug. I assumed this would be a small craft suitable for the purpose, but what eventually appeared out of the Medway was a huge ocean-going tug with twin funnels called *Hercules*, used for towing aircraft carriers and suchlike. Her crew were evidently delighted. As it was the weekend they were on overtime and because they were actually being used they were on double time, and they did not mind at all coming out on a Sunday afternoon. She was so much bigger than us that there was no point in her towing us, but we made fast alongside and she steamed in with us ignominiously tucked in beside her, as if tucked under her elbow. We had to leave her at Chatham and make our way home by train. One way and another it had been a fairly exciting trip.

It was in actual fact the last trip we ever made in *Dorset Commando* as the decision was made the following year to close down Sherbourne House, and disband the unit. It was more a case of shortage of staff rather than boys; there were so many different boys' clubs and organisations in that part of London that we were all competing and I had found myself practically running the unit single-handed.

Despite our rather ill-fated final trip, a few weeks later I was invited to accept an honorary rank as a Commander in the R.N.R. by the Admiral Commanding Reserves. I had had advance notice of this from a friend, Mike Garnett, who had been the First Lieutenant of a minesweeper I had sailed in after leaving the Gulf and who was now Staff Offer to the A.C.R. He telephoned to tell me that the Admiral Commanding Reserves had it in mind to promote me to honorary rank and asked whether I would prefer to be a Captain or a Commander. I said that I thought I would rather be a Commander; I had had a brass hat in the Merchant Service as a Staff Commander; and had I chosen Captain and had then used the title (as they fully intended me to) it would be hard for anyone to know whether I was a naval officer or an army officer. I was duly appointed Commander which, as an honorary rank, lasted for life. I still use the title, in the right places. When I was an Alderman, for example, prior to becoming Lord Mayor and a Sir, I used to refer to myself as Commander and Alderman, partly because I was the only one but also because I felt that I owed it to the Navy.

My father was retiring from the City that year. He was to be 82 in November and had finally given up work, having already moved into the Chamber of Commerce building in Canon Street where he just kept an office to deal with the various directorships that he still had. Although he liked Frinton, there was not much for him to do there and he really wanted to retire to Wiltshire, where his mother's family came from and where he had spent many of his schooldays. There was an old thatched cottage in the village of Biddeston, which had belonged to his mother. It had been sold to cousins who farmed nearby and had been occupied for most of the time by the village schoolmistress. She was by now too old to live on her own, and my father decided that this was where he wanted to retire. He thus bought the cottage back from the cousins and had it refurbished for the purpose. This meant he no longer had need of the house in Frinton and announced that he would give it to me. I asked him if there were any strings attached. By this time I was tiring of the place myself, rather; it had lost its character and was not the place it had been before the war; coming down by train every night was a nuisance and it was easier for me to stay in town and, not least, the boys had outgrown the place. He said he would not insist on my keeping it, and that I might do what I liked with it. I immediately called a family conference with Libby and the boys. When I asked them if they would mind not coming down to Frinton ever again there was great rejoicing. Some of the furniture had already been removed from the house; of the remainder we gave some to Libby's brother John, cleaned out the place and then brought the remainder of the effects to London and put the property on the market. The market did not happen to be very buoyant at the time, but we were rid of it and a chapter in my life had closed. I have only been back to Frinton once, to find it had become overcrowded with housing and the elderly (the standing joke was 'Harwich for the continent and Frinton for the incontinent'); all the big houses and gardens had been divided into flats and small plots and there was very little for young people to do. It boasted a tennis court (if you liked that sort of thing) and a golf course (I did not play golf) but apart from that there was very little. It was all too clean and nice: no pubs, no charabancs, no cinemas, no fish and chip shops. When some enterprising young soul did open a fish and chip shop a few years ago, the event made national news!

That summer we spent our holidays at Wivenhoe, where Libby's sister Stella and her husband Richard now lived. Their garden backed on to the river, where they moored their yacht. Whilst they were away cruising they had suggested that we make use of the house. We took *Tequila* with us, together with an Avon sport boat – a 10'6" large rubber dinghy – which I had bought in the early part of the holiday for £200. I had already acquired a 25 h.p. Johnson outboard engine, which had been given by Johnson to Sherbourne House but had not been used a great deal and which they had sold on to me for £50, and so now I had a boat to go with it. She became known as the 'bomber' because the boys would 'bomb about' in her at high speed. The river was fairly quiet there and there was plenty of opportunity to have some fun in her. The last weeks of that year's holiday were spent in London before the boys returned to Pangbourne.

Moving swiftly forward to the following year, the most significant event in January 1973 proved to be when Nicholas passed his driving test. This meant that we had three drivers in the family, and when visiting the boys at school and taking them for an exeat Nicholas was able to drive and allow me to rest.

In February I was admitted as a Younger Brother of Trinity House, which meant a great deal to any sailor proud of his profession. It also fitted in nicely with my service as a warden of the Honourable Company of Master Mariners (my Livery Company).

Christopher Rawson had purchased a new 4' motor sailer in Holland – a real yacht for him at last – and in March she needed to be collected from Ostende. A Dutch delivery crew would deliver her to

Littlehampton where the British agency would fit her out. Christopher and I flew out to Holland and accompanied the delivery crew back, although this was most frustrating for Christopher who by now actually owned her but was not permitted to do anything. She had a covered steering compartment – a sort of half wheelhouse, open at the back – which was equipped with plastic covers which one could zip up in inclement weather. The crew zipped themselves in and then proceeded to smoke quantities of very strong Dutch tobacco, which Christopher was most annoyed about. He was unable to do anything, however, as they were in charge. We were just off Newhaven (Newhaven again!) when the engine failed. The weather was not terribly exciting so rather then hammer on to Littlehampton we decided to stop there. We did not need the lifeboat to get us in this time – in fact the Dutch sailed her in – and we left her there.

On 16th March the Queen opened the new London Bridge. This was a brand new construction designed by the city engineer, Mr King, to replace the previous bridge which dated from 1837. The main reason for replacing the old bridge was the weight of modern traffic, which of course it had not been designed to carry and which was gradually forcing it down into the mud of the riverbed. The new bridge was built alongside the old one and, except at weekends when it was closed for working, the two bridges ran in tandem as construction developed. The old bridge had been sold to the McCulloch organisation and was to be transferred, stone by stone, to Arizona, where it was to span the Colorado River in Lake Havasou City. The aim was to put this place on the map, which it certainly succeeded in doing. The story surrounding the purchase, which has now entered the history books, is that the Americans thought they were buying Tower Bridge, and actually got the wrong bridge. This story was absolutely untrue, as I heard myself from the lips of the architect who was designing Lake Havasou City. He had already done Disneyland and the suggestion was put forward that they needed a gimmick to really make the place go. At a press conference they all had their photographs taken standing on the bridge. Down river Tower Bridge could be seen, and the architect grabbed Mr McCulloch, President of the organisation, and said, 'That's the one we ought to have had!' Of course all the journalists present scribbled the comment dutifully in their notebooks, and thus created the legend that the silly Americans had bought the wrong bridge. Also contrary to commonly held belief, they did not take the whole bridge but merely the granite facings, which were taken down and reconstructed *in situ*. And very nice it looked, too. In London the bridge had been permanently covered in soot and pigeon droppings, and was difficult to see at the best of times on account of all the buildings and warehouses surrounding it. In Arizona, however, the air is clean. It graced a greenfield site and was restored to its original glory, repaying in full the investment by the Americans, as it became a focal point for visitors to Lake Havasou City. The City was very much involved in the purchase and transfer. When they were ready to lay the first foundation stone in its new home, the Lord Mayor went out, and then again when the building was complete and it was opened he attended another big ceremony over there, accompanied on that occasion by pipe men and plenty of English pomp and circumstance.

On a much more domestic note, it was becoming evident that Christopher needed a piano. We began to look around to see if we could find a second hand one, since those in Harrods sale were out of reach of our pocket. We eventually located one in a warehouse in the Kings Road in Chelsea, which traded in second hand furniture. I went with Christopher to investigate and we selected an upright German model for £45. It was not a particularly beautiful piece, but it worked and served the purpose. I explained that it would have to go on to the second floor of our house, which they agreed to. The following Saturday the instrument appeared in a van outside our house with two rather weedy looking characters accompanying it. Nicholas was around, however, and I felt that the four of us between us should be able to manage it. 'You realise that this has to go on the second floor?' I enquired.

No, they did not realise. They had been told that they delivered to ground floors only. The stairs in our house are steep and rather narrow. It was obviously going to be an awkward job, but I had already removed the banisters and with a little persuasion and the help of a crisp five-pound note they eventually agreed to the task. It was extremely heavy and very awkward indeed, but we managed to get it up to the first landing, where we stopped for a breather. Christopher was above us, supervising and offering encouragement. We turned the corner to the half landing and began climbing the second flight of stairs. I had thought that we would manage to manoeuvre it on this section without removing the banister, so I had not bothered to take off this section. However, the ceiling was lower here, and we became completely stuck. We could not move it one way or t'other. The only solution was to cut off the banister here, too. At this point Christopher had to climb over us while we were holding on to the damn thing, to get down to the basement to get a saw. He returned and sawed through the posts of the banister and then at last, with much heaving and puffing, we arrived on to the floor of Christopher's bedroom where it was to remain. It took us the whole of the next day to replace the banisters and repaint them. I declared that if we were ever to sell the house we would have to sell it With Piano, since we would never manage to get it down again. The only disadvantage was that we would be unable to put up married couples; the boys had a bunk system in days gone by but the bunks were of the kind that could be dismantled and form two single beds, but with the piano now installed there was no room to do this. However, it was all in a good cause. Christopher was happy and now had somewhere to practise. A few years later, when Christopher had left home, we happened to have some decorators in. Whilst they were up on the top floor, Libby had asked one of them, 'You don't want a piano, do you?' 'Ooh yes!' came the reply, 'I would love a piano for my boy. How much do you want for it?'

'If you can take it away, you can have it!' Libby quickly replied.

Apparently they succeeded in getting it down without further damage to the house or any removal of banisters, although I think that in order to do so they had to dismantle the piano. So much for music.

Christopher went off to France that April, with an organisation called E.F. Tours. These were educational tours. The boys stayed for a fortnight with French families, doing lessons in the morning and then having the afternoons free to spend with their hosts. The intention was, obviously, to improve their grasp of the language. Christopher actually went on two of these trips; in this first year he stayed with a family who had three or four children about his age who unfortunately all wanted to practice their English on him, and probably gained more than he did from the experience. However, the following year we made sure that he stayed with an elderly couple who had no children and who spoke no English. Nicholas went away to Nottingham for the rowing, that holiday, as he was in the First Eight.

Libby was admitted to St. Mary's, Paddington, in May. She had an under-active thyroid, which was giving her a weight problem, and in view of our shrieval year on the horizon it was felt that she should go into hospital under a controlled diet, in order to prepare her for the marathon ahead. She was put on a low calorie diet and given plenty of exercise. Although she was not in bed all the time, she was surrounded by other patients who were, for the most part, anorexic, who were being fed plates of chips and other foods all the time while poor Libby was restricted to a meagre 600 calories a day.

We were now getting perilously close to the election as Sheriff, which actually took place, as tradition would have it, on Mid-summer's Day – or as near to it as possible, since Midsummer fell on a Sunday that year. However, on Monday 25th June, Tony Hart and I were elected unopposed as the lay and aldermanic Sheriffs for the ensuing year. Libby was out of hospital by this time and was able to attend. So there I was: Commander, Alderman and Sheriff elect until September, when I was due to take office.

At the beginning of August we went back down to Wivenhoe to collect the dinghy and the bomber (we deflated the latter and put it inside the dinghy with most of our baggage) and set off for North Wales to spend a fortnight with Christopher and Rosemary at Morfa Nevin. This was to be the last of our visits, and with the two boats there we were able to have a fine time. After this I sold *Tequila* since I knew that I would not have time to use her during my year as Sheriff. On our return to London, we knew that Nicholas's 'A' level results would be lying on the mat. Libby, Christopher and I sat in the car whilst he went in ahead of us to read them on his own first. He came bouncing out to announce that he had got an A in Physics, a B in Mathematics and a C in Chemistry. Not bad at all. The Chemistry result may well have been higher had it not been for the fact that we had managed to lose poor Nicholas's Chemistry notes on the M4 when we were returning from Pangbourne the year before; they had been on a box which was strapped to the roof of the car. I recall as we saw the papers strewn irretrievably across the carriageways that Nicholas had remarked: 'Well, there goes my 'A' level in Chemistry'. There were only two of them taking Chemistry and these were very much his personal notes. However, we were able to save the day partially by borrowing the other chap's notes and I took a day off to photocopy them. Christopher's 'O' level results arrived a few days later and he had successfully passed all eight.

Chapter 6

In my Civic career I had, as you will recall, been appointed Sheriff, enjoyed my first Sheriff's Breakfast and had my first overseas trip on the weekend after my appointment. I will now proceed to give you a flavour of those duties, although will avoid a blow-by-blow account. It was a full and varied life, although I still managed to keep an eye on things at the firm – unlike my later term of office as Lord Mayor during which I had to become totally divorced from the life of the firm for the year. If, as Sheriff, I was staying at the Old Bailey, I would get up early and after a light breakfast, would walk to the office across the City, where I would stay from 8.30 a.m. until about 10.10. A car would then come for me and transport me back to the Old Bailey, where I would be in time to put the judges in at 10.30. This was a very formal affair; a little procession was formed of under Sheriff, the Sheriff on duty, the Alderman on duty and the judge. All would be upstanding, everyone would bow to everyone else and then the 'put him in party' retired and the judge would start his trial. If I was on duty that day I would stay there, although I did have an office at the Old Bailey where I could still get quite a lot of work done. If I were not on duty, my day would depend very much on what the Lord Mayor was up to. At times he would require a Sheriff to accompany him and I would have to report to the Mansion House accordingly. At the beginning of each week we received what was referred to as the 'hymn sheet', issued from the Mansion House, which gave the Lord Mayor's programme for the current week, with a provisional programmed for the following week. On top of this, a daily programme was also issued with rather more detailed information, including who was on duty where, what dress was to be worn and the timing of all events. It ensured a very smoothly run operation.

Had I been a Lloyd's broker, I would have found the two roles impossible to sustain. However, I found that as an administrator, I was quite able to delegate sufficiently in the time I was in the office and inform my staff of everything that needed to be done. Indeed, I made it my business to let my staff know exactly what I was up to and what my thinking was – I have always believed in this policy rather than one of secrecy, which I am sure is a measure of insecurity.

There were five working days in a week at the Old Bailey, Monday to Friday. Only one Sheriff was needed on duty each day, so the lay Sheriff would have Mondays/Wednesdays and Fridays, whilst the aldermanic Sheriff took Tuesdays and Thursdays. Both Sheriffs were allotted a number of places for guests to lunch at the Old Bailey – generally a good but light meal, given that the judges were back in court fairly promptly in the afternoon. Having to spend all day sitting in their courts listening to the tales of murder, rape and robbery, lunch was always a welcome break for them and a pleasant change to meet some outsiders. The Sheriff's guests were therefore spread out among the judges; the list was always selected with care, from a list of personal friends and colleagues, bearing in mind their potential to make interesting conversation over lunch. The chosen guests would arrive at about 12.30 and be introduced to one another before going to meet the judges who would be gathered enjoying their pre-prandial orange juice (no alcohol before judging) before a prompt entry into lunch. One of the Aldermen would be present representing the Lord Mayor. He was there to put the judges back into court (or at least into the four old courts – there were 23 courts running in total and he would have spent all afternoon putting them in had he had to do all of them) after which your guests were given the option of sitting in court to observe the progress of a trial.

The whole procedure was a great deal more formal than the American way of doing things that one is accustomed to seeing on television. I am in favour of a degree of ceremony and believe it lends a civility and sense of importance to the tone of the proceedings. As one used to wearing a naval uniform and then the robes of my civic career, I do know that a uniform or formal dress changes one – you feel different wearing it, and it bestows a certain sense of responsibility. Perhaps I am old-fashioned in my beliefs, but I suspect a little dignity leads a criminal to believe that he has been 'done' correctly and that proper justice has been dispensed.

Historically, the Sheriffs would have had their own courts, where they would have been represented by an Under-Sheriff. The Under-Sheriff remained now as a permanent paid hand ensuring that Shrieval duties were carried out correctly. He was usually a retired serving officer, the discipline of a military background proving to be highly suitable for this largely administrative role.

I was provided with accommodation at the Old Bailey for myself and my wife, with bedroom, bathroom and dressing room and a sitting room/office. I also had a liveried footman to accompany me when I went out who sat with the chauffeur in the front of the car. It was his duty to ensure that you had everything you needed about you and that you were also dressed in your right gear for the occasion. The dress of a Sheriff at the Old Bailey was similar to court dress (something that might have been worn by Dr Johnson or his contemporaries) with a cutaway tail coat, black waistcoat and black trousers, all worn with a stiff reverse collar with a lace jabot. Around your neck you would have your chain of office and your badge. This is also what the judges wore under their gowns. When we were putting judges in we wore our scarlet gowns over the top of our 'Old Bailey', which was worn with trousers by day or with knee breeches and silk stockings (or in my case a pair of large ladies' tights which stayed up much more effectively) and buckled shoes for evening occasions. Shortened to 'O.B.B. & C.', the 'Old Bailey', breeches and chain was the standard uniform.

Generally speaking, if an assembled company were wearing dinner jackets, then the rule was to wear the Old Bailey with trousers; if they were sporting white tie and tails then it was knee breeches and buckled shoes. The whole assemblage was quite comfortable – certainly more so than a stiff shirt. For really special occasions we wore court dress – a very similar cut of dress, with tailcoat, waistcoat and knee breeches, but made of black velvet and with cut steel buttons, which would catch the light most effectively. When I first started as an Alderman, we also wore lightweight swords with our court dress, although this tradition was abandoned in the early seventies. The court dress also included a soft lace stock rather than the stiff jabot. In addition to these two main pieces of kit we also had two gowns: a scarlet gown trimmed with ermine and sable, and the working gown, blue in colour which was trimmed with black bear. These had to be bought, and they had a good second-hand value (as long as the previous owner had not spilt too much soup down his). They were worn over the top of other gear, and usually during the day, rather than the evening.

The formal dress of the court all lent weight to the sense of theatre attached to the proceedings. There are arguments against the unnecessary pomp and circumstance, but I have listened to those in countries other than our own who have either never had such a thing or who have dispensed with all such traditions, who inevitably warn against getting rid of it. Once such formality disappears, it can never be reclaimed. My thought for those who deride uniform and formal dress as impractical and comical is that what counts is the nature of the person wearing the outfit. The dress of a uniformed Yeoman at the Tower of London is appropriate because it reflects the genuine character of the Yeoman himself; if actors were to dress up in the same gear to show tourists around, the whole point would be lost. For my part, I always felt as proud of my civic dress as I did of my naval uniform, as an outward visible sign of something important inside.

Once you were appointed Sheriff, all magisterial duties came to an end for the year. Not that I missed it, since my time was taken up by plenty of other activities. I kept a fairly comprehensive journal at the time, from which I might give an example of some of my days' work, as a flavour of the whole:

> To office by car, 9.00 a.m. To Old Bailey, 12.15 and to Mansion House to pick up Lord Mayor. Lunch with Committee of Lloyd's. Back to Old Bailey 3.00 p.m. Boys (i.e. my sons) plus six other cadets from Pangbourne to tea at the Old Bailey. Seafarers' service at St. Paul's at 5.30 – Bishop of Buckingham, preacher. (This I recall as a very nice occasion for me, since Pangbourne was parading its Colour, to be laid up on the altar. My elder son was in the Colour Party, whilst Christopher was singing in the choir). Back to the Mansion House at 7.30. Collected Lord Mayor for Music Committee Dinner. L.M. went home with the chauffeur and I stayed on at the Old Bailey for the night.

The following day:

> Up at 8.00 a.m. Coffee. Walked to the office, collected by chauffeur at 11.45. To Old Bailey for duty. 12.30 to Mansion House. Drinks with Secretaries. Trinity House lunch – very good – sat next to Lord Wansford of Oxford. To Old Bailey, 3.00 p.m. Wrote letters. 6.00 p.m Savoy for Iranian Ambassador's party. Thence to Clockmakers Company at Goldsmith's. Home 11.45.

Two days on, and another day is recorded:

> To office by car, 8.30. Collected to Old Bailey and thence to Guildhall at noon for General Purposes Committee of Aldermen. Lunch after. Collected 2.45. Picked up Libby at Old Bailey, then to Quit Rent Ceremony at the Law Courts. Tea after with Queen's Remembrancer. Back to Old Bailey, then left Mansion House at 5 o'clock for Deal. Arrived at 7.30 for Royal Marines 309th birthday dinner. Commandant General presided. Very good. Left at 1.30 a.m for London.

A busy day. To explain the Quit Rent Ceremony: it was the custom in centuries gone by for a Sovereign to reward one who had done some service to the country with land, perhaps with a manor house thrown in. Although such land was a gift of the crown, it was actually rented to the subject, although for a token in kind rather than money (hence the term 'peppercorn rent' although another example was payment in wolves' heads, as a means of keeping the wolf population down). The rent had no value, as such, but retained the status of the property, which remained under the ownership of the Crown. The City has paid two lots of Quit Rent to the Crown over the centuries – one to a forge in St. Clements Dane, which has long since ceased to exist (indeed I'm not sure that anyone ever knew where it was); the other to a plot of land in the West Country. Every year the Sheriffs go to the Law Courts where the Queen's Remembrancer formally receives the rent, which the City Solicitor brings with him in a bag. One lot of rent consists of a blunt hatchet and a sharp hatchet; the other six war horseshoes, with 64 nails. The said items are duly produced, and the efficacy of the hatchets tested by chopping up some faggots. The 64 nails are then ceremoniously counted out. The public are invited in to watch this ancient ceremony and a great display is made of it, with gasps being emitted as the City Solicitor slowly counts the nails – woe betide if he has not brought the requisite number with him. After the ceremony, the hatchets and nails are returned to be re-presented the following year. An interesting piece of theatre, and one which could never be invented, which reminds us just how long the City has been going and what part it has played in the history of our country. And afterwards we would all go up to join the Queen's Remembrancer for a drink. It was a late night, that night, with the long drive back from Deal, although of course drink-driving was never a problem, as I was whisked along to my destination in the upholstered comfort of a Rolls Royce.

On to the 28th October:

Up at 9.00. Down with Libby to the Old Bailey. Changed, and St. Bartholomew the Great [a church just by Smithfields meat market] for Remembrance Service for the City of London Yeomanry. Lord Mayor under doctor's order to rest so stood in for him and inspected the Guard of Honour, etc. [this was unusual: a Sheriff would not normally stand in for the Lord Mayor. I suspect that here he was in attendance but it was probably too cold for him to be standing around outside. Obviously feeling the effects as his Mayoralty came to an end.] Drinks in the Mess after. Back to Fairholt Street and an early night [probably just as well].

The time was approaching for the changeover in the Mayoralty. On 9th November (which of course used to be Lord Mayor's Day) the Silent Ceremony (the Silent Change, as it was called) was held at Guildhall, after lunch at the Mansion House. The only speaking in the ceremony is when the incoming Lord Mayor takes the oath.

The following day was, that year, the day of the Lord Mayor's show, once described as the largest un-rehearsed spectacle in the world. The procession commences at Guildhall, goes past the Mansion House where the Lord Mayor takes the salute and then gets into his coach, then proceeds to Temple Bar and the Law Courts where it stops and the Lord Mayor gets out and goes inside to be sworn in as Chief Magistrate to the City before the Lord Chief Justice of England. The party then moves on to the Master of the Rolls court where another welcoming speech is made, before re-embarking into their coach and returning with the whole procession via a different route (along Embankment and Queen Victoria Street). Each Lord Mayor has a theme, chosen by him, which is expressed in the floats and the representatives present. It is a mixture of the military, marching bands and Territorial Army units, and some magnificent floats produced by those companies supporting the Show and its theme. The whole object of the exercise is to satisfy the Charter of 1215 that after the election of the Lord Mayor the successful candidate must be presented to the Sovereign (or the Barons of the Exchequer in the event of his absence) for Royal approval. Over the centuries the ceremony has evolved into a Show for the people, although it did originate with a specific purpose. At one time the procession took place on the river from the City to Westminster, but for some 250 years it has taken place on dry land as a vehicular and mounted parade.

At the outset, there is a little ceremony in Guildhall, where the Lord Mayor and the two Sheriffs are presented with illuminated addresses by their Livery Company and appropriate institutions. The Lord Mayor and his Sheriffs sit in the Crypt at Guildhall whilst these things are brought forward, as the Remembrancer calls out the name of the organisation or institution presenting the address. The Master, Wardens and Clerk of the particular Livery Company will then come forward and read out the address, which is then rolled into a scroll and presented to the Lord Mayor or Sheriffs, in turn. All three in turn then thank those presenting. In my case, I was presented with an address from my Livery Company, the Honourable Company of Master Mariners; the Bassishaw Ward Club, representing my City ward; the City Livery Club of which I was a member, and the City branch of St. John's Ambulance, where I was the Treasurer. And, best of all (a bit of one-upmanship here) the Remembrancer announced 'The Deputy Master of Trinity House' and, God bless them, my brethren came forward in their frock coats and swords, and a little bit of history was made, as I was the first Younger Brother ever to be a Sheriff of the City.

The Sheriffs have their own carriages in the Lord Mayor's Show, as co-sponsors of the event. The Lord Mayor's Show and the Lord Mayor's Banquet on the following Monday are paid for by the Lord Mayor (a half share) and the Sheriffs (a quarter share each). If there is a shortfall on the Show, then they have to split the difference, although if a profit is made (which it generally is) then the money is given by the Lord Mayor to his favourite charity.

We had a fine day for the Show that year, and it was a great success. I managed to persuade the Lord Mayor to include Pangbourne's marching party. What made it particularly personal that year was that Nicholas, now Chief Cadet Captain of the College, was marching in front of his men and giving the 'eyes left' as they passed the Mansion House, whilst ahead of them marched the College Band, where Christopher was the First Fife. This was in fact Nicholas' s second stint and he was to appear in the Show again when he was at University. It was a good day for the Gilletts.

On the Sunday a service was held at St. Paul's Cathedral which we attended with the Lord Mayor, who took the salute before going to the Royal Exchange to lay wreaths at the War Memorial there. Monday 12th November then saw the Lord Mayor's Banquet. The afternoon was taken up with various group photographs before going at 6 o'clock to the Guildhall for the Reception of the guests, which takes place in the Old Library. The Lord Mayor and Sheriffs flanked by their ladies, behind which are the Maids of Honour and behind those some of the Pikemen from the Honourable Artillery Company, all in our best court dress with gowns over. The guests come in the door of the Old Library and 'run the gauntlet' between the lines of Councilmen and lesser guests, up three steps onto the dais and then forward to be received by the Lord Mayor and Lady Mayoress. They then move off to the left or right as appropriate. First guests are

Nicholas as 2nd in command of the Guard (using my sword!), Pangbourne.

generally the Court of Aldermen and their wives, who sit on one side, followed by various Ambassadors and heads of industry. The Lord Chancellor has a procession of his own, with the Great Seal borne before him; the Lord Chief Justice comes up; the Prime Minister; and of course the late Lord Mayor, in whose honour the banquet is held. Each received guest shakes hands with the Lord Mayor and Lady Mayoress and bows to the Sheriffs before taking his place. We had arranged that my father would be coming as a guest; he made his appearance in white tie and tails and immediately behind him came the boys, both dressed in uniform. This got a good round of applause – my father had always been very popular as a Lord Mayor – and then, despite Libby's instructions, Christopher came up and gave his mother a smacking great kiss, which was extremely well received. We had a very good banquet, as you might expect. The Prime Minister of the day was Edward Heath. Tradition once demanded that the P.M. speak on foreign affairs but this had already been broken by Harold Wilson, who had made it more of a state-of-the-nation speech, and this has now become more of the norm. The Prime Minister's speech is in reply to that of the Lord Mayor, who begins the round of speeches by proposing the health of Her Majesty's Ministers. The P.M. is then followed by the Archbishop of Canterbury, who proposes the health of the late Lord Mayor; the late Lord Mayor, who replies to the Archbishop, and finally the Lord Chancellor who proposes the health of the Lord Mayor and the Lady Mayoress. All four speeches used to be broadcast in their entirety; nowadays we get edited highlights, mostly of the Prime Minister's speech. It is a great occasion, the Guildhall sparkling with the City plate, an orchestra playing and, by modern standards, a generous menu. The Guildhall seats 700, out of which the Lord Mayor gets a ration of 35 couples and each Sheriff gets 20 couples, plus extras if any on the official list are unable to attend. After the Banquet, there is sometimes dancing for those who wish, thus spreading the load of those waiting to get away.

On 11th December we had our first state visit, both Sheriffs joining the Lord Mayor at Victoria Station to greet the President of Zaire, Mr Mobutu, who arrived in a train (slightly late) to be met by the Queen and the Duke of Edinburgh and other members of the Royal family. The Queen then took him down the presentation line, starting with the Prime Minister and moving through the Lord Mayor of London and his Sheriffs down to the Chairman of the G.L.C. and the Lord Mayor of Westminster. A great choir of black faces lined the platform, and as soon as the President arrived they burst into some sort of tribal chant – something that took me right back to my Boy Scout days, when Baden-Powell used to produce African-style songs. The procession moved out into the main concourse outside where the President was to inspect a Guard of Honour. As the support group moved out and took up their chanting again, the poor horses waiting with the carriages took fright and began jumping restlessly, much to the annoyance of the Crown Equerry who was cursing the enthusiastic chanting under his breath. Not that anything could be done; eventually they quietened down and the procession moved slowly off. The President was on the usual three-day state visit; after being entertained at Buckingham Palace the first evening (not attended by the Sheriffs) the next day was our turn, with a banquet in the Guildhall for him and his retinue. Tony and I were sporting our new medals; it was customary at this sort of thing for an exchange of gongs between the two parties and we had duly been made 'Commanders of the Order of the Leopard of Zaire', for which honour we were presented with a medal each which looked more the sort of badge which would let you in to the greyhound racing at White City.

The country was at this time under the grip of fuel shortages as a result of miners' strikes. To show willing in the City we cancelled the normal Livery banquets which were generally held nightly and only used Rolls Royces when absolutely necessary – either sharing one between us or, on occasion, using my car. This habit rather caught on throughout the City and those in high office were eventually vying with one another to be seen to be doing 'the right thing'. Smaller and smaller cars appeared; the Lord Mayor was seen in a Morris Minor shooting brake and the Archbishop of Canterbury turned up to the Lord Mayor's Banquet or some grand function in a very small car. I suffered at the hands of the design of this shooting brake; the Lord Mayor had decided to use it on the occasion of the Royal Warrant-Holders' lunch held at Grosvenor House, at which Bobby Popham, the Sword-Bearer was the esquire on duty. Bobby was a large man and he had to sit in the front with the chauffeur. The only trouble was that in doing so the seat went down so much that it nearly cut off the legs of the person behind. I happened to be that person, although this was not in itself the problem. I was sharing the back seat with the Lord Mayor who sat in the middle and a footman on his right, clutching a lectern, which he carried about with him for the Lord Mayor's use. Over the rear wheel arches in this car was a sort of map compartment; there was so little room in the back that I was forced to sit with my right buttock perched on the seat and my left in the said map compartment; added to which, being tall, I was bent double like a safety pin. The chauffeur informed us that as the traffic was bad he would take us the back way from the Mansion House which involved whizzing up side streets and round corners and by the time we arrived I was so uncomfortably stuck in my position that I had to be hauled out by my arms. Compared to the luxuries of some terms of office, I think ours was rather curtailed in that department, at least until the warmer weather arrived and the need for fuel subsided. Having said that, it was probably much better for our health, since the Shrievalty would normally see one dining out night after night with some Livery company or other.

My son Christopher had earlier that year won the boys' photographic competition run by the Missions to Seamen. On 21st December we took him down to Gatwick, from where he was to fly off to Tangiers to join the school ship *Nevasa* for a trip down the West African coast by way of his prize. He wasn't entirely happy about it – it would mean missing Christmas at home, and he was to be attached to another school party for the occasion, which meant that he knew no-one on the trip, but it was a marvellous opportunity for him. Nicholas had by now finished at Pangbourne and had signed up to Imperial College to take an honours degree in physics for three years, so was around at home. Christopher arrived back on 6th January, and Libby and I went down to meet him in the car. He was looking very brown and very pleased with himself; despite being on his own he had gained popularity very easily, helped by the fact that he could play the piano and would gather people around him for entertainment. He also succeeded in winning the fancy dress competition by donning a Monty Python-style brown raincoat and pork-pie hat, under which he wore nothing but a pair of small underpants. Covering his crotch was a piece of card with the word BOO! writ large across it, and he merely 'flashed' at the judges who were evidently impressed – although rather ironically his prize was a camera! I subsequently used the costume myself with similar effect when on a cruise in the Barrier Reef.

No sooner was Christopher back than Nicholas took off. I felt it was advisable to take a year 'off' between school and university and I supported both boys in this. Nicholas opted to go to America, staying with various friends. It had been his burning ambition to visit Cape

Canaveral – ever since acquiring his first chemistry set at the age of eleven he had been a committed scientist and took it all very seriously. On 10th January I saw him off at Heathrow on a flight to New York, where Libby's sister Stella now had a flat. From here he travelled to visit his godfather, General Biddell, who lived in Philadelphia, thence down to Cape Canaveral to inspect the space museum. He then took a Greyhound bus to Cincinnati and then on to Chicago, where one of his school chums was on an exchange with an American family and attending High School there. Nicholas was permitted to attend the school with his friend Steve, which I believe was an interesting experience but one which did not leave him terribly impressed. The students seemed reasonably well-versed in knowledge of their own state, but knew very little of anything outside of it. He became rather uptight when they asked in all sincerity whether we had television in England. Drawing himself up to his full height he said, 'Yes. We invented it.' They were the sort of people who did not know the difference between Australia and Austria – and more to the point, did not really care. Nevertheless, it was an experience for Nicholas. From there he went to Gross Point where our friends the Russells lived and he stayed on there for a further four weeks. At the end of the trip I went to meet him at Heathrow, feeling somewhat anxious that America might have proved to offer everything he wanted and that he might now consider emigrating.

'Did you like it?' I enquired.

'It was alright,' came the somewhat taciturn reply. 'Interesting to visit. I wouldn't want to live there, though.'

I breathed a sigh of relief. At least he was not going to rush off and become an American, and the Baronetcy would be safe for another generation.

As I write, he is actually working out in America. But he retains his English accent!

Chapter 7

The year ahead (1974) was to be a busy one. On 21st January Richard Blackwood joined as my assistant administration manager at Bevington House. I had recruited him on the instruction of the new Managing Director, who had taken Ron Bowers away to be the computer manager. I knew exactly where I should seek out a new recruit; I wanted an ex-serviceman who had left either the Navy, Army or the R.A.F. in the rank of Lieutenant Commander, Major or Squadron Leader, who would have done a course to orientate himself and who was therefore bound to have had sufficient experience in administration. Richard Blackwood had been a Major in the Royal Signals and had been responsible for the hard graft of the withdrawal of the British presence in Malta; he would certainly be well equipped to handle a move of offices or some such. I put him through a process of induction and he shared an office with me, which enabled him to observe my working practice at first hand. If anything, his only fault was that he was rather too dyed-in-the-wool military and he would produce vast sheets of daily orders and suchlike. This level of detail was somewhat incomprehensible to his colleagues, who took some getting used to it, but nevertheless his heart was in the right place. He subsequently masterminded our move to Barking and then went down there to oversee that end of things when I was back in harness.

On 25th January we honoured Robbie Burns by having haggis for lunch at the Old Bailey, which provided a change from our usual diet. Mr Justice Thompson gave the address to the haggis.

The large silver Ford Zodiac was by now beginning to feel its age a bit; the plugs were always oiling up and it was clearly time for her to be pensioned off. So, on February 8th I went down to collect my new car – another Ford, but this time a Granada GXL and the first automatic transmission that I had owned. It was a rather extraordinary copper colour, which I did not particularly care for, but I did like the car and it was the only colour available at the time. In those days it was possible to change the licence number and I kept my distinctive *1 DLX*, which I had had since the original blue Ford Mark II. It made it very easy to locate my car in a crowded car park although the downside was that the police could spot it just as easily! I planned to give the old car to the motor club at Pangbourne where they could take her to pieces or drive her around if they so wanted, but for a while we became a two-car family, which was most convenient. On 16th March we went down to Pangbourne where Christopher was playing Damis in *Tartuffe*. His performance reinforced my opinion that he was a very good actor, which was to be affirmed in his later operatic career.

On 21st March there was a farewell party for Sir Edward Nicholls, the retiring Town Clerk. He had held the post since 1954 and in his twenty-year stint he had seen both the Gilletts serving as Aldermen. He had been knighted a few years previously and had, indeed, been one of the great Town Clerks. He was succeeded that year by Mr Clayton. Two days later the whole Mayoral party took a train down to Cardiff to take part in an official visit on the occasion of Cardiff ceasing to be a corporate city – its local government powers were being transferred to South Glamorgan. We were met by the stationmaster sporting his top hat who, thus attired, saw us safely on to the train at 12 noon. We arrived at Cardiff at 2.35 where we were met by the Lord Mayor of Cardiff and driven to his Mansion House to unpack and have tea. In the evening a motorcade sped us to the Town Hall for a meeting of the Council and an exchange of addresses. This was followed by a reception and then a civic banquet. The Council Chamber, like many a municipal chamber, was circular in shape, with the Lord Mayor at the front, flanked by his Aldermen and the officers of the court in tiered rows filling the rest of the circle. We sat in the middle clad in our gowns and with all the formal paraphernalia of office (the mace etc.) around us. It was a solemn occasion, being their last formal meeting as a council. Long and eloquent speeches were made to which we listened dutifully. It was in the midst of all of this that I suddenly noticed a spiral of blue smoke rising from the front benches; it took me a while to work out that this was a lit cigarette, and that one of the Alderman was having a smoke! I glanced round to see if anyone else had noticed; when I turned to look back at the Common Council I saw a councilman in his gown puffing away at a great curly pipe. That evening at the banquet I was sitting next to the wife of the Bishop of Llandaff. I commented to her that I had found it most extraordinary to see people smoking in the Council Chamber. 'That's nothing,' she replied, in her Welsh lilt, 'They also smoke in the Cathedral!' This was something of a turn-up for my Book of Traditions! We had a comfortable night at the Mansion House that night, and the next day proceeded in another motorcade to the Civic Centre and then for lunch at Cardiff Castle, where the Lord Mayor was presented with one of the white peacocks that roamed the grounds – I believe it was for his house in Scotland. We returned by train to London on Sunday 24th March.

My chauffeur, Grey, had by now given in his notice and on 1st April my new chauffeur reported for work. Martin Phillips was the son-in-law of Andrews, one of the Lord Mayor's chauffeurs. He looked terribly young – I believe he was only about 22 – but he had been taught to drive by his father-in-law and certainly knew how to handle a Rolls Royce. We were still on 'rations' at that time, and there were still very few of the customary evening gadabouts that would normally go with our office. However, most of the Boroughs were still holding Borough receptions. These events have all but died out now, but at that time every London Borough would hold one at some time in the year, with the Lord Mayor of London as the principal guest and the Chairman of the G.L.C. also invited. It would often mean breaking off whatever else one happened to be engaged with at the time and speeding off to Bromley, or Croydon or some other far distant place for their receptions. It has to be said that the Labour controlled boroughs always had much more fun than the Conservatives who, in my view, tended to be rather proper and staid and very conscious of the presence of the Lord Mayor. But the redder they were, the more they would let their hair down, and would sometimes be partying until four in the morning. We would, however, retire gracefully at midnight – particularly if it seemed likely that they would break into 'The Red Flag' rather than 'God Save the Queen'.

Christopher Rawson's new yacht, *Hodzah*, was now at Cowes, and that Easter we all went down, accompanying Christopher and Rosemary and their two girls, Gina and Caroline. Some of the party stayed on board but the girls stayed at the Royal Corinthian Yacht Club. The weather was kind to us and we had a relaxing break over the Easter weekend, which proved to be the first of many. *Hodzah* was named after an Albanian phrase Christopher had picked up whilst on his travels. The word was used when glasses were raised and he had assumed it meant 'cheers' or some equivalent. Subsequently it transpired that they had been toasting the local mayor and that the term was translated as 'magistrate' or 'chief citizen'. Not that it mattered too much, as Christopher was a magistrate himself anyway!

On 22nd April a farewell party was held for Mr Chandler, the Chief Clerk of the Guildhall Justice Room. He had been there for many, many years and had been very kind to me when I first became a tenderfoot magistrate. He had served my father as well as me, always on hand to guide new magistrates on the job but without ever being obtrusive in any way. He became a stipendiary magistrate in his own right after that, but I was sorry to see him go.

The 23rd April was a big day for the Royal Marines in the City, with a special service being held for them at St. Lawrence Jewry, the City church, where they had provided a screen between the Commonwealth Chapel and the main body of the church, made out of wrought ironwork and some steel from H.M.S. *Hermes*. The screen was dedicated by the Bishop of London, who also gave the sermon. The service was followed by a march past the Mansion House, the salute being taken by H.R.H. the Duke of Edinburgh and the Lord Mayor plus the Commandant General and the First Sea Lord. This rather special relationship had been encouraged by Basil Watson, the incumbent of St. Lawrence Jewry, who had been chaplain to the Royal Marines at their barracks at Portsmouth. Because the Marines had been raised in the City originally, they were also one of the few privileged regiments permitted to march through the City with drums beating and colours flying.

The Easter Banquet at the Mansion House was held on the evening of the 24th April. This is an annual event held by the Lord Mayor for members of the diplomatic corps and their wives. They all sit in order of precedence as ambassadors to the court of St. James, so the 'doyen' is usually from some very small country who just happens to have been in post for a very long time. The only trouble from out point of view was that because the American and Russian High Commissioners usually changed after three or four years, they were always in a heap down at the bottom of the table and we were always stuck at the top with the rather more obscure lot. It was usually a very colourful affair, even though sometimes we struggled to know what those at the top were saying! Another banquet was held on 26th April to celebrate the 150th anniversary of the R.N.L.I. As I write, now, we have just celebrated their 175th anniversary, which is an indication of how time flies.

On 29th April – another gong! This one was rather more prestigious than my last: a Commander (Class II) of the Dannebrog. It came from the Queen of Denmark who arrived the next day so I had it ready to wear when I met her. This one was a neck order, rather like a C.B.E., and came with a little lapel button. We had the usual state banquet for her on the Wednesday, 1st May. She must have stayed for rather longer than the usual three days as I have a record of her presenting colours to the H.A.C. on Saturday 4th May.

On May 7th we had the Aldermen's Dinner at the Mansion House. This usually takes place at the beginning of the year but had been postponed this year because of the fuel rationing. This was another annual dinner, given each year by the Lord Mayor to his brother Aldermen and I was asked to reply to the toast to the Sheriffs. It was a very good evening, although was a difficult one to speak to, I always thought, since all of those present were 'family', as it were, and well used to both hearing and making speeches of their own. It was rather like being asked to get up at a large family Christmas party and make a speech; I would far rather do it to a large company of people whom I have never met before than an intimate group of acquaintances.

On Saturday 18th May the whole party went to Christ's Hospital Girls' School in Hertford for Speech Day. It meant missing the motor sailor race at Cowes, although Nicholas was with *Hodzah* and won.

The 22nd May saw St. Paul's Cathedral packed for the service held every four years for the Order of the British Empire. The Lord Mayor carried the pearl sword in front of the Queen. It was a magnificent service, although I did not realise then how many more times I would be attending it in an official capacity in the years to come.

On Monday May 27th we were off on our travels for an overseas visit by the Lord Mayor, accompanied by both the Sheriffs and their ladies, to Geneva and Baden-Baden. We all drove to London Airport and arrived at Geneva at 12.15, where we were met by the mayor and taken to *La Reserve* (the hotel where we were staying) for drinks and lunch. There was a reception and an exchange of civic gifts in the early afternoon and then on to *La Grange* for an official dinner and entertainment. When I got home that evening (we did not get back until 12.30) we had a nightcap with the Esquires until 2.00 a.m. Libby informed me that she had been speaking to the British Vice-Consul during the party who informed her that the men of the party would be visiting the Rolex factory whilst in Geneva. Here, inevitably, the Lord Mayor would be presented with a gold Rolex Oyster and, she was informed, the Sheriffs would probably be receiving a stainless steel one. This bit of news pleased me greatly. I was in need of a good watch and stainless steel would be fine, as far as I was concerned. I went to sleep a happy man.

On the day following, the party duly set off for the Rolex factory. It was a large, modern building. We were received there by the President, who escorted us to a small cinema. Here a very slick presentation was made on the history of Rolex and the production, in particular, of the Rolex oyster watch. After this we were taken to the factory itself to see these watches being made. I was being particularly enthusiastic, for the benefit of the manager who was escorting me, saying how much as a sailor I appreciated the importance of time in navigation etc. etc. and generally trying my best to earn the watch I thought awaited me at the end of the visit. On the other hand the Lord Mayor, who knew quite a lot about clocks and watches and happened to be a member of the Worshipful Company of Clockmakers as one of his Livery Companies, kept on interrupting and whispering loudly into my ear (rather too loudly for my comfort) that this was not *real* watch-making, just production line stuff. I hoped that his disparaging remarks could not be heard by the members of the Rolex staff who hovered about us. The tour over, we were escorted into the Boardroom. 'Ah – present time!' I thought, eagerly. Sure enough, the President made a fulsome little speech to the Lord Mayor and presented him, as expected, with a beautiful gold Oyster watch in a small leather case. The Lord Mayor equally fulsomely accepted the gift, although I could not but help thinking how hypocritical it seemed. The presentation over, I looked about to see what was coming next. Unfortunately the only other gift-wrapped parcels in evidence were far too large to be watches. The Vice-Consul had got it wrong. All other members of the party received books on the history of Geneva, the history of watch making in Switzerland and the history of Rolex and how the Oysters were made.

We retired then to a lakeside restaurant, the *Lion D'Or* (the Lord Mayor sporting his glistening gold watch) to join the ladies for a good lunch. Lunch over, watch making was on the agenda yet again, but this time at the workshops of Vacheron et Constantine. As far as the Lord Mayor was concerned, this promised something quite different.

The morning had seen the Ford production line; now we were going to see *real* watch making. We arrived at the workshop (it was not big enough to merit the term factory) and were ushered into the Boardroom. No films, no videos, no slick presentations here – just the senior staff members to welcome us. The Lord Mayor had with him a Vacheron pocket watch of which he was very fond; he produced this and they immediately whisked it off, returning a few minutes later to tell him who had made it and when. He was highly delighted and gave me a satisfied look as if to say – the real thing at last! We then went into the workshop itself to see the watches being made. The place was full of elderly gentlemen with spectacles balanced on the ends of their noses who looked as if they had been making watches for about a hundred years. The workshop produced only about sixty watches a year, each one individually hand made. We were invited to look through a large magnifying glass at what looked to the naked eye like the debris from an electric razor after shaving; looking through the lens revealed that each was a tiny cog or part from the inside of a watch. If you had sneezed you would have lost about a year's worth of production! I had absolutely no expectation here, of course, of receiving a watch at the end of the tour, and I doubt that the Lord Mayor had either. Nevertheless, it was down to the Boardroom at the end of our visit, where he was presented with the slimmest evening watch I have ever seen. It was beautiful, with a fine crocodile skin strap. And what did I get? Some more books on how watches were made.

Early evening we flew to Basel and were met by a German delegation. After dinner we drove to our hotel in Baden-Baden, arriving there at 11.45 p.m. Our programme in Germany was a pretty punishing one, so much so that on any one day we never managed to complete our schedule. They got us up for breakfast at 8.30 and then we drove through the town to Brahms' House. We had lunch with various civic heads at the Kirk House and then a state drive in carriages to a meeting with the Council and an exchange of gifts. It was extraordinarily warm there at that time of year and we had to sit and listen to a number of lengthy speeches of welcome. It was a case of 'thinking cool', sitting as still as possible in one's gowns. After the speeches were over, the Öberburgermeister clapped his hands. Now we have a special gift, Lord Mayor, for you to take back to the citizens of London. Whereupon four Rhine Maidens entered bearing a large tub in which was a very sizeable Christmas tree from the

Black Forest, to be planted in the City somewhere. This was all part of a P.R. exercise on the part of the spa town of Baden-Baden, I believe, rather than an act of political *entente*. That evening we visited the local theatre – not unusual in small German towns, which tend to be better endowed with that kind of thing than we are over here – although we were, as ever, short of time. It was worse for the ladies, who were of course expected to look their best but who were given no time in the schedule to have their hair done or recover from their journey. They had to arrange for a hairdresser to come in early in the morning to prepare them for the day. The following day we had breakfast in our bedroom, as usual, and then went to the Casino for a press conference and a roulette game. A competition was staged between the Lord Mayor and the Öberburgermeister to bid for toys for disabled children; a nice idea of course, but not terribly exciting to watch. For lunch we drove to a villa in the country (I think it was an old monastery) where our presents were picnic baskets. It has to be said that the British press corps, who had been invited along for coverage of the trip, behaved pretty badly. They attended all the parties; whether they reported anything I don't know but they made their presence known and were seen to be very noisy and drunk. That afternoon we returned to our hotel to pack and then drove to Strasbourg to catch the plane back to London. Strasbourg is not a large airport; there are sheep grazing on the runway between flights. The Öberburgermeister arrived to see us off bearing a pile of large teddy bears, intended for the Lord Mayor's grandchildren. A nice gesture – but unfortunately or plane was very small and the only place to accommodate these large soft toys was in the loo; too bad if anyone needed to use the facility en route. The other slight hiccup was that the Lady Mayoress was very suspicious of flying with thirteen people in an aeroplane. I was doing a quick headcount; including the two pilots and stewardesses I am sure we were thirteen in number. However, she asked Peter Milo, the City Marshal, to count the people on board, declaring that she would be unable to fly if there were thirteen of us. He quickly reassured her that we were fourteen. I am not sure that she was 100% convinced, but away we went. Throughout the flight the stewardess hardly came near us; the door of the cockpit was open and we were able to see that she spent most of the time there chatting up the pilots! Not quite the treatment we were used to, but we arrived home safely at last. In order to recover from the rigours of our first overseas visit,

Libby and I went down to Cowes and managed a bit of sailing over the weekend.

On 7th June we embarked on a series of mini-visits to various places throughout the U.K. The Lord Mayor was very good at organising this sort of thing and managing to mix business with pleasure. He had a 'country seat' up in Scotland and we were to go and stay there for a long weekend, calling in for official visits at various places on the way. We formed a motorcade comprising the five Rolls Royces (the two Mansion House Rolls Royces, the two Sheriffs' Rolls Royces and the Lord Mayor's privately owned Corniche convertible) and a large shooting brake as a sort of 'baggage wagon'. Although the restrictions of the three day week were by now easing off a little, we were by no means back up to full steam, and given the amount of petrol our party would inevitably consume on the trip we pre-arranged stops to fill up with fuel on the way. The party consisted of the Lord Mayor and Lady Mayoress, both Sheriffs and their wives, the Chief Commoner, the Esquires and their wives and Judith Dagworthy, a P.R. representative from the Mansion House who came along to partner the Chief Commoner. In addition there were footmen and chauffeurs making up the party. We steamed off up to Birmingham, looking not unlike a funeral procession, and were entertained to lunch in the Civic Hall there by the Lord Mayor of Birmingham. Then it was back into our motorcade and on to Rydal Mount, Wordsworth's house on Lake Windermere, where we were shown round and given tea, before heading off up to Galloway, where the Lord Mayor had his 'seat', arriving in time for dinner at 9.30 p.m. Not everyone could be accommodated here, but within the grounds was an ancient Scottish fortified house – a sort of mini-castle – which had been restored and which was occupied by Bridget D'Oyly Carte, of the operatic family. Some members of the party were able to camp there. Caterers had been laid on for the weekend. On the Saturday we had a free morning and went up on to the moors for some loch fishing and then after lunch it was to Kirkcudbright in state and a march past of pipers, followed by a move on to New Galloway for a similar exercise. The natives were most impressed. New Galloway was the nearest village to the house, where the provost doubled as the local butcher. We disembarked from our vehicles just around the corner, where the main village street turned into a country road, and donned our gowns before processing with due pomp and ceremony down the village street to the accompaniment of cheers from delighted locals. It was then tea and buns at the Town Hall. On the Sunday we looked over the castle and spent time walking through the grounds before an afternoon ceremony to 'christen' the castle with a reception for the locals.

On the Monday we were up early and the motorcade steamed off to Newcastle, where we arrived at the Civic Centre at 12.20. We had lunch at their Mansion House with their Lord Mayor and then there was the usual exchange of gifts before embarking in our convoy once more, this time for Sheffield. We arrived at the City Hall here at 3.30 for the usual pleasantries. We were staying at the British Steel Corporation's guesthouse and went there to change for the evening celebration, which was the Cutlers' Forfeit Feast. This was a good do, with good speeches, and we got back to the guesthouse at midnight. Then it was up at 7.30 for departure at 9.30, and then we drove in our motorcade to London, where we arrived at 12.15 (I suspect by exceeding the speed limit) in time for lunch at the Old Bailey. It had been a good weekend, during which we were all able to get to know one another a little better.

In June the Öberburgermeister of Baden-Baden made a return visit to the Mansion House with his wife. Later on that month we made a visit to Bury St. Edmunds. Bury is one of the 'Magna Carta towns', which include London, Winchester, Runnymede and Canterbury. Every four years a parade takes place in one of these towns, at which the Master of the Rolls puts in an appearance – at this time it happened to be Lord Denning. I am quite convinced he slept with a copy of the Magna Carta under his bed, so keen was he on it. He had is own copy, which was rather battered and held together with Scotch tape and he would carry this thing through the streets as the parade made its way to the cathedral for a service. This year was the 750th anniversary of the signing of the Magna Carta. We had lunch in a very nice Georgian building known as the Athenaeum. Here the Master of the Rolls made his 'Magna Carta' speech – one which I had heard on several occasions previously, in which he always quoted from Kipling. On this occasion, I recall, he began (speaking without notes) with the usual 'And in the immortal words of Rudyard Kipling, which are indelibly printed in my memory...' and then got stuck. We all knew what they were, and for what seemed like hours but was probably only seconds, we sat with bated breath whilst he struggled to recall those 'indelibly printed' words. At last he found them, and continued, and we breathed again, but it had been a dodgy moment and a lesson learnt: never declare anything to be indelibly printed in your mind in public!

Back in London it was a quick change and then down to Pangbourne for a concert where Christopher was performing.

On 18th June one of my guests at the Old Bailey for lunch was Harold McMillan, who had been prime Minister when my father was Lord Mayor. He was getting on a bit by this time but was still as bright as a button and sat with a glass of whiskey in his hand, enthralling us all with anecdotes and stories of his time in office.

By this time my father had moved down to the cottage at Biddeston and I put his flat at Kingston House on to the market on his behalf. The only slight fly in the ointment was his younger sister, my aunt Frances, who had for years looked after her parents (my grandparents) in their flat in Holland Park. The flat had been left to her when they died and she stayed on there, even though with six bedrooms it was really far too big for her. She was a tough old stick but it now seemed right for her to move on. At the age of 75 she had survived a very unpleasant mugging. On her return from a shopping trip one day she had been accosted by a couple of thugs who had forced entry, tied her up and stuffed her ignominiously under the bed rolled in an eiderdown whilst they helped themselves to the family silver. She had managed to get out and raise the alarm but by this time it was too late and they had got away. The experience had not damaged her unduly, but she was persuaded by this incident, coupled with rising rents, to move elsewhere. She expressed a wish to move in with my father. He was not at all keen – his sister was a strong-minded woman, accustomed to getting her way and although he would visit it her at weekends he would not go out of his way to spend time with her. When my mother died he had moved into a smaller flat in Kingston House. Although it had two bedrooms, one of these had been turned into a dining room and there was really no room for Aunt Frances. We persuaded her that the best thing to do would be to move into a residential hotel in Queensgate – it was the sort of place where you could have your own furniture and your own room. My father continued to visit her there and she seemed happy enough. However, when he proposed to retire Biddeston she announced her intention to join him there and look after him in much the same way as she had her own father. This was not his idea of a joke, but he nevertheless found himself unable to refuse. She discharged herself from the hotel and moved lock, stock and barrel in with my father, proceeding to make his life something of a misery. She succeeded in alienating the locals in the village as well as the woman who used to come and cook, and she did not even make amends by feeding my father or looking after him properly. However, this anticipates another part of my story. I merely wished to point out that it was at this time that I was burning his bridges for him by putting the London flat on the market.

On June 23rd, a Sunday, Nicholas and I both drove down to Pangbourne, he in the new car and I in the old car. We left the old car behind, as a gift to the College motor club, as planned. The following day was the election of the following year's Sheriffs, although we would still be in post until the end of September. This took place in Guildhall; both were uncontested and Peter Vanneck as Aldermanic Sheriff and Hugh Olsen as the Lay Sheriff.

On 25th June we had a private visit from the President of the Gambia; he was a doctor who had been educated at Edinburgh, and proved to be very good company. He came to lunch at the Mansion House, where I was seated with his Foreign Minister. Being an Edinburgh man he was very keen on golf, and had established some golf clubs in the Gambia, although he was at pains to explain to us that of course in the Gambia they did not have 'greens', they had 'browns'. The Gambia itself is just a thin strip of a country and one of his objects on this visit was to purchase a yacht, which was to become the Gambian navy. Apparently they were having some trouble with Portuguese fishing vessels poaching in their waters and he wanted a vessel he could stick a gun on to act as a deterrent. I believe he succeeded in acquiring one from somewhere.

Tuesday 9th July saw another state visit and my third and final gong from an overseas visitor. This time we were to meet at Victoria the Agong of Malaysia, who arrived at 12.30 and was introduced by Her Majesty to the usual line up of guests. The Agong is an elected monarch and one of a number who rotate every seven years. I received the Order of Johan Sedia Mahkota (Commander of the Order of a protector of the Crown). It was another neck order and one I was very proud to wear. There was the customary banquet that night with an exchange of addresses and speeches.

We were at this time having our shots in preparation for our long overseas trip during the summer recess. It was down to Pangbourne on 13th July for Founders' Day, where Nicholas received the Founders' prize – the runner up to the Queen's Gold Medal.

Christopher, needless to say, got the music prize. The weather was not too good – it rained in the morning, but had cleared up in time for the cadets to beat the retreat in a formation they had invented themselves, which was most impressive.

Chapter 8

On the 2nd August the Old Bailey closed for the summer recess. Four courts were kept open for the duration, but the Aldermen on duty covered for the Sheriffs, who did not attend until the courts resumed again. This was normally the time for the Lord Mayor and Sheriffs to have a short rest and/or to have an overseas trip – and we did both. I went back to the office until the end of the following week, just to ensure that everything was alright while I was away, and on 15th August we took off to Cowes with the two boys to join the Rawsons in *Hodzah* for their summer cruise. Gina and Caroline were with them, so there was quite a crowd of us on board. Libby and I were in the main cabin, with double berth and Christopher and Rosemary had the after cabin. The rest of the party were distributed according to size: Nicholas (who was the largest) and Caroline (who was the smallest) had the wheelhouse, which was covered at night; Christopher and Gina had the two berths in the for'ard cabin.

On the 16th we sailed at night to Guernsey. It was very rough as we passed the Needles and we were bounced around quite alarmingly, which was not very conducive to sleeping. I was on watch with Christopher Rawson and the girls tried to sleep as best they could; suffice to say they were still in their night attire when we arrived at Guernsey at 3 o'clock the next afternoon, emerging from their bunks as we berthed in the Victoria Marina. I had never been there before; it was a truly delightful spot and I have returned nearly every summer since. We stayed for the rest of the weekend and on the Monday, 19th August, we sailed at 10.00 a.m. for St. Malo, where we arrived at 6 o'clock that evening. The plan was to sail up the River Rance, which leads up from St. Malo to Dinan, and then to navigate the canal system to emerge in the Bay of Biscay. Our plan, however, failed to materialise in quite the manner we had envisaged...

We spent one night in St. Malo and the following morning we proceeded up to Dinard, where a great hydro-electric system and barrage was sited. When the tide came in the water was let through into the river; at high water they shut it and then when the ebb started they opened the sluice gates, great turbines started whizzing round and from the combined force of tide and river, electricity was generated sufficient to provide power as far away as Paris. It was indeed a marvel of French engineering, attracting coach loads of visitors who would come to admire it. At one end was the lock, which gave access to the river. We entered, tied up and turned off the engine and waited as the lock filled. There were only about three yachts in the lock; but they were at pains to get us out as quickly as possible the other side. There was one more outward-bound lock to go that day, and there were people waiting on the other side to come in.

However, the engine refused to start. The lock staff were growing more and more agitated and, without consulting us, they whistled up a chap in a small motorboat and instructed him to tow us out. We gave this boat a line and he proceeded to tow us slowly out of the lock and into the river. I was up on the fo'c's'le and Christopher was steering. On the starboard side of the lock the water was very shallow and there were some artificial rocks – put there presumably either to support the walls of the lock or make it look more attractive – just below the surface. I am not quite sure how he managed it but one way and another he succeeded in towing us off into this shallow water and, inevitably, went aground. He got off and went astern, rocking his boat from side to side in an attempt to free it. It suddenly came off in a rush; the rope, which had been slack, tightened suddenly and the rather weak and ineffectual little cleat that it was tied to came adrift. The whole thing came flying back on board and hit me across the shins. I was in a great deal of pain and thought at first that my legs had been broken; they were, in fact, just heavily bruised but I was forced to go and lie down to recover. Our chap meanwhile had decided that his job was done and he could waste no more time. The tide was dropping with the same effect as pulling the plug out of a bath and before you could say Jack Robinson he had gone, leaving us aground! Rocks and boulders started appearing around us and it was clear that something would have to be done quickly before she fell over. The boys of the party leapt ashore and secured ropes from our masthead to convenient trees and bushes that were about the place. We found a pile of timber – they may have been railway sleepers – which we were able to use as props, shoving them underneath *Hodzah*'s rubbing strake on the port side. When the water went down the props and the ropes kept her list to about 35°. Luckily she had lodged between rocks and her hull had somehow remained undamaged. The water continued to drop and the rocks around us started drying out. Below us a road appeared and it was obvious that we were well and truly stuck. It was very uncomfortable on board and quite an eerie feeling to be on a heavily listed boat, which was not moving. So, looking rather like the Swiss Family Robinson after a shipwreck, we abandoned ship, taking ashore various items we needed, such as rugs to sit on and a picnic lunch. We then just sat looking forlornly at our poor vessel. There were a number of passers-by, with coaches bringing visitors to admire the hydroelectric station, and we provided an interesting spectacle. The younger members of the party took the opportunity to scrub down *Hodzah*, and clean her bottom whilst it was thus exposed. However this did not take long. The sun was high in the sky and it was becoming unbearably hot. Christopher Rawson stomped off to see the lock attendants and give them a piece of his mind and also to find out when we might be able to get off again. It was, after all, their fault that we were here – had we been allowed to sail out this could have been avoided. They were not much interested, however, dismissing him with cries of 'Allez! Allez! Allez!' They also provided the depressing news that we had just had the highest tide and it would be another *month* before we would be able to float off again. Our only alternative was to get a crane to lift us off and swing us across to the deeper water. This would have cost 1 million francs, which we did not imagine would please the underwriters greatly. It was agreed that for the comfort of our ladies we would find a hotel for them in Dinard and that Christopher, Nicholas and I would stay on board. The next high water was due at midnight and we felt there might be a slim chance that we could get her off. We also managed to get hold of the local yacht repairers – twin brothers who came to inspect the situation and advised us to stand by just in case the water was high enough. Christopher was still trying to contact others who might be able to help; there was no British Consul locally and anyway the only option might have been to have closed the barrage to let the water rise and in so doing cut off electricity for half of France. This again did not seem a viable solution to our problem. He did get through to the British Embassy in Paris where the woman on duty was sympathetic but not very helpful.

We joined the ladies at their hotel for dinner and then went back on board to wait for the next high tide. It came in, but was, as predicted, not high enough to float her off. We spent an uncomfortable night attempting to sleep at an angle of 35°, and the next day saw us still sitting there in the sun. We were by now becoming something of an embarrassment – 'le pauvre bâteau anglais' was being gawped up by sightseers and people were demanding to know what we were doing there. Le Directeur had obviously spoken to a higher authority and finally it was agreed that in order to get rid of us they would hold up the sluices for long enough to allow sufficient water to build up to get us off. The two brothers from the shipyard came down with a tractor and wires, removing one rather nasty looking rock that was directly in line with us and setting up their equipment in the car park above us. We all went on board; all hands were standing by as the water rose and as soon as we could they heaved away on the windlass and she came off, thankfully without any damage. We waved them a fond farewell and floated off at 11.00 a.m. heading for St. Suliac, the next town up river. We anchored here and remained for the rest of the day, venturing ashore for dinner that night. The following day saw us sailing on to Dinan, where we arrived on the Saturday. By this time, of course, our plans had been completely thrown. We decided to stay for the day at Dinan, before returning to St. Suliac, both very pleasant towns, and then returned through the lock. They looked at us rather askance as we returned – but we kept the engine running this time and got safely through, back to St. Malo. One of the reasons that we had been rather anxious about the hold up was that Libby and I were due to fly to Nairobi on the following Saturday, where, together with the other Sheriff and his wife, we were due to join the Lord Mayor at the start of our long overseas tour. By the time we got back to St. Malo it was Tuesday, so on the Wednesday we flew from Dinar back to London, leaving the two boys on board to continue the holiday with the Rawsons. They eventually brought *Hodzah* back to Cowes with Christopher via Guernsey, from where Rosemary and the two girls flew home. It had been an eventful first cruise!

Libby and I arrived safely in Nairobi on the Saturday, 21st August, where we were staying in the Norfolk Hotel. The Lord Mayor had already arrived from the Seychelles, and we were to discover that his trip had, like ours, not been without incident. It had begun badly when, on the flight over, he had discovered that he suffered from altitude sickness. The extent of his illness had alarmed him rather and it was just as well that he had found out about it on a large, well-equipped plane rather than the small aircraft we were to be using to travel around Africa. His party in the Seychelles had included the

Chief Commoner and Judith Dagworthy, the P.R. girl. Their stay had gone well and when the time came to leave, they were driven to the airport by the Governor's chauffeur. This chap had evidently become very fond of the group throughout their stay and the prospect of their departure filled him with distress. As they climbed the steps into the plane the fellow had tears streaming down his face, quite overcome with emotion. They took off, and their plane climbed steadily into the sky, leaving the chauffeur behind them. It was, alas, only at this point that the poor chap discovered that, in his heightened state, he had overlooked one of the Lord Mayor's bags, which remained in the boot of his car. For some inexplicable reason, all of the Lord Mayor's suits had been separated for packing purposes, with jackets in one suitcase and trousers in another. The bag which remained in the Seychelles, alas, contained the Lord Mayor's entire collection of trousers, apart from the pair he happened to be wearing at the time. Frantic messages were transmitted to British Airways; the errant suitcase was sent out from the Seychelles on the next flight but, needless to say, did not find its way to Nairobi. It was traced to Heathrow and then poor St. John Brook Johnstone, the Sergeant-at-Arms with our party, went on seemingly endless and fruitless trips out to Nairobi Airport to meet incoming flights that might have brought the trousers. Eventually Sir Hugh became totally fed up with B.A.'s inefficiency in dealing with this situation and got the Savoy staff themselves to track down the suitcase, which was finally despatched and arrived safely at Nairobi. The story is a salutary one, reminiscent of the tale of the Crimean War, when left and right boots for soldiers were despatched in separate consignments; the ship carrying one consignment was sunk and the army were left with no pairs of boots at all. Having lost luggage myself in Belgium I am now always careful to carry with me a spare shirt, toothbrush, clean underwear and pyjamas in my briefcase.

Chapter 9

Our first three days in Africa were spent on 'civic business'. We called on the Mayor, who happened to be the daughter of President Kenyata (he was not in Nairobi at the time himself). She was very welcoming and took us to visit the usual civic buildings, schools etc. whilst the ladies were taken on tours of hospitals and suchlike. We were given a civic dinner, where I was puzzled by the apparent lack of guests. I enquired of my neighbour the reason for the number of empty places, wondering whether the event was being boycotted. I was assured that this was not the case, with the explanation being that the custom there was never to refuse an invitation, even if you knew you were unable to attend; a refusal or an apology would mean that it would be highly unlikely that you would ever be asked again. In order to preserve your place on the potential guest list you would always accept, but attendance was not then obligatory. It seemed to me that such a system made it awfully difficult to organise the catering. I now understood why, when we entertained the President of the Gambia at the Mansion House and invitations had been sent out to Gambians resident in the U.K., the number of acceptances was not matched by the number of those who attended on the day. Clearly the same principle had applied. Nevertheless, we had a good evening, and 'prezzies' were exchanged (we were given various items such as a shopping bag, a tie of the Council of Nairobi and a number of gongs – not the medal-sort but a dinner gong, suspended between a couple of tusks). We were taken on a tour of a small domestic game park, which was actually more like a zoo, but more was to come on that score. Sir Hugh, always good at this sort of thing, had arranged a number of visits to game parks and reserves in Kenya to vary our trip and ensure that business was mixed with pleasure. On the way to the formal visit of a sugar plantation on the banks of Lake Victoria, for example, we spent one night and one day at Keekorok, an hour's flying time from Nairobi. We flew in two little twin-engine Barrons, which were very comfortable; behind the pilot there was room for two rows of two people, which meant that Libby and myself, the Chief Commoner, and Tony Hart and his wife fitted in one plane, with the Lord Mayor and Lady Mayoress and the Household Officer in the other. Keekorok was most interesting. It is almost on the border of the Masai Mara game reserve; as with most of the sites there was a central area with small huts and chalets about. Our bedroom had a big picture window looking out across central lawns. After a comfortable night, we awoke in the morning to a rather strange, munching noise. I rose from my bed and pulled back the curtains to reveal to a remarkable sight: a herd of zebra grazing just outside. They strolled off, not looking very perturbed at all!

From Keekorok we went on to Lake Victoria, where we spent a morning being shown around the sugar plantation. From there we were due to fly to Kerichio, up in the mountains, to see the Brooke Bond tea plantation. However, the Lord Mayor decided that because of his altitude problem he would not attempt the flight but return to Keekorok instead and spend two days there, leaving his two Sheriffs to fulfil the engagement at the tea plantation. Before we took off, our pilot was chatting to the Lord Mayor's pilot, asking him if he might follow him out as he was unfamiliar with the territory. The other pilot agreed, since the first parts of the journey were the same. The Lord Mayor's plane took off and we duly followed; it was a beautiful sight against the deep blue African sky. However, twenty minutes into the flight a terrific rainstorm hit us and in zero visibility the pilot was forced to fly on instruments. Mercifully the deluge was short lived, but when it subsided and we hit clear skies again there was no sign of the other plane, from which we had become separated. This meant that we were on our own and flying above unfamiliar territory. The pilot gained height and we flew around with views of dramatic mountains, gorges, and escarpments below. We were now all looking out for the tea plantation, but all we could see below us were the occasional Masai villages, and then endless parched desert country. Not surprisingly the atmosphere in the plane became tense as time went by. We were particularly concerned for Tony Hart's wife Noreen, who did not like flying at the best of times – especially in small aeroplanes. She was asleep at the back of the plane. As the pilot stared frantically out of the cockpit window trying to pick up his bearings the situation became more fraught. There was no doubting that we were completely lost. In desperation the pilot handed a map to the Chief Commoner in the hope that he might be able to identify our position; he was a solicitor and, luckily, had been a Royal Marine, so hopefully might be skilled at orientation. Amid these scenes we were concerned that Noreen would wake up and have a panic attack, but fortunately she remained dozing. As Libby and I stared out of the window, also looking for signs of tea, the pilot suggested we might be forced to return to Lake Victoria, get our bearings, and try again. At this point my main concern was the amount of fuel we had left and how long we could stay in the air!

Fortunately the pilot was able to communicate with the tea plantation by radio and having finally discovered our location was directed to continue flying north for five miles then look out for a red dirt road, turn ninety degrees and follow it until reaching a cross roads. After flying for another two miles we would see the plantation airfield and factory. The pilot duly followed these directions and, thankfully, there were in view below us before long. Even from low altitude the airfield looked no larger than a cricket pitch, but despite its small size the pilot was able to make a faultless landing, much to everyone's great relief. Once we were safely on the ground Noreen awoke and innocently enquired if we had arrived. No one had the nerve to tell her what had happened during her slumber in case it frightened her too much for the return flight. The pilot was extremely apologetic and explained that he did not know the country very well as he had only arrived in Africa for the first time the day before! Apparently he had been a Fleet Air Arm pilot, which would explain his ability to land the plane so perfectly on such a tiny airstrip.

With this traumatic experience happily behind us we were taken to our accommodation by the plantation staff. We were given a guided tour of the factory and the art of making tea was demonstrated to us – although in this factory they specialised in making granular instant tea. Interestingly, the technique for this procedure is to drop tealeaves from the top of a massive aluminium tower and dry them with huge fans as they descend. By the time it reaches the bottom of the tower the tea has been completely dehydrated and transformed into dry (and thus instant) granules. Later in the evening we were pleasantly greeted and entertained, not only by the 'high hegions' of the tea company, but also by some local tribal chiefs during which speeches and gifts were exchanged, before a hearty dinner was consumed.

The following day we travelled on to Nakuru, happily without excitement or incident. This place is well known for its salt lake, inhabited by vast colonies of pink flamingos, which are a spectacular sight – particularly when the flocks are disturbed and they all take off together and fill the sky. Libby and I spent the early part of the morning watching this breathtaking activity before the day got too hot. Later we flew on to Samburu where we met up once again with the Lord Mayor and we were able to swap the tales of our adventures before proceeding to our hotel, which was at the centre of the game park. Here were welcomed by the assistant hotel manager (the actual manager being on leave) who was quite obviously far more interested in meeting Sir Hugh in his capacity as the Chairman of the Savoy Group than in his capacity as Lord Mayor of London. Indeed, as the former he clearly regarded Sir Hugh as some kind of god in the hotel world, and he was out to impress!

The assistant manager took us the short distance from the airstrip to the hotel in a fleet of Range Rovers. The hotel consisted of a main one-storey administrative building with a bar, restaurant and reception area, surrounded by chalets and cottages for the guests, which were low brick built, thatch-roofed buildings with ventilation holes at the top of the walls covered in wire mesh. After registration the assistant manager proudly escorted the Lord Mayor and his wife to his chalet, with my wife and I in close attendance. As we approached the chalet it became obvious that the hotel staff had gone to a great deal of time and trouble to prepare things perfectly for no less a luminary than the Chairman of the Savoy Group himself, whose high office clearly warranted the highest luxury possible. We approached the front door and after it had been unlocked, the assistant manager threw it open with an extravagant flourish, confidently assuring the Lord Mayor that he would be more than happy with the room – but as he did so his jaw dropped, his face went as white as a sheet, and he quickly slammed the door. Peering through the door I could see why. The room was in a complete shambles. It had been ransacked by a pack of small monkeys living in the nearby trees, who had obviously spotted all the fresh fruit bowls and other goodies being brought in to the chalet by the hotel staff and had gained entry by climbing in through a hole in the wire mesh. In the space of about half an hour they had trashed the room and left a huge mess, with banana skins and fruit peel everywhere, and ash trays strewn all over the floor. The place was a complete wreck. As the assistant manager opened the door there was pandemonium as the monkeys all tried to flee back out through the wire mesh, fighting and scrabbling to escape the wrath of the staff. This excitement caused the monkeys to defecate and urinate all over the room. It was a frightful mess. The Lord Mayor took it all in good heart but the assistant manager was completely abashed, and although it was not his fault one could not help thinking that he had it coming to him for being so pompous. The net result was that the Lord Mayor and his wife were allotted my room, and everyone else equally went down one room in sequence. Alas, the farce did not end there.

The Lord Mayor's wife, a lady of a genteel, calm disposition and Edwardian manners was, by this time, evidently feeling quite peckish. She enquired about the possibility of nourishment, and we were duly guided to an al fresco lunch situated beside the river that ran through the hotel grounds, with a low wall that separated the crocodiles on one side from the human guests on the other. Tables covered in white cloths and chairs laid out behind provided an excellent view of the wildlife. We settled ourselves down to enjoy the spectacle, with myself sitting next to the Lady Mayoress. The waiter approached with a basket of bread rolls and placed one on her side plate with a pair of metal tongues. Much to her horror, as the Lady Mayoress reached out for her bread roll, a little brown hand suddenly shot up between us and snatched it from beneath our very eyes. It turned out to be another monkey and after it had grabbed the roll it scampered up a nearby tree and hungrily devoured it. To have your bedroom ransacked by monkeys was one thing but to have your food taken from your plate was quite another. Thus ended the second saga of the monkeys. There was yet more to come!

Next day just before lunch, we took the Range Rovers to look at some of the local game. It was a hot day and we returned feeling tired and dusty and so decided to refresh ourselves with a swim in the hotel pool. Afterwards I was sitting next to the Sergeant at Arms, Colonel Brooke-Johnson, having a pre-prandial drink in the bar. This was a large circular, thatch-roofed open sided bar overlooking the river. We were enjoying our drink when I happened to glance down the line of the chalets towards the household regiment flats, which were two-storey buildings with balconies further down, and noticed something odd happening. I turned to the Sergeant at Arms and informed him that there was a monkey trying on his bathing trunks! These had been left draped on the balcony to dry after the swim, and the monkey was looking at them quizzically – about to eat them or possibly rush up the nearest tree with them. Clearly the monkeys were serious pests. It was light-heartedly debated as to whether they should shoot a few of them to make an example of them, although in fact as they were a protected species this was quite out of the question. There was, however, no doubt that if you left anything about they would have it (including photographic film wrapped in foil, which the monkeys thought were sweets).

Our visits to safari parks started early in the morning. First there was something to eat, and then we would be driven out in suitable transport to the game reserves to observe whatever wild animals were about. I was frequently amazed at how nonchalant the animals appeared to be in our presence. We were able to get very close indeed to a pride of lions, young cubs playing about as their mothers dozed in the heat of the day. Further off we came across the male lion, stretched out in the sun, evidently enjoying the peace away from the family. One paw lazily flopped in the air as if in greeting; you could almost hear him saying casually 'Hi! Isn't it nice here – do let me go back to sleep...' On one occasion a lioness actually brought her cubs right up to our vehicle, as if she were pointing us out to them; 'These funny white things – they're human beings and they appear from time to time here.'

We had seen most sorts of game at Keekorok where there were herds of wildebeest and zebra; at Samburu we saw elephant, giraffe and lion as well as smaller animals and horned game such as antelope. I had my camera and my cine buzzing away the whole time. The only animal we had not seen in the wild was rhinoceros, although we had seen one in the small zoo-type park in Nairobi which was mentioned earlier. However, our next call after Samburu was to be the Mount Kenya game park, where the terrain was quite different.

The Lord Mayor, Lady Mayoress and St. John Brooke-Johnstone went off with the 'great white hunter' who was to show him around the following day, whilst Libby and myself, together with Tony Hart and Noreen, were to stay at the hotel. Our accommodation consisted of two 'cabins' with a communal lounge area between them, again with big picture windows looking out over the countryside. We were enjoying a pre-dinner drink here, just as dusk was falling. Suddenly a crowd of Zulu dancers appeared on the lawn of the neighbouring chalet, chanting and beating drums excitedly. We assumed that this must be some form of entertainment laid on by the hotel for their guests. The problem we were faced with now was that we did not have any money. Like royalty, we all travelled without carrying cash. I assumed that if these dancers came and gave us our own display they would expect a contribution. We decided to switch off our lights and pretend that we were not 'at home' and, as the dancers did not proceed to our lawn, we assumed that our ruse had been successful. At dinner, I made enquiries. It was explained that the entertainment had been especially for the honeymoon couple in the chalet next to ours and we would not have been visited by them anyway. It turned out that they were the hotel waiters, who donned their tribal regalia as a sideline to provide the floorshow.

Early the following morning our guide turned up in what I refer to as 'a poor Japanese imitation of a Land Rover'. We set off down what might be described as a leafy African lane, the object of the trip being to catch sight of some rhino. At one point we passed a great pile of fresh elephant droppings. Our guide observed that they had been past recently and said he hoped that we did not encounter the one he had met the previous day who had tried to push the vehicle off the road. Very reassuring! We emerged from the forest track onto the grassland, where we came first of all across a herd of buffalo, who stood and stared at us rather disinterestedly. From here we dropped down a hill into a dried riverbed and then began climbing the slope the other side. The tyres of our vehicle were clearly lacking in tread, and this steep climb proved too much for them; half way up the side we ground to a halt, our wheels sinking into the sand. There was no alternative but to push and we all got out. Unfortunately Tony Hart, quite unused to this kind of thing, got himself into completely the wrong position, just behind the rear offside wheel. When it spun he was splattered from head to foot in mud and sand; the vehicle, needless to say, did not budge an inch. Our next ploy was to try putting something under the wheel – but what? The jeep was hopelessly ill equipped, with not even any floor mats on board. We found some scrubby bushes and cut these down with machetes to stuff under the wheels. Again, no joy. She was going to have to be towed out. At the front of the vehicle was a padlocked box, which allegedly contained a winch: a wire with a hook on one end which could be tied around a tree and then pulled through on a ratchet system to winch the vehicle out. Of course, no one had the key to the box, but they managed to force it open with a crowbar. Now, we needed a tree. This found, we fed the wire round it. So far, so good. But where was the handle for the winch? There had been a handle at some point, of course. But it had been lost and never replaced. We needed to find a makeshift replacement. Again, more hacking with machetes to produce an appropriate sized stick. By this time over an hour had passed; it was hot and humid and our legs were being uncomfortably attacked by insects. Tony's wife was becoming increasingly distressed and Libby and I were doing our best to keep up morale. Eventually we fashioned a handle and managed to attach it and, finally, tow the vehicle out of its predicament onto less steep ground. Our guide pointed ahead into the middle distance. 'We shall have to walk up there,' he said, 'until we get onto flat ground if we don't want to get stuck again.' Agreeing that we did not want to get stuck again we trudged off behind the vehicle. We were in open ground and I felt very exposed indeed. I remarked to Libby that I felt as if we were being watched and imagined lots of little piggy eyes observing us from behind the bushes. Our guide reassured us that rhino did not like this sort of weather and would all be hiding up. 'Yes,' I thought, 'Hiding up and watching us, I'll be bound.' At one point I told the others that I was convinced I heard a leopard cough. We walked on – but we saw no leopard, and no rhino. In fact we did not see anything; it was just us and the open plain.

We had agreed to rendezvous with the Lord Mayor at a certain point for lunch but by the time we were able to get back into our vehicle the appointed hour was well past. Our guide had a radio and said he would try and contact the other party. Did his radio work? Of course not! We continued on our way, eventually coming across the Lord Mayor and his party at the agreed spot, where they were relaxing in deckchairs with ice-cold drinks after a good lunch. We emerged hot and filthy, having not seen any game at all. By now Tony Hart's knee was swelling up from the effect of the insect bite and we had to find a hospital for him that afternoon. All in all our visit to the Mount Kenya game park had not been the most successful of the trip! It was certainly a relief to return to the comfort of the Norfolk hotel in Nairobi that evening.

The visit had been an excellent one on the whole, however, and quite different from anything we had done before. We vowed we would return one day to the African bush, although unfortunately we have never done so. It was certainly a remarkable experience and one that has remained with us. We have found that when watching wildlife programmes on television we have been able to recapture the atmosphere of seeing the animals in real life, the excitement of which was truly unforgettable.

Chapter 10

Our next scheduled visit was intended to be to Ethiopia, which I was looking forward to. Ethiopia was not an obvious holiday destination and a state visit was always a good way of seeing somewhere 'behind the scenes'. We set out to Addis Ababa from Nairobi on 9th September. On landing, however, we were met by the British Ambassador who informed us that there was 'trouble at 't mill' and we were advised not to get off the plane. Haile Selassie had just been arrested; the state visit had been cancelled and we were to be transferred, instead, to Cairo. Sadly, we saw nothing of Ethiopia other than the runway at Addis Ababa airport.

We had to stop for re-fuelling at Khartoum, where strict security prevented us from getting off. We were flying with Abyssinian airlines, and we were given an amazing Abyssinian meal. It was served on a type of 'trencher' – what looked like a piece of grey foam rubber but which was actually a type of bread, which you tore off with your fingers and ate with the curry-type meat served on top. Delicious! The tall Abyssinian stewardesses were what can only be described as 'handsome women' and looked after us well. We arrived at Cairo late in the afternoon, to a heat of 120°. My God was it hot! When the cabin door opened it was like walking into an oven.

We were glad to get in to the V.I.P. lounge, out of the scalding heat, where the party was met by the Governor of Cairo and the Chargé d'Affaires for the British Embassy. We then dispersed to the homes of our various hosts, 'billeted out' with a number of people around the town. Libby and I were to stay with Dr Daniel and his wife. He was the head of the British Council in Egypt – an organisation heavily involved in the educational process in Cairo and very highly thought of. They were a most pleasant couple who welcomed us into their home. We were cautioned never at any time to drink water out of the taps, not even to brush our teeth with, and it was explained to us that we would find bottles of water conveniently placed throughout the house, which would have been filtered by the staff. The Daniels' personal servant was a tall fellow named Ahmed. He stood in the doorway, dressed in his long white robes, as we were warned of the severe effects of 'gyppy tummy'. If we wanted water, Ahmed would always bring us some more. More of that anon.

On the first night we dined with our hosts and then went for a walk along the banks of the Nile. Cairo was, we had been informed, one of the few places where it was considered safe to walk about at night. The river looked splendid by moonlight, and the distinctive heavy aroma of the east filled the night air, permeating the senses. We had an early night, weary from our long journey, and the day ahead promised to be a busy one.

We met with the rest of our party at the British Embassy the next morning. The Ambassador himself was back in England at the time and it proved a convenient meeting-place. We were also promised the prospect of a swim in the Embassy pool, and we had brought along swimming things in expectation. The men of the party were first of all taken to the Cairo museum, where we were met by the Director. As I have pointed out, the advantage of being a V.I.P. on these trips meant that one was taken around by the top man himself; the disadvantage was that you could never linger, but had to whisk round at whatever pace was set. Invariably there was much more to see and places you would have liked to have looked at more closely than time allowed. Compared to museums in this country the place had a somewhat neglected air, but was nevertheless full of the most marvellous treasures, including the mummified body of Ramses II, lying looking much as he might have done all those centuries ago. Most impressive of all was the Tutankhamun collection. Some of us had seen the more famous bits of this discovery in London when it was given a world tour, but these highlights did not really compare with the totality of the treasures which were on display here. Just about everything you could think of was represented: furniture, chariots, scientific instruments, and models of people undertaking all manner of activities, all beautifully crafted. Looking at these objects placed in the Pharaoh's tomb all those thousands of years ago, one could not help but think that – apart from the transistor and the internal combustion engine – there was very little which would not be familiar to us today. The furniture one could have quite easily bought at Waring and Gillows; the chariot was very similar to the sort of trap our grandfathers might have travelled in, with a harness that might still have been used today. There were medical instruments for trepanning skulls, and sets of forceps and scalpels; and carpentry tools which any modern-day craftsman could have used with ease. It made you realise that actually we had not advanced very much at all – indeed, in some cases we had probably slipped backwards. The collection was certainly a great insight into the civilisation of the time and as such quite fascinating.

We were whisked on rapidly and before long found ourselves back at the Embassy for a well-deserved and very welcome swim in the Ambassador's pool. We then returned to our houses for lunch with our hosts before leaving at 5.00 p.m. for a tour of the city. This consisted of a visit to the two mosques, situated right in the middle of the city, cheek by jowl with narrow streets and the hustle and bustle of traffic. Here of course we had to take off our shoes in order to walk around. In the evening we returned to our hosts in order to change for a dinner given by the Chargé d'Affaires. We each had a car and chauffeur allocated to us, and each car was equipped with a siren, much to the delight of our driver. In Cairo everyone drives on their horns and their brakes; our siren did not make the negotiating of traffic any easier but the driver clearly loved playing on it and we screamed along with a great cacophony of noise accompanying us. There were no automatic traffic lights, but lights controlled by policemen who stood on a little raised island in the middle of the road. He would turn the lights red for one stream of traffic and green for another, at which those on 'go' would scream off at a terrific rate whilst those on red would all immediately commence blowing their horns, presumably under the principle that if they kept it up for long enough the policeman controlling the system would eventually give in, not being able to stand the noise any more. It seemed to work and the lights would change, although without any particular regular interval. Of course immediately all those then on red would begin the noise again. Buses passed us, not only full to capacity on the inside but on the outside as well, people clinging on to every conceivable handhold.

The Chargé d'Affaires had some interesting guests in his party, including some of those connected with the museum and the collection of antiquities. It was interesting to talk to them and listen to their problems, which were largely financial. Another temple had recently been discovered but had had to be filled in with sand again in order to preserve it as they did not have the money needed to excavate the site properly.

We were to have a first hand sighting of some of the antiquities the following day, when we were taken to Saqqara to see the Step Pyramid – the first of the great pyramids to be built. It is built in a layered style, hence its name, and it is possible to enter into the tomb inside, although there is nothing much to see. Of more interest was a small temple alongside it, which was allegedly the first building ever constructed out of stone. The stone was remarkably well dressed and the building very finely constructed. At the end of each wall, carved stone represented the papyrus blocks which would have been put at the end of the walls of clay buildings to protect them from weathering; although this protection was not needed in the case of stone buildings, the traditional style was maintained. The doors, too, had been constructed of stone – they did not open or close but stood in a permanently open position, with hinges also carved in stone. Below the temple, one could descend to the tomb of the architect responsible for the design of the building. I suppose he was a sort of latter day equivalent of Brunel. His name was Imhotep and his mummified body lay there in the gloom for all to see. It was quite something to look at the evidence of such a great culture, in existence at a time when we in Britain were not even running around in woad. There was something about Egypt and its history that excited me greatly and I had a great desire to return to the country again – an ambition I have not yet fulfilled. Perhaps I am a reincarnation of some Egyptian spirit. Who knows?

We were taken from here to see a collection of tombs of the sacred bulls – a long line of sarcophagi. The bull was of great importance in Ancient Egypt. The young pharaoh designate would have to fight a bull in order to prove his suitability and his manhood. From the tomb of the bulls we then went to see the traditional pyramids and the Sphinx, which, although quite close to Cairo, are all situated in the desert. We had a traditional ride on a camel. Quite a tricky procedure getting on and off but once up there are stirrups to put your feet in – although I sat with my legs crossed in front of me, as this is how I had seen it done in pictures of my uncle, who had been in the Camel Corps. The Sphinx looked rather sad, I thought – battered by the ravages of time and vandals.

After a very good lunch we returned to our hosts once again and then in the early evening the men of the party were taken to the war graves cemetery at Heliopolis where the Lord Mayor laid a wreath. Then it was back to prepare for the evening's entertainment. That evening the Governor of Cairo held a banquet in our honour at the

Sheraton hotel, where Libby and I were presented with an Egyptian coffee service. And so, to bed – to be up again at 7.30 the next morning to bid our farewells at the airport and head for home, via a change of planes at Geneva. Our overseas visit was over, and it was back to reality at the Old Bailey and the firm.

Before leaving Heathrow, however, there was one last reminder of our jaunt. We did not have to queue for customs like everyone else, but wait in the V.I.P. lounge for the officials to come to us. As we were waiting I suddenly felt extremely uncomfortable and had to whiz to the nearest loo – gyppy tummy had struck! I do not recall ever having broken the rules by drinking tap water, but I rather suspected that Ahmed was not terribly conscientious about the filtering process. I am sure he just held the bottles under the tap and then stuck them in the fridge so that they looked appropriately frosted and cold. With a dose of Imodium pills I was able to get rid of the bug the next day, but I had not escaped unscathed. Let it be a warning to you all!

Christopher as Drum Major.

Chapter 11

We arrived back on the 12th September (a Thursday) and, after a rest at the weekend, Monday saw me at the office in the morning and then to the Old Bailey at lunchtime. In the evening we had a very nice trip in the Port of London Authority's yacht, the *Royal Nore*, a large 60' motor launch, with a pleasant dinner on the river as the guests of the Chairman of the P.L.A. On the Wednesday the Mayor of Geneva paid us a return visit and that morning I took him to see Lloyd's and the stock exchange, whilst Libby took his wife to Harrods. I had arranged for the economics class from the Upper VIth at Pangbourne (which included Christopher) to come up to the Old Bailey to see the court in operation followed by a tour of the stock exchange. Christopher was by now a Cadet Captain and also the Drum Major, and fast approaching the dizzy heights of Cadet officerhood which he had been so scornful about when his elder brother was doing it.

Our term of office was by now drawing to its close. As a sort of early warning, we now saw the presentation of Shrieval chains to our successors. It was hard to believe that a year had passed since we had been in the same position ourselves. So much had happened, and so fast, and it had shot by very quickly indeed. On Friday 27th September at Guildhall we divested ourselves of our chains of office and hung the new ones around the necks of the two new Sheriffs, Peter Vanneck and Hugh Olsen, before attending their Sheriffs' breakfast at Fishmongers' Hall, where we both spoke, briefly, in reply to a speech by the Recorder thanking us for our services. And that was it. We were back to normality, down from cloud nine, but in my case now qualified to go forward to the final hurdle: the Mayoralty. I was coming up for it a year sooner than I had thought, and in fact two or three years sooner than I had originally expected when I was elected an Alderman, for the simple reason that three of the Aldermen senior to me had retired/resigned/fallen off the ladder in the intervening period. It was now going to be only eighteen months before I was due to stand for election.

On Wednesday 9th October I fulfilled one of many a sailor's treasured dreams: I was invited to dine aboard H.M.S. *Victory*. This was, of course, made doubly exciting by the fact that my great-great-grandfather had served in the *Victory* in Nelson's time. It was a men-only do. I stayed at Admiralty House with my host, Sir Derek Emerson, who was the C-in-C, Naval Home Command at the time. On 30th November I was down at Pangbourne with Libby, to hear Christopher singing in the college production of *Oliver!* He took the part of Bumble, and very well he did it, too.

The following week found me wine-tasting, ready for Mayoralty – an indication of just how far one has to think ahead! The red wines were purchased by a committee of 'taste'; a collection of Aldermen knowledgeable in that direction who bought wine of the right vintage for a reasonable price at the right time and laid it down ready for each Mayoralty. It was stored away and carefully nurtured; if it came on too fast it would be brought out and served at various banquets, if too slow it would be stored for longer. Each year the Aldermen and potential Mayors-to-be subscribed to their wine fund, and the wine syndicate purchased the red wine and ports with this money. Each year you were informed how much money was needed and in the time between becoming an Aldermen and reaching the Mayoralty (between seven to ten years) you would have purchased sufficient quantities of wine to supply the banquets that you would be obliged to give. The wine tasting I was going to was for the white wines which were also bought from the fund, but not quite so far in advance. It was up to you to select the wines you liked best, although the expertise of the wine committee was there to guide and advise. The supplier also provided quantities of sherry at a greatly discounted rate for the necessary pre-prandials. Of course it was not required to purchase wine in this way and if you felt you could get a better deal elsewhere (by having connections in the wine trade, for example) it was entirely up to you. I felt that it was a good way of buying good wine quite painlessly and considered my wine-tasting day one well spent. I had by this time already purchased my cigars, which were then still expected after dinner, before today's anti-smoking climate. I had bought two kinds in sufficient quantities to cover all the lunches and dinners I would have to give – shorter Jamaican ones for lunchtime smoking and a decent Havana for the evening occasions. I had two Gillett cigar maxims: if you were given a cigar when the speeches started at the end of dinner and you were not still smoking it by the time the speeches were over, then either the speeches were too long or the cigars were too short. If you yourself were called upon to speak and had a lit cigar, recourse to a further match after your speech would mean that you had spoken for too long! I was glad indeed that I had made my purchase well in advance, since taxes increased substantially not long afterwards. In subsequent years a wine syndicate was started at the Old Bailey as well, for the benefit of the Sheriffs. The principle was the same although the quantities were somewhat less.

It had been a busy year. I have barely touched on half of it here, but have, I hope, provided a little taste of the duties of the office of Sheriff of the City of London.

Chapter 12

On 18th March, 1975, history was made in the City when Lady Donaldson was admitted as Alderman for the ward of Coleman Street. This was the first time in the City's long history that there had been a lady Alderman, and, to date, the only one. She had been on the Common Council since 1966, when, again, she was the first woman to be elected. Now, as Alderman, she was a potential Lord Mayor. A turn up for the books, indeed.

Easter came early that year (1975), and once again we went down to Cowes to join the Rawsons on *Hodzah*. My father was, by now, living at Biddeston with Aunt Frances and we visited them on several occasions at weekends for lunch or tea during the subsequent months. Things were not going terribly well; Aunt Frances was not really capable of looking after my father and I worried that he was ageing faster than he might have done. His eyesight was failing and the glaucoma that troubled him was eventually to rob him of his sight. This was a great disappointment to him as he had always been an avid reader. It was also sad to see him, by nature a gregarious and sociable man, confined to his cottage where she would turn visitors away at the door, alienating locals with her strident personality. But there was little one could do about it. His London flat was by now on the market and actually being rented out to someone, and his furniture had been put into storage, for future use by the boys if they needed it.

On the work front, things had been proceeding apace in my absence. The new office was ready to be occupied. Slater Walker had, thankfully, disappeared from the scene and we had merged with Poland to become Wigham Poland Ltd, with a new Managing Director, John Smith, and a new Financial Director, Michael Livingstone, to whom I reported. They were very nice people and quite different from the previous incumbents. My assistant Richard Blackwood, whom I had recruited before my time as Sheriff, was very busy masterminding the moves in various departments. We also had to clear out Armadores House because that had been sold by Slater

346

Walker, and the offices of Walker Young, in Moorgate. To recap on the history of the organisation thus far: I had started with Bevington, Vaizey and Foster, which had merged with P. Wigham Richardson to become Wigham Richardson and Bevingtons; we were then merged with Walker Young, Jim Slater's company, and now we had taken in Polands to become Wigham Poland. There had been a number of changes over a relatively short period of time, but this is common practice all over the city and continues to be the case, with small firms either merging together or becoming absorbed under the umbrella of a larger company.

We now had a considerably increased staff (over 800) and two large separate buildings to look after. Fortunately we were able to reorganise my section (administration incorporating personnel) with a strong team and a very good man who joined us from Polands called Charles Buckingham. He took over all of the administrative side and dealt with the buildings, whilst I confined myself to personnel and training. We were also introducing a graduate training scheme. This laid the foundations for the smooth running of my department during my impending absence in the not too distant future, when my role as Lord Mayor would prevent me from coming into the office at all for a year.

In May that year we took part in the annual City Livery Yacht Club motor sailor race. We went sailing again, in August, this time retracing our steps up the River Rance – navigating the lock without any difficulty this time, apart from the rather supercilious looks of the officials there. We were no doubt by now the stuff of legend! We went up to Dinon and then retraced our steps and went along the coast of Brittany, returning via Guernsey. Nicholas was not with us on that trip; we just had the two Rawson girls and Christopher.

September saw Christopher start his last term at Pangbourne. He was now Chief Cadet Captain of Hesperus Division, as his older brother and father had been before him. The boys had been discussing college life together at home during the holidays, Nicholas taunting Christopher by claiming that discipline there now was not as strong as it had been in his day. Christopher replied by claiming that Nicholas had imposed discipline only by senseless shouting, whereas now order was maintained through reason. We were down visiting later on and walking back after the parade with Christopher to his divisional house, when suddenly Christopher's voice projected at my side – a voice which was one day to be heard across the footlights of Covent Garden – shouting at a young cadet ahead of us, 'Jones! Come here!' The boy froze in his tracks, and then came doubling up to Christopher, who gave him a hell of a bollocking for having his top button undone. The lad was sent away with a flea in his ear and I smiled wryly to myself recalling Christopher's protestations about reason accompanying all discipline these days. *Plus ça change, plus c'est la même chose . . .*

In October Christopher went up to Cambridge for the auditions that were taking place for King's College Choir. The auditions were held in the Chapel and the various Colleges with choirs all sent representatives to listen to what was on offer. There was then a sort of pecking order for selection, with King's having the first pick, St. John's the next, and so on. Each day (it continued for some three days) the rejects were weeded out. At the end of the first day Christopher rang to let us know he was still in with a chance. He rang again with more excitement at the end of the second day, when the Dean of King's College had whispered in his ear that he thought he might get the tenor scholarship for King's. There was only one on offer, with about 250 people up for it. He did, indeed, get it and when he came back home he was floating on air. He could not, of course, go up until the following September since he was still too young, which left him with two terms to fill. The Headmaster at Pangbourne invited him to return for the Lent and Summer terms where, for a small remuneration, he could help with the musical activities at the College and teach clarinet. He also had an offer from St. Mary's Catholic School at Ascot, who wanted him to go over there once a week and to tutor four girls. I found it hard to believe that the Mother Superior would consent to a reasonably good looking Protestant lad of 16 being let loose with her charges, but nevertheless he got the job. He also enrolled at the Guildhall School of Music and Drama as a sort of 'out-patient' to continue with his voice training. All in all, therefore, he was kept busy for the duration. Ascot was difficult to get to by train from Pangbourne, so I offered to buy him a cheap car. We scoured advertisements and found an old Ford Escort that would suit the purpose. The only problem was that he had not yet passed his driving test. He explained the predicament to the Mother Superior at Ascot who assured him that the nuns would pray for him when he took his test. Perhaps it was because he was a Protestant, but he failed the test. He was able to take it again when two weeks had elapsed, so he informed the Mother Superior once more. She assured him that

With the family, 1975.

the nuns would pray even harder. He failed again. However, the third time he decided not to inform the Mother Superior, changed the test from London to Reading and, eventually, passed.

By the early autumn, father's health was deteriorating quite noticeably. It was difficult to get anyone to see him at all – Aunt Frances would not even admit the District Nurse. Eventually I sent for the doctor who announced that he would have to go into hospital at once to have a gallstone removed. The doctor was keen to have Frances out of the house and installed in the hospital as well, in order to be near her brother. This meant that I could get into the cottage and begin clearing and cleaning – by now father had become incontinent and there was an unpleasant odour permeating the place. Father had an enormous stone the size of a quail's egg removed from his bladder. Although he seemed a little better there was clearly no way he could return to the cottage and it was to be a nursing home from now on. Aunt Frances, whilst in the hospital, was difficult to contain and when paddling about in the corridor one night had slipped and broken her arm. She must have been about 83 by this time, so it was no small thing. However the next day she was sitting up in bed protesting about the cast on her arm and trying to pick it off. The doctor expressed his view that my aunt was a tough old bird and I related the anecdote about the muggers. It was certainly a relief to me that they were both now in medical care. When father recovered they were both transferred to a home in Bath. By now I had power of attorney for father and could deal with his affairs as well as sort out the cottage. This included the felling of a large elm tree which dominated the front garden, whose roots covered the entire garden and reached to the house and which now had Dutch elm disease. Libby and I were able to stay down and get on with the lengthy process of clearing and sorting at weekends.

By the end of 1975 I was already having to turn my thoughts to the Mayoralty, in the expectation of being elected at the end of 1976. So much takes place throughout the year, that it is imperative to plan and shape it well in advance, which includes the planning of the Lord Mayor's Show. This in itself was no small undertaking and I had a committee to help deal with various sides of it, including representatives from the Territorial Army, the city police, and the pageant master who was the director of the whole thing, as well as a team who helped to raise the money. As explained before, the Lord Mayor's Show is self-financing. The floats that enter the show have to pay a substantial fee, and are restricted as to the amount of self-publicity and advertising they are permitted to do. Anything over the mark would mean that the BBC would cease to broadcast; ITV would not broadcast at all because it would upset those who paid them advertising revenue. I had already decided upon the theme for the show: the City and the Sea. A parallel of my own career, this would emphasise London as a centre of maritime services, with places like the Baltic Exchange, and Lloyds whose history is tied up with marine insurance.

It was a tight run programme, featuring the Royal and Merchant Navies, shipping companies and their services and marine insurance services, as well as voluntary services such as the R.N.L.I. and Trinity House – anybody, in fact, who was directly connected with the sea was a candidate to join in. As well as planning the Show, I had to start thinking about how I was going to play the Mayoralty, with details such as the design of the Christmas card and menus. Obviously one was constrained to a great extent by tradition and by other local events in the calendar. In my case, the local event that year was going to be the Queen's Silver Jubilee, which was due in 1977. Everything would have to be in place for that, including which charities you would support throughout the year. In actual fact this latter decision was taken out of my hands by the Queen herself who had written to all the major charities to ask that they refrain from holding special event appeals themselves because she wished the money that year to be devoted to the Prince of Wales Jubilee Trust. During the time of the previous Jubilee, of George V, money had been raised for the National playing fields. This time it was rather different; the money raised was intended for young people to help old people. At the end of the day over £19million was raised for this cause, with the Lord Lieutenants of each county responsible for fund-raising in their own county. Half the money raised in the first year could be spent immediately on local projects throughout the country.

The Lord Mayor's wife, potential Lady Mayoress, has almost as much to do in the way of planning as the Lord Mayor-to-be himself. There was her wardrobe to consider for a start (she would need to supplement the shrieval wardrobe and have sufficient variety so she would not be seen wearing the same outfit twice). Libby was off all the time buying dresses and building up an appropriate collection. She also had to think ahead to menu planning and the type of entertainment she wanted for her guests.

In the early months of 1976 my father became a registered blind person, although he actually continued to pretend to see. When he was assessed at the nursing home by an external inspector (a bit of a cheek, I thought, even to think that an ex-Lord Mayor of London would want to try and fake such a thing) he was found sitting with a copy of The Times across his lap. The inspector was obviously suspicious that he was not as blind as made out, but was eventually convinced; my father just tried to continue as normal, offering comments and observations based on prior knowledge rather than on things he could actually see. When, for example, I gave him a picture of the boys to look at, he commented on it warmly, even though he was holding it upside down in his hands. Or he would cross to the window and mention the colour of my car – which was, of course, something he already knew. He did not get on too well with the talking books that were provided for him, lamenting the loss of the historical novels which had always been his favourite to read. His mind was also beginning to wander. On one occasion he asked me if I knew what that bloody fool Kitchener had asked him to do. 'Asked me to go round London and round up all the dray horses.

They're going to be shipped to Gibraltar. Of course I told him that they would all die in the heat.' He had, in fact, done this and the horses had died, but he told the story as if it had happened last week, not in the First World War. He would look round his room in the home and comment 'Quite a good hotel, this' or tell me that I would have to be going soon as mother would be there to collect him. It was sad to see such an intelligent and active brain disappear in this way, although he was not unhappy – just in a world of his own (most of it in the 1914-18 war). He continued to be interested in the boys and what they were doing and aware of the prospect of my Mayoralty. It was a great shame that he would not be in attendance when the time came.

In June, the BBC dropped a bombshell by announcing that they would not continue to televise the Lord Mayor's Show, giving as their reason the fact that there was not sufficient national interest. I felt this was absolute nonsense – people turned up from all over the country to be at the Show. I also knew I would have great difficulty with the firms wanting to participate if they knew it was not going to be broadcast. I went to see various directors at the BBC and kicked up a bit of a fuss and, after a lot of persuasion, they decided to overturn the decision and broadcast after all. It had already been drastically reduced in timing and now we were given an hour as part of 'Swap Shop' or some such magazine programme.

At Guildhall on Midsummer's Day, 1976, the two Sheriffs who were going to serve with me for the majority of my Mayoralty were elected. These were Alan Lamboll and Colin Cole. I was very happy with these two as 'running mates'. They were not going to take office until September, but it was nice to know whom we were going to have.

The BBC having agreed to broadcast the Show, some of the main pressure was off and preparations continued as planned. There were many small details, which needed to be prepared well in advance. In July we had a meeting with the caterers Ring and Brymer. John Combes was their 'man on the spot' and we had to discuss with him the menu for the Lord Mayor's banquet. We talked at length on the matter; Libby and I decided we should like to offer guinea fowl as the main course, but John Combes was not over enthusiastic about this suggestion. He could not, he said, guarantee seven hundred guinea fowl of the right quality being available. He could, however, guarantee sufficient quantities of roast duck, and in the end this is what we settled upon – a decision which was to result in a number of unusual meals in the first few months of the Mayoralty, as I shall reveal later on.

Father's health had not been getting any better and the matron at the home was expressing concern about him. Libby and I were due to go off on our summer holidays, and as this was to be the last holiday we would have for over a year, we felt it was important. Matron also encouraged us to go, since, as she pointed out, there was little we could have usefully done by staying around. We thus went ahead and planned a cruise in *Hodzah* with Christopher, Rosemary and the girls. This time we intended to be rather more adventurous and head 'round the corner' to explore the Morbihan area in the south of Brittany. As we were going west of Brest we were able to ship duty free on board, and we enthusiastically piled on vast quantities of alcohol – somewhat in excess of our needs, but with the excuse that we would be able to trade bottles of whiskey with French fishermen. I was the only gin drinker on board, yet an entire case was included in the store, despite my protestations. The Rawsons had worked *Hodzah* down the coast at weekends, and by 6th August she was lying at St. Mawes. Christopher Rawson and I went down by train to get her finally ready for sea, and on the following day we sailed for Brittany. Our course around to the south coast lay west of Ushant. I had intended to spend the afternoon catching up on some sleep, but must have spent the entire time talking to Christopher. By about 11 o'clock that night he announced that he was going to turn in, leaving me to do the night watch. This was an agreed division of labour between us; Christopher did not like night-time sailing whereas, ever since my days on the North Atlantic, I had always enjoyed the peace and tranquillity of being alone at night under the stars. So off he toddled to clean his teeth, say his prayers, don his pyjamas and settle down in the after cabin, leaving me in command. As we rounded Ushant we came face to face, quite unexpectedly, with a huge fleet of French fishing boats, busily going about their trade. I managed to avoid hitting any of them, luckily, and navigated my way through, despite the fact that we only had side lights and a makeshift torch lashed to the mast, as our for'ard steaming light was not working. At about 7 o'clock the next morning Christopher came bouncing up on deck looking very bright after a good night's sleep. It hardly seemed worth telling him of my night-time escapade, as we were just about to arrive at our destination, Concarneau. The harbour there was full of yachts but we managed to find a berth. We then contacted the rest of the party back in England to let them know of our safe arrival and that we were now ready to receive boarders, so Libby, Rosemary and the girls flew out to Quimper to join us the next day.

We stayed there for a couple of days before sailing of to the Île de Pontfret on the 11th. We anchored here for the afternoon and one night before continuing on to the Morbihan, where we anchored at a buoy that some friends of the Rawsons had arranged for us to use. The tide is very strong there; as we put the dinghy over the side we had to keep the engine running in order to keep her alongside. It is a fascinating place, with a mass of inland creeks and rivers running in various directions, not unlike Chichester Harbour. The weather was fine – we had hit upon the hottest summer since records had been kept and the conditions were perfect for a holiday. We visited Vannes for a day and met with the Rawsons' friends who owned the mooring. They came on board and a couple of days later we set off for Houat, an island lying off the entrance to Morbihan, where it was the day for blessing the fishing boats. Decorated in gay bunting, all the boats went out to sea, making a ring with their bows inward. The priest on board one of the boats gave the blessing and there was singing and then on the signal they all raced back to their moorings. We joined in with them, having hoisted some underwear up the yardarm to flutter in the breeze as we were a little short on flags ourselves.

On 17th August we went up into Auray and then came out again the next day and went to La Trinité, which seemed to be a French equivalent of Cowes. It was packed. However, the summer heat wave was by now taking its toll. The drought had hit and all water had been turned off. All the public lavatories and showers which served the marina were without water apart from one hour a day, and the smell was ghastly. We stuck it out for a couple of days and then moved off to Port Haliguen. We were hoping to get water, but even here there was only one tap available which we had to row to in the dinghy with a five gallon container to fill. Thence to Belle Île. Here we moored off a little harbour on the north of the island, where we had been warned to watch the moorings, as they were not particularly strong. We were a little worried as there had been a gale warning for the Bay of Biscay. However, we took the dinghy into the harbour and had a very good dinner at the hotel. Back at the boat, Christopher's eldest daughter Gina announced she was feeling unwell, so I took Christopher and her back to the harbour to spend the night at the hotel, returning to the boat once I had dropped them off. It was just as well I had done so. Those of us on board had one hell of a night. The gale blew very hard, the boat was pitching up and down and there was a horrible noise coming from the roller bearings for'ard where the rope went over to the buoy. None of us got very much sleep; at one point we were even debating as to whether we should slip our moorings and head out to sea, out of the gale. However, it eventually blew itself out, although by the next morning it was still fairly rough. Unfortunately, when we examined the dinghy, which had been lying astern, we discovered a great puncture in the bow section. The front section had deflated entirely, but since the air is compartmentalised, enough of the dinghy was still seaworthy. I folded the bow section in on itself and set off in what now looked more like a coracle in towards the landing place, where Christopher was waiting for me. Having collected him safely we all got back on board and set off, heading back on our tracks towards Île de Croix, where we stayed for the night and I was able to repair the damage to the dinghy. There was a big slash in the side, which I had to sew up like a surgeon first before I could patch it. However, this done we glued the appropriate patch on and she survived the rest of the journey.

On our return to Concarneau, whom should we meet but one of the secretaries from the Mansion House, who was on board a yacht called *Mr Cube*. Prue and her husband, Jeremy Seddon, were on their way back from the Mediterranean and we enjoyed a very fine boozy afternoon with them – or I did, certainly. Once back on board I had no option but to turn in, to sleep it off, missing the firework display on shore that night. Libby tried to persuade me to watch it; I was only able to groan and roll over, complaining that it sounded to me more like a Russian convoy.

By the following day I was feeling a bit brighter and we sailed 'round the corner' to Benodet, which was a rather nice little Brittany town. We were by now working our way home, and were joined by an extra crew member, Sue Maxwell Scott, who was a friend of the Rawsons. Our plan was to go back to Cowes, after Libby, Rosemary and the girls had flown home. She came with a good reputation as a sailor and cook and the plan was that she should help us on the long journey back. The following day we went up river and then on 26th August we sailed for Douarnenez. Here the girls left us to fly back from Quimper, leaving Christopher, Sue and myself to set on our merry way out into the Channel.

We had not been out in the Channel for very long when a hell of a gale blew up. *Hodzah* was a good sea boat but nevertheless it was very uncomfortable. It finished off Sue Maxwell Scott completely. She retired to her bunk, and was not seen again until we arrived at Cowes. Unfortunately, before she retired, she had gone into the heads and had somehow managed to break the seat off the loo. This left the two of us something in the lurch (quite literally!). Each time it was necessary to sit on the loo you had to hold on to the seat with one hand and keep it between yourself and the porcelain, whilst the boat pitched up and down like a pea on a skillet. Not an easy task! I have a feeling that Christopher did not actually 'go' in the whole 48 hours it took us to reach Cowes. We took turns on watches, sleeping between times in the after cabin, which was reasonably comfortable, but I must say the whole experience was rather a miserable one. I was convinced that the tide was taking us further out into the Atlantic. We made headway for a full day and a night and then, on the next afternoon, we finally caught sight of the Devon coast. We were not sure which bit of the Devon coast it was, but it was land and it was in the right place, which eased our concern. The next day (the 29th) we passed the Needles and were on the home stretch. During the whole voyage I don't think either of us ate anything at all. We did not see any other craft, which made it rather a lonely experience and it was without doubt a great relief to arrive in Cowes.

Apart from this last episode it had been an extremely good summer holiday. It was to be our last until the November of the following year. In fact it was the last trip I ever made in *Hodzah*. I had always planned to get a yacht of my own and once the Mayoralty was out of the way and the children had been put through their education there was no reason not to do so.

Libby and I were back together in London. The following weekend we went down to Biddeston. Poor father was not at all well and was admitted to hospital the day after to be operated on for a twisted bowel. He survived that, and returned to the home, and that was the last time that I ever saw him. I think he knew that he was dying and although it was terribly sad I knew that it was for the best. I was very disappointed that he did not live to see me get my own 'K' – in those days the Lord Mayor received the G.B.E. at the beginning of the Mayoralty, on the day that he was presented to the Lord Chancellor, when he was gazetted as a Knight Grand Cross of the Most Excellent Order of the British Empire. Of course when father died I was to inherit the Baronetcy, but I would have been very proud for him to see me get my own, rather than the second-hand title, so to speak.

However, on the 21st, two days after I had last seen him, the matron rang up in the morning to say that my father had died at 8.20 a.m. *Nunc dimittis*, I rather think. It was, for me, the end of an era. The funeral was held on the 24th, which was, ironically, the same day as Nicholas's 21st birthday. Not a very jolly occasion for him. The four of us drove down to Bath where father was cremated. The service was a small and intimate affair, attended only by members of our immediate family and close friends – cousin Alan and that branch of the family, and Mr and Mrs Westcott – and conducted by Frank Trimmingham, who had been father's chaplain when he was Sheriff and Lord Mayor. We all returned to a hotel afterwards, and then Libby and I and the boys came back to London. Eight days later I was elected Lord Mayor.

As Lord Mayor of London.

My father, as Lord Mayor of London.

Chapter 13

The Mayoralty is not a nepotistic office. I was only the seventh son who had ever succeeded a father who had himself been Lord Mayor, in nearly 800 years of the Mayoralty. I think that father came the closest to ever being alive to actually see it.

There was a Labour government in power at the time, under Jim Callaghan. There were some feelings amongst my younger brother Aldermen that, because I had inherited the Baronetcy, the prime Minister would say that I did not need another title. It might have conveniently been slipped for a year and then fallen by the wayside altogether, since it was already being tampered with. The Baronetcy awarded to my father, for example, no longer existed. It had stopped being awarded in 1964, when they had substituted the G.B.E., and they had also stopped knighting the Aldermanic Sheriff, which had been customary in days gone by (since it was likely that he was going to be Lord Mayor, this ensured that he was a knight when he went in and then he was awarded a Baronetcy at the end). In later days it was to get even worse, when they stopped giving out an automatic title at all. Fortunately, it became a sort of custom (although not obligatory) for the Lord Mayor to receive a knighthood halfway through his year. However, Callaghan put paid to this flutter in the dovecote and proclaimed that since I had earned the title in my own right I should be awarded the G.B.E.

We decided to hold a memorial service for father after I had become Lord Mayor. It seemed appropriate, under the circumstances, that since he had been a Lord Mayor, the current Lord Mayor should give the address at his memorial service. And if that Lord Mayor happened to be his son then so much the better. By that time, too, I would have got over it and would be more capable of speaking. His ashes were scattered at Golders Green where my mother's ashes had also been scattered.

The Mayoralty was now approaching fast and I shall attempt, here, to recapture my feelings at that time. I certainly wanted to do the job, and now that father had died, that wish was even stronger. I felt I owed it to father to do it well, so that he could look down and be proud of me. Did I have any misgivings? I don't think that I did. In some curious way I felt that it was ordained, and I felt quite prepared for it. I had studied the job assiduously, and had made notes during my time as Sheriff as to what I would and would not do when in office – rather as I had studied the role of Captain in my seafaring days. Above all, I was young. I was coming up for 51 and Libby was only one year younger, which meant that we were fit and able to carry out the duties required of us. When father had been Lord Mayor in 1958 he had been considerably older, and although he was very robust, there was certainly a difference when faced with the demands of the job. Because of the advances in travel the Lord Mayor was now expected to travel widely abroad – not just in the summer, as had traditionally been the case, but at any time throughout the year. One could be expected to fly off at the drop of a hat: flying in Concorde, for example, to take breakfast with the Mayor of New York and then be back in London in time to attend a dinner that evening. I knew full well that the pressure would be on, but I did not have any qualms. I had now been in the City for seventeen years and felt that I knew it well. Of course, with hindsight, I now know that I was not at all prepared for the troubles that were to beset us in the early part of my office, when we were faced with the problems with the G.L.C. However, in the event I was able to rise to the challenge and actually rather enjoyed it (particularly as we won!). However, I am anticipating. At this stage I was, frankly, looking forward to it. All the necessary preparations were in order and, although it had been an immense disappointment that father had not lived to see me in office, it meant that I did not have the worry of his demise hanging over me any more. Reading through the duties of the Lord Mayor one might be astounded at the arrogance with which I felt able to do the job, but it is true to say that at that time I felt well equipped to tackle what lay ahead.

One of the things I was working on at this time was the speech I would have to make at the Lord Mayor's Banquet. This is probably the most important speech that the Lord Mayor has to make as it sets the tone for his year of office. It has to be a tribute, of course, to the outgoing Lord Mayor in whose honour the banquet is held, but it also encapsulates the intentions of the new incumbent. One also has to propose the health of Her Majesty's ministers, to which the Prime Minister has to reply. The Prime Minister expected to see what you were going to say, so of course it had to be written well in advance, and with some considerable care. I spent some time working at this. If you gave a good speech, then people would look forward to hearing you again, and you could always be excused for not delivering quite such a sparkling speech on the many occasions that you would have to speak during your term of office. However, if you started off on a bad note (and some did) then it was a uphill struggle to convince people that you were capable of speaking decently, since they were pre-conditioned to assume it was going to be poor. In those days, there were no such things as speechwriters. It would have to be all one's own work, but this was the way I liked it. Having got the thing done, and sent off to the Prime Minister, it occurred to me that for the 365 days of my term of office I was going to be speaking once, if not twice, every day. It was a daunting thought. 'Can you keep this up, Gillett?' I wondered to myself. Another important speech loomed on the horizon, which would be the one I would have to deliver for the Queen's Silver Jubilee. Generally speaking, I do not write my speeches in advance but just plan them in my head, but this would again have to be written and inspected in advance.

I managed to get in to the office quite a bit at this time. They were having a float in the Lord Mayor's Show and I was able to impart some advice to them. Everything seemed to be working smoothly and I felt confident that I could go away for the year and leave them to get on with the job. The firm were very much in favour of the idea of my impending role, and very co-operative.

The system of election in the City is unlike any other local authority. But then, the City is not like any other local authority. For a start, there are no politics in the City. This means that as apolitical ambassadors abroad we can do a selling job without the worry of having bricks thrown at us. And because it is a system that has been tried and tested over so many years ('archaic' is a label that some of our detractors apply to it) it does mean that it is a system capable of producing the right man for the job at the right time.

In other Councils, the Mayor is elected by the Council from their general membership. This is not the case in the City. Only those Aldermen who have been Sheriff can be elected, which means only between three or six, at the outside, are eligible. They are all well known to their brother Aldermen, they have been vetted and any weaknesses ironed out, or even advised that, if they are not considered suitable for the post, they would not be supported by the court of Aldermen to proceed for election to the Mayoralty. The process is one of continual review, and from the moment you become an Alderman you are really being trained up for the job ahead.

The actual procedure is still carried out in the old way, by a show of hands. Those who have the right of nomination are the Liverymen (all the members of the Livery companies of the City of London) who today number somewhat in excess of 24,000. The list of those eligible for election are read out in order of seniority by the Common Sergeant and the Liverymen then choose two of those names to be put forward. The order is paramount and ensures that the proceedings are carried out in a civilised manner. Basically what happens is that the first name is read out (say, Snooks). The call comes, 'Those of you who will have Snooks, hold up your hands'. All raise their hands and say, 'All!' loudly. Then comes the turn of the second on the list (say, Jenkins). Again, the request, 'As many of you who will have Jenkins, hold up your hands.' Then comes the cry, 'Next year!' In other words, he will be first on the list next year. The other names are called out and the response comes, 'Later, later'. There have of course been occasions in history when the Liverymen have not voted in accordance with the priority on the list, and in this case it is taken to the court of Aldermen. Those in the court of Aldermen who have served the office of Sheriff then leave the room so that, as the Recorder will tell the Liverymen, their choice may be 'free and unfettered'. Then, once the election is over, those who have not been Lord Mayor process out to join them in the Livery Hall and the two Sheriffs and the secondary will come in and report to the Lord Mayor that the vote has fallen on Snooks, or Jenkins or whoever. At that point there is a secret ballot and, hopefully, there will be a 100% vote, although this is not always the case. The answer is then announced and the successful candidate is brought up by the City Marshal to the Lord Mayor and then all the court of Aldermen come by in turn and shake him by the hand. He makes a little speech at this stage, thanking the Aldermen and assuring them he will do his best throughout the year. Then they all process back into Guildhall, the successful candidate walking on the Lord Mayor's left, to thunderous applause. The whole procedure is, therefore, highly predictable, although their have been occasions in history when there have been hiccups. It is such an important office and it is important to get it right. It is also fair for the prospective candidate to have sufficient time to prepare; with the amount of work involved it would not do at all to impose the office on someone without warning. Unlike other Mayors, the Lord Mayor of London has a national profile, and he is enshrined through history in the woof and web of the whole country. To our enemies, or course, the system just seems undemocratic and part of the Old Boy network. This is not the thinking behind it; the system is evolved because it is crucial to get the right person, and this has proved the best and most effective way of getting it right.

Back at the Guildhall you proceed to the dais, where you sit to the left of the Lord Mayor, and then you are called upon by the Town Clerk to 'stand forth and declare yourself willing to take upon yourself the office'. There is a fine of £1,000 if you decide to back out at this stage! You then go up and address the Livery, thanking them for their support. You tell them a bit about your plans for the year, and you usually mention your wife and the support of your family. It has to be brief and pungent, and, again, is a tone-setter for your year, inspiring confidence in your qualities of leadership and I repeat here the content of my speech:

'My Lord Mayor – Brother Liverymen,

In thanking you for the honour you do me in proposing me for this great office, and to my Brother Aldermen for endorsing your selection, I trust that I come to it well prepared to discharge its many duties to your satisfaction.

I was born a Londoner – on Lord Mayor's Day, 1925 – and have spent half my working life at sea and half in the City at Lloyd's.

Between us, my late Father and I have served this City continuously for half a century as Common Councilmen, Aldermen, Sheriffs and now as Lord Mayors. Alas, he died within 8 days of making history and being the first past holder of this office to see his son elected Lord Mayor.

May I take this opportunity to thank his many friends in the Livery for their kind condolences at this time.

When I addressed you on taking upon myself the office of Sheriff, just over three years ago. I ventured the opinion that those who aspired to lead must first learn to serve. Now that my day of testing has arrived I approach the forthcoming year strengthened in the knowledge of your continued confidence expressed here today.

That election to this unique position should fill me with pride goes without saying; the attendant feelings of humility are purely personal; for the office of Lord Mayor of London is, to my mind, nothing to be humble about, and I will seek to do nothing to diminish its prestige.

As a sailor and the first Master Mariner to be elected Lord Mayor, you will not be surprised to hear that I shall be seeking throughout next year to emphasise the importance to our national fortunes, nay survival, of the maritime services, both sea borne and City based. I shall continue the tradition of providing, through the Mansion House, a forum where Government and City can meet, and I hope to travel to Europe and the Far East to further the cause of good relations and trade.

Next year we celebrate the Silver Jubilee of our beloved Queen, and as a permanent expression of thanks for those 25 years of devoted service an appeal is to be launched under the leadership of the Prince of Wales.

The resulting funds are to be used to help youth to serve the community. It is Her Majesty's wish that expressions of goodwill towards her on this occasion should be made through this channel. I know that as leader of this appeal in the City I will be able to count on the generous support of the Livery, as my predecessors have done over the centuries.

As my guideline for the coming year I can think of none more appropriate than that expressed in the prayer of another sailor, Sir Francis Drake, 'Oh Lord God, when thou givest to they servants to endeavour any great matter, grant us also to know that it is not the beginning but the continuing of the same unto the end until it be thoroughly finished, which yieldeth the true glory.'

With the example of my Father before me, my dear Wife at my side and my Sons behind me, I pledge myself to this precept and declare myself ready and willing to take upon myself the office.'

The office of Lord Mayor carries with it no executive powers, he is only a constitutional monarch, but nevertheless he is a man of great influence and can effect change in various ways. Once you have given your commitment you become, truly, the Lord Mayor elect. Your Sheriff's chain is hung once more about your neck, and you will wear this again after you have been Lord Mayor, with the Cap of Dignity sewn on to your Alderman's gown to indicate that you are a past Lord Mayor.

There was one rather amusing aside in all of this. We were sitting down for the secret ballot, pens poised and slips of paper in our hands upon which to write the name of the candidate we wished to elect. Kenneth Cork was sitting next to me. Being a bit of a wag he leaned across and said to me, 'How many 'n's in Vanneck?' Vanneck was second on the list and had been the one they had shouted 'Next year!' for.

The election over, there are various other speeches to be made to the outgoing Lord Mayor and outgoing Sheriffs. It all goes on for quite a long time, but eventually all is over and as Lord Mayor elect you go out of the Guildhall to the awaiting press, accompanied by a trumpet fanfare. Back at the Mansion House there is a lunch in your honour and again you speak.

This is all followed by a period of 'purdah'. The City is very good at this sort of thing; when you have finished being Lord Mayor you go into 'purdah' until Easter of the following year, and when you have been elected Lord Mayor you go into 'purdah' between your election and your taking office in November. This prevents from you from buzzing around in public and being acknowledged as the new Lord Mayor before your time, and saves the existing Lord Mayor the embarrassment of being made to look redundant. It also gives you time to prepare. You are relieved of all your Aldermanic duties, you do not have to sit on the bench and, if your firm is willing, you do not have to turn up at work, either.

It also gave me time for my family. On 1st October I took Christopher up to King's College, Cambridge, to start his three years reading for an Economics degree. He was very excited and certainly ready to move up. He was staying in lodgings run by a woman who only took in choral scholars at King's; she loved music and enjoyed listening to her students practising in their rooms. Her walls were adorned with photographs of ex-King's men, many of whom were now King's Singers.

Having seen him settled in I returned to London. The next occasion was to be the presentation, on 13th October – again different from all other Mayors. The ceremony had been laid down by King John in the Charter of 1215, which decreed that the Lord Mayor was to be presented to the King and the Barons of the Exchequer for the Royal approval. The ceremony continued to the present day, and no election was complete or fully legal until it had received the Royal approbation. The Lord Mayor goes in procession by car with his brother Aldermen to the House of Lords. Here, in the Prince's Chamber, they all line up and the Lord Chancellor comes in with his Seal and his Mace and various other bits and pieces of his retinue. The Recorder of London then presents the Lord Mayor elect to the Lord Chancellor, with a few choice and, in my case, humorous words. The Lord Chancellor will say that he has it on the command of Her Majesty to grant her approbation to the election of the citizens, and he duly hands over the Order signed by the Queen. Nowadays, this procedure is something of a formality, but it has on occasion in history been challenged. I believe the last time anyone actually objected was George III, who had a bit of an argument with the City since they tended to support the American Revolution, but I do not believe that any Sovereign has actually stopped the appointment of a Lord Mayor. It is now regarded as a *fait accompli*, and that same day at noon you are gazetted as a Knight Grand Cross of the Most Excellent Order of the British Empire. That evening it is customary (everything in the City is, you will have gathered, always 'customary') for the Lord Mayor elect to give a dinner to his brother Aldermen and to the Lord Chancellor. It is held in his Livery Hall (if he has one – if not, then in somebody else's). Its purpose is really to thank the Lord Chancellor for his message from the Queen but it also serves as a test of his hospitality. The menu is scrutinized by the gourmets who assess whether the prospects look good for the year ahead. Much to Libby's annoyance, women were not invited to this occasion, at least in my day, although this rule lapsed in future generations. Sons could be included, so Nicholas came along (Christopher could not get down from Cambridge). I gave a fairly sumptuous feast; some friends had very kindly given me several tins of caviar and there was smoked salmon and oysters, much to the approval of at least one of the Aldermen who came up not just for seconds but for thirds. I also supplied generous cigars. Not having a Livery Hall (*Wellington* was not even equipped to provide hot food) I used Trinity House, which was quite exciting as many had not ever set foot inside the building.

We actually managed to escape the following week to Biddeston. The cottage had now been finished and fully re-decorated and was habitable once more. Whilst we were there we held a local memorial service for my father, for those in the village who knew him. It was the last time we were able to get down there for the entire year.

On November 2nd a press conference was held on board *Wellington*. I had invited the well-known broadcaster and presenter Richard Baker to chair the conference. Richard Baker was not only an officer R.N.R. but was also the descendant of the Pageant Master in the reign of Queen Elizabeth I. Various participants in the Show came along to the press conference, which went extraordinarily well. Many had turned up in uniform for the benefit of the cameras. London Transport were now producing posters advertising the Show. My own personal logo was a little robin, a character I had invented during my days in the passenger ship for children's autograph books, in lieu of being able to think of anything funny or witty to write. My robin sported a naval cap and boots and had a telescope under his wing.

The *Daily Telegraph* reproduced this little robin and it became a feature of the Show. The first float carried a sculpted model of my robin and stickers were handed out to the children. Of course a couple of days after the Show the telephone rang, querying what I wanted to do with this fifteen-foot high polystyrene robin. I had not given the matter much thought, it has to be said, but I had paid for it and it belonged to me. Fortunately Nicholas offered to take it for Rag Week at Imperial College. I do not know what its eventual fate turned out to be, but was pleased to have it off my hands!

On 3rd November I went to Buckingham Palace to receive the accolade for the G.B.E. This was quite unusual since I was already Sir Robin Gillett, with my inherited title. Still, I had not gone through the ceremony and now had to receive the accolade. I was second in line, after Sir Terence Lewin, who was on for an Order of the Bath. You had to kneel with one knee on a stool, which had a rather convenient handle with which to pull yourself up. The Queen did her thing with the sword, pinned the star on my chest, put the sash over my shoulder and said a few words – and that was it. It did of course, provide me with the opportunity to quip 'Twice a knight at my age . . . ' (although not to Her!). Unfortunately Christopher could not be with us, once again, but Nicholas came along and we all had our photographs taken outside the palace.

The next day Libby and I went to the Mansion House, where we had a session with Peter Drury, the steward there. He had been there in my father's day as my mother's footman, so it felt very much like family. He went through with Libby and me all the things he would need to know in order to make us comfortable, in a litany reminiscent of a school matron's list. I was advised, among other minutiae, that I would need 12 white shirts, 24 stiff white collars, and 16 pairs of underpants. I rather wondered what I would do with all this kit, but realised that as soon as one coughed one would be required to change clothes. Other fine details included what temperature our baths should be, how we liked our eggs boiled, what sort of soap we preferred: details which we promptly forgot but which was stored away by those who would be looking after us, to ensure that we always got what we wanted. Our staff would include the steward and three footmen, the housekeeper and her housemaids, the secretarial staff and someone who kept the diary and their assistant, the carpenter and electrician, the three people who looked after all the plate, two chauffeurs, three chefs and kitchen staff provided by the catering contractors. All had to be attuned to the comfort of the current Lord Mayor and Lady Mayoress, and they would have bitten their tongues off rather than make reference to the previous incumbent and their way of doing things. What you wanted was what mattered and they would have done all in their power to ensure it happened.

On 9th November I celebrated my 51st birthday. That was the day that a young Glaswegian journalist appeared, smelling strongly of whisky, to interview Libby about her former life. On the day that I went in to the Mansion House, the banner headline in the Glasgow Evening Times ran: 'Lady Libby – First Glaswegian in the Mansion House.' Up until that point, Libby had only been known by that name by close family and friends. All other acquaintances and the public at large knew her as Elizabeth. From that point on, however, she was Lady Libby.

On the evening of the 9th, a dinner was traditionally held for the Lord Mayor elect by the Master and the Wardens of the Grocers' Company. Each warden selected a course and it was one of the richest dinners I have ever eaten. We had caviar, lobster thermidore, pheasant in cream and goodness knows what else.

The Lord Mayor's Show is the biggest unrehearsed event in the world. There is, however, one small element of rehearsal involved, and Libby and I were duly collected at 5.30 a.m. the following morning to take part in the rehearsal for the coach which had to stop in front of St. Paul's and at H.M.S. *President*. It is quite a difficult procedure. This done, we proceeded to Butchers' Hall, where the Butchers' Company had laid on an extravagant breakfast for us. We felt as if we were getting fat even before we had started! We were interviewed again, this time by the *Daily Telegraph* and then, for me, yet more eating that day, with the Lighting Up dinner that evening. This was so called from the days when the Guildhall was lit by candles and would be inspected by the committee to ensure that all was in order. You were given the same menu as for the Lord Mayor's banquet, as a trial run, so to speak. Nicholas accompanied me, as it was a men-only do. The next day we packed up all our gear from home, which was collected from Fairholt Street and taken to the Mansion House. There was a very quick turnaround, with only about two hours in between the last Lord Mayor leaving and the new one being installed. We actually moved in on the 12th and attended a lunch, traditionally given by the outgoing Lord Mayor to the incoming. It was supposed to be a frugal meal, demonstrating the host's lack of remaining funds. We all then trooped into Guildhall in our gowns for the Silent Ceremony – so-called because, apart from the Lord Mayor taking the oath, no words are spoken. The old Lord Mayor sits at the head of a long table with the Lord Mayor elect beside him; when the latter has taken his oath the outgoing Lord Mayor surrenders his seat to the new incumbent who, for the first time, dons his tri-corn hat. It felt quite peculiar the first time around, until one got used to it. All the various insignia are then presented by the officers to the outgoing Lord Mayor; the officers retreat backwards out of the room, the insignia are handed over to the new Lord Mayor and the officers re-appear to collect their items again. It is a very dignified representation of the transferral of the symbols of power. The new Lord Mayor, after shaking hands with all the officers, then exits, preceded by the Sword and Mace, with the old Lord Mayor now walking on his left hand side. Back at the Mansion House the new Lord Mayor gives tea to his predecessor, and that's it – he's out and you are in!

Chapter 14

And there I was – holding the most important civic office in the land. I did wonder, for a moment, what on earth I was doing there. But it was too late to go back now. I spent the rest of the evening down in the office, arranging things as I liked them. It was much the same as moving into any new office, in any new job.

The next day was Saturday, and the day of the Lord Mayor's Show. I looked out of the window first thing with some trepidation, to ascertain what sort of weather we were going to have. A light rain was falling, but every prospect was that it would clear later on. And so it did. The sun came out in time, and we had a fine run. The Lord Mayor's Show does seem to be blessed in that respect and I can only call to mind two Shows which were really soaked in streaming rain the whole time. Libby and I breakfasted together in the private dining room, where the table would seat 16 if required. My boiled eggs duly appeared on the sideboard beneath a huge silver cover; displayed on a platter beneath two little cosies, and done just as I liked them.

It was then time to get ready for the Show. The Lady Mayoress does not take part in the procession, but is driven to the Law Courts by car, and is on the balcony when the Lord Mayor takes the salute. The Lord Mayor is required to wear court dress – knee breeches, buckled shoes and his scarlet, fur-trimmed Aldermanic gown. In my case, the BBC had requested that I be wired for sound. This was the first time such a thing had happened; they had attempted, the previous year, to get some comments from inside the coach by wielding one of those huge fluffy microphones, but it did not work terribly well. So on this occasion I had to have a microphone concealed under my jabot, with two little transmitters attached to my braces. I asked how I would know whether or not it was working, imagining myself in private conversation with my chaplain and having some untoward remark broadcast to the nation. They explained that they would switch it on from the control point and that I would be able to hear the commentator speaking to me. I enquired at what stage this was likely to happen, and they again reassured me that, having been on a recce

371

the day before, they had earmarked the spot at which they would want to 'go live' to the carriage.

'Just as you are on the approach to St. Paul's, you will pass a lamp post, with a litter bin attached to it. That's the point at which we'll turn it on.'

'*When* did you say you checked this?'

'Yesterday'

'That's all very well, but yesterday there were no people about. Today the road will be packed; I may well see the top of the lamp post but there will be no way of knowing if it's the right one!'

They admitted that I was probably right.

I asked them to get the commentator to wave his handkerchief or give me some signal, instead, since I would be able to see him from the carriage. They agreed to this plan and I was led off carrying my added weight of microphones and transmitters to begin the proceedings for the day.

We went off first of all to Guildhall for the presentation of loyal addresses. It is customary for your Livery company (or companies if you belong to more than one) and your City Livery club, the Guild of Freemen and any other organisations with which you may be connected, to present you with an illuminated address. This takes place just before the Show in the crypt of Guildhall. As when I was Sheriff, the Elder Brethren of Trinity House were there to present me with mine. There was then a short break for coffee, after which it was time to board the golden coach, which was drawn up outside the Church of St. Lawrence Jewry. I climbed aboard with the sword and the mace and my chaplain and, as tradition demanded, leant out to wave the tri-corn hat at the cheering crowds, for the customary photograph. Preceded by the Sheriffs in their carriages we formed a mini-procession to the Mansion House, led by the mounted police and with the Pikemen of the Honourable Artillery Company marching at the side. We went round Princes Street and up by the Mansion House, where we disembarked and went up on to the balcony to take the salute as the main procession went past. Various guests were with me on the balcony, including Libby, of course.

When we were ready, the parade commenced and the floats and bands and marching parties began their procession past. They were led by the carved polystyrene figure of my robin, as mentioned earlier, mounted on a concealed forklift truck. The marine theme was evident, with representations from the Navy and Royal Marines,

The Lord Mayor's Show.

Lloyd's Register of Shipping, the Port of London Authority, the Baltic Exchange, insurance companies connected with maritime trade, the R.N.L.I. and, in short, anything and everything connected with the sea. There were some marvellous floats. I had permitted Nicholas to bring 'Jezebel' into the Show. 'Jezebel' was an early twentieth century fire engine and the mascot of the Royal College of Science (the division of Imperial College in which Nicholas was studying). It had illegally infiltrated the Lord Mayor's Show on other occasions, but this year it was there legitimately, despite the fact that it did not exactly have a maritime connection. Nicholas rode past on this, carrying a placard which he held up as they drove past the Mansion House with 'Hi, Dad!' on one side and 'Hi, Mum!' on the other. Christopher was unable to join in the Show as he had to be back at King's for Evensong, but he was there on the balcony and took photographs for us. Canadian Pacific had put in a float with planes, ships and hotels represented on it. On the curtain of the low loader on which this was displayed was a sign saying 'Come back, Robin – all is forgiven!'

Bringing up the rear were the Aldermen, riding in the Queen's landaus borrowed from the Royal Mews for the occasion. It was now time for me to get back into my coach and, escorted by the Household Cavalry, off we trundled to the Law Courts. It must be remembered that the whole *raison d'être* for this Show is to take the Lord Mayor to the Law Courts to be sworn in as Chief Magistrate of the City. Through the centuries it has become a family occasion and carnival, but there is meaning behind the merrymaking. Our journey took us along Cheapside and round New Change, past the south of St. Paul's.

Just as we were approaching the cathedral I found to my horror that one of my concealed microphones had come loose and was swinging down between my knees. I picked it up and concealed it in my hand, hoping that it would still work. Brian Johnson was doing the commentary and the signal duly came for me to be on air. He asked me what it felt like to ride in the coach and I replied that I felt like a cross between Cinderella and Clare Francis (who had previously completed her transatlantic crossing which had received much television coverage). I wished everyone well and hoped they all had a good day.

We stopped at St. Paul's where the choir was lined up, and then proceeded down Ludgate Hill and into Fleet Street and Temple Bar.

Here we disembarked and I went into the Courts, preceded by the Aldermen. In the Lord Chief Justice's court I was presented by the recorder to the Lord Chief Justice, where speeches were exchanged. I took the oath, then processed to the next court, that of the Master of the Rolls. Here there were similar greetings and presentations. A quick glass of champagne and a smoked salmon sandwich and then it was back into the carriage for the return trip. This followed a different route; down Norfolk Street to the Embankment and then up Queen Victoria Street.

I began a new tradition for this Show, which, I am glad to say, has continued to this day. The carriage stopped alongside H.M.S. *President*, which in those days was still the headquarters of the R.N.R. Subsequently this changed to become a 'stone frigate' by St. Katharine's Dock, but in fact they still parade a guard alongside the old ship, and the Lord Mayor stops and gets out of his carriage to be greeted by the Commanding Officer and offered a tot of rum from the rum tub by a pretty Wren (I also got a kiss from her, which was rather nice!). My chaplain Basil Watson (who had been a naval padre) got out of the coach too and managed to get a tot for himself.

It is always amazing to see how many people turn out for the Lord Mayor's Show. Of course it used to be held on my birthday, 9th November, on whatever day of the week that happened to be (unless it was a Sunday). Having changed to a Saturday in 1958, the Show became much more accessible for children (particularly disabled children) who would arrive in coach loads. It became very much an audience participation event, and the Aldermen would do their best to whip up the crowd, vying as to which side of the road could cheer the loudest. On occasion they would even use glove puppets, ensuring that the theme of the day was fun, rather than pomposity.

Back at the Mansion House I disembarked and inspected the guard drawn up outside before reappearing at the balcony to take the final salute. The British Legion marched past, forming the very last of the procession. This was followed by a lunch for the invitees, during which the Lord Mayor was expected to circulate and chat to people. By the time the last guest had gone it was about 4.00 p.m. It had been a busy day, indeed.

In my father's day, the Lord Mayor's Banquet would take place on the very same evening, which made it an extremely long and tiring day. Now that the Show was fixed permanently on the Saturday, the Banquet was now held on the following Monday, which certainly made life a lot easier for everyone. It also meant that I was now free to go to the Remembrance Celebration in the Albert Hall that evening. We had seats not far from the Royal Box and enjoyed the various displays that took place before the finale of poppies falling from the roof.

I was now fully fledged as Lord Mayor. I had taken the necessary oaths, I had been shown to the people, and life would not be the same again for the next twelve months. The following day (which was Remembrance Sunday) we went off to St. Paul's Cathedral for the Remembrance Day Service. The City Territorial Units took part in the service and afterwards I took the salute as they marched past the Mansion House, prior to laying wreaths outside the Royal Exchange. Back at the Mansion House there was food and drink for the officers who had taken part. I was then able to put my feet up for the rest of the day and contemplate the activities for the following day. I should point out that all of these events were very finely stage-managed. The Pageant Master for the Lord Mayor's Show had overseen all the planning, which was meticulously detailed and very precisely timed. On one previous occasion the Lord Mayor did not get seen at all on television as things had gone on for so long that by the time his coach appeared they had run out of air time. This was now avoided by holding back some of the floats and displays at the start, in case of any unforeseen snag. Depending on circumstance and how things were going, the retained floats could either be slipped in front of the Lord Mayor's coach or, if things were running behind, they could then be added afterwards. Although this would mean their missing the cameras it would still allow the public to see them and would ensure that the main body of the procession was not delayed and the Lord Mayor was always on view.

For the general day-to-day running of the Mansion House, the 'hymn sheet' for the next day was always brought out the evening before, giving a blow-by-blow account of the activities of the Lord Mayor and Lady Mayoress for the following day. It included fine detail such as what to wear, and who the chauffeur and footmen would be for the day. This was in addition to the weekly rolling programme, which informed you of events for the next fortnight. It all worked very well. I feel that the secret for a successful and enjoyable Mayoralty was to leave the detail of the organisation in the hands of those who had done it year in and year out, and knew exactly what they were doing. You were the *prima donna*. Your job was to come on stage at the right moment, wearing the right clothes and perform in the right way. The stage-management, the scenery, lighting and props would all be done for you. If you performed well, the backstage crew basked in the knowledge that their work had not been wasted. If you failed to perform well, this somehow reflected on their stage management duties. But the important thing was not to worry or interfere with their job, and you could rest safe in the knowledge that their expertise would get you where you needed to be at precisely the right time. This left you free to get on with your job (speaking, mostly) and looking as if you were enjoying it. And not having to worry about the background detail meant, on the whole, that you *did* enjoy it. I suspect that some of my predecessors did not get as much personal satisfaction out of the Mayoralty as they could have done if they had just allowed those with the relevant experience to get on with the jobs they knew best. I imagine it is much the same on the stage; the actor or singer who is constantly trying to interfere with how things are done backstage only makes their own job more difficult.

Here I am, less than 48 hours into the Mayoralty, and pontificating already! I must apologise to my readers for anticipating here, but these are thoughts which had formed before I took office and which were confirmed as my year progressed.

Chapter 15

Day Three, the Monday, was to culminate in what was probably the biggest production that I would have to perform in all year, with the exception of the Queen's Silver Jubilee. The Lord Mayor's Banquet was at that time broadcast on both television and radio, plus the seven hundred guests who were actually at the Banquet, watching and listening closely to your every move, to see just what they had let themselves in for by electing you.

The day began with a call from the Governor of the Bank of England, who came across the road with the Deputy Governor. He used a wonderful phrase, telling me that he 'placed the facilities of the bank at my disposal'. It gave me a delicious notion of being able to ask him casually for a couple of a million quid! It was in fact possible to hold a bank account there if one wished, although the fact that you had to keep £100 in it at all times rather daunted me and I did not greatly desire the snob value of being able to sign Bank of England cheques.

That morning I made my first appearance on the Bench as Chief Magistrate. I was concerned to appear on the Bench as much as possible, and to take my role seriously. My father, who had been very popular on the Bench, had been presented with an engraved Schaeffer pen when he retired and I used this very pen on the Bench that day. The Lady Mayoress was involved in preparations throughout the day. At about 4 o'clock in the afternoon photographs were taken of the Mayoral party, much akin to a bridal party, with the Sheriffs and their ladies and the maids of honour – eight young 'bridesmaids' who would accompany the Lady Mayoress on to the dais. The eight were all friends of the family and all looked very pretty indeed.

The Banquet started with an early evening reception at 6 o'clock at Guildhall. I was now in my best bib and tucker: the black and gold gown. This came quite high in the hierarchy of gowns, and was topped only by the long, ermine-trimmed gown used for receiving heads of state (which I was to wear for the Jubilee) and the very finest gown which was reserved for Coronations – not one I would have the

378

opportunity to wear during my year! Flanked by our maids of honour and then by a small escort of the Pikemen of the Honourable Artillery Company (the Lord Mayor's personal bodyguards) we stood up on the dais in the Old Library to receive the more important guests. This was quite a lengthy procedure and took about an hour. The more important guests, such as the Prime Minister, the Lord Chief Justice, the Archbishop of Canterbury and the Lord Chancellor all arrived with their retinues of various office-holders and were announced with a fanfare of trumpets from the state trumpeters of the Household Cavalry.

The Banquet was of course held in honour of the outgoing Lord Mayor (not the Prime Minister, which is a commonly held belief). When all the guests are in, the Lord Mayor and Lady Mayoress, together with the Prime Minister and his wife, exit to the Old Print Room just outside the Library for a pre-prandial drink, whilst the rest of the company get into Guildhall and find their places. This takes a good fifteen minutes, although the guests are not abandoned and are all given a glass of sherry while they wait to be seated. Once they are all settled trumpets sound once again and the Lord Mayor processes in together with the Prime Minister's wife, the P.M. and the Lady Mayoress, to the accompaniment of Handel's *Scipio*, which is the Lord Mayor's own 'little tune', so to speak. They proceed around the hall and up to the top table. Grace is said, and the feast begins.

The excellent food apart, it is indeed a marvellous occasion. The gold plate sparkles in the middle of the tables and around the walls, glowing in the light from the candelabra, and the orchestra (in my case the Royal Marines) plays from the musicians' gallery, and all this in the setting of a grand historical building. Although it was burnt down in the Great Fire of London, and also fire-bombed in the Second World War, much of the original still remains and all that was damaged has been carefully restored. The building dates from 1415, the time of the Battle of Agincourt, and it is steeped in history. It was once a court, as well as the seat of the City government, and it hosts receptions for visiting heads of state and royals at various stages of their career. One could not help but be moved by the great sense of occasion.

As has been mentioned previously, the meal has several traditional components, including turtle soup and a baron of beef, followed by a fowl of some kind (the duck à l'orange proved a success, in the end) and the sweet, with of course a number of suitable wines for each

Before the Lord Mayor's Banquet: Back Row: Maids of Honour, The Sword Bearer, The Chaplain, The City Marshal, The Sergeant-at-Arms, Maids of Honour. Front Row: The Lord Mayor and Lady Mayoress with the Sheriffs and their wives.

Processing with the Prime Minister, Jim Callaghan.

course. It must be remembered that the Lord Mayor's banquet is paid for by the Sheriffs (who pay a quarter each) and the Lord Mayor himself, who pays half. It is, as you may imagine, an expensive affair, and there is some assistance in the form of an allowance. However, it is, largely, a personal thing, kept that way because it is characteristic of the nature of the Mayoralty. A certain contribution is required from the incumbent in terms of hospitality, which goes with the job. I would argue that anyone in public life has a certain responsibility, and above all requires enthusiasm for the job, which is a voluntary position.

The meal concludes with a toast to Her Majesty the Queen and the passing of the 'loving cup'. This is an ancient custom, whereby a lidded vessel (gold) with some wine of rather dubious quality is passed from one person to another. At any one time, three people stand for the purpose. One takes the lid off, the drinker drinks from the cup and wipes it with a napkin tied around the handle, the lifter replaces the lid, takes the cup and turns to the next in line, where the process is repeated. The one who has just drunk does not sit down but turns around with his back to the drinker. The idea is to protect the drinker, whilst he is thus engaged, from any passing malcontent who may decide to stab him whilst he has his face in the mug. The custom is preserved as a sign of friendship and unity, in much the same way as the communion cup, I suppose. Nowadays, of course, there are those who would rather not drink from the same cup as others, but they are not required to do so and can merely go through the motions. The custom is practised in Livery Companies as well. Once this has been concluded and grace said again, the speechifying commences.

The Lord Mayor kicks off with a speech, which has to be divided into three parts. I began with the anecdote of the schoolboy whose mathematics was as bad as his Latin and who translated the opening lines of Caesar's 'Gallic Wars' – *Omnia Gallia in tres partes divisa est* – as 'all Gaul is quartered into three halves'. The first part of the speech is a reference to the guest of honour, the outgoing Lord Mayor, although one must not go into too much detail as his health is proposed later by the Archbishop of Canterbury and it is important not to steal his thunder. The second part is a statement of his intentions. He has done this to an extent, of course, to the Liverymen at Guildhall at the time of his election. He will also use this opportunity to introduce his 'pet theme' for the year. If he has a charity, for example, he will give it a plug at this juncture. In my case, I explained a little about the Prince's Jubilee Trust, and, as you might expect, I also took the chance of hammering home my concern about the decline in our maritime power – not only our dwindling Royal Navy but also our mercantile fleet which at that time was still quite strong but was diminishing rapidly. We live on an island and have always relied upon the sea for our livelihood and I felt we could ill afford to allow our power to diminish. Finally I had to propose my toast to Her Majesty's ministers. This I did in what I hoped was an amusing manner. Harold Wilson, Prime Minister and leader of the Labour Party, had suddenly and quite inexplicably resigned in the earlier part of that year. The government of the day had had to go through the process of selecting a new Prime Minister and this had been through the customary tortuous process, swinging first one way and then the other between the likely candidates, who included Callaghan (the Foreign Secretary) and Healey (Chancellor of the Exchequer). I referred it by way of a nautical analogy, commenting that the passengers aboard the ship had been somewhat alarmed when the Captain had walked off the Bridge and had wondered who was going to take command: would it be the Purser (the Chancellor of the Exchequer), or would it be the Chief Engineer (the Trade and Industry Secretary) or perhaps the Pilot, experienced in foreign waters (the Foreign Secretary)? Callaghan had actually been a sailor himself and was President of the Pilot's Association. I went on to say that we had been somewhat relieved when it turned out to be the Pilot!

I already knew that Callaghan approved of the speech since he had told my wife that he liked it when he met her after the Remembrance Service evening in the Albert Hall. What I had not anticipated was the standing ovation I received, the first to have been given after a Lord Mayor's speech in living memory. It was of course very pleasing, and I sat blushing modestly, feeling both very proud and relieved. As I have indicated before, it is probably the most important speech you are likely to make in your Mayoral career as it sets the tone, and you can always be forgiven for being less good later on. As one of the youngest ever Lord Mayors I had felt it doubly important that I should have got it right at this point.

Proceedings continued with the Prime Minister's reply and then the Archbishop of Canterbury's speech and, finally, the Lord Chancellor, who proposed the health of the hosts, that is, the Lord Mayor and the two Sheriffs. A few more words of thanks from me and that was more or less it. We all then rose and processed down to the Crypt, where there was dancing for the remainder of the evening, as a way of staggering the exodus of the 700 guests. The dancing after the Lord Mayor's Banquet normally takes place in the Livery Hall but Libby had insisted on it being in the Crypt, despite opposition from the traditionalists. In fact it worked very well indeed there, with an atmosphere akin to that of a stylish nightclub. The Prime Minister stayed, as did the Lord Chancellor, and great fun was had by all. Once the last guest had gone and all farewells said, Libby and I sank gracefully and gratefully to bed and I felt quite happy that we were off to a good start. It was, of course, just the beginning...

Although I had intended to use my speaking time during my year to develop my theme of the danger of allowing our maritime skills to pass away and diminishing our merchant fleet, I think I only made one more speech on those lines (and that was the next night, at the Mercers' Company) before I was having to concentrate on a completely different tack. The mood amongst the left wing in the

Greater London Council had been simmering for some time, and was now coming to a head with an attempt by them to abolish the Corporation of the City of London, to destroy it as a unit of local government, and to carve up its territory (and of course its rateable value and its wealth) amongst the adjacent socialist boroughs of Camden, Tower Hamlets and Hackney. They had been working on this secretly for some time, and now decided to make a frontal attack. It has to be said that this move actually helped me considerably in the defence. The main accusations were that we were undemocratic, unrepresentative and anachronistic. They were making overtures to the financial institutions of the City by a drip feed method of propaganda, claiming that we were unnecessary and that we ourselves laid false claim to being instrumental in producing the wealth of the City. Within a week or so of my appointment this move was becoming headline news and I was constantly being asked for my opinion on the situation. I have to say that my response when asked what I thought about the abolition of the City Council was to question why the G.L.C. should not be abolished instead! It was interesting to note that there was no suggestion of our being merged with the Council of the City of Westminster, which might have been a more logical step, since we shared an M.P. – but oh, no! They were a stuffy conservative lot and could not be trusted! I found myself having to switch my speaking to the Livery companies, many of whom I am sure did not realise the potential danger they were in, since they would have been discarded under the new regime. Many did not know, some did not care, and I knew it was up to me – speaking to them as I did more or less every night – to educate them and to muster support for our cause.

I must confess that in a way I rather enjoyed this (I enjoyed it even more, of course, when we came out of it alright in the end). I felt that I had a corner to fight, because I did not believe for one minute the rubbish that the left were talking. I knew, from personal experience, that the archaic ceremonies and traditions they derided so strongly were in actual fact a great 'come on' to foreigners. I knew that if we lost such traditions now, they could never be regained. Provided the people inside the 'funny clothes' were genuine professionals, which of course they were, then the system worked. The Lord Mayor of London, whatever his profession, would be a man of intelligence and probity who could promote trade overseas and speak not only for his City but also for his country. I thus embarked on a crusade of speechifying more or less every night, and systematically demolishing the arguments put up by the other side. These were becoming more and more ridiculous, and what's more they kept on changing their minds. In our favour, it became evident that there were divisions in the ranks on the 'other side': some of the other socialist boroughs under the G.L.C. were not that enthusiastic about carving up the City and the proposed division of the spoils, and did not see why the demise of the City should benefit only a few selected boroughs. They were not wholeheartedly in favour of the G.L.C., which took a lot of money off the borough councils and did not always spend it wisely. And against the criticism that we were claiming undue worth for our contribution to the wealth of the nation we countered that we never had made such a claim, but what we did achieve successfully was the creation of the right climate for the financial businesses to flourish. Under the G.L.C. such businesses could well be taxed out of existence. It was becoming evident that we were winning the argument on this last score, and so they began changing their tune; they would not abolish the City altogether, but create a system of local government by a committee of twelve, to be appointed by the G.L.C. They would do away with the Aldermen and the Sheriffs and the Lord Mayor – although this of course then left them with the problem of the Lord Mayor's Show, the popularity of which they could not deny. Well, they might just keep some of the positions, but for ceremonial purposes only. This played right into my hands. How much more undemocratic could you get than an appointed committee – a quango, so to speak – to replace an elected institution which had evolved over 800 years?

The process was a fascinating one, and provided material for many a television debate. Tony Banks, M.P. was one of the protagonists, but would get quite easily riled and on occasion lost his temper on air, thereby losing his cause. They had managed to produce a private members' bill in Parliament proposing the abolition of the Corporation and it was not until April that it was thrown out by the Labour government. I was at dinner when the result was announced. It was evident that, at the end of the day, political persuasion mattered not; those in government fully appreciated that the traditions of the City were an asset to them and to the country. The role of the Lord Mayor as ambassador cost them nothing, as the City paid for the travel; entertaining of visiting heads of State was undertaken by the Corporation at no cost; and above all the role had no political axes to grind. It was not an institution they could afford to lose. The debate was finally put to bed, but the for the first four months of the Mayoralty I was on my feet every night, telling the Liverymen what to do, explaining the implications of the threat to the City and what it could mean for the country. It had given me something to get my teeth in to, and on the whole, as I have said, was an experience I fully enjoyed.

Following the standing ovation I had received at the Lord Mayor's Banquet, I then had the City Livery Club's annual banquet, which was a mini-version of the original, delivered in much the same style as the speech in Guildhall. By that time, I was getting well into my stride and received yet another standing ovation. A week later I had a different audience again with the Guild of Freemen, and by then had worked up quite a head of steam, delivering an impassioned speech on the subject which by this time was closest to my heart. There was stamping and cheering, and at one point in the course of my speaking I even heard a cry from the back of the hall: 'Lord Mayor for prime Minister!' The Town Clerk told me afterwards that such was the fervour I succeeded in whipping up that, had I urged them to follow me down the street to go and smash all of the windows at County Hall, they would have followed me like sheep; once again I received a prolonged standing ovation. Perhaps it had been a little over the top; I recall at one point quoting grandly from one of Macaulay's *Lays of Ancient Rome*: 'How can man die better than facing fearful odds, For the ashes of his fathers, and the Temples of his Gods?' Talk of rabble rousing! I felt perhaps better qualified to join the Trade Union movement rather than being Lord Mayor of London. Nevertheless, it was all in a good cause – and it worked. I was not trying to deliver a political message, merely to stand up for what I believed was common sense. I was accused of being political on one occasion when speaking in a Livery Hall, by an M.P. who had been warned against any politics himself. I was quick to defend my position with the riposte that I was merely standing up for the City. I did not care who had attacked us, be it left, right or centre. If the City was attacked, then I was there to defend it. In fact I had a visit from the opposition leader of the G.L.C., Mr Cutler, who came to Mansion House one day with the message: 'You must come down off the fence, Lord Mayor, and nail your colours to the conservative mast!'

'I am sorry Mr Cutler, ' I replied, 'But I am not nailing my colours to *anybody's* mast, other than the City's. If I try and fight this on party political basis, then we shall suffer the same fortunes as the political party with whom we claim allegiance. I do not care who criticises us, I am just sure that what we are doing is right.'

On the second day after the Lord Mayor's banquet, we held a Memorial service for father in the church of St. Lawrence Jewry. I gave the address, Nicholas read the lesson, Christopher sang a solo and Libby did the flowers, which made it a fittingly family affair. The service was very well attended, as was to be expected, not only by people from the City but also by representatives of my father's old regiment and his firm and the various clients that he had. His death had been a sufficient distance away in time to enable us to feel quite able to carry out our parts; I do not think I would have had the strength to give the address shortly after his passing. He had had 'a good innings', and it was with pride and love that I was able to speak, rather than from any feelings of grief and sadness.

Chapter 16

I have no intention of going through the Mayoralty day by day, but rather to pick out the highlights of my year. Having said that, I should relate that the very next day I took my first Common Council, where the Lord Mayor acts rather like the Speaker in the House of Commons, rather than a party leader. He only speaks, in fact, to read the prayer at the beginning of the service, or to make any reports that he has to present (if he as been overseas, for example) or to give out any special announcements. Even if he should have to make a pronouncement (to announce the results of a vote, for example) the Town Clerk speaks for him. This does not, however, diminish his power in any way and he could, if he so wished, adjourn a meeting or cut a meeting short. The Common Council is always held on Thursdays, in Guildhall. That evening we dined with the Grocers' Company and then went off to Buckingham Palace for the Diplomatic Reception. This takes place once a year, and is where the Queen receives all the Ambassadors and High Commissioners at the Court of St. James. The Lord Mayor merely has to sit in the gallery and watch her shake hands with all those present, but afterwards there is an intimate little party to which we were invited. The Queen, the Duke of Edinburgh, the Prince of Wales and the Queen Mother all retire to one of the smaller reception rooms, for a small gathering with drinks and eats which is attended by the Lord Chancellor, the Foreign Secretary and the doyennes of the diplomatic corps, together with the Lord Mayor and Lady Mayoress. There was one rather amusing incident that occurred earlier in the evening, before the start of proceedings. We were talking with the Queen's Equerry, Colonel Miller, who was responsible for general ceremony and in particular for equestrian ceremony (he came with the carriages to the Lord Mayor's Show) which had earned him the nickname 'Miller the Horse'. He approached us in great excitement to say that he had persuaded the Queen, on Jubilee Day, to come into the City in the golden coronation coach. This was, he claimed, a first; the coach had never been in the City before. Although strongly tempted to wager a bet

The Lord Mayoress, Lady Gillett (Libby).

against this claim, I forbore taking any money off him for I knew full well that it was not the first time the coronation coach had made such journey. There is a famous painting – often used as a Christmas card in the City – which depicts Queen Victoria, as a new Queen, preceded by the Lord Mayor, on her way to the Lord Mayor's banquet at Guildhall (custom once held that the sovereign attended the banquet in the first year of his or her reign). I merely corrected him, and informed him that the coach had been seen in the City in 1837. I'm afraid I rather spoilt his fun, but felt that it was better that he found out now, rather than later.

I think it might be useful to describe here a typical Lord Mayor's day. The Lord Mayor and Lady Mayoress would rise and have breakfast in the private dining room (usually at 8.30 a.m.). I insisted on having all the mail sent up to me at breakfast. Some preferred to have it opened for them and sorted but I liked to open my own mail; I rather suspect that in doing so I saw much that would have otherwise been filtered out for me by a secretary. There were, indeed, some extraordinary correspondents. I am sure the Queen receives similar missives, but people tend to write to the Lord Mayor on all sorts of subjects. Many were obviously cranks, but some were rather amusing, and anything of interest I could then read out to Libby or pass to her. So I would eat my boiled eggs and toast and marmalade, and drink my orange juice, whilst perusing the morning's mail. Breakfast over, I would then go down to the Venetian Parlour, the room on the first floor of the Mansion House which serves as the Lord Mayor's private office, where he would receive visitors. The half hour between 9.00 and 9.30 would then be given over to domestic arrangements. In would come the Esquire on duty, and go through the day's programme with me. If we were going to give an entertainment in the Mansion House, he would be followed by the steward. Having discussed the menu with the chef and the Lady Mayoress prior to this, he and I would select the wines. If the Private Secretary had anything he wanted to discuss he would also come in at this time and we would deal with anything that might have been received in the mail and needed attention.

From then on, a variety of things could happen. I might, for example, spend the morning on the bench. In those days, the Mansion House Justice Room was actually in the Mansion House – the only private house in the world with an active court of justice in it. Alas, nowadays it has been merged with the larger court of

Guildhall, in the building the other side of Walbrook, since it was, admittedly, rather small. The Bench was built for the days when the Lord Mayor sat on his own, and to get three on the Bench was a bit of a squash; the Magistrate sitting on the Chairman's left could practically shake hands with whoever was in the witness box. There were a number of cells down below, just for keeping those who were brought in from the remand prison and waiting to be tried. Several of the cells were for men and then there was also the 'birdcage' – a larger cell where all the female prisoners would be kept together. When showing visitors round the Mansion House custom was that you showed them the cells; the birdcage was of particular interest as Emily Pankhurst had been there on one occasion. There was an incident in a Mayoralty previous to mine when a guest had said: 'I've always wanted to know what it felt like to be in a cell', went in and shut the door only to find out too late that the doors are self-locking. The jailer had gone home and taken the keys with him and a taxi had to be sent in order to retrieve him and release the unfortunate guest.

If I did sit on the Bench, it would be from 10.30 to perhaps midday, just to exercise my right as Chief Magistrate. Alternatively, I might receive a visiting Ambassador, or a new Ambassador appointed to the Court of St. James (it was customary for them to call on the Lord Mayor for a cup of coffee and a chat after they had reported to the Queen), or a visiting overseas Mayor. Along with that, I had to play the 'present game'. An exchange of gifts took place on frequent occasions, but one never quite knew whether or not the visitor was going to produce a gift, and it was the duty of the Esquire to try and 'suss out' whether this was the case, or not. We had a cupboard in the adjacent parlour stocked in readiness and he would go to this cupboard and select a suitable return gift. Often the visitor's gift was quite small, and they would merely whip it out of their pocket and present it to the Lord Mayor. Ideally, if the game had been played correctly, I would be able to put my hand out and the Esquire would produce a return gift. In anticipation, I had ordered a firm to strike me a set of silver crowns with the Jubilee hallmark on – on one side it had a Jubilee cipher and on the other the civic arms, with the civic shield and a crossed sword and mace and my name round the edge – which came in a rather nice leather case with my coat of arms embossed on the front. There was a certificate inside to say that it was a limited edition. I had 300 struck for myself; a further 300 were sent to Canada, to collectors' shops and others were for retail in this country. These were very handy, as they could just be slipped into your pocket and produced if required, and saved the Esquire all his detective work. The exchange of gifts was a matter of considerable tact and diplomacy, particularly with the representatives of certain countries, who might have been offended if the gift given to them was obviously considerably more expensive (which might be construed as an attempt at one upmanship) or obviously less worthy (a put down) than their own gift. As well as my own medallions, Libby also had a collection of Wedgwood china birds to hand, in the event of any of the wives producing gifts. We abandoned these after a bit; if we were packing to go abroad they were very vulnerable and we opted, in the end, for a selection of prints of views of the City. Other potential recipients for gifts included the outriders accompanying motorcades (usually given a pair of cufflinks bearing the City arms). I built up quite a collection of gifts I received myself, and kept them on display in the Mansion House. A popular gift from the mayors of small American towns was the key to their city – over the year I managed to acquire a drawerful of keys to various American towns. Books were also popular, particularly the well illustrated coffee table type and I would be able to reciprocate with a fine publication called 'The Flowering City' – an account of the City of London with particular reference to its gardens. Moving up the scale (a visiting Ambassador being entertained with a dinner or banquet, for example) the stakes were obviously higher, and it would be necessary to ascertain beforehand what kind of gift might be bestowed, if any, so that one could offer a return gift of equal value. Other possible morning activities, as well as presiding over the Courts of Common Councilmen and Courts of Aldermen, included perhaps going out on visits or to open something. One was certainly never idle.

Lunch was mostly outside the Mansion House, and generally with a City institution. Many of the banks in the City would invite the Lord Mayor to lunch (this included the many foreign banks, as well as our own), as would the Baltic Exchange, or Lloyd's Register of Shipping. The hope was that you would be given a fairly light meal, and you would have to go carefully on the wine, bearing in mind that you still had a long day ahead of you. There were also *en famille* lunches when members of the Common Council would come for lunch in the Long Parlour – the Court of Common Council would be invited in its totality throughout the course of the year, usually divided into four separate groups. You usually had to give a light speech over lunch, often no more than a formal thanks, although during the course of the attack I would use the opportunity to provide an update on the situation. The twenty-five wards in the City each had a Ward Club, made up of members and those who worked and voted in the ward, and they would also have lunches to which the Lord Mayor would be invited.

In the afternoon, there would often (perhaps two or three times a week) be a charity A.G.M. Many charities had been started in the City and would have had their first meetings in the Mansion House, and they liked to continue the tradition by holding their A.G.M. there, where the Lord Mayor's presence would also be a draw for their members to attend. In the case of many big national charities (such as the R.N.L.I. or King George's Fund for Sailors) people would attend from all over the county; the Lord Mayor, who was often a patron, would address the meeting and tea and buns would be laid on for them all afterwards. As well as A.G.M.s, afternoon activities might include prizegivings at the various schools to which the City was connected – the City of London School for Boys and the City of London School for Girls, the Freemans School, Christ's Hospital and King Edward's Witley would all expect to see the Lord Mayor at Founder's Day, in addition to which institutions such as the Chamber of Commerce would have occasions to hand out prizes to best secretary and what have you, again held at the Mansion House.

The late afternoon might be taken up with visits to hospitals, nurses' homes and other such places. It was important at all times to exercise a degree of caution, since it was a commonly held belief that the men in public office were permanently starved and one would invariably be presented with an array of cakes and buns to eat; food would be pressed upon you at about 5 or 6 o'clock and it would be politic to accept offers of sausage rolls and cakes which had been made especially, knowing full well that you had to attend a banquet later that evening. After this indulgence it was back to the Mansion House and, in the evening, one was either out or entertaining at home. Some of the Livery companies were without halls, since a great many had been lost in the last war and had never been rebuilt. The Egyptian Hall at the Mansion House – the big banqueting hall, which holds some three hundred people – was available for hire to Livery companies wishing to hold their banquet there. It was used particularly if ladies were invited, since many of the Livery companies' own halls were big enough only to hold the members, but not their wives as well. On these occasions the Lord Mayor would be a guest in his own house, as it were. As at every occasion where the Lord Mayor was the guest of honour, a speech was required. Some would bemoan the fact that as Lord Mayor one had to make over three hundred speeches a year. My complaint was not with having to make the speeches, but the fact that for every speech you made yourself, you would be required to listen to at least four others, of varying degrees of quality, presentation and content. However, it was great fun, if you went into it with a sense of humour. The quality of the Livery banquets varied enormously. You would sit to the right of the Master, and on your right would be the Master's lady. The Lady Mayoress sat on the other side of the Master, and they would engage in conversation, which meant that much of my time would be spent talking to the Master's lady. The tenor of the conversation was always very much the same, and I felt as if I could have carried a tape recorder with me to churn out the responses to tentative questions such as 'Are you enjoying it?' and 'How do you watch your weight?'. But of course you had to answer each question as it was the first time anyone had asked you that in your life. I used to have one or two standard quips up my sleeve, particularly in response to questions about the quantity of food I was obliged to eat in relation to the lack of opportunity for exercise (my answer to this last was that I never took any exercise before I became Lord Mayor, and therefore never missed it). I would control the food problem by always taking very small quantities, but in answer to any question on the subject I would claim that my principle was that: 'The most effective oral contraceptive was the word 'no'. I would apply the same to drink – I have seldom drunk red wine, which does not agree with me, and would confine myself to one glass of white for an evening and a glass of port for the toast. It was essential to keep a clear head for speaking, which was the part I enjoyed the most. Along with 'putting the boot in' for my 'Save the City' campaign, I would always try and make my speeches as amusing as possible. I enjoyed having an audience – particularly a mixed audience, rather than all male – and if you were able to make them laugh and they were clearly having a good time, I would get as much a buzz from it myself as one might from quantities of alcohol. A typical Mayoral day would end as one kicked off one's buckled shoes at about 11.00 p.m. We would try and draw things to a close at the Mansion House at 10.30, although there were often the lingerers who liked to hang around. However, it was up to the boudoir (the private drawing room) once they had all gone, and a quiet smoke of my pipe whilst discussing the evening with Libby before turning in ready for the next day.

Chapter 17

Having painted a very general picture of the lifestyle, I will select certain out-of-the-ordinary events and some of the travelling that we did, in addition, of course, to the Jubilee – for no sooner was the threat to our well being lifted, than we were in Jubilee mode. It must be said that one thing we did not do was to gloat over our victory or the defeat of the private members' bill to abolish the City. Once the threat had gone, there was a tacit agreement amongst ourselves that it would not be mentioned again. We fought our battles hard, but, once over, normal service was resumed and we did not wallow in the events. The G.L.C. was of course later abolished, but even then not all of us were in favour of such a decision and were not jumping up and down on its grave. Personally I favoured reform rather than complete abolition – I felt that the organisation needed its wings clipped, which might have saved all the current furore (happening as I write) in search of a new Mayor of London.

Quite soon after my appointment, on 21st November, I was persuaded by the studios of Thames TV studios at Teddington to present the prize on the Hughie Greene show, 'Opportunity Knocks!' We had great fun, going down there for lunch and rehearsing the thing through, although I do recall that Hughie Greene was consistently unable to get my name right. However, I have got quite used to this over the years: Gillett – rhymes with fillet, I always say, helpfully, although it still comes out as Gillette, as in razor. I would often work at weekends; attending events where I thought my absence might be seized upon by the G.L.C. and used as evidence against me ('the Lord Mayor only attends toffs' events – he's not interested in meeting the people' and that sort of thing).

On 23rd November, we had our first official visit. This was a banquet at the Mansion House for the President of Venezuela. I should explain here that there are really three sorts of overseas visits. At the top of the rung is a State Visit, where a Head of State is a guest of H.M. The Queen and the government. It is usually a three-day visit, and the incoming visitor is met, usually at Victoria Station, by the

Queen, other members of the Royal family, the Lord Mayor and various other V.I.P.s. The Queen then takes the visitor in one of her open carriages to Buckingham Palaces, where he may be staying. On the first night the Queen gives a banquet either at the Palace or at Windsor. The next day might be spent in meeting members of the government; the following evening the Corporation hosts a plush banquet in Guildhall, as prestigious as the Lord Mayor's banquet itself and then, on the third evening, there is often a return match, and the visitor will host a dinner at an hotel or other appropriate venue, to which the Queen and the Lord Mayor are both invited. Second in line is the Official Visit. This is when a Head of State comes over to discuss loans or trade or some other business with the government. The Queen is not involved on those occasions, although the government might use Hampton Court or Lancaster House for a lunch, and the City will give a banquet in the Mansion House, hosted by the Lord Mayor. He then may, or may not, host a return dinner, although it will depend on the length of his stay. At the bottom end of the scale come those who are not necessarily Heads of State but may be a Mayor or a government minister. The Lord Mayor would not necessarily be involved in the arrangements for the latter.

The President of Venezuela fell into the second category. He and his wife were quite charming. He did not speak very good English, but the Foreign Office would produce marvellous interpreters for such occasions – usually a young woman who would place herself on a kind of 'milking stool' between you and your guest and then instantly translate everything that was said. She would literally be only one or two words behind you, and it meant you did not have to wait patiently for whole sentences or paragraphs to be relayed. Once you became used to it, it was certainly a most helpful means of communication. The customary gifts were exchanged, and I recall that his wife presented Libby with a very stylish brooch, fashioned from a large piece of jade set in gold. The Corporation employed a firm of P.R. consultants. Among their duties was to write speeches for the Lord Mayor on occasions such as this, and, this being my first visitor, I thought that I may as well give them a go. Background information was supplied by the Foreign Office, who would provide details of the country and its economy as well as useful information about the man himself. I duly passed all of this over to the P.R. department, with an instruction to draft me a speech – without, it has to be said, a great deal of optimism on my part. I was not wrong. The speech which came back was absolute rubbish, which went straight into the bin, and I quickly sat down to write my own. Although I do not usually speak from notes, on this occasion my guests wanted a preview of what I was going to say. A translation of the visitor's speech is often also provided for those at the table so that everyone can follow what is being said. The brief from the Foreign Office had suggested some quotation in Spanish, which I decided to attempt. I do not think my pronunciation was terribly good and I gave up after that, apart from one reception at Guildhall when I managed a few words in French.

Shortly after this, we entertained Mrs Thatcher to lunch. I had met her before, as her husband Dennis had been a client of my father's and she had visited my father's firm when she was first elected as an M.P.

An occasion not quite in the same category as a State Visit, but perhaps of passing interest, is when Morecambe and Wise were given the Freedom of the City, which took place on 1st December. They came with their families and took their oaths as Freemen, and following the formalities the Chamberlain gave a lunch. The pair were both extremely amusing and entertaining – more humorous off the stage than on, in many ways, with constant displays of quick wit. Following the Chamberlain's speech, Ernie Wise stood up to reply. As he stood, he knocked his chair over backwards. Standing in attendance was the beadle to the Chamberlain's court, dressed very primly in frock coat and top hat. He rushed around the table to pick up the chair and just as he did so Eric Morecambe called out, 'Don't worry Ern – Frankie Vaughan's on his way to help!'

The following day the private secretary came in to my office to announce that Morecambe and Wise's agent was on the telephone, wanting to know whether Eric and Ernie could drive a sheep across London Bridge, thus exercising their traditional right as Freemen of the City. Despite the fact that this was one of the ancient rights of Freemen (to be able to drive a flock of sheep across the Bridge) it seemed to me that such an exercise would prove rather unfair on the sheep, and furthermore I had visions of the R.S.P.C.A. and sheep lovers everywhere coming down on me like a ton of bricks. I thus turned down the request. 'Anyway,' I asked, 'Why are they asking *me*?' Apparently they had first approached the police, who had turned down the request as contrary to some Metropolitan Streets Act, but had suggested they ask the Lord Mayor. The agent thus dutifully rang the Mansion House. Subsequently I believe that some other celebrity did get permission to drive a sheep across the bridge, from a future Lord Mayor.

I was to come across Morecambe and Wise on several other occasions throughout my year, including the Midsummer Banquet for the Arts and Sciences. It was here that Eric Morecambe thoughtfully asked me if I would like him to shout 'Rubbish!' in the middle of my speech, if I were to ask my audience how I was doing. I decided to decline his offer. I would add, however, that Libby would sometimes take it upon herself to prick the balloon of my pomposity and shout 'Rubbish!' when I was speaking – an act which many erroneously thought was rehearsed! On another occasion, a big lunchtime banquet was being held at Guildhall for the Sportsman of the Year. Eric was once again in attendance, sitting in the main body of the hall. He sent one of the waiters round to me, at the top table, with his place card on which was written a note of complaint – his name had been spelt wrongly. Giving as good as I got, I quickly wrote back, 'Obviously not you then – get out!'

Also in December the Queen opened the new London museum – the Barbican. Following this, the next excitement out of the normal run was another Official Visit, this time from the Prime Minister of Poland, Mr Jeroszewicz. Again, he was unable to speak a word of English. Libby entertained Mrs Jeroszewicz in the private apartments upstairs, whilst he came to lunch in the Egyptian Hall. As with the Venezuelan visit, we had an interpreter again, and got on well. There was, however, a slight hiccup with the present exchange. My staff had contacted the Polish Embassy to find out in advance if he was likely to present me with anything. They were told that he would not, although word did reach us that Libby might receive an amber necklace. I had planned to give one of my medals and Libby was going to give a bird to his wife. As the lunch was drawing to a close, a footman approached me and whispered in my ear that a great parcel had just arrived from the Polish Embassy and was now in the Venetian Parlour. I told him quickly to open it and find out what it was. The message came back that the parcel contained a full coffee service, hand-painted with scenes of Warsaw. A crisis. Fortunately, after lunch, the Prime Minister was to go off to the Long Parlour with some chaps from our Board of Trade to sign an agreement for the sale of 50 half completed hulls, for shipment to Gdansk. With him out of the way I shot into the Venetian Parlour to inspect the gift – a splendid coffee service, encased in a vast hinged box. I quickly called Libby on the internal telephone, enquiring as to whether she had been given an amber necklace. No, she had not. 'Well bring the bird down here at once!' I urged, explaining the situation. Together we went to our treasure chest of reserve gifts to try and equal as best we good the very fine coffee service we were about to receive. We found a rather nice pewter tankard, engraved with a coat of arms, a leather bound copy of 'The Living City', the medal and the bird which together made a sufficiently interesting package. When he emerged from his meeting, I thanked him profusely for his gift, which he came to inspect, not being aware of it himself. I rather suspect that our telephone call to the Polish Embassy had alerted them and they had done a quick scurrying around themselves! Anyway, he went away as happy as a sand boy with the assortment of gifts he received himself.

Another problem I faced at the beginning of my Mayoralty was a dietary one. As mentioned, we had roast duck at the Lord Mayor's banquet. I failed to understand why, at the next few dinners at the Mansion House, roast duck appeared on the menu on nearly every occasion. At this time, I had to make a visit to Essex to open a new comprehensive school. The reasons I had been asked to do the honours were a) there was embarrassment at the amount of money that had been spent and they did not want to incur local political odium and b) it happened that my secretary's daughter was a pupil there and she had put forward my name. I agreed to the task, which involved being taken out to lunch by the representatives from Essex County Council. The Chair of the Education Committee sat next to me and then turned to me and announced, 'We've got your favourite, Lord Mayor – roast duck!' The day went smoothly enough and I returned to London for the Boar's Head Feast that evening, in Cutlers Hall. This involved six courses, accompanied by great jollification and merrymaking. We tucked in to the traditional slices of boar's head, but then I was dug in the ribs by the Master who turned to me and said, 'We've got your favourite, Lord Mayor – roast duck!' I was beginning to get suspicious. I asked the girls in the outer office of the Mansion House if there was any procedure for choosing the menu when Livery companies were entertaining me. 'Oh yes,' they explained. 'They usually ask what the Lord Mayor likes to eat'. 'And what do you say?' I asked, archly. 'Oh, we always say roast duck!' they chirped.

'For heaven's sakes!' I responded. 'I've been eating nothing but roast duck for the past x weeks! The next time you get asked, tell them the Lord Mayor will eat anything. Let the host choose!'

The incident became something of a standing joke. I was being entertained one evening by the Finance Committee. They had had a menu specially printed, just for me, with the main course listed as Roast Duck (it was, in fact, roast beef). I do not usually bother glancing at the menu – it seems to me that there is little point, since there is no choice in the matter anyway – but I was pressed to do so, as they awaited eagerly for my reaction. I realised as soon as I saw, and took the joke well.

One out-of-routine gastronomic experience I had to attend at this time was a Christmas Pudding tasting. Among those invited to the tasting were the Chef of the Savoy and the Lord Mayor of London. The event was held at the Savoy and we were presented with an array of about ten different baby Christmas puddings, each about the size of an apple, all made by a selection of different manufacturers. We were given forms to complete with a number of questions about different aspects of the puddings. The whole thing was conducted rather like a formal wine-tasting, although of course, unlike wine, one cannot spit out Christmas pudding. Eating was obligatory. The press were in attendance, eager for pictures of us all with our mouths open, chomping on these puddings. Unfortunately they also published some of the comments we made, which I feared might result in my being sued by the manufacturers of the puddings I did not care for. At the end of the day we were presented with a large Christmas pudding ourselves, which I took to Bart's Hospital, although it could not be given to the children there since it was so liberally soaked in brandy.

On the Sunday before Christmas, I was asked by the Bishop of Southwark to attend a Carol Service in aid of CRISIS – the charity for the homeless. I agreed, since I felt it was a good cause. At Southwark Cathedral we were met by the Bishop at the gate. He was dressed in a cape and did not quite look the part. 'Marvellous of you to come, Lord Mayor,' he said. 'Hope you don't mind, but I'm not attending the service – I'm off to the Russian Embassy.' I thought this was a bit off, since I had given up my Sunday evening for this. However, the running of the service had been delegated to the Bishop of Woolwich, and between us we did out stuff, with me reading the lesson.

The 23rd December was the day appointed for the staff Christmas party at the Mansion House. Following this we went home, armed with a stuffed Christmas turkey, which had been presented to Libby by the chef. The next day we went up to Cambridge for the Service of Nine Lessons and Carols at King's. I had threatened Christopher that I would arrive dressed in my academic robes as Chancellor to the City University, but since Christopher's reaction had been 'Over my dead body' I decided against this. I had of course heard the service many times before on the radio. It was quite different being there, listening to one's own son singing – although in a way I have to say I do rather prefer sitting in a darkened room listening on one's own, without any distractions. But we went that year and every year following throughout Christopher's time at Cambridge and it was indeed a marvellous experience. The only drawback was that Christopher's presence in the choir was required on Christmas morning, and we never had him at home for the Day ourselves. I suppose that is the price of fame!

As Lord Mayor, one is awarded an Honorary Degree. You have a choice of two – either letters or science. I plumped for the science, since as I do not spell very well I thought that to have D.Litt. after my name might be embarrassing. However, Nicholas, who was in his final year of a physics degree at Imperial College, considered the whole business quite corrupt. On looking at my degree which bore the words *Honoris Causa* he would remark, 'Hmmph. Very little *honoris* – and certainly no *causa*!' Subsequently, of course, I was to be made a Fellow of the Royal College of Music, which was even worse, in the light of Christopher's qualifications.

With Christopher in Cambridge and only Nicholas at home with us, Christmas felt somewhat disjointed that year. We made little of Christmas lunch, and then went to the Rawsons for Christmas dinner. Christopher returned home after lunch on Boxing Day and we had our Mansion House Christmas turkey that evening.

The following day was given over to rest and digestion and then on the 28th we went down to Biddeston for a change of air. We were having a good white Christmas that year, and the cottage was snug and warm. We stayed there until the New Year, when the boys came up to London for their own engagements and Libby and I spent Hogmanay together at the cottage – one of the quietest New Years we have had for a long time!

Chapter 18

It was then back to London and the Mansion House to resume my duties and kick off 1977. On January 8th we hosted the Lord Mayor's annual children's fancy dress party. This was quite an occasion, with about 650 children aged between 6 and 12 in attendance. They were the children and grandchildren of the Aldermen, the Common Councilmen, the Borough Mayors, and the High Commissioners. Callaghan's grandchildren were all there, and Terry Wogan was also present with his brood. He was at the time running his 'fight the flab' campaign on BBC Radio, and would from time to time refer to us on his morning programme – if the traffic was bad, for example, in the City, he might genially say 'Look out Sir Robin – traffic's bad this morning!' across the airwaves. It was all very good humoured. All the children had to attend the party in fancy dress and although they were permitted one adult to accompany them it was, on the whole, children only. They used all of the public rooms on the first floor, and the Lord Mayor and Lady Mayoress, the Sheriffs and their ladies, the maids of honour and the Pikemen all received the children in the same way as they did for the Lord Mayor's banquet. Dressed in my finery I sat on my throne in the salon as the children filed past and went through into the Egyptian Hall, where they sat on the floor and waited for the Lord Mayor to process in to begin the festivities. I had with me the daughter of one of the past Sheriffs, who undertook this kind of event fairly frequently. She was dressed, for the occasion, in a full cat suit, lying curled up at my feet when I sat down or padding along beside me as I walked around, as the traditional Dick Whittington cat. Thinking back to my passenger ship days, I decided that I would warm up proceedings by getting the children to sing. An orchestra was in attendance, and as I announced a chorus of 'Three Blind Mice' a canvas sheet dropped down from the gallery with the words of the song on it. However, as soon as I said the word 'mice' the cat went spare, leaping to her feet and pawing the air and miaowing. 'Oh dear,' I said, solemnly. 'I don't think this is going to work – because puss here gets very excited when I say 'mice' (whispered here for effect). Tell you what, we'll sing the song but leave out That Word.' I knew full well what would happen, with that number of children, as we launched into the song with gusto. As soon as we got to the end of the first line, the smaller children all forgot, sang the word 'mice' and the cat, on cue, leapt up feverishly once again. 'Oh dear,' I said solemnly once again. 'This isn't working at all. We'll have to do another animal. Tell you what, we'll sing 'Three Blind Wombles'. A small boy sitting near the front shouted out helpfully, ' Wombles don't have tails' This completely flawed me – I simply had no idea whether wombles had tails or not. The Household Officers upstairs were now enjoying themselves immensely – obviously wondering, with relish, how I was going to get myself out of this one. 'Oh,' I said, somewhat surprised. 'Don't they? Well, in that case . . . we'll have to think of *another* animal. How about Three Blind Weasels?' (I was fairly sure that weasels had tails). Well, we managed it without further interruption, everyone joined in with gusto, and the ice had been broken. The party then dispersed and visited the various activities on offer – there was a conjuror in one room, Punch and Judy in another, and in the Long Parlour I had a whole series of Tom and Jerry cartoons running. As I was walking around, introducing myself to various parents and ensuring that all children were having a good time, I ran in to one of the Directors from my firm, accompanying a small boy of six or seven. I asked him if he was enjoying himself and he commented enthusiastically that he thought it was all going extremely well. 'I'd love to get my hands on that lad who said that Wombles didn't have tails, ' I confided. The small boy holding his father's hand, beamed up at me. 'It was me!' he piped up. An unrehearsed moment of pure innocence. I beamed back, patted him on the head and said 'Nice boy!' – refraining politely from giving him a cuff around the ear. Tea was made available in various places, and at 6 o'clock they were all taken home. It was an exhausting event, for myself and the staff, who considered it the most tiring day of the year, but it was certainly enjoyed by all.

This was not the end of children's parties, since the two police stations in the City – Wood Street and Snow Hill – both hosted children's parties which I attended; there was a staff children's party in Guildhall and I also went along to the Press Club children's party. It was, all in all, quite a season. My little robin logo, which had featured in the Lord Mayor's Show, had appeared on the invitations to the various parties. This was, however, to become something of a problem. I recall a little mite approaching me at one of the parties and asking if I would draw my little robin for him in his autograph book. I took him behind a pillar, and drew the robin for him, but warned him not to spread the word as everyone would want one. Off he toddled and of course the first thing he did was to tell all his mates, which meant that I was immediately bombarded by a hoard of youngsters all waving their autograph books and wanting robins. I ended up with quite a sore wrist!

The Monday following the children's party at the Mansion House was 'Plough Monday', traditionally the day (more in the country than in the City) when hired hands were mustered and hired on by employers who needed them. In the City the day was celebrated by inviting various retiring members of the corporation staff and other employees to the Mansion House – N.C.O.'s, as it were, rather than Heads of Department. The next event in the annual calendar was then given over to the brethren in the court of Aldermen and officers of the Corporation (the aforementioned Heads of Department), which took place in the Egyptian Hall in the Mansion House. I always felt that this was one of the most difficult gatherings to speak to; I had spoken at it as a Sheriff, since the Aldermanic Sheriff had to reply to the toast to the Sheriffs, but I always felt that this small and rather discreet audience was much more difficult than, say, a large and anonymous crowd of 3000 plus. This was a group of people – including past Sheriffs – who had all done it before, and who were all probably thinking they could do it better; in short, a very challenging and critical audience. It was important to make the speech a good one, and, if possible, to make them laugh. On this occasion I hit upon the idea (fairly late on – it may have been the day before or even the day itself) of producing a piece of writing which I claimed I had discovered to be a lost Shakespearian fragment, which had, consequently, to be delivered in a 'Laurence Olivier' voice; this was all wrapped around the threat to the City and followed the format of a Shakespearian play, thus:

Act I, Sc. II: A banquet at the Mansion House. Tucket without. Enter a Household Officer... Then followed a little speech by the messenger telling the assembled company of a debate taking place on the South Bank, promoting a bill to abolish the City of London. The Lord Mayor's response included a mustering call to all the assembled company to exhort their wards to defend the City. I succeeded in mentioning every Alderman by name, giving about four lines per ward, and quite getting into the flow of things once the muse had struck. I recall getting to Lime Street ward, where Christopher Rawson was the Alderman, and starting off: *Stout Rawson...* (he was fairly plump, although I did mean to refer to valour) and the company all burst out laughing. This happened several times, and each time I was prevented from proceeding by raucous laughter, although eventually I managed to get it out and proceed with:... *from their goose-feathered beds/The sleep-drugged stallholders of the Leadenhall shall rouse/And with him to the Lime Street ward shall call.* The ending of the whole read: *I'll to Guildhall, and there, with Bassishaw at bay/Direct our fortunes on this day/To arms then, trusty brethren all/Cry Havoc! For Gillett and St. Paul!* It was a little bit of nonsense but nobody was left out of the act and it seemed to go down well, with plenty of requests for copies once I had finished. This was the kind of ploy that I used from time to time, as appropriate. Although not always easy, and not something that could be done at the drop of a hat, I found that once I had got my pen to paper, the muse would take me and it would flow quite naturally. It was certainly very useful and a great help to my speech-writing to be able to resort to these 'funnies' from time to time. Perhaps, one of these days, I shall publish the collection as a 'slim volume'!

Still on the subject of parties, Libby and I had decided that whilst we were in the Mansion House we would use the opportunity to have a party there for the boys. Nicholas had of course had his fourth birthday party there, when my father was in the Mansion House, and Christopher had also been there, although he was very small at the time. We felt it would be an excellent plan to commemorate their 21st and 18th birthdays in one grand party whilst we still had the Mansion House to play with. It was agreed that they could each have 50 guests, and that we could have a similar number (some of whom would be the parents of the boys' guests). We would have liked to have held it on New Year's Eve but this proved logistically impossible with the lack of transport and staff. So we settled, in the end, for Friday 14th January, which was a free night in the calendar. A buffet and bar (with real ale for the young lads) were put on in the Long Parlour, and they ate in the North and South drawing rooms, on the other side of the Salon. The Salon itself was rigged as a discotheque. The 'oldies' used the Venetian Parlour as a proper bar and we ate outside at tables set up in the access area. A large curtain separated us from the salon, although the two sides could mingle if they wished.

Nicholas and his friends were responsible for rigging up the discotheque, and Christopher, who brought with him all the other choral scholars, provided the cabaret, with harmonised swingle singing to entertain us. The first time, I think, that the King's College Choir have ever sung in the Mansion House! The whole thing was a great success. In the manner of a Hunt Ball, we all piled down to the kitchen at about one o'clock in the morning and had breakfast – sausages, egg and bacon and the like, which everyone thoroughly enjoyed, including the staff. We finally got to bed at about 3.30 a.m., putting up as many people as we could in the various State bedrooms and the family accommodation upstairs. A few more actually camped in sleeping bags in the Egyptian Hall. It was certainly a night to remember.

We were now back into the general round of Livery company dinners. I was still, at the time, beating the drum on the City's behalf. Representatives of the City and the G.L.C. were interviewed together on the London Programme, and I must say we came out of it rather well, partly because Tony Banks on the G.L.C. team became very needled and began losing his temper – which is just what you want, of course.

It was also at about this time that I gave the annual Dinner of the Common Council and the Governing Bodies of Greater London. This event needed to played, this year, with particular care. The Chairman of the G.L.C., Lord Ponsonby, was going to make a speech. All the Borough Mayors who were thirsting to get rid of us were in attendance, as well as those who were not in favour of the G.L.C. and those who were fairly indifferent. It was not uncommon for any one of them to get up and walk out if they felt aggrieved by what was said and I knew that haranguing the masses on this occasion would have been quite inappropriate – akin to Arthur Scargill addressing a Conservative party conference! I would, in my position as Lord Mayor, have to be seen as being completely apolitical. Once again my guardian angel came to the rescue. As I was upstairs getting changed and waiting to go down, something made me look at a copy of the *Evening Standard* – not a paper I normally have time to peruse. However, on this occasion I happened to look at the daily horoscope. I knew that it was Tom Ponsonby's birthday, either that day or the next, and on reading the birthday prediction found it to be an absolute gift. 'Do not seek to upset or disturb things that are working well' was the general gist of the horoscope, which could not have been more fitting. I cut it out from the newspaper and put it carefully in my pocket. During the course of my speech I was able to address Tom Ponsonby, congratulating him on his birthday and enquiring if he had happened to read his stars. I was then able to produce my cutting and read it out, which of course produced great laughter as everyone knew full well what I was referring to. Undercutting the subject in this way, I managed to defuse what might have been a very difficult situation. It also proved to 'the other side' that we were not just a lot of stuffy toffs, but that we knew how to enjoy a joke and had a sense of humour. I suppose it harked back to the 'exercising his ready wit on his superiors' jibe from my cadet captain at Pangbourne. Whatever, it worked and the evening went off very well.

We were now beginning to have some idea of where I would be travelling overseas. The Foreign Office would produce a list of suggestions as to where the Lord Mayor might travel – either somewhere that had been neglected for a while, or somewhere with whom they were hoping to do trade, or somewhere that needed patting on the head, so to speak, because they were upset about something. The visits were officially city to city, rather than to country, although it often turned out to be much broader than that, since the office of the Lord Mayor of London carried with it a certain charisma and mystique all of its own, and Presidents and their like would always want to get in on the act. Everyone, it seems, has heard of Dick Whittington. There was a little confusion surrounding the difference between the City of London and London itself, (although of course historically the City *had* been London) and some may have thought that they were receiving an equivalent of the Mayor of New York, who was Mayor of the whole place, rather than just the Lord Mayor of the financial centre of London. However, it mattered little, and of course it was the financial heartland that they were interested in most. The Lord Mayor's brief was to promote the so-called 'invisible' services (rather than manufactured goods) and to put in a plug for the country as a whole. He was a safe pair of hands to send precisely because he was not political. The role was therefore an important one and used by governments of all political persuasions. Nowadays the whole business of foreign visiting is conducted even more efficiently than I believe it was in my day, when it was really just the Department of Trade and the Foreign Office who came up with suggestions and organised the trips. You could not, of course, just go to a country – they had to engineer an invitation through their Ambassador, who would diplomatically suggest the procedure. On occasion they were not terribly systematic about it all; it was a case of sticking a pin in a map and finding somewhere that had not had a visit for a bit, without checking up first on the status of our relations with that country. Today there is a committee, comprising not only representatives of the Foreign Office but also the Bank of England, the Chamber of Commerce, the Committee of Invisibles and many other people who are able to have their say. The whole process is much more informed and successful.

Various suggestions were now on the table, including Turkey (Ankara and Istanbul), Vienna, and Helsinki. The latter invitation came from Finland, since we had entertained the Lord Mayor of Helsinki (I am unsure as to why he is a 'Lord' since they do not have such a system there) and that trip did not need any particular organising. One silly suggestion was for Greece and Turkey. 'Whose idea was that?' I asked, knowing full well the situation in Cyprus at the time. Neither side was talking to the other, and had I visited one I would have almost certainly been cold-shouldered by the other. The situation was resolved by sending the Lord Provost of Edinburgh on a trip to Athens, leaving Turkey to us.

This was all to take place at the end of February and the beginning of March. Looking ahead to the summer there were plans afoot for Singapore, Jakarta, Manila and Hong Kong, and subsequently, there was a wish for me to go to Poland, where they wanted someone to open the new British pavilion at the Poznan fair. Normally a Royal would have been fielded to do this, but as the Jubilee was in the same week, the Royals were all pretty tied up. Libby and I had had our first TAB shots already in preparation – which I had of course experienced before I went out to the Persian Gulf. They make you feel pretty miserable, and rather as if you have 'flu coming on.

On the rare occasions we had an evening free we would try and fit in a private dinner party in the private dining room upstairs, which could take some sixteen guests. These occasions were used to meet the Ambassadors of countries we might be going to visit, so that we could get to know them better, or possibly to bring together parties who might be negotiating with one another; on one occasion, for example, we hosted a dinner for some people from shipping who urgently wished to speak to someone from the Ministry of Transport. Such occasions were few and far between, but were actually one of the uses that were made of the Mansion House, by those who could not otherwise get past their civil servants to talk freely.

On the 3rd February we dined, in the evening, at the Skinners Hall. The message came through, during dinner, that a debate in the G.L.C. that evening, about promoting a private members' bill in the House of Commons to abolish the City, had been carried by 40 votes to 31. It was not as bad as we had expected, but nevertheless bad enough, since it meant that the bill was now to be debated. Battle lines were drawn. Two nights later we were to go to Tower Hamlets – one of the boroughs which was hoping to profit from the takeover. It had been the custom at one time (certainly in my father's day) for each of the London boroughs to give a reception during the course of the year. The Lord Mayor of London was always invited as the principal guest. The tenor of the reception varied enormously from borough to borough (Tower Hamlets was always a bit of knees-up although some were much more sedate affairs) although the form was usually a dinner followed by dancing. The Lord Mayor quite often had to attend a Livery Company first, and then leave early in the evening to travel out to the particular borough. By my time these occasions had been somewhat reduced. They were quite expensive affairs and paid for out of public rates, and they had, in many cases, been done away with altogether. However, Tower Hamlets still held their reception. I was somewhat anxious, given the situation, but need not have worried at all. It was a very jolly evening, with a good dinner followed by a floorshow and dancing to round it off. I did feel that it would be politic for us to withdraw before the end of the evening, since it was often the custom in the left wing boroughs to conclude proceedings by singing 'The Red Flag' instead of 'God Save the Queen', which would have given me cause for embarrassment. As midnight approached, and with the party still in full swing, I suggested to my party (the two Sheriffs and their wives, household officers and various attendants) that we make a move. We were beginning our discreet exit when the Toastmaster, who happened by now to be dancing with one of the girls from the floor show, spotted that we were going, left his partner and came over to us. I explained that we had to leave, and that we would just slip quietly away, but he insisted that we could not possibly just depart like that, and that he would make an announcement. It was really the last thing I wanted. 'Yes,' he went on, 'I shall make an announcement so that the assembled company can applaud your departure'. That certainly had a double edge to it! I did manage to persuade him otherwise, in the end.

The following week we held a press conference prior to the forthcoming overseas visit. The sword and mace were on display and I said a few words about the programme. I was explaining to my audience the background to the collar of S's – the Lord Mayor's chain which comprises Tudor roses and 'S' shapes – and the jewel that hangs below it. Jokingly, I explained that, the collar of S's having been given to the City in 1545, it was very valuable and I treated it with great care, counting the diamonds in the badge every night to make sure I had not lost one. My quip was picked up by a cartoonist and a few weeks later (by which time we were in Finland) a piece appeared in the *Telegraph* with the heading 'Collaring the S's and Counting the Diamonds' with a cartoon of me sitting up in bed in my pyjamas with the chain round my neck and fingering it, whilst Libby was hanging up my gown in the cupboard in the background.

The host country selected for a visit was sent, in advance of my visits, various bits and pieces by way of preparation and they generally mounted a display of regalia and background information explaining who the Lord Mayor of London was. The above article was sent out to Finland and I was, later, able to get a copy of the original for myself.

On the domestic front, we decided once more to make use of the Mansion House while we had the chance. Libby's eldest niece (her brother's daughter) was getting married and we decided that it would be very nice if she were to be married in the church of St. Lawrence Jury in Guildhall Square, with a reception in the Mansion House afterwards by way of a wedding present. She was duly married by my chaplain and after the service everyone returned to the Mansion House. One hundred and forty guests were entertained to lunch in the Egyptian Hall and it was a most memorable occasion.

On the following Monday there was a big lunch at Guildhall for the Sportsman of the Year award. The recipient that year was Nikki Lauder, the racing driver, who had had a terrible disfigurement to his face after a crash. He had a very positive personality and it was easy enough to chat to him without being disturbed by his appearance. This was the same lunch at which Eric Morecambe had complained to me about the wrong spelling of his name.

The next evening there was another banquet at Guildhall – this time the Metal Exchange Centenary Banquet. The guest of honour was the Prince of Wales, who sat next to Libby. The pair had a very amusing time exchanging Scottish accents – the Prince imitating downtown Edinburgh and Libby speaking in a upper class Glaswegian. In my speech, I made reference to the statues which adorned the room, for the benefit of those present who were visiting Guildhall perhaps for the first time. The statues included Nelson, Wellington, the Earl of Chatham, Pitt the Younger and Lord Mayor Beckford. I knew that the Prince of Wales happened to be a great admirer of George III. The statue of Beckford has underneath it an *extempore* speech that he had made to King George III, couched in very loyalist eighteenth century rhetoric, but which was to some extent a remonstrance. It was well known that George III did not see entirely eye to eye with the City, since the City were in favour of the American Revolution. I explained to the assembled guests the content of the speech, telling them that despite its flowery language, it would in effect be like the Lord Mayor saying 'knickers' to George III. My words started a ball rolling. A few days later I paid an official visit to the Metal Exchange. Trading ceased for a few minutes while the President of the Exchange made a brief speech of welcome. In view of my speech at Guildhall a few days before, he had a present for me from the Exchange. I wondered what it might be, thinking along the lines of an ingot of silver or some such. He then produced a pair of black, lacy kiss-me-quick knickers! Subsequent to this, I met the Prince of Wales at an event on the South Bank one evening, which was being held in honour of the Jubilee. Over drinks at the interval I related to him this incident at the Metal Exchange. 'Oh yes,' he said, 'I know the sort of things you mean. You can buy them in tins, you know – I often give them to my girlfriends!' (this was in the days before he was married, I hasten to add). Those knickers were destined to haunt me. Not knowing quite what to do with them I consulted with Libby, who suggested giving them to my God-daughter, Christopher Rawson's teenage daughter Caroline. This is jumping the gun, rather, but our itinerary at that time included a visit to Atlantic College and a stopover at the Mansion House in Cardiff, following on from which we were going to join the Rawsons at Cowes for a few days. Libby had the kickers in her suitcase, ready to present them to Caroline. At the Cardiff Mansion House we had tea with the Lord Mayor, whilst upstairs our bags were being unpacked by the butler. When we went up to our rooms we were greeted by the butler who held out the knickers at arm's length and said in a very deadpan, butlerish sort of way, 'What do you want me to do with *these*, m'lady?' Quite what he thought we got up to I really cannot imagine. Libby refused to let anyone unpack her cases ever again, but thankfully that proved to be the end of the 'knicker' saga, after a few innocuous remarks on my part about George III!

On a more maritime note, the 17th February saw Libby christening the new Port Health launch, *Londinium* at Fishmonger's Stairs. After smacking a bottle of champagne across her bow we went for a little trot in her. At the end of her life with the corporation I was to get her for my emergent Maritime Volunteer Service which we were forming, and she was to become the first of our training craft. Her career came full circle, as it were, and Libby re-commissioned her in St. Katharine's Dock for that purpose, twenty years after she had originally christened her.

Chapter 19

Two days later we were off on our travels. Leaving London at some early hour we flew to Istanbul, where they were experiencing their hottest February since 1935. Having left a wintry England we were quite overdressed in our fur hats and boots. We had to wait until 5.45 p.m. for a plane to take us on to Ankara, where we eventually arrived at 6.30 p.m. – almost twelve hours after leaving Heathrow. We were met by Sir Horace and Lady Phillips, the British Ambassador, and the deputy Mayor. The Mayor of Ankara himself could not be there. He was an architect who designed mosques and he was off for the opening ceremony of a mosque he had designed in Pakistan. Unfortunately the deputy Mayor's wife did not speak any English, which was problematic for poor Libby who was to be going around with her and had to use the services of an interpreter the whole time. Libby and I were staying at the Embassy. We had our own footman with us and settled in that night, with dinner at the Embassy. Our footman, Tony, was an immaculate dresser. When we were having drinks before dinner he came down to see if he could help. The Ambassador clearly thought he was one of the party and enquired what he would like to drink – only to be somewhat embarrassed to find that Tony was there to serve the drinks, not enjoy them himself! Tony was in fact an excellent footman and, rather usefully for Libby, a former hairdresser.

The Embassy was one of the first to be built in Ankara – a purpose built town situated in a basin, surrounded by hills. This had the effect of keeping the city permanently clouded in a sort of smog, but the British Embassy had been built in the hills, away from the pollution of the city and with a marvellous view. After a day of orientation, we were joined by the rest of our party from their various hotels, in preparation for our tour of the city which would enable us to view at first hand the problems faced by the local government there. Often on overseas visits one is often only shown the 'best bits' of a particular place, but to give the Turks their due, they wanted us to see their city 'warts and all', in order that we might be able to impart advice to them. They were most interested, for example, in our smokeless zones and the cleaning up of the Thames, two programmes which they would evidently benefit from themselves. Our tour took us to the outskirts of Ankara, where we were intrigued to find a great number of piles of rocks about the place. It is the law in Turkey that anyone who builds himself a house in 24 hours does not need planning permission. The rocks would be brought to the location in readiness, and then family and friends would be recruited and, within 24 hours, they would build a house. This created enormous problems for the city, which then had to provide services and utilities for this unplanned building programme. Roads weaved in between this jumbled collection of houses, which were linked by spaghetti-like collections of electricity cables. The residents of these houses were also classed as squatters, rather than proper residents, and were therefore not included in the population figures of the city. Unlike our rating system, whereby householders pay for the services provided for them, the Turkish system is based on a per capita allowance, which is distributed by central government. The local government in Ankara was run by the opposing political party in power at the time, which did not make life any easier – clearly they were not going to be given any more money than the absolute minimum. Consequently, the local authority in Ankara was permanently struggling to save itself from bankruptcy, feeling obliged to provide services for all these people but not being given the money to do so. We were unable to help with this problem, which was one of internal politics, but we were able to offer advice on the problem of the smog, which hung over the city as a result of all the cheap local coal that was burned. We explained our legislation against this, which had made a remarkable difference to our own city (I can still recall the thick yellow fogs of my childhood – real pea-soupers in which you were unable to see your hand in front of your face – which nowadays just do not occur). However, it was all very well telling them what we had done; their capability of doing similar was somewhat limited as they just did not have the resources available to provide the alternative fuels required. Despite the high level of poverty and unemployment, I was aware that throughout our tour I never saw a neglected child or an adult who was not wearing a clean shirt. They appeared to be a proud and dignified people, and I found this most impressive.

We returned to the Embassy for lunch and the afternoon was taken up with a visit to the Hittite Museum. Dinner was in a large restaurant, hosted by the Municipality, where we sampled some excellent Turkish food. Presents were exchanged in the usual way and we were given a Turkish carpet.

There is an English school in Ankara which had been started for the benefit of the ex-patriots, but which is also popular with the locals. The next morning, children from the school were brought in buses to the Embassy, to meet me dressed in my black and gold gown. They were all well turned out and extremely polite. The ladies had gone off shopping and Libby returned with a very nice coat with a fur collar. The deputy mayor and I then went off the Mayor's parlour for a chat and to meet the local press. This was followed by a tour of the city centre, which was reminiscent of Egypt in its chaos and bustle. The traffic was appalling, with no apparent order at all. It was said that if you wanted a panel beater this was one of the best places in the world to come, since drivers treated the roads in the city centre a bit like a dodgem car rink, bashing in to one another all the time. The place was littered with garages and repair shops. A reference to this nearly got me into trouble with the press at home, when I was reporting back on my trip; I was reported in the Evening Standard as having said that if you wanted a 'camel beater' Ankara was the place to visit. I envisaged the R.S.P.C.A. coming down on me like a ton of bricks!

My visit provided a good opportunity for the Ambassador to make some connections of his own. I had not appreciated quite how difficult and problematic it could be for an overseas Ambassador to get to those in power when he wanted to. Since the Prime Minister had heard we were in the country and had requested to see us, the Ambassador was able to use the opportunity to get to see the P.M. himself.

That evening we returned to Istanbul and were met by the Consul General. We were put up there in a penthouse suite at the Hilton. The next day we were off on tours again, although as this was not the capital the content was rather more tourist-like. I went to see the Governor, and we visited the English Boys and English Girls schools, where, again, there was a mix of English and Turkish pupils. We dressed in our finery for them, which they loved. It must be said that one of the greatest criticisms we faced from our opponents at home was the fact that we strutted about in medieval garb for official duties. However, when abroad it was, almost inevitably, a great attraction.

Countries would be asked, before the visit, what sort of manner they would like us to appear in: whether it be in state, rigged in our finery, or in civilian clothes – we would dress according to their desires. Ninety per cent (certainly pretty well everywhere outside of the United States and Canada) requested that we dress up. Some of the countries used to have such traditions and had now lost them, and they loved it. It also made much more of the visit, and of the V.I.P. status; it was more of an occasion than being visited by someone in a suit, for example, who could have been anybody.

We went off to lunch after the school visits and then to a restaurant overlooking the sea, which was very good. The lunch was given by the Mayor of Istanbul, accompanied by his wife and the Governor. He only spoke French but we managed to communicate successfully. Lunch was followed by a visit to the Civic Hall and the customary exchange of presents. The girls then went off on a spree whilst we went into the Council Chamber, where I addressed a packed house. That evening the Consulate General hosted a reception at the Consulate, and again I was asked to wear my full rig, which, as usual, provoked much interest. We then gave a dinner ourselves back at our hotel for the Mayor and his wife and several other dignitaries.

The following day, 23rd February, was devoted to sightseeing. We visited the Blue Mosque, which is the biggest and most famous of the 550 mosques in Istanbul, and the Saint Sofia Mosque, which had, of course, been the Christian cathedral in the days of the Holy Roman Empire and before the invasion of the Turks. It was not un-mosque like in its design, and both buildings were most impressive. I went to lunch at the Chamber of Commerce – an opportunity to make a connection with the local expatriate community and give them a chance to feedback on what the situation was like for them on the ground. After lunch it was back to the hotel and then a trip to the covered bazaars – fortunately Libby had come without any money, and thus was prevented from having a field day! There was yet another reception and yet again we were asked to wear our gowns, which we did, and we finished up with a dinner hosted by Mr and Mrs West, of Barclays Bank. They produced the *Telegraph* cutting 'Collaring the S's and Counting the Diamonds' referred to earlier.

It was then off to Vienna, a city I had always wanted to visit. Mr Hugh Morgan was the Ambassador there, and welcomed us with his Bulgarian wife, a very chic and vivacious lady. The Embassy was lovely, genuinely old and beautifully furnished. Our footman stayed with us but the rest of the party were put up in a hotel. That evening was an official civic ceremony – the signing of the Golden Book – and again the exchange of presents which took place at the Rafthouse in the evening. I arrived dressed in my finery and I shall never forget having to climb up a vast staircase to reach the top, where Herr Gratz, the Öberburgermeister, stood with his retinue. A Viennese orchestra played in the background and at dinner a menu was produced which had been used to commemorate the visit of the Lord Mayor and the Common Council in 1910. I am not sure why, but Libby awoke early the next morning feeling really very poorly. She was out of action for the next day, and missed our visit to the Spanish Riding School although she did manage a totter around the porcelain factory later on. She also missed a performance of *The Barber of Seville* at the Opera House that evening. We took Tony with us in her place and he loved it, never having been to the opera before, and looking every inch the part as one of our party in our box. Libby had made a full recovery by the next day, when we made a visit to the hospital and a garbage reclamation plant. This latter proved most interesting, with machinery to sift through all the rubbish and extract any recyclable items. Anything that could not be recycled was burnt, and the heat from the incinerator was used to heat the hospital and various other public buildings. Not quite so impressive was our next visit, a trip by minibus to view a sewage plant, awaiting completion. They were very proud of it, although I was rather horrified when they advised me that it was their first sewage plant, and unlike our full treatment works at home, it just 'removed the solids'. I shall spare my reader and go into no further detail here, although I did enquire rather hesitantly, if this were their first sewage plant, what had happened to the 'solids' before? They explained that everything had gone into the Danube, which seemed quite extraordinary given that we had not pumped raw sewage into the Thames since 1860. It did, perhaps, explain why the Danube was not looking terribly blue.

Lunch was in the city's revolving tower restaurant (every major city in the world seems to have one) which afforded fine views of the city. Vienna did not quite live up to all my expectations, but perhaps I had been confusing it with eastern European cities, which did not boast so much modern development. The afternoon was taken up with museum visits and a drive through the Vienna Woods and that evening a dinner party at the Embassy. The Ambassador there told me the same story as our Ambassador in Ankara. They had not had a visit from anyone for a very long time, and it was proving very difficult for him to get to see the people he needed to see, but with my presence he was able to invite all the people he had been trying to get hold of and know that they would turn up to dinner to meet the Lord Mayor of London.

That was Vienna, and so to Helsinki. The Ambassador came to see us off, together with the Burgermeister. As if we had not received enough presents already, he presented me with a lovely ciné camera, with electrical controls, zoom lens and what have you. The weather was deteriorating fast; we had had a few flakes of snow in Vienna and by the time we arrived in Helsinki we found them in the grip of a severe cold snap, with more snow than they could cope with in the city and temperatures falling to below –20° at night. The Ambassador there, Sir James Cable, and the Lord Mayor, Mr Auira met us off the plane. I never quite discovered why the Mayor of Helsinki described himself as the Lord Mayor, since the country did not have any lords. I believe he had recently been remarried; certainly he and his wife seemed to be very preoccupied with one another, and kept going off for saunas. This is, in fact, common there, where sauna time is sacrosanct and seems to be indulged in by everyone. People would go off for a good sweat and beat themselves with birch twigs or what have you, and I must say they all looked very fit on it. The Ambassador's wife, Lady Cable, was Swedish and the Embassy once again was a fine building. That evening they hosted a dinner party for Embassy staff and we retired reasonably early. We were joined in Helsinki by Alan Lamboll, the other Sheriff who had stayed at home to look after the Old Bailey, and the Coles, who had been accompanying us as far as Vienna, returned home. Our first day included a bus trip to visit the Finlandia Concert Hall – an impressive new building – and then on to the Rock Church, an extraordinary place which had been made, literally, by blasting a hole in the rock. We had lunch at a restaurant overlooking a frozen lake. All the lakes were, of course, frozen at that time, as was the sea in the harbour, which quite altered the landscape, as you can drive across the lakes, and all the many islands become part of the mainland, so to speak. I asked what happens in the autumn and spring – at what point is it determined that the lakes are safe, or unsafe, to drive across? They told me that they used the army for that – a truck was sent across to find out if it was safe or not. I did not enquire further as to what happened to the truck driver, but left it to my imagination. That night we had dinner in the City Hall and again dressed up in our regalia, and I was able to speak to the guests through an interpreter. Tuesday 1st March was a beautiful, clear day. The roads had been cleared by snow ploughs so it was possible to get out and the plan was to take us out in an ice-breaker. As usual, the women were to be fobbed off with a shopping expedition, but on this occasion Libby stepped out of line, and requested that she join us on the ice-breaker instead. They deferred to her wishes, which delighted the Mayor's wife and other women in the party, none of whom were terribly excited at the thought of yet another shopping expedition. We all got on board, my new ciné camera whirring, and set off, plunging into the ice of the harbour. We were off to visit a shipyard, which meant leaving the harbour and travelling around the coast for a bit. The sea outside the harbour was not quite so iced up, but we cracked out way through, leaving a mushy pile in our wake which then began, almost at once to freeze over again. At the shipyard we found them building huge ferries under cover. Our next jaunt was into the countryside to visit a hotel – a series of three houses designed by famous Finnish architects at the beginning of the century which had been turned into a hotel complex, where we given smoked reindeer meat and roast ptarmigan to eat. The landscape there was quite magnificent, the air as clear as glass and acres of deep white snow startling against the blue sky. Libby, loving the Christmas-card purity of it, took great gulps of air, exhorting us all to do the same. Unfortunately her enthusiasm got the better of her, for in the act of breathing in the clear sharp air so deeply she managed to freeze her larynx! I did advise her that the Good Lord had designed a perfectly good air-intake system (her nose) and a suitable exhaust (her mouth) and that she was doing it the wrong way round, but my words came to late and she was unable to speak for a day and a half.

We left Helsinki on 2nd March, seen off by the Lord Mayor and his wife, after a supper with them the night before at which I recall consuming a fair quantity of schnapps. The flight home was fairly brief and we arrived to a fine sunny day in London. We could well have done without a dinner that night, but duty prevailed and we attended the Fishmongers' dinner at Fishmongers' Hall.

Thus ended our first batch of overseas visits. We wrote fairly comprehensive reports on our activities, but there was no formal de-briefing system, which I felt rather annoyed about. The Foreign Office seemed surprised at my complaint, but it did seem a serious omission, given the level of preparation that had gone into the trips. After all, no business would send a salesman on an exploratory trip abroad at vast expense and not expect them to report on it once back home. It seemed a great waste of money, in my view, if no one came and spoke to us on our return to find out what we had done. However, once I had raised the matter it was rectified and from then on it has been common practice.

Chapter 20

We were now back in harness. On 10th March the Private Members' Bill came up under the ten minute rule in the House of Commons and I am glad to say was defeated by a majority of 41 – and this with a Labour government in power. I can only conclude that those who had to govern the country appreciated fully what we were doing and had no wish to start upsetting a situation which worked perfectly well. They knew full well what the City did for the country, and the highly successful ambassadorial role played by the Lord Mayor. As mentioned before, there was a tacit agreement amongst those of us in the City that we would not jump and down and blow trumpets at our victory; we had won, and that was sufficient.

It was at about this time that a Dutch television company came over to make a film about the City. It was to be called 'Land of Hope and Glory', and was being produced for Dutch television. They took pictures of the Common Council at work, and I was asked to go down the river driving *Londinium I* whilst giving a running commentary and pointing out sights of interest from Tower Bridge to the city boundary. They subsequently took pictures of the Mansion House – of Libby and I have tea in the boudoir and me sitting making imaginary telephone calls in the Mayoral Rolls. They took one picture of Tony Banks leaning against the wall of the Embankment outside the G.L.C., asking him what thought of the Court of Aldermen and the City of London. Looking straight at camera he described the Court of Aldermen as 'the dead smile on the carcass of capitalism.' – a phrase culled from Karl Marx which I thought was a little rich. I met him on occasion afterwards – sat next to him at dinner, even – and he was gracious enough to say that it was nothing personal.

The threat had been put to bed, at last, but throughout the first three months of my Mayoralty I had been distracted from my original intent, which was the demise of the country as a maritime power. There were now other things to think of. The Jubilee was in the offing and the appeal was now well under way. Our Austrian friend, Herr

Gratz, paid a visit, and we held a dinner for him at the House of Commons. We also had a special dinner at the Mansion House for the Jubilee of the London Division, Royal Naval Reserve. That was a great naval occasion, with everyone in mess kit and many naval traditions observed and I felt it appropriate that it should have coincided with a naval officer being Lord Mayor. They presented Libby and me with a very nice gift – a silver four-wheeled 'gun carriage', holding two decanters for port and Madeira, used in naval messes to pass the port. On our small dining table at home it had to be on hard lock all the time to get round; nevertheless it was a fine piece to look at.

On 6th April we had a lunch at the G.L.C. – an annual affair, held at County Hall. The battle was over by now, although tensions still ran a little high and it could have proved somewhat embarrassing. However, the day was saved (quite unintentionally) by Libby interrupting my speech. Without wishing to stir things I still felt that it was important to indicate my feelings on the subject. 'I have always quoted Alexander Pope,' I began, and then proceeded with the extract: 'For forms of government let fools contest/Whate'er is best administer'd, is best' (meaning, of course, that the City surpassed all others in its administration). No sooner had I finished the quote than Libby piped up, 'I've never heard you say that in my life!' Collapse of present company into gales of laughter. A situation well diffused.

That Easter we went down to Cowes to bring Christopher Rawson's yacht back into commission after the winter. Easter was early, that year, and it was pretty chilly down there. On the Saturday we went up the Beaulieu river and had some lunch there and the next day, Easter Sunday, we were back in Cowes, where it snowed, with similar weather the next day, too. We returned to London and duty on the Tuesday, after a somewhat disappointing weekend.

On the following Saturday, we took off at 9 o'clock in LMO with the City Marshall as our Esquire and went to York – an annual pilgrimage made by the Lord Mayor to stay with the Lord Mayor of York at the Mansion House. We had quite a good drive up, taking a picnic with us, which we had on the edge of York racecourse just before arriving. The York Mansion House is, in fact, older than the one in the City, although very much smaller. The room we were in was really very pokey – there was hardly room for the two of us and you practically had to get out of bed one at a time. The Lord Mayor, Mr Archer, had only just taken up his office. He was a railwayman and really quite frightened at the prospect of the Lord Mayor of London arriving. We managed to thaw them out fairly quickly and it transpired that he had taken office at very short notice, and had not known at all that he would be undertaking the role. The steward there seemed to have various functions – he acted as toastmaster, and carried the Mace as well. He had been there for years, and it was he who ran the place. However, he had one rather disturbing habit. We went to a dinner given by the Guild of Freemen (at the Merchant Adventurers' Hall). It seems that the further from London you get the more importance is bestowed upon the role of toastmaster – I have even heard, on occasion, the toastmaster telling stories and almost becoming part of the entertainment. This particular chap stood up and announced The Right Honourable, the Lord Mayor . . . and then went on to say 'who will propose the toast of Her Majesty, Queen Elizabeth, Queen of England and Northern Ireland and other territories beyond, the Defender of the Faith . . . the lot, in fact, instead of just introducing the Lord Mayor who would get up and say 'The Queen'. Then the Lord Mayor fumbled through the next bit, trying to list all the parts of her title, instead of just saying 'The Queen' – and then blow me if the toastmaster did not come in again, with an echo, to say 'The Toast is: . . . ' and then go through the whole rigmarole once again. He obviously liked the sound of his own voice and nobody had the guts to tell him that it was not the way it was done.

The next day was Sunday. We went to church, the two Lord Mayors preceded by Sword and Mace and then we paraded through the streets, marching through the Shambles (the old, cobbled part of the City) to lunch at the banqueting hall with various other city dignitaries. Our trip included a brief visit to York Minster and the Castle Museum, where one can see the cell where Dick Turpin spent his last night. The museum also contains a very good reproduction of a full Victorian street.

We returned to London on the Sunday, arriving home late afternoon, having invited the Lord Mayor of York and his lady wife to visit us when he finished his term of office, which would be in May. The following Monday we went on a regular visit to the Maritime Museum at Greenwich, which I thoroughly enjoyed, although I had been before in my own right. Little did I know then that I would eventually become a trustee of the place, myself. On Wednesday 20th April we went in the morning to the Stow Commemoration service at St. Mary Undershaft – another annual performance by the Lord Mayor. There is a bust of Stowe, the great surveyor of the City, who holds a quill in his hand. Tradition holds that the Lord Mayor must, each year, replace the old quill with a new one – a rather fiddly process since it is rather poorly lit and quite difficult to get it in exactly the right place first time around. The day concluded with the traditional Easter banquet at the Mansion House, which is given to the diplomatic corps. This is one of the few occasions when it was not permitted to do what Libby was always trying to do, which was to break up husbands and wives. She always disapproved of the fact that in the City generally you were sat next to your spouse at a banquet. In her view, since it was possible to sit next to your husband every day of the week, it was much more interesting to be able to speak with someone else. However, the diplomatic corps have a very strict pecking order, with wives taking the same precedence as their husbands. Many of them, also, were unable to speak English and needed their husbands nearby to assist. The level of seniority in the diplomatic corps dates from the time of their appointment at the Court of St. James. This meant that there were countries represented such as America, Canada and Australia, whose High Commissioners were changed regularly, whereas other countries left their Ambassadors in place for years and years. These latter would become the doyennes of the top table. It was often quite a colourful affair, as many of the wives would come in national dress. The number of countries gaining independence is steadily increasing and consequently the Easter banquet is becoming more crowded. The Easter banquet is also usually the first occasion when the late Lord Mayor comes out of 'purdah' and appears as an Alderman in public for the first time, having had a well-earned rest until now.

On Friday 29th April we had a corporation lunch at the Mansion House in honour of the Mayor and Mayoress of Lima, Peru. They were a very nice couple and at the end of lunch he invested me with the Grand Cross of Municipal Merit of the city of Lima. This consisted of a brassy star and a yellow sash, hung with a tassel at the side – yet another gong to add to my collection, although I knew I could not actually wear it, unless I happened to go to Peru or to an event at the Embassy. Nevertheless it was impressive to have. That same evening was an important one. We were going down to Deal to have dinner with the Royal Marines. The route to Deal conveniently lay past the town of Ricksborough, where they built the yacht that I was interested in and was thinking of buying. I knew that Captain Warwick, the first captain of the *Q.E.II*, who was a Master in the

Honourable Company of Master Mariners, would be at the same party and I asked if he would drop in on his way down and cast his eye over her. I felt that she was exactly what I was looking for but I wanted a second opinion. As we arrived at the yard ourselves we met Captain Warwick just coming off the yacht. I asked him what he thought, and he said that if she sailed, she would certainly be OK. He then got in his car and drove off, and we all climbed out of our Rolls Royces and I went on board to look round. It was only a small place, and I don't think the designer knew what had hit him: first he had the Captain of the *Q.E.II* looking round his boat and then the Lord Mayor of London – dressed, of course, in Old Bailey! I decided that, subject to a test sail, I was certainly interested. I would be able to design the interior myself, which was a great advantage too. I said that I would return for a test sail as soon as I could find the time. We went on to have a good night with the Royal Marines, returning late to the Mansion House feeling quite satisfied at having killed two birds with one stone.

On the 10th May the High Commissioner of Canada came to the Mansion House and we both received the Squadron of the Royal Canadian Mounted Police who were over by invitation to parade to St. Paul's Cathedral in close company with the Queen's carriage for the Jubilee. It was a nostalgic occasion for me, bringing back memories of the time that I had carried the horses over myself in one of my cargo ships for the Coronation. Things were now beginning to warm up for the Jubilee, which was now only one month away.

The next day we had a Festival Sons of the Clergy – this was an organisation formed way back in the time of Christopher Wren, which provided educational support to children of members of the clergy. After a service which the Lord Mayor attended in state we had a dinner in Merchant Taylors' Hall. I was speaking at the dinner. The main speaker was unable to attend so the Dean of St. Paul's stood in at the last minute. I recall the toastmaster coming round and asking 'Are you going to speak now, Sir, or shall I top them up all round beforehand?' – the implication being, of course, that the speech would be so boring that they needed a drink to see them through it. I added this to my collection of funny things that toastmasters have said – not quite as bad as 'Are you going to speak now or shall we let them go on enjoying themselves for a bit longer?' – but pretty nearly.

On 16th May it was time for the second of the degree ceremonies of the City of London University, the first having been quite soon after my appointment, when I received my honorary degree. As on the previous occasion, this was a Long Day – gently hitting a seemingly endless line of graduates over the head with a Tudor hat. I reckoned that by the end of the year I had earned my Doctorate of Science, whatever my elder son might say about it – the hordes of graduates awaiting admission seemed interminable. The day was rounded off with a Livery company dinner, which was probably just as well as I needed to calm down a bit. I had visions of getting into bed and hitting Libby over the head with a hot water bottle saying 'I admit you, I admit you'.

On the 19th there we attended another naval occasion: Ladies' Guest Night, at the Royal Naval College, Greenwich. The next day saw a Queen's Silver Jubilee Appeal committee meeting; this was the first of a number of meetings at which it would be decided who would be receiving grants from the money raised.

The following weekend it was down to Cowes, where we took part in the City Livery yacht club motor sailing race, sailing in *Hodzah*. We won the race, which was most satisfying and spent the rest of the weekend down there, before returning to the Mansion House with the cup on the Monday. I brought our cup back to the Mansion House so that the lads in the plate room could give it a good burnishing before I handed it over to Christopher Rawson.

Our state of euphoria on arriving home was abruptly cut short on hearing the news that a Sergeant Footman, Denis Chalk, had been murdered whilst we had been away. Apparently he and a friend who shared a flat together were 'picked up' by a couple of Scots guardsmen at a pub frequented by homosexuals. They took the soldiers back to the flat only to find that they were queer-bashers. The guardsmen bludgeoned Dennis and his friend to death with bayonets, hacking them about so much that they were unrecognisable. It was a truly dreadful tragedy. Denis was a very kind and gentle man, who had served in the Mansion House during my father's time before leaving for a while to work for Lord Mountbatten as a valet. He had subsequently returned to the Mansion House some three years previously. Needless to say everyone was very upset, particularly the domestic staff. The police moved in quickly and had captured the culprits within six weeks, but there was a veil of gloom over the place for some considerable time.

Shortly after this I went to open an exhibition at Guildhall of a series of paintings by one John Hamilton, depicting the events of the war at sea in the North Atlantic. They were beautiful paintings and as a sort of *quid pro quo* he said that he would like to paint a picture of my first voyage to sea. It so happened that I had some photographs which had been taken of the *Empress of Russia*, the ship which had been taken off the troop convoy because she had been smoking so badly, after being stoked with cheap coal. From these pictures, he managed to paint a very good likeness of her, which was hung in the exhibition. Rather amusingly I overheard some crusty Admiral point out this picture and claim that it was quite unrealistic; such a ship would never have had smoke coming out of her funnels like that – although I of course I knew perfectly well that this *had* been the case; indeed, that very smoke had been the cause of all our trouble in the first place! Subsequently the exhibition was moved and is now permanently housed on board H.M.S. *Belfast*. The artist was commissioned, after this, to do a similar series on the Pacific war for the Americans, which I happened to see when I went to visit him at his home in Trescoe on the Isles of Scilly some years later. The Prince of Wales came to see the exhibition and I was able to show him round.

A run down of the activities that took place on Thursday 26th May provides an excellent example of the Mayoral lifestyle and a fairly typical slice of life at the Mansion House. At 10 o'clock in the morning Libby received the President of the Egyptian Red Crescent – by dint of the fact that, as Lady Mayoress, Libby was herself the President of the City Red Cross. At 10.30 I had a meeting of the General Purposes Committee of the Court of Alderman and half an hour later I received a party of representatives from the Amsterdam Volunteer Police. Then at one o'clock it was Common Council. That evening to Knightsbridge to present a Queen's Award for Industry to Graf Diamonds, Ltd. (I think in the course of my year I presented no less than six Queen's Award for Industry to various firms in the City). This was followed by a Livery Company dinner back at the Mansion House in the evening. Such was the flavour of life, and it would be quite possible to provide details of every day that passed more or less in this manner. But the intention here is to provide only a flavour, and to recount in more detail some of the more interesting or out of the ordinary anecdotes and incidents that occurred during my term of office.

On 27th May our friends the past Lord Mayor of York and his wife – Mr and Mrs Archer – took up our invitation to spend a day with us. They seemed to enjoy themselves thoroughly, as we showed them what a Mansion House really ought to look like and worked them into our programme as best we could that day.

On the afternoon of Monday 30th May we carried out a rehearsal for the lunch that was to take place in Guildhall subsequent to the service in St. Paul's Cathedral on Jubilee Day. This was just an example, I suppose, of just how thoroughly these things are rehearsed. When one sees state occasions on television they all seem to go seamlessly well – ceremony being our artform, as I always say – but this is only because we do ensure that we get it right, rather than relying on chance or throwing things together at the last minute. We were still days away from the actual event, but we were busy making sure that all the little bits of the ceremony for which we were responsible would run like clockwork. It was mainly a question of timing. When the guests were all assembled in Guildhall ready for lunch, the Queen and the Duke and Libby and myself would make our entrance accompanied by a blare of trumpets, whereupon the band of the Welsh guards would play two verses of 'God Save the Queen' to give us just enough time to process between the tables, divide in front of the dais and finish up at our places on the top table, facing down the hall towards the assembled company. We had to be sure that the timing was correct to the second, and that we arrived at our places at precisely the same time that the 'God Save the Queen' finished. It took us about three goes to get it right, so that those processing and those playing were absolutely synchronised. Our job would also be to take the Queen and the Duke of Edinburgh up to the Chief Commoners' Room when we arrived at Guildhall, to refresh ourselves before joining the rest of the Royal Family for a pre-prandial drink; this, too, was rehearsed so that we knew exactly how long it would take to get up in the lift. That evening we actually met up with the Queen and the Duke in person at the Royal Opera House where there was a gala performance of opera and ballet to celebrate the Jubilee. Things were now beginning to hot up.

The 1st June was a very nautical day, commencing with a demonstration of equipment of Decca Navigational equipment on the river, on board the demonstration yacht, the *Navigator*. It was most interesting, not least because the chap driving her was an old contemporary of mine from Pangbourne. This was followed, at 12.30, by the inauguration of the jetfoil service, from London to Zeebrugge. These were the craft that sat up on three legs and crossed a high speed. I went down to meet her coming across with a whole load of

Mayors from Belgium; the hope was that I would accompany them on their return trip but I had a Midsummer Banquet to attend and it proved impossible. They did promise me a trip across at high speed, however, which I was to have in the future.

The Midsummer Banquet was the banquet to the Arts and Sciences. It was rather difficult to arrange and a sub-committee was needed of experts in the various fields to determine who should be invited. Given the nature of the arts, and in particular the performing arts, it was always difficult to get hold of any well-known names as they were usually busy working, with only the out-of-work actors free to attend. You never quite knew who you were going to get to sit next to on these occasions; it might, for example, turn out to be the *Regis* Professor of Zoology from Edinburgh University on one side and Benny Hill on the other. Needless to say Morecambe and Wise put in appearance and helped the evening go well.

The next day there was a lunch in honour of the Prime Minister of Australia, Mr Malcolm Fraser and his wife, who were over here for the Jubilee, given in the Mansion House on behalf of the Corporation.

The following Saturday 4th June, the opportunity at last arose to have a test sail in the yacht I had my eye on. I went down to Ricksborough with Nicholas and my God-daughter Caroline and took her out on the river and out to sea just to the south of Ramsgate. I was very happy with her performance, and before I left I placed my order and put down a deposit, the idea being that she should be ready for me when I had finished the Mayoralty. I recall my elder son being horrified as I signed a cheque for £3,000 but I felt it was money well spent and I knew I would enjoy spending time planning her interior.

The next day there was a big rehearsal for the Temple Bar ceremony. In order to miss the crowds, we had to start proceedings at 7.20 in the morning. The Queen's coach stops at Temple Bar, where the Lord Mayor symbolically surrenders the City sword to her, then receives it back and carries it point upwards thereafter. In a rather incongruous scene the coach was duly brought to Temple Bar at the crack of dawn, with the Yeomen of the Guard marching beside the carriage in brown raincoats and pork pie hats and with all other participants also in mufti. Another little piece of the jigsaw rehearsed, with timings again worked out to the second. Having completed the ceremony I had to go ahead to St. Paul's to be there at the steps when Her Majesty arrived. This too was a difficult manoeuvre to complete and they had to be sure that the coach would stop in exactly the right place. Getting all of this detail right took up the whole morning. At 3 o'clock in the afternoon there was a special Queen's Silver Jubilee service for the people of London, held in Westminster Abbey. We were now in full Jubilee mode!

Chapter 21

The following day was an official public holiday, declared in honour of the Jubilee. It was no holiday for us, however, as we spent the whole day in St. Paul's Cathedral going through procedures. Firstly, we all rehearsed individual little bits of ceremony – parts of the whole – in various parts of the cathedral, working out exactly where to stand, and what to do, and when. I treated it as a full dress run and wore my processional robes, and was very glad I had done so. I had at one point to walk up the nave, carrying the sword in front of the Queen and then below the steps of the Chancel I had to lay the sword on a table. This necessitated turning round to face the Queen and the Duke and then bowing as I placed the sword on its cushion. I discovered that if I took a pace forward, away from the table, my gown, which was trailing the floor, swung in behind me, so that when I stepped back again before turning round I would have trodden on the gown, a move which could have had disastrous consequences. I devised a system whereby, instead of taking a step forward, I came up close to the table and then took a pace back with my right foot – which meant I was actually pushing the gown back with my heel and I could turn without tripping. It was vital that such minor detail was ironed out in advance – discovering 'on the night' would be too late! When everyone had finished rehearsing their own little bits we went back to square one and, all on the stopwatch, we did the whole thing in real time, up to the point at which the service was to begin, and then picked it up again after the blessing. The Cathedral confidently said that they did not need to rehearse, since they knew how long their bit would take, although they were proved wrong in the end and overran, which meant we were late getting to Guildhall! However, every other fine detail was timed to the second and once everyone was happy we were allowed to leave, in preparation for the real thing the next day.

The crowds were already beginning to gather outside, some coming to watch the rehearsal and some even believing that the rehearsal was *it*. Libby was flattered to overhear someone nudging her neighbour and pointing to her with the words, 'That's the Queen Mother!' Most things had gone smoothly, although there was something of a *contretemps* over the exit procedure. Having picked the sword up again at the end of the service I proceeded back down the nave, to be followed by the Queen and the Duke. When we got to the West door, they would be stopping to say goodbye to the Archbishop of Canterbury, the Bishop of London and other attendant clergy. When we got out through the door, where the sword bearer was waiting, I handed the sword over to him and waited to escort the Queen and the Duke down the steps. Libby had 'snuck out' of her pew and had come round the back and was also waiting there ready to be presented to the Queen and the Duke; the four of us would then go down the steps and start the walkabout. At this point in the rehearsal the Dean came up and said to Libby 'You can't stand there!' I asked him why not, and he explained that that was cathedral ground and she would have to wait down the steps. I imagined this would look ridiculous, particularly if it was pouring with rain – a lonely figure standing waiting half way down the steps of St. Paul's. I got hold of the Remembrancer and explained the problem to him. He had a go, but no, the answer was the same. We tried the Lord Chamberlain, but the Dean was intransigent. It was Cathedral ground and no one could wait there. So poor Libby had no choice but to stand half way down the steps, a little lone figure, waiting until we got down to that level, when she stepped forward to be presented. She was then able to team up with the Duke and the four of us could commence the walk. I failed to see the cathedral's logic in all of this, and also felt irritated that it was they who, in the end, overran and held up proceedings. The timing of the whole thing was absolutely crucial; it was being broadcast worldwide and certainly as far as our speeches at Guildhall went everything was timed to the second.

Tuesday 7th June was the Great Day itself, and a day I shall certainly never forget. We left the Mansion House at 10.20 a.m., with the deputation to Temple Bar. I was in my coach, leaving Libby behind to make her way independently by car to St. Paul's. The rest of us mustered at Child's Bank, all dressed in our finery. I had my long processional robe with the white ermine top and the sword bearer had the pearl-scabbarded sword at the ready. The Queen arrived in her golden coach, escorted by the Household Cavalry and the Mounties. We had a slight problem with the latter; I do not know whether it was the English climate, or possibly a new diet which did not agree with them, but they all seemed to lift their tails as one just at the spot where I was going to have to walk forward to the Queen's carriage. The Queen was met first of all by the City Marshall, on his horse, and escorted to the spot outside the law courts where I was waiting; I stepped forward – squelched forward, might be a more appropriate way of putting it – and duly presented the hilt of the sword to the Queen, before whizzing off with my entourage to get into my own carriage which awaited on the other side of the road, and make best speed to Guildhall. I had to have a ten-minute lead on the Queen in order to be ready on the steps of St. Paul's to greet her when she arrived. Lifeguards and heralds flanked the steps and the congregation was already assembled inside the cathedral. When she and the Duke arrived we proceeded up the steps, with me in front carrying the sword. There was a breeze blowing and as I walked slowly up the long flight of steps the wind caught my ermine-trimmed gown – unlike an Alderman's gown with slits for one's arms, this was a long, heavy cape – and I could feel it billowing up like a balloon around me. There was very little I could do as both my hands were holding the sword, and I recall feeling slightly anxious that a strong gust might pull off the cloak and chain all in one. I overheard the Duke say to the Queen at that point, 'I think the Lord Mayor's going to take off!' I must say I did have visions of sailing off like Mary Poppins over the west face of St. Paul's Cathedral, the sword still in my hand. I was immensely relieved as we reached the top of the steps and everything fell back into place.

The clergy greeted the Queen and the clerical procession began, followed by the heralds and then me, carrying the sword, up the long, long nave of St. Paul's. I have a video recording of the whole thing, and it shows a great picture taken from above. You can see the red carpet laid out all the way up the nave but it is taken from so far up (the Whispering Gallery, I believe) that the figures walking up are barely recognisable; in my great white ermine trimmed cloak I rather resemble a giant ping-pong ball, followed by two little black dots, which were the Queen and the Duke of Edinburgh. I am glad to say that we followed a very straight line all the way up. Thanks to the rehearsal the laying of the sword in front of the Queen went without a hitch; I made my bow and proceeded to the sanctuary, to my seat in the choir. Then away we went with the service.

My last worry was that the Archbishop, in his address, would steal some of my lines, since the subject matter of my speech was to be very similar. I am glad to say that although the sentiment was the same he did not actually come out with any of my words. The service came to an end; I had to go and pick up the sword and then lead the Queen out. This, again, had been well rehearsed. Normally in St. Paul's cathedral the Lord Mayor is escorted everywhere by a verger or other body and does not have to worry too much about precisely when things happen; on this occasion I was under my own steam and responsible for my own timing. I had to come out of my pew, bow to the altar, turn about and then go past the choir to where the sword rested on its table. If I left my pew too soon I would run into the back of the clergy who were going down ahead of me; if, on the other hand, I left it too late, there would be a gap in the procession. I had decided for myself that I would leave my pew just as the Archbishop was passing the last choirboy on the left; this would mean arriving at just the right point after the clergy. All went smoothly; I went out through the door, the sword-bearer took the sword off me and I then waited until the Queen and the Duke had finished saying goodbye to the clergy. We then went down the steps to where Libby awaited, halfway down as instructed; she came over and I presented her to the Queen and the Duke and we paired up and launched into the walkabout.

After a short burst of the public at the bottom of the steps, we turned in to go through the gardens of St. Paul's to meet the Master Gardener and his wardens who were to present the Queen with a bouquet, which was an exact replica of the one she had been presented with when she was crowned. It was then out into New Change, heading for Cheapside. The place was absolutely packed, the crowd lining the streets about four or five deep. The Queen seemed quite surprised. 'Where have all these people come from?' she enquired. 'I thought it was a Bank Holiday.' 'They have come to see you, ma'am,' I explained.

I should say here that whilst we had been inside the Cathedral, she had been looking rather strained; several people commented on this after the event and wondered whether she had been feeling unwell. I suspect it was the occasion itself and all that it signified for her, perhaps bringing back memories of her father of whom she had been so fond. However, as soon as we were outside and we hit the crowds, her countenance altered. It is hard to describe exactly how it felt, but I can honestly say that the feeling of affection and love that poured from those ranks of people gathered to see her was palpable. You could feel it coming across in waves. Within yards, she looked as if she had shed twenty years. She was absolutely radiant, smiling and happy and genuinely delighted to see her people. I discovered only later that Her instruction had been given to the police to stay clear two hundred yards either side of her, so there were no ranks of police standing between her and the crowds she was passing. Indeed, none were needed. Everyone was extremely well behaved, with no one thrusting cameras into her face or pushing and shoving; just wanting to touch her and pat her hand and congratulate her.

Our first stop was Bow Church, where we paused for the Church Wardens to be presented. There was a visitor's book for her to sign and she was given a little silver bow bell. We then proceeded down Cheapside and round to the left up King Street towards Guildhall. The Queen and I were on the south side of the road and the Duke and Libby were on the other; once round the corner we swapped sides. The Alderman of each ward was on duty at each ward, but apart from this it was just the Queen and her people. She was so happy it was hard to believe how sombre she had looked earlier.

We made good time and we went into Guildhall yard and into the west wing, where we were to join the rest of the Royal family, who were already assembled there having their pre-prandial drinks. As I have said, this was all rehearsed and Libby and I knew that we had to take the Queen and the Duke up to the Chief Commoner's flat to refresh themselves before lunch. For some reason (probably security) when we got up there Libby turned the door handle only to discover that it was locked! We managed to find another room and all was well, but again it proves how rigorous every last detail needs to be planned.

The procession into lunch consisted of the Queen, myself, the Duke and Libby, the Queen Mother, the Prince of Wales and Lord Mountbatten. They took us down to the ambulatory leading up to the entrance to Guildhall; as often happens on these occasions they paraded us too soon, which meant that we had to stand and wait at the entrance before we could actually go in. There had been a rumour in the press at that time that Idi Amin of Uganda, who was causing a lot of trouble and who had not been invited, was threatening to gatecrash proceedings. As we stood waiting for the fanfare of trumpets that would announce our entrance, we could still see one or two people arriving to take their places. The Queen at that point turned to me and said, 'What are we waiting for?' I am afraid that at this

The Silver Jubilee of H.M. Queen Elizabeth II – the walkabout.

With H.M. Queen Elizabeth II and H.M. The Queen Mother.

438

was subsequently to join the Worshipful Company of Coach Makers and Coach Harness Makers. The first step on the road, so to speak. That evening was the Judges' banquet and the following day we went up to Sheffield to attend the Cutlers' Forfeit feast in the evening. – an annual do given by the Master Cutler. It was a very good evening, and a rare occasion for the Lord Mayor who is not required to speak. We stayed at the house usually used by the visiting judges and the next day visited a steel works, where I was presented with a very nice yachting knife.

On Wednesday 20th July the Queen gave a reception at Buckingham Palace, which began at 10 o'clock in the evening. People came and went and the Royal family were in attendance talking to people throughout. There was dancing in the main ballroom and suppers being served in various side drawing rooms. The guests were a cross section of people who had achieved significantly in their respective fields or had contributed to the community in some way during the first 25 years of Her Majesty's reign. It was a very jolly party, which went on until about 4.30 in the morning, although we took our leave somewhat earlier. The next day was the Royal Garden Party, which we attended, although I had to leave this to catch a helicopter to take me to Portland where I was to be the guest of Rear Admiral Pritchard, who was Admiral Sea Training, and his Staff Officer Anthony Dring who had been my best man. It had been engineered that I should visit his unit in my capacity as Lord Mayor and I was able to stay over with him and his wife, before going to sea the next day. I had taken Teddy Ellis, the Private Secretary with me as well as the Sergeant-at-Arms who both came to sea with us. One of the pieces of activity was to jackstay us between H.M.S. *Active* and H.M.S. *Sheffield* whilst we were steaming along at twenty knots off Portland. I had never been jackstayed before; the Admiral went first, and then I went over followed by the others. They did not do anything silly like try and dip the Lord Mayor in the ocean, but it was all very exciting. You were hooked to a wire between the two ships and you whizzed across to land safely on the deck the other side, although there were chaps in wet suits standing around in case of emergency. We returned by helicopter to the heliport at Battersea where we had started.

On 25th July I presented letters patent to the newly founded Livery company, the Worshipful Company of Chartered Accountants in England and Wales. This was the third I had given to new livery companies in the course of my Mayoralty; the Chartered Secretaries were supposed to have theirs but had not got their paperwork ready, but I did the Chartered Surveyors and the Builders Merchants. Together with the Accountants these formed the new tranche of Livery Companies, comprising professional bodies with all the powers of the governing bodies, which encapsulated all that the Livery companies had done in the past. It did not mean that every Chartered Accountant would have to become a member of the Livery company, but it did mean that the avenue was open to them should they wish to pursue it.

On Tuesday 26th July I received at the Mansion House, at the request of the Foreign Office, a Japanese gentleman by the name of Mr Sasakawa. He arrived in full Japanese dress with about five henchmen dressed in short black jackets and striped trousers who wrote down everything he said. A prominent Japanese industrialist and philanthropist, he was reputedly a great believer in world peace, although I understand that he came close to being indicted as a war criminal at the end of World War II. Amongst other titles he laid claim to, he happened to be President of the Japanese ship building federation. He was over in this country to present £1 million to the Lister Foundation and was very interested to learn that I was planning to visit Japan in the summer, when Libby would be launching a ship for Canadian Pacific. He offered me hospitality when I got there, and then produced a number of presents for me, including a short 'happy coat', two small glass cubes which, with their magnetic qualities, were reputedly good for one's health if rubbed against the body, and, finally, he announced that he was going to make me a karate black belt of the seventh dan. I had always thought that considerable training would be required to reach such dizzy heights, but he produced a white suit which I duly put on and then posed for photographs with him in the salon in various martial-art style positions. To my horror these appeared in the *Daily Telegraph* the next day! More of Mr Sasakawa, anon.

The same day I had lunch with the President of the CBI, as part of my briefing round prior to my overseas travels. The following day I took the salute at the Royal Tournament – another annual feature in the Lord Mayor's diary. Alas, the event no longer exists.

Chapter 23

On Friday 29th July we were off on our long overseas summer visit. We were embarking a full party on this occasion, leaving the Old Bailey in the hands of the duty Aldermen. We took with us both Sheriffs, the Chief Commoner and two of the household officers – the Sergeant-at-Arms, Colonel Brook Johnstone and Colonel O'Thacker the City Marshal. Such a party was quite common in those days, although nowadays the entourage is somewhat more restricted. A nice little earner for British Airways, who were to fly us around on this trip – although Japanese airlines had in fact offered us free flights there and back. We had to politely refuse such an offer, as there would have been a terrible row if we had not gone BA (viz: my flight back from Poznan). Our first stop was to be Singapore, after an overnight flight from Heathrow. We left London at 7.45 on Friday evening, and did not arrive in Singapore until 7 o'clock, local time, on the evening of the following day. I had deliberately advanced the programme by a day to give us a day to recover after such a long haul before we had to start on our round of official duties – bearing in mind, too, that our trip was to be an extensive one. We were met by the British High Commissioner, Mr John Tripp, who saw us safely to our hotel. We were put up at the Shangri-La Hotel, Singapore, which was having some building work done on it at the time, but was nevertheless a very pleasant hotel indeed. Our first day was spent relaxing, before the rigours of the tour commenced. In the afternoon we took the opportunity to do some shopping. I wanted to purchase a telephoto lens for my camera and I knew that this would be a good place to acquire this. We went into a camera store, asked to see some lenses and found one I liked. I then asked the price. I was told that it was $120. The shop was about to close so I said that I would be back the next day. By the time we returned the following day, the staff had been alerted to my official status and I was greeted by the manager at the door, asking if there was anything at all they could do for me. I explained that I had been in the store the previous day and told him about the lens I was wanting. The manager went over to the counter, where the same member of staff who had served me the previous day was standing. Not a glimmer of recognition, so I explained again which lens it was that I was after. The lens was duly produced and I asked him to verify the price. 'You told me yesterday that it was $120.'

'Oh no lah,' he said, hastily. 'Eighty dollar, eighty dollar'.

I found this a little curious, but assumed that the manager had indicated to him that I was important and should be offered a good price. I was to encounter a similar experience in other parts of the Far East throughout my travels.

After a day recuperating, we attended an official ceremony at the Public Utilities Board on the Monday. Lee Kuan Yew, the Prime Minister, had a few years previously abolished the local authority of the city of Singapore on the grounds that the whole of Singapore was a city state and did not need a two-tier government. In its place was the Public Utilities Board, the Chairman of which was the closest they had to a Mayor. It was to him that we presented the customary piece of plate and received in return a piece of pewter. They were somewhat embarrassed at the exchange of gifts, since Lee Kuan Yew's crackdown on bribery and corruption. All the usual trappings of the Mayoralty – the Mace and chains and what have you – were consigned to a glass case as mere exhibits and one had to tread very carefully to make sure that all was above board, since we were being televised at the time. We conducted the usual discussions, exchanging information about our respective cities. The press then had their stint and we proceeded to a luncheon attended by various government ministers. After lunch the ladies of the party went off to do ladies-type things (Libby often objected to this, claiming that we got to do far more exciting things) but they were taken to the famous Botanical Gardens and then to a social services home for retarded children. We, on the other hand, visited Jurong New Town industrial area on the south west corner of the island. This was a major project, reclaiming a mangrove swamp to construct a huge industrial estate with some one hundred companies represented there. They were quite ruthless about moving their population, having torn down most of the old part of the city. I had last visited Singapore in 1945, taking troops out to restore the airfield there. It was then a bustling Chinese town, with all the usual bazaars, sights, sounds and smells, overlooked by imperial-style Raffles Hotel. Now the old city was unrecognisable, with gleaming new skyscrapers dominating the landscape as far as the eye could see. Vast numbers of the population had been moved compulsorily into high-rise blocks

afternoon we went to the Urban Council Chamber and were received by the Chairman of the Council. I went in to address the Council and gifts were once again exchanged. The gifts this time included a beautiful silver model of a Chinese junk, which I admired enormously, although unfortunately it had the Corporation's name on it and not mine, and I could not claim it as my own. However, I did rescue it from being consigned to the basement of Guildhall but secured it with the Lord Mayor's plate, so that at least it would be seen at the Mansion House. Libby was meanwhile off to visit another Cheshire Home. That evening there was a dinner party at Government House. On the Saturday we were taken on a tour of the harbour, and this in turn was followed by a tour of the New Territories by car. The drive takes about an hour and a half, to Island House, home of the Secretary, where a traditional Chinese meal of claypot chicken was served. The country setting was delightful and in sharp contrast to the concrete of modern Hong Kong we had left behind. After lunch we went off to embark in a couple of helicopters. Ours carried the pilot, then Libby and myself on a bench seat in the front, and behind us the Coles. They were tucked in to the back and fairly secure, but up at the front we were open to the elements at the side, with only the glass bubble of the helicopter in front of us. I suffer from vertigo a bit and found it very hard to cope with the fact that there was absolutely nothing at the end of our bench seat. Taking off was not too bad, as we rose straight into the air, but I snuggled up to Libby who sat in the middle and tried not to look out as we banked round. We landed on a cliff top and got out to look at Sho Tin New Town. A racecourse had been built and we inspected this and all the other new facilities that were awaiting final completion. We then climbed back into our helicopter and took off once more. Unlike the first time, when we had risen slowly and the ground fell away beneath us, this time we just pulled away from the cliff top, directly over a 300 foot drop below us. I spent the time busily scrutinising my camera and fiddling with the knobs, and trying very hard not to look down. We were taken on to look at the High Island damn, before returning back down to the city and eventually coming down to land. Never have I been so relieved to get out of an aircraft. It must be psychological, since I was subsequently to fly in a helicopter in Canada with no problem at all. However, in that case it was possible to get in and shut the door. Had there at least been a bar I might have felt easier, but I think it was just the fact that there was absolutely nothing to hold me in, should I slide across the bench, that I found most disturbing. Recovering from that experience, we had a quiet dinner with the acting Chief Secretary that evening.

On Sunday 14th August we went 'on the banyan' – the Naval equivalent of a picnic. We drove down to H.M.S. *Tamar*, embarked on some Royal Naval launches and spent some two hours steaming off to a little cove off the New Territories, where swimming conditions were ideal, jellyfish apart. After a couple of boozy hours we returned back feeling quite relaxed. I was presented with a little Chinese compass, which I still have, and which I believe tells you your fortune as well as pointing north.

This was really the end of the official overseas tour for the rest of the party. The Sheriffs returned to the U.K., and Libby and I stayed on to await our trip to Japan with Canadian Pacific. As far as I was concerned, my official duties were not yet over and I was still expected to act the part of Lord Mayor. On the following day I offered to give a press and television interview to some 40 journalists, fielding a wide range of questions. I was certainly put through the mill, although I think I acquitted myself quite well and felt it was a good P.R. exercise. I certainly felt I earned my lunch that day. In the afternoon I took the opportunity to meet with some Old Pangbournians and some of our firm's clients who also happened to be out there. Dinner that night was again with an ex-member of the Council. Libby had had a more exciting day than I had on that occasion, having been taking to Shaw's film studios.

On the next day we had a trip to Macau at the request of the Governor of Macau. We sped by jetfoil across to Macau, which they allowed me to drive at one point (fly, I think is the correct term). It was certainly great fun whizzing across the mouth of the Yellow River at 52 m.p.h., dodging junks and what have you along the way. We were accompanied on the journey by the Consul of Macau, and were met on arrival by His Excellency the Governor of Macau.

Our first call in Macau was to meet the Governor, Colonel Jose Garcia Lenandro, at his HQ. We had a long and interesting talk about the history of the Portuguese colonies, and about Macau in particular. He spoke excellent English, and communication was not a problem. He was a fairly young man, in his early forties, and quite new to the post, and was full of enthusiasm and ideas. Unlike Hong Kong, which buzzed night and day, Macau had a somewhat lazy air; the atmosphere was more like that of a sleepy hacienda at high noon, with Chinamen dozing in the sun and no real sense of anything happening. The Governor's palace was somewhat down-at-heel and in need of decoration. He was certainly going to have his work cut out! He took me to see the President of the Urban Council, and then we went to lunch at the Governor's residence where his wife and Libby and several ladies of Macau were assembled. The ladies all seemed to be dressed up to the nines, leaving Libby feeling somewhat underdressed in what she termed her 'tourist rig'. After lunch, Libby and I and the Governor took off for a tour. He was boundlessly optimistic and full of plans. We arrived at a rather shabby looking bay with a solitary junk looking as if it had seen better days, and he announced that this was where they were going to build a container port; he then showed us where the new airport was being built; we crossed the causeway to a neighbouring island where he pointed out a deserted beach with black sand, which he wanted to turn into a tourist resort. I cast doubt on this latter notion, unconvinced that people would flock to a beach with black sand. I did return to Macau some fifteen years later to find that they had indeed built a fine hotel there, although I rather think that visitors stuck to the hotel pool and did not venture on to the black sand too much! We visited a museum with what looked like an interesting collection, although the Director did not seem to know an awful lot about his exhibits; he would take out a pot for us to look at, for example, and then have to enquire from our host what it was. The only place that was really smart and clean and beautifully kept in Macau was the English church. It was really quite immaculate, with a manicured lawn surround. All the graves were kept in excellent condition, with the lettering on the upright gravestones recently re-blacked; I have really never seen anything quite like it, and it was in such sharp contrast to the dilapidated area around. The Church was apparently very well off – indeed, it would appear that they had more money than they knew what to do with. The headstones in the graveyard there were particularly interesting to read; many were those of sailors drowned at sea.

Macau was due to be returned to the Chinese slightly later than Hong Kong and I understand that there has been considerable development in recent times. The Portuguese had in fact tried to return the colony to the Chinese some years before, but the Chinese were not interested then, preferring to use it merely as a port, like Hong Kong, and to let others worry about the administration.

The only evident success in Macau, it has to be said, was the casino, which had been built near to the jetfoil terminal. The Chinese are of course inveterate gamblers; needless to say the casino was run by the Hong Kong Chinese, and being only 45 minutes away from Hong Kong it was a popular destination, particularly with women who crossed over for a bit of a flutter. There was a racecourse, too, which was equally popular. Gambling apart, however, there really was very little to recommend the place, and I felt quite sorry for the young Governor, so full of ideas and enthusiasm but clearly up against centuries of apathy.

We returned to Hong Kong and that evening we were taken by launch to see Aberdeen Harbour, a floating village of junks, where an evening market was held. However, security was tight at all times in Hong Kong, and there was very little opportunity for us to see the place properly. Staying at Government House brought certain restrictions and, although we wanted for nothing, our movements were carefully controlled. This inhibited Libby in particular, who liked to wander around the shops and discover things for herself. Even at the market in Aberdeen Harbour we had the Chief of Police with us and a couple of hefties trailing behind. We were able to return to Hong Kong later in life and see the place properly, as tourists, but for the time being we were only permitted to see what they wanted us to see. This is true, of course, of most of the places we visited on an official basis, as I have said before. You do get shown interesting places and get to meet interesting people, but it is always on their terms, not yours, and there is never time to dally. Whilst in Hong Kong I had a dinner jacket and a suit made by the official tailor appointed to Government House. He had a thriving business, with a shop in Kowloon as well as his book of V.I.P.s whom he had kitted out in his time. He came round to measure me and within twenty-four hours was back to fit with a complete suit. I also managed to buy a watch whilst there, but, again, I was swept off in the Daimler to a particular shop recommended by Government House and was swept back again, with no time to linger. However, we were not there for a holiday, we were there to work!

The following morning I gave a radio broadcast, with snippets of interview interspersed with records of my choice. Coincidentally the chap who interviewed me happened to be the son of one of the members of the Common Council. A small world, indeed. It has to be said that the record collection there was somewhat limited, which meant that I did not always get precisely what I asked for. Having requested Handel's *Music for the Royal Fireworks*, for example, they came up with the *Water Music* instead, and there was one which annoyed Christopher particularly when he listened to the tape, as I had requested King's College Choir and they played a recording by a completely different choir, which to his horror included women singers!

We had our final lunch with the Governor and then it was time to set off for Japan. The remainder of our trip was to be at the expense of Canadian Pacific. Our arrangements were to be undertaken by a P.R. person from the company, who did all the sorts of things that my team would have done in ensuring that everything went smoothly, so I did not have to worry on that score. And I was still Lord Mayor and could operate in that capacity, but I was no longer representing the City on my travels.

Chapter 24

We flew from Hong Kong to Osaka, where the ship that Libby was to launch was being built. As we descended the steps from the plane on to the tarmac we were met by a group of 'heavies', which puzzled me rather as I had thought we were to be met by a representative of Canadian Pacific. As we stepped down they came forward, bowing, and said 'Ah Lord Mayor! We are from Mr Sasakawa.' They took our hand baggage and marched us off to customs and immigration where they threw their weight around and the customs officials visibly cowered in deference. Mr Sasakawa's name obviously meant a great deal. Without even having our passports checked we sped through and emerged into the main airport concourse. Here a large limousine awaited us – but also awaiting were the Canadian Pacific lot, who had not been allowed in to the Arrival lounge. They too had a car for us. The plan was to spend our first night at a hotel in Kyoto. After a bit of a tug of war, we were taken eventually by Mr Sasakawa's representatives, who already had our baggage in the boot of their car, and we sped away to Kyoto, promising to meet the Canadian Pacific men in the morning.

They turned up at the hotel the following morning as promised and we spent a day sightseeing with them in Kyoto. Our tourist bit over, we then went back down to Osaka to view the ship. She had been built in dry dock so it was just a question of naming her: she would not be sliding down the slipway to be launched. She was big – a 22,000 ton bulk carrier, and one of a series that Canadian Pacific was building. Since I had left the company the passenger trade had disappeared completely, and they had moved into tankers and bulk carriers. This particular class was being named after the Royal Canadian Mounted Police forts across Canada and our ship was to be named the *Fort Walsh*.

We were taken out that night by the dockyard firm to a geisha restaurant, which was a most interesting experience. I must point that we had our wives with us, which was of course unusual, since they are generally men-only venues. There were only a couple of dining rooms and I believe that it was phenomenally expensive. You sat at long low tables and the 'girls' (I think that the youngest geisha girl was probably about fifty) hovered about to entertain. Some of the entertainment was pretty grizzly, it has to be said, particularly the musical offering, when they 'sang' to a guitar accompaniment – to my ears it sounded more like a wail. Otherwise they sat by you and helped you with your food, popping little squares of sizzling beef into your mouth and keeping your *saki* cup full. Quite a lot of giggling went on throughout. The meal took place at a very leisurely place, with various little bits of food appearing at intervals. We stopped for photographs at one point and the girls attempted to use a camera, which entailed a lot more giggling. It was certainly a genuine Japanese experience.

On the Friday we were taken to a more conventional restaurant where we ate *kobi* beef for lunch (prepared in a particular Japanese style which gave the meat excellent flavour and made it very tender), prior to the naming ceremony at the dockyard that afternoon. We were taken up on to a platform adjacent to the bow of the ship, which was bedecked with flags. A great balloon contraption was suspended from the stem and a bottle of champagne was on hand to swing against the hull. The champagne bottle was released at the critical moment by a string, which came from the release gear up on to the bow and back on to the platform where we were standing. The string divided at the end into a 'Y' and was placed across a kind of chopping block; the sponsor (Libby) was given a small hatchet which she had to swing across the string and release the bottle; the balloon contraption then burst open releasing a great flock of doves and there was a great cheer from the dockyard workers, waving Japanese and Canadian flags. There then followed a scramble to get the string; Japanese folklore held that it brought great good luck to tie the umbilical cord of your first-born with a piece of string from the launch of a ship and everyone was eager for a piece of it. Libby did extremely well: she had got someone to translate her words into Japanese, which she wrote (phonetically) on a card carefully concealed at the top of her handbag. She was then able to perform the ceremony in both languages, which got a huge cheer. There were, I understand, a number of fail-safe devices to ensure that the process went smoothly, with concealed razor blades poised to cut the string if it had not been severed by the

Libby names the Fort Walsh.

hatchet, so that the release of the champagne bottle was more or less guaranteed.

However – no show without punch! During our lunch at the kobi beef restaurant, who should have turned up but Mr Sasakawa. There was great bowing and scraping from all present and in he strutted, like some sort of turkey cock, followed by his henchmen, there to write down his every word and take photographs at every opportunity. Mr Sasakawa was dressed in western clothes for a change, rather than his customary Japanese dress, and from that point on more or less took over the proceedings. He accompanied us to the dockyard and came up on to the platform with us, with his henchmen practically pushing the shipyard managers out of the way to make way for him. Not that they seemed to mind, all deferring to him without question. He had his photograph taken with Libby and it was his picture that appeared in the press rather than that of the people who had actually built the ship!

The ceremony over, we were whisked off to a hotel for a reception, where I noted a conspicuous absence of women. Apart from Libby and the wife of the Managing Director of Canadian Pacific, none of the other men had wives present; when I queried this I was told quite clearly that the place for Japanese women was in the home and they were never expected to attend this kind of thing. There was great speechifying; inevitably Mr Sasakawa got up to make a long speech in Japanese and presented Libby and I with gifts, and then the shipyard manager got up and spoke and presented Libby with a string of pearls, and then someone else spoke. Eventually the day was over, and we were able to retire to our hotel for a good night's rest.

The following day we travelled to Tokyo on the famous bullet train, having shaken off Mr Sasakawa for the time being. I must say that compared with British Rail it was quite an eye-opener. The station at Osaka was spotlessly clean and the interior of the train was spacious and extremely comfortable. We whizzed through the Japanese countryside, passing neat little villages, and arriving eventually at Tokyo where we were staying at the Imperial Hotel. We were housed in the executive suite here, which was very sumptuous. The following day Mr Sasakawa's representatives appeared and we were taken to the Museum of Maritime Science down in the harbour. This was their equivalent of a national maritime museum, except that it had been paid for by Mr Sasakawa, who was there to greet us in person. It was a very good museum, and not aggressively Japanese, containing pictures of Nelson and Cook and other European navigators who had preceded the relatively recent development of their own nation as a maritime power. The museum was aimed particularly at a younger audience and there were several school parties wandering around trying out the various hands-on exhibits. What impressed me most of all – and frightened me, slightly, again bearing in mind the excellent Marine Academy at Jakarta – was how well they were educating their young as to the importance of their nation as a maritime power. When the young people had finished their tour of the museum they were taken into a cinema where they took part in a quiz, which was all disguised as being great fun, with little buttons to press at the side of their cinema seats. Pictures appeared on their screen, for example, a picture of a tanker with a multiple choice question about its weight. Parents and teachers had to take part as well, and when the answers appeared on the screen the children could tell whether or not their teachers had got it right, which produced great hilarity at times. This was a far cry, I remember thinking, from my own school visits many years ago, when any trip was always rather spoilt by having to write an essay about it when one got back to school. And of course this entertaining method of learning ensured that the information was retained. Hundreds of thousands of children were going through this process every year, all of whom would be conversant with maritime facts and information. What were we doing about this at home? Very little, it occurred to me.

The museum was built to resemble a ship, and once our tour was over we were taken up to Mr Sasakawa's personal suite for lunch, and then we proceeded out to the cars. Our route was lined with flag-waving schoolchildren all cheering Mr Sasakawa who strutted self-importantly along with us, obviously enjoying the attention. He took us, then, to the Sasakawa Foundation, where his main office was housed. This was a very grand affair, as one would have expected. It was a Sunday, but all the staff were there lined up to greet us and as we ran the gauntlet of these people to reach the escalators at the other end they all bowed practically in half as we passed by. The office was huge, adorned with life-size stuffed lions and tigers. He showed us around the Medical Centre housed in the same building, and then we had a formal Japanese tea ceremony in his office. One of the serving girls tripped on the mat, poor thing, as she came to serve us and looked completely terrified. I had to be photographed with Mr Sasakawa with my arm round a tiger, or something. Clearly this man had his finger in all sorts of pies – we discovered that one of his many sources of income was motorboat racing, on which people gambled in the same way as horse racing. It seemed to me that everyone was bowing and scraping the whole time, and he evidently enjoyed it all immensely.

There was only one time that I saw him subdued and put in his place, and that was that afternoon, when we were taken to see Prince and Princess Takamatsu. The Prince was the brother of the Emperor, although he had no particular role to play himself. They were a charming couple who both spoke perfect English, even though they had only been out of Japan once in their lives, in 1933, when they had been married. They had visited London, on that occasion, and produced some photographs of the then Lord Mayor and their visit to the Mansion House. Mr Sasakawa was at last put in his place, and sat quietly on the sofa whilst we chatted away with the Prince and Princess.

I must say, however, that Mr Sasakawa had been most generous in placing at our disposal one of his Rolls Royces and also the services of his secretary – a very pleasant middle-aged Japanese woman who arranged his affairs for him. She took us on a guided tour of Tokyo, but this was only after I had performed my official duty for the following morning. This was a call on the Deputy Governor of Tokyo and the members of Keidanren – the Japanese equivalent of the C.B.I. I had assumed that this was to be a fairly informal get together which would merely entail a chat over a cup of coffee, and so I was more than a little surprised when the Rolls Royce from the Embassy called at the hotel to pick me up first thing, with the First Secretary and an Adviser from the Bank of England on board. The First Secretary handed me a piece of paper and told me that this was the agenda for our morning meeting. 'Agenda?' I queried, glancing at the heading. 'VISIT OF THE RIGHT HONOURABLE LORD MAYOR OF LONDON TO THE DEPUTY GOVERNOR OF TOKYO AND MEMBERS OF THE KEIDANREN' together with the date. Underneath this was written, 'Agenda for Discussion: World Economic Affairs'. I groaned inwardly. I had been briefed fairly thoroughly on various Japanese matters but this looked all too heavy. What was I going to do now?

We arrived at our destination and I was ushered into the conference room. Tables were arranged on either side of the room, with our side and theirs opposite one another and television cameras and the press in evidence. The Deputy Governor kicked off with an opening speech and I replied in appropriate terms about how good it was to be here and what have you. He then launched into the main agenda, saying how they would now very much like to hear my opinion about the current world economic climate. I have a Guardian Angel who sits on a small cloud above me and fortunately he awoke with a start at precisely the right moment. The muse struck me. 'Well,' I began, with all due seriousness and gravitas 'I will give you an analogy.' (thank goodness for analogies!) 'You are, as we are,' I went on, 'a maritime nation. You will know that in times of threat, it is necessary to sail ships in a convoy to protect them against the ravages of the enemy, if they are to arrive safely at their destination'. (Ah! so!) 'They are protected on their journey by a screen of warships around them. If, in this convoy, there is one ship that is old and not in such good repair as the rest of them, she will not be able to keep up with the speed of the convoy. Unless something is done, she will fall out of the back of the protective screen and she will be torpedoed.' (Ah! so!) 'It may be necessary to slow down the speed of the convoy to accommodate this weaker ship. On the other hand, it may be that one ship on the convoy is so new, and so well-built and well-run that she is capable of going much faster than all the others.

If she does this, she will go out at the front of the screen. She will be in as much danger as the ship that fell behind, and she will be torpedoed.' (Ah! so!) 'When is Japan going to slow down, and allow the rest of the fleet to keep up at a reasonable speed? Because if you do not, you are going to be in serious trouble.' (Ah, so!) 'Because,' I continued, now warming to my subject, 'Your economy at the moment is so far ahead of everyone else in the world that, if you carry on as you are doing at the moment, you will become isolated. People will not tolerate the imbalance of payments. Barriers will go up, trade restrictions will be put in place, and you will be in trouble. Take our own country, for example. You are flooding our market with Japanese cars, Japanese television sets, Japanese electrical equipment and Japanese cameras. The man on the street sees all this, the man working in industry understands what is happening, and he begins to fear for his job. He has the right to vote. He will eventually say to his politician that this has to stop. And because politicians listen to the voters they will begin to put in place trade restrictions. This will do you no good at all. However,' I suggested, 'If you were to make a gesture in the right direction, for example, offering to purchase a number of our aircraft, this will be headline news in our country and we will look more kindly on your exports.' (Ah! so!). I thought that this was really the best I could do. It was a very simplistic message, which they could not have failed to understand. It was now their turn to respond. 'It is not quite as you say,' they claimed. 'Our invisible exports are not so healthy'. I knew I had to tread carefully here, for I had been told by the Bank of England that in fact the way they presented their figures was erroneous as far as we were concerned. In the re-insurance market, for instance, they might re-insure through Lloyd's, through the London market, and they would attribute the total of the re-insurance premiums they paid to London, whereas in fact London was only a clearing house which re-insured against a risk spread out across America, Italy, Germany, France or wherever. The balance was not ours alone but was spread out to numerous other different countries. I did not point this out here, but I did infer that the presentation might be misconstrued, since we re-insured worldwide. They then went on to claim that they imported a lot of our whiskey although I did argue that whiskey alone was not really going to affect the balance of payments to a great extent. I pointed out, too, that they made very good whiskey themselves, almost indistinguishable from true Scotch. I suggested that more encouragement was needed to those countries wishing to export to Japan. They did express interest, but of course made no promises, and that is really where we left it. I came away feeling mightily relieved that the ordeal was over. I had not anticipated anything of the kind, but thought that perhaps, in a way, my ignorance was my best ally: it enabled me to put a very straightforward point in terms that I felt comfortable with myself and perhaps might have been more use than had I been some sort of financial expert with complex economies theories. At the end of the day it was the man in the street back home who was going to vote with his feet and determine economic policy anyway. Maybe I protest too much – but that was my get out, I felt I had conducted myself with reasonable grace, and we parted in good heart.

I gave an interview for an English magazine that afternoon, and that evening the Ambassador gave a party in our honour, to which they invited all sorts of people that they themselves needed to see. That was a most fruitful evening. I recall that in the drawing room over coffee, after we had eaten, I encountered the Japanese Foreign Minister. He had drunk sufficient quantities and was at the stage which might be described as 'maudlin tight'. He put his arm around me, and asked why the British hated the Japanese so much. I of course protested that we did not, but he refuted this, putting it all down to the War. I said that the War had happened a long time ago, that it was no reason to continue hating someone perpetually and that we all had to live together now. He continued in his vein. 'We ought to be much closer than we are,' he argued. 'We are an island nation and so are you; you are a kingdom and so are we; we all rely on our exports to survive and we need the resources one another can provide'. Tears were rolling down his cheeks at this point, so overcome with emotion was he. Somewhat embarrassed, and quite unable to console him, I managed to extricate myself eventually.

Our visit to Japan had now come to a close. The following day was Tuesday 23rd August, which we were to see twice as we crossed the dateline that evening and saw the day all over again. We spent the morning shopping for Christmas presents, purchasing a number of miniature Bonsai trees, beautifully wrapped for transit, with each leaf being wrapped individually.

After lunch with our Canadian Pacific agent we flew out on a Canadian Pacific Jumbo (I noticed that they had started calling their planes after the North Atlantic ships, and it was the *Empress* of something, although I cannot recall what) to Vancouver. It was a rather bumpy flight, with a strong tail wind, with the result that we arrived in Vancouver about an hour and a half earlier than expected. The poor Mayor of Vancouver was caught on the hoof but managed to get there in time to welcome us.

Chapter 25

We arrived to find Vancouver in the middle of a bit of a security flap, in which the I.R.A. were involved in some way, and there was great concern over my safety. We consequently had two city police force men, plus a corporal of the R.C.M.P. (plain clothes) escorting us everywhere we went, the whole time we were there. It was real James Bond stuff: we were instructed once in our hotel to put a drinking straw into the door every time we left; if we returned to find the straw lying on the floor we had to call the police immediately.

That afternoon Libby went to the hairdressers on the lower ground floor of the hotel, and was accompanied by the R.C.M.P. who sat outside pretending to read a newspaper. We had a quiet first evening, being entertained to dinner with the Pritchards – he was the Managing Director of Canadian Pacific Steamships (U.K.) who had initially trained as a marine architect and had been responsible for building the new *Empress of Britain* which I had joined in 1956. They were a very nice couple and we had a pleasant evening, retiring to bed after a very long day at about 11.00 p.m.

On our first day, feeling bright eyed and bushy tailed, we were taken to see the Maritime Museum before being entertained for lunch by the Mayor of Vancouver at the Queen Elizabeth Theatre restaurant, which was followed by a tour of the city. One of the places we visited was the dolphinarium, where we watched tame dolphins performing and a killer whale, which also did tricks. For P.R. purposes I was asked to put my head into the mouth of the whale. I decided that at least it would make a newsworthy story ('Lord Mayor has head bitten off by Killer Whale') and consented. It was brought into a small pool and encouraged to come up; it certainly looked friendly enough as it poked its head up at us, but then it opened its mouth to display an array of very vicious looking teeth. As the press clicked away I stuck my head more or less as far as I could between its jaws; one wrong move and that would have been it, most definitely, but it behaved and did not suddenly snap its jaws shut as I feared. As a reward for my bravery I was presented with a tie, which I wear quite often.

Later that afternoon the Master Mariners Company of Canada greeted me as a long-lost brother and gave me another tie. I was made an honorary member of their organisation, which comprised a number of ex-Brits. We were then picked up by the Mayor of North Vancouver, who took us up to a restaurant high up on Grouse Mountain, reached by cable car which took us seemingly endlessly up and up and up until we were high in the clouds. Here we enjoyed a very good meal and I was given a nice piece of dark green jade, a characteristic of this part of the world.

On Thursday 25th August we were to have another helicopter flight. This one was quite different from the rather hair-raising experience in Hong Kong – a civilian helicopter which looks rather like a small car, with secure doors protecting one from the elements outside. I was quite happy with this and we set off for a spectacular tour of the Fraser River area and into the foothills of the Rockies. There was a marvellous view across forests and lakes, ascending until we reached a glacier and then higher still up into the peaks of the mountains. Way up high we saw a mountain goat skipping nimbly on what looked like a vertical rock face. We then dropped back down and landed at a hotel for lunch, and then off again to retrace our steps. The helicopter was used by the forestation department and on our return journey we were treated to a display of their work as we hovered above a pine tree to enable our pilot to remove a branch for inspection. We returned safely to our landing point and were taken back to Vancouver. That evening we were taken by the Mayor to the Pacific National exhibition which was on at the time – a large expo-style affair, where we had dinner and were entertained to a stage show in a huge auditorium.

The following day we were airborne again, this time in a seaplane. We flew from Vancouver to Victoria, the island lying off in the Pacific. There was a big Canadian Pacific hotel there, which we visited briefly, before going to see Lester Pearson College, the third of the international colleges. I think if I was choosing one of the three to attend it would be this one, if for its location alone. It was virtually buried in the edge of a pine forest, with log cabin style buildings and accommodation, and looked a marvellous place to study. We also went to luncheon at Government House (Victoria, not Vancouver, is the capital of British Columbia) with the Lieutenant Governor of the province. Amongst the guests were some old chums, now retired, who were living out there and it was a very happy occasion. Then it was back in our seaplane and we returned to our hotel. That evening we were entertained by the President of Canadian-Pacific railways in his own special train, equipped with living accommodation, kitchens and dining rooms, in which he travelled. This was not before the usual rigmarole with sniffer dogs and people looking underneath the train and what have you. This was now par for the course. There was a rather interesting incident the next morning, when we went off on a shopping spree to the big store in Vancouver. I wanted to buy some film and Libby wanted one or two things, and we were accompanied by our faithful hound, the Corporal R.C.M.P., who kept with me, lurking close by but pretending to be an ordinary customer. I purchased my film from the photographic department and as the girl handed it to me and I paid, she thrust the receipt into my hand. I did not particularly want the receipt, but she insisted that I take it in case I was stopped by the police. Little does she know, I thought, that the man standing over there is my own personal policeman! I was touched by her concern but decided not to blow his cover. It did occur to me that I must look decidedly suspicious if she thought that I might be stopped and asked for evidence of my purchase. We managed a bit of local sightseeing that day, and then in the evening we boarded the Canadian Pacific train heading for Montreal. We were to get off at Lake Louise, which was an overnight trip.

Once we left Vancouver the police decided we were out of their care, but the Canadian Pacific Police remained with us in the shape of one of their security men. He was a large man, who sat in the smoking car after dinner with a Colt .45 stuck in his waistband, looking most conspicuous. He had the carriage next to ours – a first class berth with shower, which was very comfortable. I did not realise how slowly the train actually went across the Rockies; they only travel at about 25 miles per hour. The following morning we went to the Observation Car and were then taken up to the engine and rode the rest of the journey 'head-end' as it is called. This afforded a much better view; at one part of the journey the train goes through a tunnel and it is possible to look back and see the tail of the train disappearing into the tunnel behind you at right angles. There were only two railway companies operating – the privately owned Canadian Pacific and the Canadian National, although the two companies worked closely together, operating alternate trains. It was also possible to drive through the Rockies, although of course air travel now held sway. Lake Louise is past the highest point, although still high up in the mountains. We arrived there at about 11 o'clock in the morning and were taken to the Lake Louise Hotel, which is Canadian Pacific owned. We were met there by the Canadian Pacific past President, Buck Crump. Lake Louise is stunning; as still and as clear as a millpond with the spectacular mountain scenery reflected in its surface as in a mirror. Canadian Pacific hotels of that period were designed to resemble a French château, and it certainly looked in keeping with the Alpine scenery. We had lunch there, and I was given another piece of jade – this time a bear with a fish in its mouth – and from there we drove by car to the next Canadian Pacific hotel 'down the line', as it were. This was the Banff Springs hotel where we were to spend the night and most of the following day. The hotel was almost in the middle of nowhere, but a very popular holiday resort, and manned largely by students. It had a strong Scottish flavour, with staff dressed in kilts. Although it was only the end of August there was already snow on the high ground. Having come from the Far East we only had summer wear with us. We did not actually get to see any bears, although there were plenty of warning signs about. They were something of a nuisance, in fact, with no fear at all of humans. To them, humans meant food and they were not above breaking into cars to find the coolbox or knocking over trash cans and littering the place.

After our sightseeing tour in the morning, we embarked again in the car. Well, it was not exactly a car, but a camper, owned by a photographer who worked fairly regularly for Canadian Pacific and beautifully equipped. It was a fairly large vehicle, with a galley kitchen and bunks, although we were not taking advantage of these. Our next destination was Calgary, and we drove through the lower levels of the Rockies, past various lakes and forests and stopping frequently to take photographs. Calgary is a bit of a boom town, and more of a thriving city. We were put in yet another Canadian Pacific hotel, which was in fact The Railway Hotel, and although very comfortable it was rather like staying in the middle of Euston Station. Buck Crump had come down from Lake Louise and threw yet another dinner party for us, inviting various people he thought we ought to meet.

The following day the Mayor took over the role of host and gave us a tour of the city followed by lunch, and also took us round the Old Calgary 'experience', a re-creation of what the town looked like in its frontier days, which was most interesting. Then we were off on our travels again. We could have completed the entire Canadian Pacific route, as far as Montreal, but opted not to do this: what many fail to realise is that it is actually further from Vancouver to Montreal than it is from London to Montreal and takes six days by train. I am given to understand that much of the journey is also pretty dull, across the prairies. We had been away from home for five weeks already and were now quite keen to start the homeward leg. So we flew from here to Toronto, which was to be our very last stop.

*   *   *

It had seemed that at each hotel we had stayed at so far, the manager was trying to go one better than the previous hotel, with the private bar, or room size or other feature. In Toronto we stayed at what was the then the largest hotel, the Royal York, where we were put in the Royal Suite, which was almost as elaborate as that provided by Mrs Marcos in Manila. There was a dining room with seating for twelve, a kitchen, two bedrooms, a large drawing room with log fire and a bar with every conceivable drink you could have wished for. We were going to be staying there for several days, since various plans were in place.

On our first day, the 31st August we were taken to the Queen Elizabeth Building where we attended a special luncheon given by the Canadian National Exhibition Board of Directors.

Living in Toronto was a distant cousin of mine (our grandmothers had been sisters, so quite how many times removed that made him I am not entirely sure). He, too, was a Baronet, whose father had moved out to Canada after the First World War. He himself had been in the film industry, but had also been a President of the Empire Club – a prestigious Canadian club which had very high profile speakers. Knowing of my trip, he was made Chairman of the reception committee and had organised a banquet for the Empire Club at which I was to speak that evening. Of course they all wanted to hear about the Silver Jubilee, as well as how things were going generally in the U.K., so I had plenty to talk about and think that my words were quite well received. Also at the dinner, but not speaking, was the Archbishop of Canterbury (Dr Coggan and his wife, whom I always refer to as 'my' Archbishop, as I do with all those who held office during my time as Lord Mayor, as in 'my Prime Minister'). It was very nice to see a face from home.

The next day we visited the Parliament buildings and paid official

With the Lieutenant Governor of Ontario, at the Empire Club in Toronto.

calls on the Lieutenant Governor and the Mayor of Scarborough, one of the suburban towns on the outskirts of Toronto. The Mayor of Toronto himself was away, so this chap was doing the honours instead. That evening there was a dinner at the Toronto Hope Club, organised again by my cousin and some friends – people I had known who had moved out there, including two brother officers of mine from my Canadian Pacific days. The following day we visited Niagara Falls, where we went out in *The Maid of the Mist*, a Canadian steamer which goes to the foot of the falls. You get given a set of oilskins (well used!) but you still get pretty wet, but I managed to get some good photographs, both from the top and the bottom of the falls. It was back, then, to Toronto for a party that evening given by the Burstons and which was another chance to catch up with old friends.

On 3rd September we shopped in the morning, before being collected by the Palmers to take us out to their summer house to the north of Toronto. Peter Ainsworth came and joined us and we swam in the pool; it was a good C.P. day and very interesting to catch up with my brother officers who had both succeeded in their chosen fields.

During our stay in Toronto we also chalked up another dinner in a revolving restaurant; this one in the Toronto Tower which is the tallest in Canada. It was most impressive, not least because there happened to be a thunderstorm going on below us, and we were treated to a light show and display in addition to the magnificent views.

September 4th was our last day in Canada. We packed first thing in order to be ready for the evening, then met up with the Chetwins for a boat trip around the islands off Toronto. They kindly drove us to the airport that evening, having been extremely generous and hospitable. They even offered us the use of their house in Barbados, where they used to go to escape from the Canadian winter, for three weeks when we had finished our term in the Mansion House. This would certainly be something to look forward to, and we knew that we would need a break when the whole thing came to an end. My firm had indicated that I did not need to return until January, so the offer was gratefully accepted.

At 9.30 p.m. we boarded our homeward bound Jumbo. Just to prove my small-world theory, the Chief Steward on this flight was the same Chief Steward that we had had on our flight to Singapore some five and a half weeks before! We were met at Heathrow by the Lord

Mayor's secretary, somewhat weary, considerably wiser and very happy to be home. We had seen a lot, met a lot of people and hopefully done a little bit of good.

Chapter 26

We could not go back to the Mansion House just yet as it was still having its annual re-fit; we had also had decorators in at Fairholt Street while we had been away and that was not yet right, but we managed.

I went into the Mansion House the following day just to pick up the mail whilst Libby sorted out the decorators and then took off to Biddeston – the only civilised home open to us. Nicholas, now in his first year with British Aerospace in Bristol, was living there; I imagine that he found it rather quiet but he seemed to spend most of his evenings taking his car to pieces and rebuilding it and was happy enough. Mrs Taylor in the village was taking care of him – washing and cooking and ironing for him. It was good to see him and we had a good time catching up on our news.

By 12th September everything was straightened out and we started to pick up the threads. The Corporation had been in recess over the summer and although the finishing post was now in sight for my term of office there was still an awful lot left to do. We had to gather momentum for the last dash, as it were. The first public engagement was a trip in the Admiral's barge of the Port of London, the *Royal Nore*, where we had been invited to dine. We went up the river first as far as Battersea and then back down again to see the progress of the Thames barrage, which was being built just above Woolwich Reach to prevent flooding in the upper river. Christopher arrived back the next day from Japan, where he been singing. Unfortunately we had just missed him, although Libby had deposited our remaining yen with the Embassy for him to collect when he was there. He had enjoyed himself very much and it was interesting to compare notes.

On 17th September we were able to take up the offer made to us by P & O for a trip in the new jet foil to Zeebrugge. We took the morning 'flight', as it is called. The jetfoils can reach very high speeds, and can function in winds up to Force 7, before conditions get too rough for them. They were discontinued after a while as they were not an economic means of getting across, but it was fun to have a go and we whizzed across the Channel. We stayed overnight in Bruges, where we were put up in a very nice hotel, more like a very good restaurant with bedrooms attached, where we had a most memorable dinner. We had time that evening to have a wander around Bruges, then left the next day and returned to St. Katharine's Dock. On the way back we had to pass through a small customs shed. The car had come down from the Mansion House to meet us, but was waiting outside. A representative from P & O was there to greet us, but of course the customs official did not know who we were, and the representative was mortified as he made a great play of going through our bags. He grilled Libby in particular over a bottle of tonic water she had taken from the flight, unused. Everyone else had gone and we were the last people there, and I could sense the P & O chap hopping up and down but unable to do anything as the customs man continued to burrow through our cases, sniffing Libby's talcum powder just to make sure it was not cannabis and taking his time going through everything. I did not mind in the least and in fact found the whole incident very amusing, although the poor P & O man was quite upset.

On 20th September we had dinner at Lambeth Palace with Dr Coggon, the Archbishop of Canterbury, whom we had of course last met in Toronto. He was a lovely man, who exuded goodness, and although one does not want to use the term 'saintly' it was possible to tell that he had a very special quality about him.

On 22nd, I had a visit in the afternoon from the Mayor of Riyadh, the capital of Saudi Arabia, accompanied by the Managing Director of a firm that specialised in environmental cleaning, who had just obtained the contract to clean the city of Riyadh. The plan was to sign the contract in the Mansion House, after which the Mayor presented me with a large cardboard box, which I opened to reveal a complete sheik's outfit. I put it on for the benefit of the cameras, although could not imagine when I would ever get the opportunity to use it. However, just such an opportunity arose several years later, when we were out attending an American conference of the Administrative Management Society of America who had invited us out. We would have a themed evening wherever we were and as this particular conference was being held in Hollywood, the theme of the evening was to be the stars. My costume came into its own.

On the 23rd we went down to Southampton, to visit the Mayor of Southampton and the Boat Show. Another motive for my visit was that one of the boats in the show was a similar model to the one I had on order. The building of my own yacht had not, in the meantime, been without incident. Two weeks prior to our round the world trip, I had had a 'phone call from the company building the boat, who told me not to send them any more money as they were going into receivership the following day. I have to say I was not unduly surprised, since I knew that they could not have been making much money, but I was not quite sure what to do now, especially as I was shortly to be leaving the country. One of my brother Aldermen, Kenneth Court (who was to become Lord Mayor two years after me) was a yachtsman and also a specialist in receivership. I gave him a call and explained my predicament to him. He seemed quite relaxed about it, and said that he had faced a similar problem. A yard had been building a yacht for him, and had gone bust. 'What did you do?' I enquired eagerly.

'Bought the yard,' was the reply.

'Not quite the answer I was looking for, Kenneth,' I laughed. However, he took all the details of the case and said I could leave it with him. He came back to me two days later, having spoken to the receiver and to the bank, and said that he had persuaded the receiver to ensure that the hull of my yacht was completed before the yard was closed down. It would cost a bit more, but at least I would have a boat, which could then be kitted out. She worked out, in the end, at £4000 above the price that had been agreed, although I do feel that this was a more realistic price for the boat I was getting. By now the hull of my own yacht was complete and she was being fitted out.

The Cheltenham Ladies' College Guild (the Old Girls' association) had asked Libby, on Old Girl herself, if they might hold their annual meeting in the Mansion House this year. This seemed a good plan, especially as I would be out of the way at the time attending a Memorial Service for the Prime Minister of Jamaica in Westminster Abbey. However, Libby had asked if I would say a few words to them before I left for the service. They turned up in droves and I duly welcomed them in the Egyptian Hall before handing them over to Libby. I then departed, confident that all would be done and dusted by the time I got home. Not a bit of it. I returned to find the place crawling with Cheltenham Ladies, enjoying themselves enormously, and it was another hour at least before the last of them went out of the door.

On 26th September I was invited to be a guest of the Port of

London Authority, little realising at the time that I would eventually become the organisation's Vice Chairman. That very same evening I was invited to give the annual inspection of the River Police Specials. And then the very next day, at last, I was visited by someone from the Department of Trade and the Foreign Office for a de-briefing after my overseas trip.

The end was now drawing nigh. The two new Sheriffs were sworn in the next day and my successor was elected the day after that, on 29th September, to become the Lord Mayor elect before taking office in November. My own duties continued apace, beginning with a rather curious duty on 30th September which was to present a medal to a dog. It was, in fact, a police dog, who had saved his master who had been attacked by some thugs and had been thrown into the river. The dog, a lovely German Shepherd, had gone in after him and pulled him out. I hung the medal around his neck with all due ceremony in the morning, before a lunchtime visit of the President of Costa Rica. As usual, this entailed playing the present game. However, on this occasion we were unable to find out beforehand whether or not a present was in the offing. We had a plate dish ready just in case, but having reached the speeches without any evidence of a present on the President's part I felt fairly confident that there was to be no exchange. It was then that to my horror I looked up to see the Yeoman standing there with the silver dish ready to give to me. The President himself was unable to see this, although it would have been obvious to members of his retinue. I managed to hiss out of the corner of my mouth an instruction to the Yeoman to put it away, which he duly did. The visit came to an end and we saw the President into his car. I was conscious that his aide was jabbering away to him nineteen to the dozen, and I was convinced that he was telling him about the un-given present. We very nearly had a serious diplomatic incident on our hands, but thankfully I heard no more about it.

We were now into October, and the clock was ticking. I accepted an invitation to the Royal Hospital at Chelsea – the Chelsea Pensioners spiritual home, where we attended a church service and were entertained to lunch. On 6th October it was time for the annual visit of the Lord Mayor to Burnham Beeches, in order to plant a tree, and a visit to Dorny House, which had been left as a gift to the nation and could be occupied by the Foreign Secretary if he wanted to live there. The Lord Mayor of London also has a claim to it if he so wishes. I had planted a couple of trees before, in the course of my duties, and was acquiring quite a collection of spades – as one always gets to keep the spade after a tree-planting ceremony.

On 17th I went to see the Black Museum of Scotland Yard, a fairly unpleasant collection of nasty bits and pieces associated with various criminals. It was interesting to see the central control system of their operations there. Two days later I attended one of my favourites – the Seafarers' Service at St. Paul's Cathedral and then on October 20th it was the Bankers' Dinner, where I gave them a potted version of my words of wisdom on the convoy analogy given to the Japanese. I am afraid to say that it was at this occasion the previous year that the Chairman of the Stock Exchange had been rather rude to the Chancellor, Dennis Healey.

An invitation had come from the C-in-C Naval Home Command to dine aboard *Victory* with my wife on Trafalgar Night, 21st October. This put me in a bit of a quandary as traditionally the Lord Mayor dines aboard H.M.S. *President* that night, but knowing they would understand, I telephoned the captain of *President* and offered to send someone in my place. Libby and I went down to stay at Admiralty House, to dine aboard *Victory* – an opportunity I would not have missed for the world. Unfortunately we were unable to dine in Nelson's cabin, which was under re-fit at the time, but dined in Hardy's cabin and enjoyed a most memorable night.

On 25th October I opened the new Guildhall School of Music and Drama in the Barbican. Embarrassingly they made me an Honorary Member, which caused a bit of amusement on the part of my younger son, after the scorn poured on me by my eldest when I was awarded a Doctor of Science. Another bogus qualification, in their eyes.

On 26th October I had another engagement dear to my heart – the Civic Lunch at Trinity House for the Lord Mayor of London. As a Younger Brother I had received loyal addresses myself and it was nice now to be on the other side of the fence. It was a very jolly party. This was followed by another good nautical occasion on the 31st of the month, when Sir Terence Lewin, the First Sea Lord, thought it would be a nice idea to present to the Mansion House plate one of the silver bells on H.M.S. *London*. To this end, he authorised the withdrawing of a bell from the naval trophy store and ordered a display cabinet to be made. He then mustered together all the captains who had ever served in any of the H.M.S. *London*'s to come to the Mansion House to witness the presentation of this bell. We all lined up in the salon, where the bell was concealed beneath a white ensign on the table. Terry Lewin made a little speech, whipped the ensign off the bell and duly presented it to me, to be kept in perpetuity in the Mansion House plate. I gave a little speech in return, we all had a little drink and everyone withdrew. A petty officer photographer was present recording the event. I had instructed the staff, when the ceremony was over, to hang on to the white ensign. That was *my* present, and just what I needed for my yacht. It was duly rolled up and put to one side. The following day came a call from the Admiralty asking after the ensign. Unfortunately some silly girl in the office helpfully told them she had seen it and knew where it was. I happened to overhear the conversation and so immediately got onto Teddy Ellis, my private secretary. 'Surely Teddy,' I reasoned, 'a white ensign can quite easily get lost without anyone getting into trouble.' I really regarded it as my perk, since the bell was not for me personally – and it was precisely the right size for my yacht. Presumably he rang up someone and said something, since it was never asked for again, and has now been pressed into service most fittingly. In fact, I recounted this story to other captains of H.M.S. *London*, and as the ensign gradually wore out they would exclaim 'You must have another!' which meant I had a steady stream of white ensigns for as long as I needed.

On 3rd November the Lord Mayor and Lady Mayoress were invited to the State Opening of Parliament. In fact we got two of these during the course of our Mayoralty, one at the beginning and one at the end. The following day I did something I had been intending to do much earlier, which was to visit all the staff in the Guildhall department and thank them for their service. This was followed, the day after, by the staff party for the Mansion House staff and on 7th November, as a sort of parting shot, I gave my third letters patent on behalf of the Court of Aldermen to a new Livery Company – the Company of Builders Merchants who were now ready to receive their livery. I had hoped to get the Secretaries and Administrators on board too, but they still did not have their paperwork in order.

This brings me to 9th November, my birthday. I held a birthday party in the salon for a select group comprising the two Lord Mayors whom I had served as Sheriff, the two Sheriffs that had served me as Lord Mayor, the two new Sheriffs, and my brother Sheriff who had served with me in 1973/4. In addition we had the Lord Mayor's private secretary, the Sword Bearer, the Sergeant-at-Arms and the City

Marshal, all with their wives. Also the Secondary at the Old Bailey and his wife – and last, but not least, Christopher Rawson. All were instructed not to bring presents; as is the way of the world they all did, but all were small and insignificant. The most amusing was from Hugh Wontner whom I had always ribbed about his gold Rolex, received when we were in Switzerland, who presented me with a fully working Mickey Mouse watch.

Various formal presents were exchanged: I gave presents to the Household Officers and the Secretary in the form of glass goblets engraved with my little robin and received some myself from the girls in the office. My time had now just about drawn to a close. On the 11th I went into court in the Mansion House for the last time in my capacity as Lord Mayor, and took the opportunity to say a formal farewell to the court staff. That day was the installation lunch and the Silent Change, when the Lord Mayor elect officially became Lord Mayor. I handed over the insignia of office and I returned to the Mansion House as the Late Lord Mayor.

It was back to normality, if life could ever be described as normal again. Was I sad? No, not really. After all, I was not going away for ever. I would go into 'purdah' until Easter but civic duties would then resume. I felt I had done the best I could, and it certainly would not have been possible to continue at the same pace. I had absorbed myself fully in the job and had enjoyed it, and hoped that those who had shared the time with me had enjoyed it too. The resumé which follows provides various facts and figures, and the answers to some frequently asked questions about the Mayoralty, and will also show that the events recounted here do not account for half of the duties I undertook during my year.

Libby and I went home, for a while, before taking up my cousin's kind offer of a house in Barbados, where we spent a very relaxing time, going to bed at 9 o'clock at night, getting up when we felt like it and gradually winding down, ready to resume a more gentle pace of life once we were back. It was certainly a well-earned and much needed holiday.

It has taken me three years to write this book, largely because I have been very busy since I was Lord Mayor. It has been completed in fits and starts and the whole has been dictated. There are another 23 years to recount, in which an awful lot has happened, so there may well be a second volume, should the first prove popular.

I wrote a poem, at this time, which I believe encapsulated my feelings on handing over my Mayoral chain of office, which I would like to include here as my parting shot:

> The king is dead; long live the king
> So runs tradition's cry.
> And so it is with Lord Mayors,
> Though not called upon to die
> But if you seek an epitaph
> Then here's a little verse:
> He could have done it better –
> But he might have done it worse!
> So looking back across the months
> As far as I can see,
> I'll try to be objective
> About what it's meant to me.
> I've tried to live each minute
> Full sixty seconds' span
> To bring to each occasion
> The maximum élan
> And this from my experience
> Has taught me to believe
> That it is more rewarding
> To give than to receive.
> That history has been more than kind
> Throughout this busy year
> With Jubilees and suchlike –
> Of this I am aware.
> But aside from special cases,
> Beyond one's power to choose,
> There have been other memories
> That I will never lose
> Outstanding and throughout the year
> And prized above them all
> The loyalty and service
> Both here and at Guildhall
> The king is dead; long live the king!
> This Mayoralty is o'er
> The obscurity of purdah
> Awaits me through the door
> So let be the chant of mourners
> Who walk behind my hearse
> 'He might have done it better,
> But he could have done it worse!'